D1275753

The
New
Expert
Handicappers

The
NEW EXPERT
HANDICAPPERS

Fourteen of the Best
New-Style Experts
Beating the Races Today

JAMES QUINN

*HICKORY
PLAINS*

WILLIAM MORROW AND COMPANY, INC.
New York

Library of Congress Cataloging-in-Publication Data

Quinn, James, 1943–
    The new expert handicappers : fourteen best new-style experts
beating the races today / James Quinn.
        p. cm.
    ISBN 0-688-07511-8
    1. Horse race betting. 2. Horseplayers—United States—Biography.
I. Title.
SF331.Q553 1989
798.401—dc20   89-32522
                                                                     CIP

Printed In the United States of America

First Edition

1 2 3 4 5 6 7 8 9 10

BOOK DESIGN BY BERNARD SCHLEIFER

Contents

1. The Screamer   9

2. The Tout   12

3. The Famous Insiders   15

4. The New Expert Handicappers   22

5. *Paul Braseth*   *27*
Three Is Enough

6. *Joe Takach*   *39*
Hard-core Philly Pro

7. Lee Rousso   50
Too Young to Be a Two-Time Champ

8. *Anton Hemm*   *62*
Park Avenue Banker

9. *Scott Finley*   *73*
International Frequent Flyer

10. *Erika Holderith*   *86*
Playing with Artificial Intelligence

5

CONTENTS

11. *George Kaywood*   96
Mensa Handicapper in the Midwest

12. *Steve Klein*   108
Angles, Angles . . . Testing for Long Shots

13. *Dan McDevitt*   118
Weekends in Boston

14. *Darryll Claussen*   127
No Longer an Aeronautical Engineer;
Not Yet a Professional Handicapper

15. *Tom Hambleton*   135
Can a Loser Ever Win?

16. *Ron Cox*   144
Captain Cover

17. *Frank Romano*   156
High Roller

18. *Tom Brohamer*   172
No. 1 in My Book

19. *Winning Time*   187
Brohamer, Quinn, and Rousso at Santa Anita
Ninety-one Days / Winter Season / 1988

The
New
Expert
Handicappers

CHAPTER ONE

The Screamer

IT'S HAPPENED AGAIN. The race is ended. The Screamer has lost. He knows he should have won. He was robbed.

He tears away from the mezzanine rail, where he has been screaming his pain for forty-five seconds. He moves loudly toward the monitor for the replay, where he can relive his angst in uninvited company, now with screams and shouts and vulgar epitaphs. His flabby arms flail about, smashing the program and *Form* into fleshy hands and a beer belly. His neck and eyes bulge, his large head spins in all directions, releasing its scowls. The vitriol pours from his mouth nonstop. The Screamer is hot and furious.

"Did you ever see anything like that bleep," he yells at no one and everyone. "That goddamn bleeping Toro. He's no bleepin' jockey.

"Hang 'em up, Toro, you scum.

"Did you see what he did? Did you catch that bleep?"

The Screamer arrives at the monitor. It's showing only results. No replay yet. The Screamer looks around, almost frantically. He spots a potential victim, a track acquaintance.

The Screamer rushes to his prey, grabs a shoulder, walks him outside, back toward the scene of the crime, shouting obscenities in his ears. His face has changed to flush red, the veins of his neck to a radiant purple.

"They're always playing goddamn games here. Did you see what happened? I'm sick of this bleep. You don't think these races are bleepin' fixed? That was a bleeping boat race. They can take this whole goddamn crapshoot and go to hell with it."

9

"What are you talking about? I didn't see anything. You just picked a bad horse."

"What! You bleeping asshole. Come look at this bleep. I'll show you the bleep you didn't see."

The Screamer picks up the replay as the horses glide into the clubhouse turn of a nine-furlong turf route.

"Watch what this goddamn bleepin' Toro does. Toro on the turf! That's a bunch of bleep. He's on the rail now. See him. In the yellow. A good color for that bum. You got that right."

The Screamer blares his call of the race to a group of bemused, annoyed customers within earshot. As the horses parade down the backside he's spreading venom like buckshot. He darts jerkily from victim No. 1's side to lean on other familiar innocents nearby. He never shuts up; that's the Screamer's imprimatur.

The horses approach the three-eighths pole. The riders begin to maneuver for striking position and advantage on the far turn.

"Look at that idiot on the outside," cries the Screamer. "He's killing his horse." The Screamer is shaking his finger at Laffit Pincay, Jr. "Now look at this goddamn Toro. He's standing up, for Chrissake. He's always standing up, standing up and checking.

"Dammit. Look at him steadying. Once, twice, three times! See that bleep. Steady, check, steady, check.

"Here he gets shuffled back. Asshole.

"Now wait till you see this bleep. Look at him. Why's he swinging wide in the middle of the turn? He's five wide. He's six, seven wide into the stretch. Can you believe this?"

The Screamer flies out of control.

"This goddamn bleep is bleep. Goddamn bleeping bleeping jockeys. Bleep you, Toro. I gotta put up with this bleep every day here. Bleep this.

"How can we bet on this bleep every day?" He's now roaring to the crowd, as from a pulpit. "This is the most screwed-up bleeping goddamn game in town. It's crazy we even come here."

While steadying, not wanting to lose ground and momentum simultaneously, jockey Toro has taken hold behind a wall of horses on the far turn, and approaching the upper stretch, has begun to angle outside for running room. The jockey has to angle out still more, but his horse has lots of late kick and he begins to use it.

"Look at this horse," shouts the Screamer. "He's still runnin'. After all this bleep, this goddamn horse is comin' on again. You tell me this horse wasn't best! Bleep this bleeping bleep! He should have won for fun. I can't stand this bleep anymore!"

After a troubled trip, horse and jockey finish a close fourth. The Screamer's rage has lost a measure of its fury. He's calm enough to sum up the day's harsh lesson again for the audience to listen and learn.

"It's those goddamn favorites. Never bet the favorites. You can't win with them. Every bleeping asshole in the place knows they're stiffing them. Every day. Stiff jobs. Every goddamn day. You can't get a bleeping break here."

The Screamer storms away from the monitor at last. Within seconds he's out of sight; for now.

The Screamer next sees a handicapper he knows on line to collect. He approaches the guy immediately, unabashedly.

"I played that favorite Toro bleeped. It tapped me for the day. I got something I like in the Ninth. I need $20. I've really had a rotten day. How about it? Just $20. You'll get it tomorrow, next time you see me. You know me. I'm good for it. Right after the race if I hit."

With a nod, the guy on line motions the Screamer away. He does not look up from his program. He knows the Screamer too well.

"Come on, guy, you're flush. What's a bleeping $20? I want to play the last. I got something good, I tell ya."

No response. Nothing. The guy's savvy.

The Screamer repairs, now quietly, to the box of a closer acquaintance. He borrows the $20. The friendly sucker just hands the Screamer the day money, saying little.

The Screamer checks the odds on his good thing in the nitecap. He goes to the window.

"Ten to win on number ten," he calls. "And $5 exactas, ten-two, ten-five."

CHAPTER TWO

The Tout

IT'S WEDNESDAY, the first day of the racing week. About mid-card, the pitiful races done with, the Handicapper sees a familiar figure, not coincidentally, striding toward him in the box section with the same customary confident grin, an animated ray of hope and expectation. It's the Tout, perhaps the most long-suffering enigma in the corridors and conclaves of thoroughbred racing.

"Who's the top figure horse on the card?" begins the Tout. It's practically protocol, an indispensable element in his armor, that the Tout affect a rational, informed, intelligent discussion of the races, especially in the presence of authentic handicappers.

"Valiant Cougar in the Seventh, by open lengths," notes the Handicapper, "and he should pay a decent price."

The Handicapper explains, not for the first time, that Valiant Cougar earned a superior figure in a claiming race featuring selling prices $9000 lower than today's top claiming prices. Though the two claiming-class levels are essentially interchangeable at Santa Anita, the public will likely discount the performance at the lower level, making Valiant Cougar a sweet overlay today.

The Tout listens attentively, nods affirmatively. He knows from experience the Handicapper is frequently correct.

A rational discussion of the remaining card ensues, as always. The Handicapper guides the discussion, the Tout listening and nodding agreeably.

But the Tout has his personal agenda.

"You might be right about that figure horse in the Seventh," the Tout observes kindly, "but there's a sleeper in there you probably tossed out. He's making a comeback here and they think he's a good thing."

The Tout pauses, to see whether the Handicapper can identify the sleeper. The Handicapper shrugs, but mentions no horse.

"First Albert. The number-one horse. He's ready, and has never been this cheap. They're going with him big."

"You say the horse is sound and ready," repeats the Handicapper idly.

"Yes. They've been looking for the right spot. This is it."

The Tout was accurate on one point. First Albert had never run in a middling claiming race, and once, at three, the horse won a division of a Grade 1 race. The tip sounded seductive, in a way. Many tips, of course, do.

Prior to getting hurt, two seasons ago, First Albert had already descended far below its former heights, losing versus high-priced claiming horses before heading to the sidelines. The horse had been absent almost two seasons. First Albert was 11–1 on the board.

When the gates opened for the 7th, Valiant Cougar took the lead handily and set a keen pace, unmolested. First Albert showed little speed, settled toward the rear.

Valiant Cougar breezed to victory, paid $13.80. The Handicapper netted $690 to win, and cashed some exactas besides. The Tout offered congratulations later that afternoon.

On Thursday, mid-card, the Tout told the Handicapper about a maiden in the Sixth.

"You know I'm not one of these touts," he said, "always looking for the inside dope. I don't go for that. You know that. This one is from trainer Mel Stute himself. I'm keying it in the triple, with the two-four-five-nine in the seventh and everything in the feature."

The Handicapper thanked the Tout for the information, without acting on it.

"Also," said the Tout, "Vienna has a turf import entered on Saturday. It's against nonwinners, the kind of race where you like the foreign horses."

The Stute maiden lost the 6th without mounting a challenge.

On Friday the Tout had nothing to boast of.

When the past performances for Saturday became available, the import trained by Darrel Vienna looked intriguing indeed.

The colt had raced with some success in England and today would be facing horses 4up that had not won even a single allowance race. The Tout was correct. The Handicapper often preferred impressive imports still eligible for preliminary non-winners allowance competition at middle distances on the grass.

When the Handicapper examined the shipper's foreign races, however, the horse had never even been entered in a Listed stakes. Its three wins had occurred at minor ovals having winner shares so small the horses remained eligible for older nonwinners of one. This horse lacked the class advantage the Handicapper preferred in these turf routes.

Vienna's tip horse raced well enough, but finished third.

When the Handicapper saw the Tout on Saturday, it was late in the day. The Tout flashed a triple card showing he was alive to a pair of low-priced contenders in the feature. The probable payoffs would be generous.

"And they're going with this horse in the Ninth today," he mentioned, pointing to No. 3, an intriguing sort the Handicapper himself had considered an outside threat in the field.

"What do you know about the horse?" asked the Handicapper.

"He was rank last time because they put the blinks on and sent the horse. Today the blinkers are off, there's a switch to Eddie D., and they're dropping to where the horse should be too much. They're betting good on him, I know that."

Neither of the Tout's contenders nailed down the feature. The Tout's angle in the 9th chased a too-rapid pace for approximately seven furlongs and quit badly turning for home.

Sunday was another day. The Tout had two tips, both lost.

Nearing the close of the season, the Handicapper studied the stats on the two stables the Tout relied upon for most of his inside information. Both were betting outfits, as many big-league stables are. Both were large, with a number of regular runners. One trainer had been uncommonly cold, 3 for 52 with twenty days left. The second stable had been 7 for 73, below 10 percent.

Instead of just another bad year, the Handicapper mused, the Tout may be experiencing his worst season ever.

CHAPTER THREE

The Famous Insiders

THE GREAT HORSEMAN Charles Whittingham likes to bet on his horses. Whenever Charlie is sighted in the turf club, ambling toward the windows, the whispers begin.

"Charlie likes his horse in this one."

"Charlie likes so-and-so. He doesn't like his horse."

"Charlie's betting a bundle on his horse in the feature."

The rumors spread like ragweed, carrying an invisible pollen. Whittingham has another betting coup up his sleeve, and the regulars want to know about it. Everyone wants a piece of Charlie's action. The native inhabitants at racetracks lay claim to certain inalienable rights, like squatting rights: the right to be in the know.

What racing's regulars have never understood is that what racing's insiders do not understand about the art of handicapping has cost them so much money, they surrendered all opportunity to catch up years ago. The deficits only grow.

Charlie Whittingham is among the best of trainers. He is just as surely among the worst of bettors.

Testimony on the point has been provided by the great man himself.

"You just can't beat them," moans Charlie, and the pain of the past is quite evident during the occasional media references he makes to playing the horses. "Anybody who bets on horses wears a size-three hat."

Ah, the famous insiders. The privileged people who know something the rest of the racegoers do not know. Aren't they marvelous? They endow the racetrack with its Runyonesque charm, its mass appeal. If only ordinary customers could know what the famous insiders know, wouldn't life be wonderful?

An intriguing subplot at any racetrack regards the famous insiders—not what they know, but what they don't know.

A handicapping companion and I once recorded the unequivocal betting tips we received from impressively credentialed insiders—horsemen, jockey agents, stable employees, reasonably rational owners—for an entire season. Of the first 100 tips, 92 lost. We stopped taking notes.

Another season, now deeper inside than ever, I toted a dozen bets to the windows for one of the nation's leading trainers. Bet size never varied; $200 to win. Of the twelve, one horse won. It paid 8–5. With one exception, the bets supported the trainer's own horses. He felt supremely confident that each horse would win.

Another day, on line at the turf club, Santa Anita, the country's premier trainer stood on the adjoining line, one ahead, a direct diagonal from me.

"Six thousand to win," he called, "on number one."

I got out of line. The No. 1 horse was the trainer's own. I had not marked the horse as a contender myself, but remained open to persuasion on the matter.

The race was carded at 1¹⁄₁₆M for 3YOs, nonwinners of a race other than maiden or claiming, often a difficult proposition. The trainer's colt had broken its maiden last out, in undistinguished time and manner, after numerous losing cracks at maidens. It would be stretching out from a sprint to route, while moving ahead against a field of solid nonclaiming three-year-olds.

On cold dope the horse looked to stand a small chance. Yet, there it was, a heavy vote of confidence from a famous insider. Six thousand dollars!

The colt attended a par pace to the quarter pole, and faded.

Another famous insider I know liked the Pick 6, but no more. He composed the same kind of $192 ticket anytime he located two singles in the series. He never cashed the ticket. Not once! Before ending the futile chase, wishing not to be undone by circumstances he calls his own, this famous insider deposited tens of thousands of dollars.

Pari-mutuel comedies aside, authentic handicappers can contemplate the famous insiders and appreciate how much they literally do not know. Most of them, I submit, comprehend very little about the intricacies of handicapping.

The Kentucky Derby annually provides a national forum for some very famous insiders to make ignorant fools of themselves.

Only days before this was written, the filly Winning Colors took the 114th Kentucky Derby field wire to wire, holding off two-year-old champion Forty Niner during the final sixteenth.

In its two prior starts, Winning Colors had a) demolished the outstanding Goodbye Halo in the Grade 1 Santa Anita Oaks (Goodbye Halo rebounded from the thrashing to annex the Grade 1 Kentucky Oaks a day before the 1988 run for the roses, flattering Winning Colors even more), and b) humbled the leading West Coast colts with a romping tour de force in the Grade 1 Santa Anita Derby.

In the Santa Anita Derby, Winning Colors had earned excellent pace figures and a speed figure only four lengths behind champion Alysheba's best figure for the Santa Anita season. For a three-year-old filly, it was a tremendous performance.

Despite that, somehow, numerous famous insiders concluded the southern California filly had little chance to win the big derby. Many mocked her chances from New York to Kentucky.

"I guarantee you the filly won't get away and win like that in Kentucky," Woody Stephens assured the nation. "We'll see what she's made of when she's pressed on a deep surface. I think she'll fold."

On congratulating trainer D. Wayne Lukas on winning the Kentucky Derby with a filly, Stephens took pains to assure Lukas that he (Lukas) would never win five Belmonts in succession as had Stephens himself from 1983 to 1987. Perhaps this constitutes the rarified logic that preserves for the famous insiders their unique place in racetrack mythology.

A few years ago, during the pre-1985 Kentucky Derby hoopla, the *Daily Racing Form* conducted its poll of horsemen as to the most probable winner. The pre-Derby favorite was Chief's Crown, two-year-old champion of 1984 and a genuinely brilliant colt which had looked sensational in its Florida campaign as a budding 3YO.

Chief's Crown possessed a high dosage index, at 5.50, indicating a pedigree too unbalanced toward speed, or brilliance, and lacking in endurance, or stamina. The colt therefore was an improbable classic winner at a mile and one-quarter. No three-year-old having a dosage index above 4.00 had won the Kentucky Derby since 1929, a controversial fact well-distributed among horsemen and other famous insiders.

In the *Daily Racing Form* poll, 98 percent of the horsemen selected Chief's Crown to win the 1985 Kentucky Derby. Exactly one horseman, trainer Dick Mandella, selected Spend A Buck to win. One famous insider!

Chief's Crown, well-placed following a perfect trip, labored conspicuously in the Churchill Downs stretch, barely clinging to third. Spend A Buck sped wire to wire in a romp, recording the fourth-fastest Derby time in history.

What did a sizable number of up-to-snuff handicappers know that the famous insiders did not? Plenty.

In certain technical areas of handicapping, as on the relations between speed and class, many famous insiders often appear bewilderingly lost.

When Alysheba won the Kentucky Derby in slow time and was harpooned for it, trainer Jack Van Berg issued a rejoinder having a long-hallowed tradition among several of his fellows, but an egregious error nonetheless.

"Final time doesn't mean a damn thing."

Van Berg rehashed the timeless observation that countless good horses have beaten bad horses in slower time than the cheaper horses have previously run. From these observations many horsemen have concluded that final time is meaningless. The quality of the opposition counts, but not time.

In fact, speed and class, final time and the quality of the competition, have a perfect positive correlation, as probability studies unmistakably show. The better the horses, the faster they run.

The raw recruits of modern speed handicapping on every circuit in the nation can deliver a more rational explanation of the phenomenon Van Berg cites.

When daily track variants—measures of track surface speed—have been calculated and applied to actual times, the adjusted final times often reveal the apparently slower horses have actually run faster. They merely ran on slower surfaces. Not many famous insiders easily comprehend the point, and fewer still can perform the calculations.

Or, when a pace analysis has been completed and the complex relations among final time, fractional times (variants applied), and running styles have been crystallized, real differences in final time are more clearly understood and compared. Horses with apparently faster final times may actually have run slower throughout the race. Not many famous insiders are quick to appreciate the distinctions.

On other relations of modern handicapping, such as the complementary or uncomplementary relationship between track biases and speed figures, the majority of insiders remain out in left field. What they do not know baffles them; betrays them.

The dull, repetitive observations of famous insiders to the racing media reflect the overwhelming emphasis they bestow on traditional factors of handicapping known now to have incidental effects on race outcomes.

The most conspicuous mistakes involve weights and weight shifts. The observation is inevitable. It's the biggest race of the season. Trainers point to differences in pounds, regularly trite, as the crucial factor bridging victory and defeat. Broadcasters and newspaper writers pick up the comments and brandish them to a starving audience that deserves better.

The weight factor constitutes much ado about nothing, a form of trivial pursuit. Weight is virtually irrelevant in handicapping. Weight not only does not bring them together, weight shifts do not reverse prior outcomes, however close. The high-weighted horses in feature events win so disproportionately to the others, mathematician Bill Quirin has asserted that handicappers having no other information about the relative abilities of horses should bet the top weights all the time.

Inevitably, the famous insiders sound the praises of favorable posts, never forget to tout the advantages of leading jockeys, and will mention whether the speed horses will be clear or pressed. All of this is repeated so reflexively, regardless of the particular field, racetrack, or other distinguishing circumstances of races, the drip-drip of the discussion takes on the oppressive character of hackneyed clichés.

Contemporary handicappers have received little intellectual nourishment from the observations of famous insiders.

This being so, and the steady stream of negative results becoming so discouraging, it's curious why racing's customers continue to solicit the worthless information of insiders.

A perfectly plausible explanation is that few racetrack customers have learned to beat the horses by their own devices. Most have learned only how to cope, losing modest or immodest amounts while enjoying the chase and clutching the possibility of a gigantic score. A practical historical constraint has been the lack of alternative forms of instruction.

And so, negative results notwithstanding, the legend of the famous insiders and the special know-how they must have gathered to their breasts continues to fascinate racegoers, perhaps because a hopeful majority want the inside gospel to be true.

A growing minority of racing's devotees no longer seek the hollow counsel passed around daily among insiders. They instead have become highly skilled handicappers, people who have learned how to appraise the relative chances of the horses in a field.

The majority of the growing minority have become notably proficient at handicapping the races, ending the season in the black. Many are authentic experts, fully prepared to extract a partial living from their expertise. Whether they treat the pastime as an occasional recreation, a hobby, an avocation, or an occupation, these new handicappers view racing as a formful risk-management game characterized by familiar predictable patterns. They understand the handicapping process as an intellectual challenge game that can be mastered well enough to win.

These modern handicappers may differ from one another markedly in their ideas and practices, as will be reflected by the selective sample of fourteen winners the readers will meet in these chapters. That is because thoroughbred racing is a richly diverse sport offering its handicapping practitioners a richly varied menu. Handicappers choose from numerous effective ways to skin the races.

The new expert handicappers also share a number of common denominators, as also will be seen, one of which is a disdain toward the blandishments of the famous insiders. That is because each of them comprehends more about the art and intricacies of contemporary handicapping than the famous insiders can even imagine. The confidence evolves from a well-documented history of successful play.

For novices, relative newcomers, unsuccessful handicappers, and longtime denizens of the racetrack yet unaware of the possibilities, this book represents an opportunity to make acquaintance with a different group of insiders who have something worthwhile to say.

In the aggregate, their message is unequivocal, and optimistic, I dare say.

Implicit in that message is a cautionary note to would-be successful handicappers.

Instead of mixing it up at the track with the famous insiders, pay attention to the new expert handicappers. The secrets of beating the races belong to them.

CHAPTER FOUR

The New Expert Handicappers

DAMON RUNYON would not recognize the new expert handicappers. The chronicler of a different era probably would not like the modern horseplayer nearly as much as he did his down-on-their-luck characters, not as much, indeed, as the new experts themselves liked Runyon's guys and dolls.

No matter. Modern handicappers are not as sympathetic as luckless bettors. They take themselves too seriously. They take the game too seriously. They strive to win, detest losing. They do not depend upon luck. They do not make excuses, will not suffer fools. Winners are not as sympathetic as losers.

Besides, the subculture of the racetrack has been changing slowly for two decades. It's a new game now. The age of information has arrived. The new expert handicappers are the celebrants of the new age. They are the best informed practitioners the game has ever known. They are the new racetrack celebrities. Their fellows salute, admire even, their unusual, savvy handicapping talents.

The new expert handicappers are younger, ages twenty-five to fifty-five. Toward the youthful pole, they are absolutely the young adults the racing industry has never been able to attract. Until thirty, young adults tend to manage limited bankrolls, and alongside larger responsibilities, tend to avoid playing a game in which they absorb a repeated financial thrashing.

Playing the races for profit is a difficult intellectual, emotional, and psychological challenge game. Their regular presence on the scene means at least the new handicappers have learned how to cope successfully, if not win consistently. Modern handicappers know what they are about, as their predecessors did not.

The new expert handicappers tend to be better-educated men and women, and many are college graduates. They understand the value of learning, and of studying the past without reinventing it. Thus they read recommended books on handicapping. Few have not come to terms with *Ainslie's Complete Guide to Thoroughbred Racing, Picking Winners, Winning at the Races, The Handicapper's Condition Book, Betting Thoroughbreds, How Will Your Horse Run Today?, The Body Language of Horses,* and other excellent treatments of the pastime widely recognized by talented handicappers as standards. Most have devoured many additional books besides, and have merged the crucial concepts of each with the prior knowledge and individualized methodology they prefer to call their own.

As trackside experience accumulates, the book knowledge and personal development are integrated continuously into broader spheres of interconnected knowledge and skill. After a time in the sun, the new experts are not easily defeated.

Even as their racetrack exploits grow, these contemporary handicappers pursue professional, managerial, and technical careers outside of the track. Their backgrounds drive the handicapping experiences; the requirements of career advancement transfer nicely to the racetrack. The new expert handicappers come prepared. They do their homework. They willfully invest the time, energy, and resources, none of it inconsiderable, they know to be prerequisites of success.

Except as recreation, few of them would choose to go to the races without the crucial figures, ratings, records, statistics, notes, or information that have sustained them well in the past. They spend from ninety minutes to three hours off-track, getting ready.

Whether or not they rely on computer technology, the new expert handicappers understand the merits of technical proficiency. Handicapping is extensively a data-based activity that lends itself superbly to numerical manipulation. If an innovative method of speed handicapping appeals to them, the new experts expend the intellectual effort to master its technique and procedures. The same applies to technical methods of class appraisal, pace analysis, and other numerical approaches to effective handicapping. Arithmetic and conversational math are part and parcel of the modern handicapping process. Experts and would-be experts, however averse to the math, do not shy away.

If they make mistakes when implementing technical methods, the new experts identify the mistakes, correct them, and continue to practice until procedure improves, and results do too.

The new expert handicappers keep copious records. They update daily a file of speed figures, class ratings, pace numbers, trainer statistics, trip notes, and other assorted information that becomes heavy artillery at the races. They keep a log of surface and post biases, a slate of hot and cold trainers/jockeys, and a selective, relatively sparse list of horses to watch.

The horses to watch, by the way, are the real turtle soup. The horses have been stickouts on performance, perhaps in relation to pars, or especially sharp runners at certain claiming levels, not horses that went wide, or stumbled, or washed out, or were blocked briefly in the upper stretch last out. The new experts deal more with the reality of performance than with the speculations of troubled trips or the promise of potential. As a result, their horses to watch win, and several win again.

Most modern experts are savvy enough to realize that personal computers and data bases can provide a tremendous assist in recordkeeping and data processing. They do not shy from computer technology or discount its promise as a handicapping tool.

If a new applications program appeals to them, they'll test it, perhaps running the program on handheld hardware they can use at the track. As to information-management programs, any aspect of data processing or storage and retrieval that can be shifted efficiently (without back-breaking input) to the computer, up-to-date handicappers gleefully shift. Experts appreciate every edge.

The new expert handicappers constantly evaluate their ideas, methods, and results, and they are neither averse nor hesitant to change. Successful players have evolved as handicappers and bettors. They do not much resemble the handicappers they were to begin. They are not the same handicappers they were five years ago. They will not be the same five years from today. They change, they grow.

The new experts especially do not cling stubbornly to a universal method for clobbering all the races at all the tracks all the time. They diversify. Their weaponry remains state-of-the-art and dynamic, without losing a sense of organization, or even central thrust, when used.

If something is not working, experts discard it. The burden of proof never changes: results. At the racetrack, results means money won. Nothing else counts.

The implication of that is enormous. Of all that might be stated and reiterated, the new expert handicappers, first of all, are winners. Winning sets them apart.

During fallow periods, which are entirely normal, experts' moods sour, and if the losing persists beyond customary bounds, they will quit for a time. The work stoppages rejuvenate the spirits. Quick comebacks are typical. Expert handicappers may lose for a week, a few weeks, even a couple of months, but rarely longer than that. Across a season, authentic experts infrequently continue to lose. A losing year is extraordinary.

Nevertheless, all is neither calm nor copacetic in the experts' private corner. How much do the real experts win? Racegoers want to know. It's a good, penetrating question.

The new expert handicappers are not, alas, expert bettors. Most of them lack as well the rarefied artistic skills of the successful gamblers. The latter shortcoming prevents the majority from becoming bigger winners. The former is worse. It prevents experts from winning even as much as their expertise warrants. This problem is correctable, yet it persists.

Why?

The weak wagering skills trace in part to an avid interest in handicapping but not betting. The art of effective handicapping has been prized, pursued, and mastered. The science of parimutuel wagering has not. Lack of instruction has played a real, if less influential, role. In consequence, the new expert handicappers generally win significantly less than they should, a sorry but not desperate state of affairs.

The winnings, if not huge, can be moderately large. They are more impressive, notably to inveterate losers and punters, in their consistency. Consistency is the hallmark of the experts' performance. Season upon season the new expert handicappers ring up the profits. The bottom line is bankable.

In the chapters that follow, racegoers meet fourteen expert handicappers. They cover both coasts and the Midwest, and all are certifiable winners. Other common denominators will become evident, but so will individual differences. Major tracks, medium-sized tracks, and minor tracks are represented here. One expert is an international traveler. One is a high roller. One is a woman. Four abandoned thriving professional careers for full-time handicapping, the fantasy of thousands of talented, motivated, recreational handicappers.

How goes the struggle? Would-be professionals can learn the truth at last.

In the lengthy concluding section, "Winning Time," handicappers can accompany the author and two of the book's experts as we challenged the difficult ninety-one-day winter season of 1988 at Santa Anita, the Great Race Place. The three of us played the entire season together in Box 136, one of our most fascinating, stimulating racetrack experiences, we agreed afterwards. We gleaned insights from one another at a keen professional level, drew upon one another's strengths, and could not fail to improve individually.

I present the material as the best depiction of the professional handicapping enterprise on record. The way it happened for us at Santa Anita is rather much the way it is.

How much can expert professional handicappers win for the season? You are about to see three bottom lines.

CHAPTER FIVE

Paul Braseth

·

Three Is Enough

WHEN ASKED TO ASSESS his strengths and weaknesses seven years following the grand decision, the one that snatched him away from an eighteen-year teaching career to play the ponies full time, professional handicapper Paul Braseth, of Seattle, responds with the most intelligent insight I have yet to hear on the matter of personal handicapping strengths.

"Maturity," says Braseth. "My strength is my maturity."

He elaborates.

"I have simplified my information needs. I have focused the information I collect and emphasize to suit the tracks I play, and my personal handicapping strengths. I understand my strengths. And I use them."

The tracks Braseth plays include Longacres, near home; Portland Meadows, in Portland, Oregon; and Bay Meadows, below San Francisco, an unlikely circuit, lacking a major oval. Longacres does not card turf races. Portland Meadows does not house stakes horses. Bay Meadows, of medium size, has it all.

"I use a hierarchy of information," notes Braseth, who encamps at Longacres, in the main, from April to October; in fact, a horrendously drawn-out meeting. "It has three levels. In this order of preference, I use (1) trainer records, (2) trips and track biases, (3) pace and speed figures.

"Three is enough."

Notice that pace and speed figures have been subordinated by Braseth to trainer records and trips/biases.

Isn't this a regimen that confuses the abilities of horses with the maneuvers of trainers and the circumstances of races?

27

Not absolutely.

"Longacres is a track especially well-suited to trip and bias handicapping," observes Braseth. "A few years ago the surface changed drastically to favor early speed. I like what I call 'negative bias playbacks,' horses that performed strongly last out when hampered by an unfavorable bias.

"Pace and speed figures are always important, of course, and pace figures can be very important here, but they are not as decisive at Longacres as at Santa Anita."

Braseth did not mention that he puts trainer records first, ahead of all else, because he is arguably the nation's leading authority on analyzing trainer patterns. I, however, do not hesitate to stress the point.

Braseth allows that trainer records will be relatively more important at minor tracks, and that compiling and evaluating those data has evolved into his deadliest weapon.

"I've analyzed literally thousands of winning cycles [short-term performance patterns], and can relate them reliably to individual trainers. I do understand trainer patterns very well."

On trainer patterns, Braseth eschews performance patterns reflected by three years or five years of statistics in favor of current updated records for all trainers on the grounds.

"Handicappers need to know what is happening now. The five-year statistics indicate general strengths and weaknesses, perhaps, but it's short-term data that helps the most. I update my trainer records every day."

Winning cycles, Braseth says, are often accompanied by generous odds and are reflected by short-term data that must be current. Who's hot? Who's cold? Is a winning cycle heating up or cooling off? Is a telltale maneuver that introduces a winning cycle happening today?

"Performance patterns reflected by years of evidence do change in the short run.

"Currently updated data also supply clues about the abilities and shortcomings of young trainers. This season at Longacres I did well with two new faces, Tom Burlingame and Tom Kidwell, by staying alert to the first printouts on them."

Braseth and colleague Danny Wheeler, of Northwest Statistics, have completed a five-year scan of trainer records that slices the data bank into forty-two angles. On trainers, no matter how obscure or idiosyncratic the pattern, Braseth will seldom be fooled or unawares. In 1985, as the author watched, Braseth cashed a half-dozen trainer bets in four days, missing once. The winners were conspicuous overlays, at least to a trainer specialist.

"The best bet at the track," asserts Braseth unflinchingly, "is an improving horse that fits a winning trainer pattern. I'm looking at improving horses more closely now, studying patterns of improvement that win. It's my next big project."

As most modern handicappers have expanded their information requirements, Braseth has narrowed and focused his. Mark Cramer speaks of opposite logics, seemingly contradictory points of view that can have equally valid practical applications. Braseth's situation has provided an apt illustration.

Handicappers can learn to apply as much knowledge as their minds can absorb, but to avoid a maddening information glut by collecting and emphasizing types of information that best reflect their strengths, their personalities, or the peculiarities of their tracks. No real conflict exists. Something lost, something gained. Logical opposites, practical alternatives.

Braseth continues at no loss of maturity on two additional complex counts, money management and the psychology of winning.

Of money management, the trick, if there is one, suggests Braseth, is to develop strategies that are not only sensible, but can be implemented literally. The handicapper must retain control, not only over bet size, but over wager value and whether to bet at all.

Distinct strategies for win wagering, exactas, daily doubles, and triples are recommended, even if a single bank will be plundered. Braseth does not comment roundly on betting to win, acknowledging he invests $50, $100, or $200 variously, depending primarily on potential value, the largest bets pursuing the greatest values.

"I prefer the exotics," he admits, steering the conversation abruptly.

"My favorite bet is the exacta. That is where the handicapper enjoys leverage. No question about it. You get the most value from the smallest risk in exactas. But you need a program to follow, and you must follow it."

For the handicapper's consideration, Braseth describes his own. On betting exactas, he recommends handicappers demand a minimum 10–1 return on investment whenever the most preferred combination wins.

"If I bet $50 worth of exactas, and my best combination wins, I must get $500 in profits. I can use other combinations, or savers, and I do, but if my top combination hits, I must collect a 10–1 payoff."

On betting daily doubles, the same strategy applies, but Braseth recommends a minimum payback of 15–1 whenever the most favored combination clicks. As to procedure, Braseth simply identifies the contenders in each half, checks the probable payoffs, and wagers in increments that guarantee a 1500 percent profit if his leading pair win.

"If I invest $100 and my best combination wins, I must get $1500 in profits back.

"If I put $100 into exactas, and my best combination wins, I must net $1000. I usually limit exacta investments to $50 to $100, and won't play at all if the required value cannot be obtained.

"The cardinal sin of exotic wagering is to win a best-combination bet but not get the desired value. No cutting back, no spreading too thin. You must be there to collect the appropriate amount when your best combination wins."

Braseth has developed no strategy for betting triples (the West Coast style of serial bet), as Longacres does not yet proffer the wager. "I understand from colleagues it's the best bet ever," he remarks wistfully, "and on my next excursion to Bay Meadows I intend to study the triple carefully."

Braseth also entertains the notion of "action" bets to win, if merely to enliven a slow afternoon. "I like the Steve Davidowitz separation of prime bets and action bets. I think $30 a day worth of action bets is just right."

Handicapping theories and money management strategies are steady lively topics for Braseth, but his keenest interest, the subject that sets his heart to spinning, the discipline he wants to explore to its bottom depths, and the factor he feels ultimately separates winners and losers, big winners from small winners, is the psychology of winning.

He has been troubled by the elusive question, Why don't good handicappers win? Or, Why do so many talented handicappers lose?

Braseth dismisses any finger-pointing at the perverse nature of the game, pointing to talented handicappers who do manage to prosper.

He also disavows the instinctive reaction common among excellent handicappers who have nonetheless continued to lose:

making an even stronger commitment to improving themselves as handicappers.

As the psychologist Howard Sartin has exclaimed, "The psychological aspects of losing cannot be dealt with on the basis of better handicapping." Braseth agrees, firmly.

"Handicapping is strictly an intellectual exercise. Playing the races well is not.

"Identifying the contenders is easy. Playing the winners is not.

"The key to success at the races is effective decision-making, and that skill contains highly psychological and emotional components.

"The psychology of winning means finding answers to the question, How can I become a good player? It does not ask, How can I become a good handicapper? Good handicappers and good players are very different species."

A partial solution, according to Braseth, is understanding the racetrack's realities, accepting them, and dealing effectively with them.

Numerous realities complicate the equation, of course.

One prized by Braseth is getting value on winners, in preference to picking winners that are undervalued. Almost no one understands, notes Braseth, that playing underlays that win is part of a losing pattern (because the low, unfair payoff will not yield sufficient profits in the long run; that is, if the same bet were placed a hundred times).

Another reality, Braseth holds, one more aligned to proficiency in handicapping, is adapting to the predominance of younger horses on the programs. The handicapping shifts, at least subtly, often dramatically. Personal practice must shift in kind.

"The past weekend at Longacres, two of the races were for two-year-olds, and five were restricted to three-year-olds. Only one race was open to older horses. Handicappers have to be aware of that change, accept the new reality, and alter their game to meet the challenge. Younger horses are different."

Handicappers must also understand themselves as players, says Braseth, as a kind of first principle—know their strengths and weaknesses, play to their strengths, improve weaknesses.

"A personal reality I have had to cope with has been a failure for years to recognize the importance of early speed. It's been my biggest weakness. Still is.

"I have always automatically looked for horses showing an

Ainslie-style 'big win.' I learned to do that early on. Those horses often come from just behind the pace, winning after the pace collapses. I have too quickly assumed that if two or more speed horses were running on the front, an off-pace horse would win.

"I know that's wrong. The superior speed horse, or the front-runner that will eventually control the pace, regularly wins. I now use speed points and pace figures to identify those horses. I must continually remind myself to be alert to the best speed horses, and play them.

"I cannot afford to throw speed horses out prematurely or discount them too much because they are likely to be contested on the pace.

"That's what I mean about knowing yourself as a player, especially weaknesses that prevent winning. I realize I have this tendency to discount speed horses, and I have to guard against that.

"The psychology of winning fascinates me, probably more than any other aspect of handicapping for profit. I'd like to write about that subject someday."

Although he had been visiting racetracks for recreation for upwards of two decades, Braseth traces his true beginnings as a handicapper to 1975, and the publication of Andrew Beyer's *Picking Winners*.

"I began developing par times and calculating variants after reading Beyer," he recalls. "Before that, I can't refer to myself as much of a handicapper."

A prominent personality on the handicapping scene in Seattle in the late seventies was James Selvidge, editor/publisher of Jacada Publications. Braseth bought trainer data from Selvidge. Massaging the data, he developed his own "trainer win analysis." Braseth credits Selvidge as having a positive influence on his growth and for stimulating his deeper interest in trainer records.

Soon Braseth found himself struggling with competing interests. Having taken an M. A. in history from the University of Washington almost two decades before, Braseth had been teaching the subject to students at Roosevelt High School in Seattle ever since. In 1980, with a decade to go before retirement—meaning a thirty-year pension—Braseth departed the ranks for the racetrack.

"People have been asking me why I did it ever since."

He is hardly unclear about the incentives.

"It was strictly the intellectual challenge," notes Braseth, inverting the driving forces that traditionally have explained participation in academe vis-à-vis the racetrack. It's a rationale the nation's teachers will find hard to swallow, but not enthusiastic handicappers.

"In my early forties, then, I had burned low as a teacher. I had been a successful recreational handicapper for a few years, and felt I could make it as a pro.

"The concept of personal freedom intrigued me a lot. Success at the races was up to me, and no one else. There were no institutional or organizational boundaries.

"I also like to write, and from the beginning had in mind to start a newsletter for racegoers and handicappers at Longacres."

The result was *The Northwest Track Review,* a newsletter and information service Braseth has circulated weekly since 1981. He immediately broadened his handicapping arsenal to include trips and biases, knowing subscribers who could not attend the races daily would relish that information. Matters have proceeded swimmingly with the newsletter, Braseth now counting more than 150 subscribers in a minor-league market.

Weren't you worried? skeptics want to know still. Like, what if you were to go broke?

"No, I wasn't worried," Braseth truthfully tells the doubters. "If I go broke, I can always return to teaching. It's turned out to be a great life. I love it."

The life Braseth adores has a formidable schedule to it, beginning three weeks prior to the debut of Longacres (a preparation phase), which itself, as mentioned, opens in April and endures until October. Throughout Longacres, Braseth works seven days a week, seven months a year. The daily routine includes two to 2½ hours of handicapping off-track, and two to three hours of record-keeping. Since handicappers spend five hours at the races, Braseth's routine lasts roughly ten hours.

On dark days he arises earlier and undertakes the nonstop heavy industry that sends forth *The Northwest Track Review* to his waiting customers.

When Longacres closes, Braseth, believe it or not, hustles down to San Francisco, where from October to December he plays the horses—he swears—more seriously than he can in Seattle.

"I do not face the responsibilities and distractions of data collection and record-keeping at Bay Meadows that I do at

Longacres. So while there I actually play with greater concentration, and I bet more.

"In 1982, the first year I produced the newsletter, I experienced one of my worst seasons ever handicapping. I was prepared for rough seas though, thanks to Ron Cox, who produces an excellent information service on the northern California circuit. Ron had warned me what to expect. I couldn't concentrate on both, my betting and the newsletter, couldn't give my total energy to myself."

If 1982 was among the worst of seasons for Braseth, it was also among the few he remembers as bad times.

"Yes, I'm now a consistent winner," he concedes. "But it only took me two, three years to become consistent. Using a flat-bet strategy, I had always done fairly well as a recreational player. It was a relatively smooth transition to pro, except for that first season."

Braseth's best season was 1986.

"Everything was going well in my life. I met a new woman I cared about. I was betting aggressively, with confidence. I worked hard at it. And I won the noses."

Braseth did not reveal the bottom line of his best season, but identified 1987 as his worst, when the bottom line was black but he had only $5000 to $6000 in profits.

Since turning pro, Braseth has experienced two big scores, each uncharacteristic of his regular play.

At Portland Meadows he nabbed a trifecta for $12,000. He yearns to duplicate the feat, but Longacres denies him the opportunity—no trifectas, no triples.

The second windfall came at Bay Meadows during fall, 1986, and then Braseth did not even select the horses, though he is not embarrassed to recollect the incident. He did make the play.

"I went to Ron Cox's seminar that morning. He was talking about a turf race, which I normally do not play. Ron liked Big Dan Ryan, a 13–1 shot, even though the horse would be ridden by Russell Baze and was trained by the outstanding Tom Roberts.

"At the track another colleague, Dr. Howard Murray, a body-language expert, fell in love with the looks of a horse in the same race in the post parade. It was Au Bon Marche. That horse was 12–1.

"I played Big Dan Ryan to win and boxed the $2 exacta ten times, using both horses. They finished one-two, Big Dan Ryan winning. The $2 exacta paid $535. I netted $6000, and complimented my friends."

Ah, racing's logical opposites! A turf race, which Braseth does not even encounter at Longacres. A body-language long shot, Braseth's admitted Achilles heel. He pairs the two, and bingo! he scores. Prodded to name names of other impressive handicappers, Braseth immediately acknowledges his buddy and colleague Ron Cox, of San Francisco.

"Ron's as good as anybody I know. I've spent lots of time with him. Handicapping is his strength. He plays erratically at times, but he's a winner. He collects tons of information. He has imparted good practical advice to me many times. I've learned from him."

Braseth talks anonymously of a millionaire and successful businessman he admires at Longacres.

"This guy understands how to play. I don't think he has a lot of time to handicap, but I've been impressed repeatedly with his betting. He makes his biggest wagers where the potential profit is the greatest. I watch him. He puts his money down on excellent opportunities. I like his style.

"I like Lee Rousso's game also. He bets against the herd instinct intelligently. He also plays for strong potential value."

Dedicated to horse racing, Braseth finds room as well for other active interests.

"I love to read mystery novels. Robert Ludlum is number one. Elmore Leonard is number two. I like the Dick Francis, William Murray mysteries about racing too.

"I love music; jazz. When I am in San Francisco, I go to the clubs as much as I can.

"I'm a physical fitness slave too. I run. I try to stay in shape. I find analogies between running and racing.

"If I'm running and get tired, instead of quitting, I try to improve my form through techniques like task analysis—(what am I doing wrong?)—and rehearsal—(how can I improve?) I do the same if I go 'off form' in handicapping. Just try to analyze my mistakes and correct them.

"I also like to cook . . ."

Enough, already. What about mental fatigue, the malaise of dedicated handicappers, notably during losing runs?

"I avoid mental fatigue by invoking an old teaching maxim: pace yourself. I organize myself well, and do not fall behind schedule. I stay aware of the fatigue problem, and take steps as best I can to prevent it or correct it. For instance, I take one hour a day for myself. Every day, one hour off. If I need more time off, I take it.

"Regarding losing runs, my way of coping is to give myself as much positive feedback as I can.

"I remind myself I'm a winner and that events will soon turn. I also try to analyze why things are going badly, and make any corrections in my play that I determine are needed. But positive feedback during down times is the key for me."

Well, all intricacies aside, does a professional handicapping career interfere with a normal, healthy, personal life, or family life?

"I was married when I turned to handicapping full time, and I'm divorced now. There was a partial impact, that's all. My kids were grown at the time, and the career change has had no negative impact upon them.

"No doubt it helps if a wife or partner understands racing and enjoys the racetrack some. It is time-consuming in a way that can suggest to others it must be a first love. My present partner likes the racetrack, and we share some times there."

What are Braseth's pet peeves about the sport and industry?

"The first complaint that jumps to mind is that Longacres still offers no triples and only four exactas. I would like a $2 exacta on every race. I could make a better living.

"Longacres has only one exacta monitor in the turf club, also, and that seems inexcusable.

"More broadly, the industry knows what its best customers need and want, but they just won't give it to them. There is too little information. There is no education on how to handicap. The sport needs younger players, but to get them you have to teach them how to play.

"The efforts made in these directions are usually misdirected. The track will take an employee who knows little or nothing about handicapping, or is not very adept at it, and will make him responsible for the handicapping activities and services to be provided. Does that make any sense?

"The correct model is Scott McMannis at Arlington Park. First of all, Scott is an authentic expert. He works at an information center inside the track on an independent contract basis. He does a first-rate job representing the track. Everybody wins, especially casual customers who want to learn something useful about handicapping.

"I also think the racing day should be shortened. Longacres cards as many as eleven races on weekends. It's a long, long day. Young people are not accustomed to it, and they don't like it. Sitting around for thirty-five minutes between races is boring. The maximum interim should be twenty-two minutes.

"Dog racing waits only twenty-two minutes between races, and I believe that's one basic reason they compete with thoroughbreds as well as they do."

The first step a novice who cares to improve should take, according to Braseth, is to buy the appropriate books. He recommends four.

"Steve Davidowitz's *Betting Thoroughbreds* provides a good general education and excellent techniques. *Ainslie's Complete Guide* is still a worthwhile introduction, though parts of it are dated.

"Then buy Beyer's books on speed handicapping. Learn how to make speed figures.

"At that point a fourth book should be Quinn's *The Best of Thoroughbred Handicapping*. Newcomers can find out where they might want to go next; which specialties attract them most.

"After that, it's a matter of developing an organized in-depth approach to handicapping that works for you and your tracks. You need good methods, good mechanics, some specialized knowledge, and sound betting strategies.

"But the literature is the most important step in the beginning. Read the good books. Study them."

And when the novice has mastered the books, has gained enough experience—successful experience—to enter the journeyman's class, and decides to depart a thriving career to attempt professional handicapping—if he or she wins, how much money can be earned in a typical year?

"It depends on too many factors to be concrete—amount of capital, betting strategy, handicapping proficiency. A fair guideline is 20 to 25 percent profit on total investment."

Switching scenes briskly, let's go to Longacres, where on August 16, 1988, the 9th race is a bottom-of-the-barrel claiming route for 4up, nonwinners of a race in 1988.

In conditioned claiming races near the bottom, Braseth knows the horses still eligible will be no great shakes. He hunts for layoff types that fit winning trainer patterns, his specialty.

This day he finds Flying Admiral, not only returning from a long layoff, but taking a triple drop for trainer Ed Mosher, a journeyman who can win with cheap claimers following layoffs. Mosher obtains the services of leading rider Vickie Aragon rarely, but Aragon is riding Flying Admiral, a persuasive switch that closes the case.

Braseth touts Flying Admiral as well on a 976 telephone

service where he staffs two lines, one to win, the second for exotics.

In the same race Braseth is attracted to a Tom Roberts horse, also back from vacation, to be ridden by Longacres' leading apprentice.

The race favorite will be sent to the post by a trainer who currently posts an 0 for 43 streak, under a jockey winning on 2 percent of his mounts.

Braseth makes a sizable bet to win on Flying Admiral, odds at 4–1, and hooks his good thing with the Roberts comebacker in multiple exactas. Flying Admiral wins handily, pays $10.20. The Roberts horse finishes fourth; no exacta.

It's irrelevant, but the favorite does not get a call.

That's a peek at how things had been going for Paul Braseth in 1988, his best season by a leap so far.

"These have really been the best of times," he admits. "I'm winning consistently at the races. My newsletter has a brand-new format and more subscribers than ever. My telephone service is going great guns. The weekend seminars are crowded to capacity. I've even been approached about a possible television show for next season.

"Do I have any dreams? Hell, I'm living them. I've done it."

But what are they saying in the lunch room back at Roosevelt High?

"Remember Paul Braseth, our former history teacher? Oh, yeah; sure. Nice guy, Paul. He went to the racetrack. It's a pity."

CHAPTER SIX

Joe Takach

•

Hard-core Philly Pro

THE SOFT-CORE PROFESSIONAL handicapper depends on race-track profits for a portion of his income. The hard-core pro depends upon handicapping skill for the entirety of his income.

The soft-core pro plays regularly for a thick slice of the season. The hard-core pro plays all year.

The soft-core pro attends to other priorities and diversified interests. The hard-core pro has no greater priority and few, if any, other interests.

The soft-core pro depends upon conventional ideas and methods, widely shared, to obtain a relative edge. The hard-core pro supplements the conventional methods with highly specialized knowledge to maintain the absolute edge he needs to pay the bills, and live comfortably besides.

The soft-core pro can be susceptible to sentiments and amusements about horses, horsemen, and races. The hard-core pro is unsentimental, not amused.

Meet hard-core professional handicapper Joe Takach, of Philadelphia.

A card-carrying pro since 1978, when he turned thirty-two, Takach tours the Garden State, Philadelphia Park, Atlantic City, Monmouth Park circuit of Philadelphia/New Jersey. At times he visits the Meadowlands. Takach's goals are 50 percent winners, these yielding ground-out profits from average bets of $250.

Bet size scales from $1000 prime to $50 chuck. Takach gets a couple of plays a day. He eschews the exotics. His vacations are unplanned, resulting either from losing runs or mental fatigue.

Takach's methods embrace the conventional and unconventional, refined in either case to suit personal tastes and temperament, and designed to provide the individual edge he shares with no man.

On the conventional side, Takach employs speed figures, a self-generated variation of Beyer speed. These play twin roles, neither decisive. A priori, they identify contenders that aren't outgunned today. A posteriori, they confirm the more decisive evidence Takach collects at the paddock.

"I'm essentially a paddock handicapper," Takach affirms, yet only in the sense it's the paddock and post parade where he completes the bulk of his work.

A caveat must be issued here. Any throwaway references to Takach as a paddock handicapper, as handicappers comprehend that topic, will be confusing. What Takach does as he observes the paddock and post parade activities bears no resemblance to what journeymen handicappers do there.

Much of the Takach technique will be uncharted territory for body-language fanciers. Yet handicappers can glean useful procedures from this impressive pro, notably Takach's guidance on watching the pre-race warm-ups.

Back to methodology.

After he has rechecked his speed figures to confirm the implications of paddock inspections, Takach takes a second idiosyncratic leap that sets the hard-core pro apart. He computes an individualized brand of pace figures, at the 2F and 4F calls in sprints, at the 4F and 6F calls in routes.

The intent is to isolate the lead horses at each point of call and relate the probable pace to today's track biases, however subtle they may be, and at various positions on the course. Biases can change from clubhouse turn to far turn, from backstretch to homestretch.

"Garden State, for example, has been favoring speed on the outside all the way in sprints the last few nights," notes Takach. "So I'm looking for horses that survive all my tests and will be benefited by having enough speed while breaking or racing on the outside.

"If you are painstakingly strict in your standards, the ready horse jumps out at you."

Takach uses the term a lot, the *ready* horses. These unusual gems have recorded competitive figures, pass muster in the paddock, and should benefit from today's probable pace and track biases. An advantage on each factor must be palpable.

No wonder Takach finds just a play or two a day. Horses with four sharp edges are difficult to spot. Takach can persevere for as many as six days without a bet. The image of the highly selective, perfectly controlled handicapper standing by resolutely as unreliable and overly contentious races run themselves out, without squandering a dollar, may not be altogether unreal after all. Takach waits patiently, arguing that his methods, the process, are sufficiently interesting to forestall the boredom of not betting.

Although recreational handicappers cannot duplicate a pro's habits or tricks, and should not commit the mistake of trying, they can learn more about the pastime from full-blown professionals. Takach, for example, promotes claiming races as the likeliest source of winners.

"Not the real cheapies," he warns. "You know, nonwinners of $800 lifetime.

"I prefer open claiming races for $6500 and upwards. And I much prefer sprints. These are simply the most predictable races. A large number of the entrants can be dismissed reliably. Not that handicappers don't or shouldn't play other races, but these are the handicapper's best friends."

A rarely remarked trick Takach passes along regards the also-eligible list. He pays attention to any horse from a maneuvering stable that has been entered in an unlikely spot. As the public does not ponder the also-eligibles as much, and the horse looks out of place, the odds should be generous. If a trainer maneuver is occurring, and the horse draws in, it will be overlooked by the crowd. Takach often bets, and scores.

This professional's forte, however, is paddock and post parade observations, and he does not mince advice on substance and procedure. His opening salvo hits between the eyes, especially those of handicappers whose numbers do not seem to work well enough too frequently.

"You can have the greatest speed figures, pace ratings, and best understanding of bias, even every possible tidbit of information that can be collected. There's always going to be that intangible—current condition.

"By current condition I do not mean how well the horse performed seven days ago. I mean what does it look like today."

There it is, horse fans, a brief on the relative importance of equine body language.

As to procedure, Takach advises handicappers to escort themselves to the rail and observe the horses up close on arrival at the paddock.

Takach scouts first for what he calls a happy horse. Here many handicappers already know the clues.

"He's already prancing, the neck is bowed. He's playful. The head will often be turned toward the groom. The groom himself is calm. There's no shanking. If that happens, forget it.

"I also look for proud horses. The coat gleams, and the muscle tone is unmistakable; well-defined muscles bulge out all over the body.

"Many of the horses won't be able to raise their heads above their shoulders and appear listless. The ready ones stick out.

"Nostrils should be well-dilated. Ears should be pricked forward.

"As the horses get closer, handicappers can inspect the legs. Look for bows and puffed ankles. Look for bad, crooked knees. If you don't know how these deformities appear, find out, and practice the observation skills alongside someone who does.

"Look for liniment on the legs or body. This indicates muscle soreness. That means the horse will have trouble generating speed. If the weather's hot, and the horse is wearing a blanket, it's the same problem. I throw these horses out at this point. They're sore, and unlikely to win.

"Once inside the paddock for the saddling, I look again at the calm, happy types. They're not resisting the grooms. They're not kicking the stalls. Unready horses will stand wide in the front, heads down, looking half asleep.

"When they leave the saddling area, probably the most crucial facet of paddock handicapping is the pre-race warm-up.

"I absolutely require a two-turn warm-up. Once the post parade is over and the horses are allowed to run, I want to see the horse in a full gallop right away. I mean within fifty feet of striding out.

"Horses that have to be trotted or walked around the clubhouse turn are leg weary or muscle sore; it's a negative sign.

"Horses that want to run move into a full gallop quickly. They're probably dragging the lead pony, maybe even biting its neck. Doing something to initiate or accelerate the gallop.

"At mile tracks, horses that begin to stride out at the finish line following the parade should be in a full gallop at the sixteenth pole. If they're not, I throw them out. They do not want to run today.

"As for kidney sweat, a little is okay. A three-inch half-moon of sweat is no problem. The biggest negative is sweating under the forelegs. To sweat under the front legs requires an extremely nervous horse. Frothing on the neck or at the mouth is also negative.

"When horses do begin to gallop, I like to see them galloping close to the ground. The horse reaches out with the fronts, like he's actually pulling the ground with him, and his rear feet will strike far ahead of where the front legs previously had put down.

"This indicates the horse is physically sound. He can stretch. His muscle tone is correct.

"Generally the warm-up will extend from the finish line to the half-mile pole, and then they will turn the horse around. The instant the horse turns around, pay attention, it's very important. A ready horse will immediately start dancing, not stand there flat-footed. He will be put back into the full gallop right away, and he picks it back up.

"Any horse that gallops like this will run. His presence will be felt at some point in the race, even if he does not win. If three or four horses gallop this well, it's difficult. I look at the figures again, but usually wind up passing.

"If you see only one horse galloping properly, the only horse really working out, and he's passed your other handicapping tests, put your money down. There isn't a better handicapping bet in the game. That's the ready horse."

A Takach dissertation on body language and paddock inspection grows voluminous and includes a provocative segment on recognizing the presence of drugs, fair or illicit. He has recorded these observations in a 250-page unpublished manuscript titled *The Ready Horse.**

If a professional handicapper, like any person, can become the product of a wayward youth, Takach's reliance on body language goes back to a telltale beginning.

At age twelve, on his first trip to Garden State, young Joe visits the paddock and notices a horse jumping around playfully, acting out, looking sharp. Joe determines this is a happy horse. The others look unhappy by comparison. Joe bets. The happy horse pays $48.60.

A formative experience? Joe's been searching out happy horses ever since.

*NOTE: For additional information about "The Ready Horse," write to Takach at 2036-B Mather Way, Elkins Park, PA, 19117.

rom Garden State to professional handicapper the long winding road has been troubled but destined. Cutting high school classes, Joe reappeared at Garden State frequently. He went every Saturday. He liked the track.

Like everyone else, says Takach, he began his book knowledge by reading Tom Ainslie. He internalized several Ainslie-type guidelines. Soon he graduated to commercial speed charts. He takes unflattering swipes at the early instruction now.

"None of it is effective for a pro. A lot of it is handicapping nonsense also. Days away, class drops, distance rules, it's all rather ridiculous, in a sense. You get a low percentage of winners at average payoffs of $4.40. Who needs it?"

While in college, circa 1968, Takach returned to the paddock area and began to generate his own figures. He was now astonished at the appearance and equipment of racehorses; blinkers, bits, bandages, patches, liniments, drugs, tongue ties, goggles.

"I knew the paddock was a big part of the whole. It was an awakening. I wanted to learn the fine points of paddock handicapping."

He had begun to take responsibility for his own play. Now the racetrack became irresistible, a refuge of personal responsibility.

Soon Takach took a B. S. in Economics and a sales position in the garment district of New York City. He would stay there five years, mainly as sales manager. The income supported his on-the-job racetrack education, which occurred at the New York/ Philadelphia tracks throughout the seventies.

If by 1971–72 Joe's appetite for racing had swelled, it was fed conveniently by his employers, who also owned a racing stable. Joe began acquiring horses for his bosses. He was suddenly operating on the inside.

"I made mistakes, had successes, the usual results. As I learned more, I made better claims, and one year the stable actually showed a profit, no mean feat."

The stable dissolved, but Takach had acquired a daily requirement for the racetrack.

He returned in 1974 with handicapping ambitions to Philadelphia and Keystone Park.

In 1975 the breakthrough occurred. Takach met his mentor.

"I met Frank, and he taught me what to look for in a horse before it runs. I picked at his brain at the paddock for four years. It took that long. In 1978 I felt ready and went out on my own."

Just as Takach was approaching the decision to turn professional, two events coalesced to shape the near future. Both would prove significant.

Beyer speed had spread across the handicapping landscape as nothing so methodical had before. The figures had begun to lower the odds of speed horses. Takach saw the trend.

"I knew you had to have good figures, but I recognized the numbers could not be an end in themselves. They had to be a tool.

"And I thought the figures would be more useful if they were self-generated; refined in a way that afforded the individual more of an edge. Speed figures are more or less the same as long as they are accurate enough, but self-generated figures at least give you a method other handicappers do not share. You spot horses they don't."

On the other hand, Takach understood at a gut level the special market value attaching to expertise at the paddock. After all, he is a closet economist.

"If there are ten thousand people at the track, no more than 3 percent even bother looking at the horses in the paddock, let alone inspect them carefully. Maybe one percent know what to look for; what's important and what's not. And only .5 percent know what to do with the information they get. When to put the money down. That edge is difficult to match."

So Takach joined the exclusive pro circuit with a vision of the information he would covet and use. Not a typical beginning.

In addition, Takach's conclusion as to the gigantic edge accorded experts on body language was valid. Outside of New York and southern California, and at those plants less often, body language can be more frequently decisive. This esoteric know-how remains poorly distributed, even among serious, studious handicappers, and winning mutuels will regularly be generous. Body language experts find overlays their colleagues cannot appreciate.

In 1977, a catastrophe. Takach suffered a losing run of unprecedented—for him—proportions. In thirty races he dropped $12,000. It changed his mentality on money management, only a year before his new professional life would begin.

"Until then I coped with losing runs by chasing until my bankroll ran out. I was very aggressive, very macho. It had worked.

"When I lost the thirty straight, I was rocked. I stopped betting. I did not make a bet for thirty days. I have witnesses.

"It took the worst losing streak of my career, but I learned to pass races. What happens when you're losing, the tendency to make poor or careless bets increases tremendously. You want to get it back too quickly. You chase. You press.

"I learned not to press. It was an important lesson, a costly lesson—but unavoidable, in my case, I guess."

How should handicappers cope with longer-than-normal losing runs? Takach is succinct. "You have to take a vacation."

Life as a professional handicapper has run a fairly even course for Takach since 1978. That year, however, he was divorced and disowned by the family, which could not condone his decision.

Takach assumes a fatalistic philosophical stance.

"They could not support me when I most needed the support. It was right for me, not for them. It has worked out for the best for everybody. I'm happier today than I've ever been. I'm doing what I love to do. I answer to no one but myself. That's the way I like to think about it."

Where the hard-core pro differs from the soft-core pro, and dramatically from the recreational handicapper, is at the betting windows.

Takach bets $200 to win, or more. He grinds out the profits, two bets a day, six days a week. One day off.

He does not dabble in the exotics. He has no huge scores to recount. Other than his bankroll for betting, which is substantial, he lays claim to no money management strategy.

"Anybody tells you they are making it with the Pick 6, the Pick 9, the double exactas, all that crap, that's nonsense.

"Yeah, everybody had a big score, once in their life. The $100,000 score. What they don't tell you is what it cost them to get the big score. Try it. You'll find out. They don't tell you, either, how fast they gave it back trying to repeat the thrill."

Takach runs a personal business, as he see it, and does not play a game. He sends forth his best business advice for bettors wanting to take advantage of the surest bet at a racetrack.

"It's the lone frontrunner on a track with a positive speed bias. They don't come any better than that."

He extends no other warranties.

Bets, he says, even for recreational bettors, must be affordable, comfortable, and represent capital.

"Scared money never wins. What a true statement that is,"

Takach stresses. "Don't ever play with the rent money."

Even today, Takach reports his strengths include speed figures he generates himself, excellent pace figures he bases upon his speed figures, and the ability to recognize either an illegally drugged horse or the naturally ready horse—"my greatest strength, and it goes with me anywhere I play.

"I might boast, too, that my pace figures are the best I've seen. They're just impeccable. I cash a lot of tickets thanks to them."

Takach confesses to a trio of weaknesses.

"I'm still a sucker for repeaters at less than 5–1. History proves you need an edge in the odds with repeaters, but I am still a sucker for these horses. Many of them look better than they are.

"I'm also a sucker for a horse stepping up off a maiden win when the figure is awesome. I guess I'll never learn to pass these horses. I don't bet a lot of money on this kind. That saves me.

"I also eat too much at the track, my third real weakness. It's a distraction I don't need."

Takach spends four to six hours a day handicapping the card. He consumes another hour in record-keeping: figures, biases, and charts. He's in attendance for four to five hours. The time and energy commitments are enormous.

Yet mental fatigue rarely sets in, is not a nagging problem.

"I don't really get tired much. I think I just enjoy it so much that I don't fight mental fatigue during the course of the season.

"When I do get tired or fatigued, it's usually following a long, long grind, and I just have to get away for an extended period.

"Last fall [1987] I took three months off, but really had not had a vacation in six years. No lie."

Takach lists no active interests beyond horses, so vacations are spent at the Jersey shore, lying on the beach.

"I just relax. Even if I just lie around the apartment. I just relax."

Takach comes back from forced vacations without lofty goals and dreams. He just pushes ahead. "My goal is the same as always, to pick winners."

He admits to wanting a publisher for his 1986 manuscript on spotting ready horses. A well-crafted tome, it's been returned with regrets by several publishers, who cite the scandalous lengthy section on drugs.

"I want to spread the word on drugs. There's so much the

bettors do not know. It's a technical area I feel qualified to discuss, though apparently nobody likes what I have to say.

"My in-depth article on first and second usage of Lasix was published in *Gambling Times*, and with much praise about the insights, I might add, but the same editor that published the article would not recommend the broader treatment on the larger topic.

"I'm somewhat bitter about that. First, I'm a genius, then I'm an idiot. The old double standard."

His pet peeves on the current racing scene draw similar outpourings.

"The so-called officiating by the stewards is just—what's a strong enough word to describe it—abominable. They are just so incompetent. Every real handicapper knows that.

"Also, it's clear the industry has no desire to clean up the drug problem. They have no universal drug plan. Certain drugs are allowed in certain states, but not elsewhere; here, there, and everywhere, it just adds to the customer's confusion."

On handicapping books, Takach bends both ways. Few of them can be helpful to hard-core pros, he feels, but he admits taking golden nuggets from each book he has read. He singles out Steve Davidowitz's *Betting Thoroughbreds* for high praise. "Davidowitz taught me the importance of track biases."

Pointers to novices flow readily from Takach:

1. Make your own speed figures
2. Understand track bias
3. Study trainers and trainer maneuvers
4. Know what the "ready" horse looks like, an imperative for handicappers who want to become professional

"I'll never get off the importance of spotting ready horses, for the simple reason it's what made a winner of me."

When waxing philosophically about winning, winners, pros, luck, and like concepts of the craft, Takach talks first about the importance of studying, playing, observing, and keeping copious records; doing, by all means, the tidy, detailed things all professionals do.

"Winners also keep their balance at the track, whether they're ahead or behind, and they handicap every possible aspect of the race, every horse, and they know when to put their money down."

Notwithstanding all of the above, however, Takach comes to rest on a kind of first principle that begs to be the practitioner's greatest commandment.

"Every good horseplayer knows that every rule of the game can be broken with remarkable success if the situation warrants it."

Playing the horses successfully is the most difficult human endeavor of all, argues Takach, precisely because there are no ironclad rules. All other games have restrictions that must be adhered to, but racing does not.

When handicappers break the so-called rules at the right time for the right reasons, it's often the smartest decision of the day, week, or season. Takach repeats the first commandment with emphasis, and delivers a veritable litany of the broken rules handicappers must tolerate:

- Horses do win carrying 126 pounds
- Horses do win six races in a row
- Females do beat males
- Horses do win off a 180-day layoff
- Three-year-olds do beat four-year-olds
- Maidens do win their first starts
- Claiming horses do beat allowance horses
- Horses do shorten up or stretch out for the first time and win
- Shippers do win races over a new track
- Drugged horses do win races every day

Finishing the soliloquy, Takach allows that he might have continued forever.

The point is, he concludes, handicappers can never say never.

CHAPTER SEVEN

Lee Rousso

·

Too Young to be a Two-Time Champ

"I WAS A BOOKWORM as a youth," muses Lee Rousso, recalling that at age nine he read his father's 1967 *Racing Manual* "cover to cover." The boy was fascinated by thoroughbred racing, and the man still is.

The steppingstone book Rousso absorbed closely on the heels of Dad's manual was Tom Ainslie's *The Complete Horseplayer*. "I must have read that one cover to cover one hundred times. Looking back, it has nothing on early speed, and too much on class, but Ainslie was a good starting point."

Rousso must have internalized the book's title, for today, at age thirty, he has become one of the most complete handicappers on the American scene. His methods encompass early speed, final speed, pace, form cycles, trips, track bias, trainers, and other factors, too, even class, and Rousso supplies the explanation for the comprehensiveness that makes irrefutable sense.

"Each of the factors produces a share of the winners. If I play 250 days a year, some 2000 races, I'll have between 500 and 600 winners. Some will be the lone early speed, some will have high figures, some will benefit from the pace, some will result from trips and biases, some will result from trainer maneuvers, and so forth.

"That's the way racing is. You have to take everything into account, and identify what should work best in each race."

Of the manifold factors, Rousso emphasizes two that have rewarded him most frequently with overlays that win. One is surprising, form cycles; the other predictable, early speed.

"I look for improving horses all the time. The form cycle is

50

far more dynamic than the public understands. Peak performances and good races will be generally overbet, improving horses underbet.

"I also prefer early speed horses that have not been clear lately but will be today. These kind often score as major overlays.

"I'd estimate that 80 percent of my biggest hits have resulted from improving form or early speed. I also think the combination of improving form and early speed is the best bet at the track."

Rousso holds thoughtful, definite opinions on the other fundamental factors as well, and they are worth trotting out up front.

On speed handicapping:

"I used Beyer figures for years but lately have switched to Quirin's methods. Quirin promotes pace figures, and handicappers today need pace figures in combination with speed figures.

"A big final figure, but slow fractional time, can obviously be misleading. If a closer wins in a race having a high pace figure but a slow or common final figure, obviously the front of the race fell apart. Handicappers must comprehend these basic relationships.

"The key pace considerations are two: how fast was the pace, and how many horses contested it."

Rousso notes that even Beyer changed his position on pace, favoring the factor once the final-figure horses began winding up as underlays and losing.

He also comments, with dry irony, on the Ragozin style sheets' presumption that pace does not count.

"No pace is the Raggies' gimmick. I guess all handicappers have gimmicks. My gimmick is that there's no such thing as class. It's not true, but I like to think it."

On class handicapping:

"Class is not an intrinsic quality. Not in the sense of one horse looking another in the eye and beating it into submission. Poor-breds beat blue-breds every day at every track. Claiming horses improve from $10,000 to $50,000 competition in a single season. It happens all the time.

"Last season at Hollywood Park, a recent graduate of a $32,000 maiden-claiming race won a Graded stakes. Class levels seem less meaningful than ever.

"What's important is to know the levels where a horse can do well. Also, know the levels where class counts. For instance, when maidens drop into maiden-claiming races, we know they win frequently. The maiden-claiming horses just run so much slower.

"A useful class maneuver not understood by the public is the change from claiming races, say $25,000 to $40,000 selling levels, to nonwinners-once allowances. Claiming horses can win those kind of allowance races, and do repeatedly.

"At Santa Anita during winter, older consistent claimers beat older (4up) nonwinners of allowance races all the time. Since the public undervalues claiming horses entered in allowance races, it's a good play.

"The point is to know the local class levels where drops and rises really do make a difference. I let the class factor go at that."

On trainers:

"A lot of bad advice is dished out daily on trainers. The key question is simply whether it's a competent trainer or not. The key statistic is the win percentage for the last year. Between 15 and 20 percent is good, 5 percent is poor.

"Percentages for subcategories are too fine to matter. The data's just not reliable. A trainer does well in turf sprints for two years and badly the next year. So what?

"Computer data on trainers is often conflicting. A printout shows that when a trainer switches from dirt to turf and employs a certain jockey, or some similar move, and the horse goes off at 5–1 or less, it's a good pattern. But the same horse is a three-year-old, and the same data shows the trainer does poorly with three-year-olds. Or the horse is coming back from a layoff and the trainer performs badly with those kind. The contradictions and inconsistencies are many.

"Certain large performance subcategories do matter: first starts after claims, first starters, repeaters, class drops.

"Knowing the hot and cold trainers is also important. Hot trainers are difficult to catch—by the time you notice the streak, it's over—but cold trainers must be avoided. And there are always numerous cold trainers."

On track biases:

"Biases are crucial. The key is to keep ahead of the crowd. A two-week bias can be spotted on the first day. At Santa Anita, 1986, inside speed was powerful for the first six weeks. About the third week the trend began showing up in the press. I perceived it early enough and cashed in very nicely.

"You have to know your tracks. In southern California, for example, biases at Santa Anita and Del Mar last for weeks, but at Hollywood Park they can change from day to day. Santa Anita's biases usually will last until the next rain. Del Mar's can continue throughout the entire season, and do.

"In looking for biases, it's important not to see what isn't there. Biases move horses up that otherwise would not be nearly as competitive. Look for unpredictable outcomes that a bias explains."

On trips:

"I like being present at the track in preference to watching races or reruns on monitors. Using monitors, I recommend the head-on monitors some tracks now provide. Santa Anita does this best.

"I look for a severely disadvantageous trip. A wide trip all the way for a speed horse outside is a common bad-trip playback I like. If the horse persevered until mid-stretch, it probably would have won with a better trip.

"I also discount easy wins that were helped by perfect trips. Speed horses often benefit in this way, and can be tossed or downgraded next time, especially if their figures are common or weak."

On jockeys:

"Not an important factor at major tracks as a rule. Certainly not in southern California. It's nice to know which jockeys are hot and cold, but handicappers can't do too much with the jockey factor. The leading jockey is often overbet, but that's just a fact of life at the racetrack."

Rousso readily recalls his first bet. Five years after devouring his first racing manual, now age fourteen, and an illegal bettor, he and two friends chipped in with $1.33 each and played two horses in the first half to a co-favorite in the second half of a Longacres' double.

One horse in the first was the 4–5 choice. It broke down. But the 20–1 shot won. So did the selection in the second half. The double paid $298. When the 2–5 shot they picked won the third, one more wayward teenager had been set on his life's journey.

Four years later, at age eighteen and legal at last, the first of the red-hot Rousso win streaks came to pass. Taking the bus to Portland Meadows for ten consecutive days, Rousso converted a $5 bill to $800. In two months, the five-spot had sprouted to $3000. This was the bellwether formative experience.

"I considered it a real accomplishment, my first in life. I realized how quickly handicappers could make money at the races. I was hooked."

From 1976 to 1980 Rousso became literally a journeyman handicapper, visiting a number of tracks on the East Coast. Two new experiences would set the tone for his handicapping.

At a boardinghouse at Saratoga in 1976, a friend handed Rousso a copy of Beyer's *Picking Winners*. It knocked Rousso over, and another modern speed handicapper sprang to life.

The other experience would be gradual in its lasting effects.

"I went to lots of tracks, as many as eighteen to twenty, and I usually won. Eventually I concluded that form reads the same everywhere. I became a devotee of form cycles and learned how to read between horses' running lines.

"In Boston, in 1979, I had a turnaround experience. I began to check the charts for horses showing improved efforts. My first play on a horse keyed to what I saw as an improving form cycle, the horse was 75–1. I bet it, and it lost by a nose. I knew then that improving horses can outrun their prices. And they do."

To complete Rousso's personal form cycle, we flash back briefly to Longacres, where two brothers he knew bet every horse on the lead.

"They were speed freaks," remembers Lee, "and they had a big impact on my thinking. They literally bet any horse they thought would be a frontrunner. When speed was winning, they had enormous win streaks. I was impressed, no bones about it.

"I backed many stoppers while learning, but I no longer do that."

In 1981 Rousso took his handicapping tack to Del Mar, near San Diego. He prepared figures and charts and was primed for his most bullish season.

Events did not proceed as planned. Scrambling, losing, moaning, Rousso, about halfway through, had little capital left. Then a freakish incident took place that would mark his style until now.

One day he had $13 remaining in his pocket. On line to bet $10 in the 7th, Rousso suffered a massive nosebleed. He got out of line.

The bleeding soon stopped.

"I would have tapped out in the seventh, but the next race I bet the $10 to win on another horse, and $2 to win on a long shot named Time For Sale."

The longshot won, paid $34. Rousso next cashed a $400 exacta in the 9th.

In the next few weeks Rousso patented the exacta score, raking in several huge pots. The $13 ran upwards of $5000.

"I'm a streak winner," says Rousso. "I do not grind it out. My big years have overcome losing years, but I have had losing years, I must admit. I do lack consistency, though I'm more consistent now than ever. The Santa Anita season [1988] was among my most consistent. But that splurge at Del Mar in 1981 has been rather typical of my play."

The next Del Mar, 1982, Rousso saw a *Daily Racing Form* ad promoting a professional handicapping tournament in Reno later that fall, and he entered.

What a propitious moment for Rousso's third lifetime winning streak!

He scored with his first bet [Hollywood Park, Mr. Reactor, $21.20] of the three-day tournament, picked a $13 winner at Golden Gate, and finished Day 1 in eleventh place.

He held position Day 2, ranking twenty-first, after backing three winners that each fit the Hollywood Park route bias on the inside.

Rousso handicapped for seven hours the night of Day 3, but knew in the initial ten minutes that two particular horses would be the keys.

"The horses just jumped out at me, the overwhelming kind of intuition. I knew I was going to use them. Both were at Hollywood."

The first was a shipper from Exhibition Park, in Canada, switching from a marathon distance to 6½ furlongs, a middling claimer named Joshie Boy. The favorite, Rousso knew, was a "hanger." From close up Joshie Boy got up in the last strides, paid $38.00.

"The sixth race that day, November twentieth, 1982, I probably made the most crucial pick of my life.

"It was a horse at Hollywood Park named Rocky Folly, who was breaking from the outside going a flat mile. Hollywood had a strong inside speed bias, but no horses drawn inside had shown speed. I felt this horse on the outside could drop over and take the lead with the bias.

"There was no simulcasting then. I listened to the race re-creation. Rocky Folly led but was under pressure. When he drew off at the top of the stretch, I had it. He paid $48.

"I was in second place, but needed only a show horse with two betting tickets left. In the feature at Hollywood I played a mare named Pat's Joy to show, with champion Sangue the favorite. Sangue won easily, and my pick got third in a three-horse photo. I was lucky on that one.

"I walked out with $83,800, just an awesome feeling."

Rousso's confidence soared, but his credibility slackened. Friends and associates thought he had been lucky, not good.

Events did not proceed smoothly. Following his best year, 1982, profits upwards of $90,000, 1983 became Lee's worst year. He dropped $12,000 at the windows.

"I thought it was just an evening-out process myself, but it hurt my reputation with some people."

Then lightning struck again. Eighteen months after capturing the national tournament in Reno, Rousso won another national title, now at the MGM Grand in Las Vegas.

"The second title eliminated the luck factor. I had proved myself to everyone. The third day of the Las Vegas tournament, if I do say so, I had my best handicapping day ever, and one of the best in the handicapping record book."

Actually, the second tournament Rousso won proved vastly dissimilar on several fronts.

Winning at Hollywood Park with a route-speed bias the first time, he now won at all tracks on the contest board. He was third after Day 1, but blanked throughout Day 2, and faltered from third to seventy-third in the contest.

"I knew I could still win it, and stayed up all night handicapping. I had picked fifteen horses by morning, and had to use nine of them."

At Pimlico, to kick off, no speed in the field, Robette won for Rousso at $19.

At Belmont, nonwinners of two, an allowance turf route at 1⅜M, Rousso found another paceless field. He isolated a clutch pick.

"He's Vivacious had shown fairly decent speed at a middle distance at Saratoga, staying within seven lengths of the quick frontrunner Vulnerability.

"Away four months, the horse had recorded fine workouts for its comeback, including a five-furlong bullet. He went off at 45–1. I used the horse in the contest, expecting a slow pace in the marathon and a chance to steal the race.''

Watching the Belmont simulcast, Rousso saw He's Vivacious grab a big early lead, still five lengths in front down the backstretch. The field came to the pacesetter nearing the stretch. As had Rocky Folly in 1982, He's Vivacious pulled away and survived as a long shot.

"There must have been eight hundred people there, and I think I was the only guy rooting. I sensed if this horse won, I'd be back in the hunt.''

He's Vivacious landed Rousso again in the top twenty.

Next play, now at Golden Gate Fields, he surprised again, this time for $17.

Staying at Golden Gate, a mile turf race for fillies and mares, Rousso spotted Dan's Way, a filly stretching out following a lay-off and two sprints, the most successful stretch-out pattern. She wired the field—what's new?—paid $28. Rousso leaped to second place.

"I almost made a mistake here. I needed to pass one person. Each bet was $600. If I had bet to win, I would have blown it. But I calculated the points I needed. Jockey Kenny Black, who was hot at the time, was named on a speed horse at Hollywood Park. I bet $200 to place and $400 to show.

"The horse finished second. I won the contest by ten points.''

Rousso's prize money the second haul was $63,900. The two-tournament total amounted to $147,700. He was twenty-six years old.

Rousso still beats the races with a streaky brand of consistency. His is a soar-and-slump syndrome, long fallow periods followed by winning runs during which he cleans the table.

Rousso bets in the $150 to $200 neighborhood to win, and invests similar amounts regularly in exactas, triples, and even Pick 6 pools. He offers short, sound advice on money management.

"First of all, it's critical to think clearly about what you are doing. People at the races seem to check their brains at the door. Remember, you are attempting to win, an incredibly important point. You must try to win, not just have some entertainment. Or else you will definitely lose.

"Also, staying cool is important. Don't chase, don't panic. Experience shows that losing bets return to good handicappers eventually. Trust that experience. They always do. The money comes back.''

Technically, Rousso follows three maxims:

1. No short prices. Not enough of them win to return profits.
2. Do not bet every race. No opinion, no bet.

"Pretend the window is a mile away," suggests Rousso. "If the horse looks good enough to walk a mile to bet, that's a strong opinion. That's the horse to load up on."

3. No side bets. No throw-ins in exotics.

"Never, never throw in a horse in exotics at 6–5 or such. Toss those types out. If handicappers toss in horses of dubious merit, at least insist the prices are attractive."

Rousso's largest bet has been $5000. Last season he risked $1000 tops, on a 9–5 favorite that won by seven.

"I have no choke point, really," says Rousso, "and I can live with negative results. I am not a coward at the windows."

Rousso's routine finds him stationed at Santa Anita and Del Mar every racing day, with time off during Hollywood Park. Off-track, he spends roughly three hours with the *Daily Racing Form* and assorted information resources.

This is something of a compromise with a too-demanding past, a ghastly regimen of year-round handicapping, seminars, and betting. Burnt-out, Rousso abandoned the racetrack for the whole of 1987.

"Handicapping at night, doing morning seminars, and playing afternoons, is very demanding. Not playing Hollywood everyday helps, and if I feel mental fatigue at other times, I take naps on weekday afternoons instead of going to the track.

"Handicappers must exercise their brains a lot, so mental fatigue goes with the territory."

Handicappers contemplating becoming professional can accept Rousso's no-money-back guarantee that the position is full-time and the activity resembles work-work-work.

"Too many guys who want to do this for a living view the handicapping life as an alternative to hard work. But it isn't, and it can be grim when losing.

"It helps to be smart, but that's not necessary. The work ethic counts most.

"Also, your income swings can be fantastic. Guys will say they want to make $50,000 a year. Hypothetically, that's possible. But it's more likely to be $10,000 one year, $20,000 another, and maybe $100,000 another. You have to be able to deal with that.

"If you have a spouse and family, that support is certainly crucial. I know my mood changes in concert with win-loss patterns, and I feel lots more social when I'm winning. I prefer to be left alone when losing. My wife understands all of that. Lucky me.

"If you're unmarried and do this full time, finding a mate will be more difficult. It shortened some of my relationships.

"And unless you're a winner, playing the races is considered a character weakness. It's perceived as a gambling lifestyle that most people will not tolerate.

"No matter what, you will not be universally respected."

The polar opposite of professionals are novices, the newcomers to handicapping. How does a newcomer transform himself from novice to competent handicapper?

Rousso recommends novices gather a good reading list from a solid veteran and absorb the books repeatedly.

"I don't think you should read everything. Be selective. But just don't read a book once and put it on a shelf. I've studied every book on my shelf several times, and so should novices."

When novices feel prepared to bet, Rousso encourages them to conduct this experiment.

For six months, go to the races regularly and bet only one race. The horse must have odds greater than 2–1. Pick enough winners to demonstrate a flat-bet profit.

Then play two horses a day. Show a flat-bet profit.

After two years of profit-making, you're a handicapper, and on your own.

"If novices take this kind of approach, at least after two years they will be less likely to go from betting one horse to betting nine horses. It teaches you to be careful and selective. To pick favorable spots."

Beyond reading and experimenting, Rousso believes learning occurs best as a function of cumulative experiences at several racetracks. Especially instructive are winning and losing streaks. Pay close attention to streaks. Try to understand what's happening and why.

"I have learned more from slumps or losing streaks than anything else. I'm more consistent now as a result.

"I also discovered my greatest weakness by studying my streaks. It's cheaper claiming races for fillies and mares. On the other hand, give me a $25,000 claiming race for colts and geldings at six furlongs. I love those. I have a good grass record too."

What are Lee Rousso's pet peeves about the sport and industry?

"I'm afraid I have a lot of those."

Rousso complains that tracks generally affect an ivory-tower mentality that disassociates executives and managers from the interests of their customers, particularly their regular customers.

"How can a flagship track like Santa Anita have such a poor simulcast policy, for instance?

"The Florida Derby of 1988 was the most glamorous pre-Derby stakes for three-year-olds, and featured a local contender, Ruhlmann. Santa Anita did not carry the race, and in explanation said customers would rather bet on low-priced local claiming races.

"Besides missing the point, that's ridiculous. Yet Santa Anita sends out its signals every day. Isn't that hypocritical, and a touch arrogant?

"Hollywood Park has become unprofessional. They ran out of programs and *Forms* even on their special fiftieth anniversary night-racing program. Windows were understaffed. You had to wait in line to bet for as long as twenty minutes."

Rousso also thought horsemen as a group oversensitive to criticism and second-guessing.

But he reserved his harshest comments for other handicappers who make a living as touts.

"I'd say at least half of them are liars and cheats. They lie outright about their records. A prominent handicapper in southern California gives five horses a race and takes credit if any of them wins.

"People, especially newcomers, lose literally thousands of dollars purchasing this information. Not betting, just buying the selections of crooked touts. It's so much bunk. I guess that's my biggest peeve.

"But I think horse racing will always be this way. I see no systematic effort by the industry, horse-racing boards, or anybody else, to get rid of the liars and cheats. I just think it's another unfortunate fact of life at the racetrack. Buyer beware, I suppose. But it's sad, and contributes to a very negative public image the sport still has. Handicapping is my field, and I don't like being associated with the nonsense."

Yet Rousso, like other professionals, relishes the companionship and communication of other excellent handicappers.

"Of the national group, I admire Andy Beyer most. He's always thinking at the track, and adjusts well to circumstances. Above all, he has the courage of his convictions. When Andy is persuaded something will happen, he puts his money down.

"My impression of him is that he's streaky, but his scores make up for any downside. He's struggled in southern California, I think, but he's the kind of guy that can make up for two seasons of struggle in a single day. And he does.

"And Andy is a good guy. Fun to be around. I like him.

"The best handicapper I've encountered in southern California is Tom Brohamer. He's very consistent, very disciplined. Tom does not play races he does not belong in, and that's one of the secrets of success. He picks his spots, knows his strengths, and in general is extremely knowledgeable.

"Tom's a grinder, but a good grinder. He's more consistent than me.

"I haven't met too many other local pros, really. You're a good handicapper, James Quinn, but if I name you it sounds like I'm touting the author to get a good write-up in your book. But for the record, an author can also be a good handicapper."

Rousso retains a few goals and dreams befitting a successful professional handicapper.

"My goal is to make more money each succeeding season or year, just like successful people in any career.

"I would also like to have the only Pick 6 ticket at the track.

"I would like to be able to retire at age fifty or fifty-five, so I can buy some nice property in Washington state and play the races for fun."

CHAPTER EIGHT

Anton Hemm

•

Park Avenue Banker

UNLESS HE FREQUENTS the service at Grand Central, an incongruous sight, even in Manhattan's Big Apple, is the finely tailored Park Avenue banker at the OTB shop. At Grand Central a handicapper can stand among the three-piece suits and bird-dog Merrill Lynch's electronic board out of Wall Street, slipping away at a moment's unnotice for the forty-yard walk to bet the feature at Belmont Park, an inglorious version of banker's hours.

The almost-new Off-Track Betting Parlor on Second Avenue uptown remedies the horseplaying New Yorker's lust for the better life in all things. There, businessmen who are handicappers don suit coats, pay admission, sit in comfort—eating lunch at tables, perhaps—and watch the races from Aqueduct on giant color screens. Per capita wagering has been $650 in the parlor, a statistic a banking manager of mutual funds can appreciate.

In fact, our Park Avenue handicapper visits neither Grand Central nor the uptown parlor on the infrequent occasions when the force of circumstances takes him from the executive office to the dusky floors of OTB.

"I have a full-time job," states Anton Hemm. "There's no horseplaying Monday to Friday, unless, that is, I see something too tempting to avoid.

"I do read the *Form* every day, either in the A.M. before office hours or after hours, but I make maybe one or two plays a week at OTB. Both the horse and its trainer have to be special."

Bankers are conservatives, of course, by definition, investing gobs of capital to earn a small return, not a typical but not an altogether impractical approach to beating the racetrack, notably when the edge to place or to show on low-priced contenders is undeniable.

Hemm does not fit the stereotype exactly, but he proceeds cautiously, deliberately, reflecting the influence of his profession. Hemm has never challenged the Pick 6. He has played maybe two or three trifectas. He disdains exactas. He wagers 5 percent of capital in the straight pools, one unit to win, three units to place. His "action" bets are nominal, $4 to $10. Bets on exotics he calls "flyers," or gambles, and he expects to lose them.

"I'm far behind on exotics," he confesses. "They look like overlays so often, but I just don't win them with any consistency. The losses have mounted up to enough that I've contemplated not playing exotics at all."

Banker Hemm has exerted comparable control over his handicapping practices across fifteen years, but personal development here has been marked by the change and expansionism that parallels major directions in the sport.

Lately Hemm's focus has shifted to NYRA's trainers, and he has studied their performance records and win-loss patterns in detail. The research has proved fruitful. Hemm has isolated a power group of twenty trainers he can trust. A horse is a horse is a horse, of course, but to warrant a wager from Hemm, the animal must proceed to the gate from one of the deserving twenty barns.

"To be successful in New York," comments Hemm, "I feel I must contrast myself to the armies of numbers players you find here. So many guys buy the 'sheets,' they can affect the tote by as much as 60 percent.

"I look for a horse with improving figures, all right, but only in conjunction with a trainer or training pattern I know to be effective.

"The weakness of the 'sheets' players is the instinct to play the high-figure horse regardless. I did this myself with my figures, but ultimately it became a win-and-lose roller coaster, too uneven. I much prefer improving figures and competent trainers hand in hand."

Hemm picks the bettable trainers before picking horses. He then smokes their horses to an extreme, searching back *Forms* to clarify ambiguous situations that might be relevant now, such as performances following layoffs, performances at distances not contained in the current record, or performances on special footing.

"I like to look at the total record, for example, when analyzing horses on the inner-dirt track during winter at Aqueduct. Or when analyzing horses coming off long layoffs. Profits are good and steady on both those types.

"It may take me forty-five to sixty minutes to study one race this way. But I'm selective about races, and time and energy requirements rarely become a problem in my routine. I prefer to understand a few races in-depth rather than take a more scattered approach to the full card."

Nor is Hemm finicky about low odds.

"If a horse I like is odds-on, no. I won't bite. But I'll accept even money, or 7–5, and my records show these bets have been highly successful for me."

Where trainers and figures have not proved sufficient to separate contending horses, Hemm does not toss the towel. He depends upon an array of plus factors to arrive at final distinctions. He adheres to the following assortment:

1. A lone frontrunner in a paceless field, especially in the slop or when aided by an S+ [extra strong speed] bias
2. Two moves, same race, last out, provided form looks intact
3. Any horse that ran competitively against a negative track bias
4. Horses exiting "key" races, or races producing multiple winners next out
5. A maiden dropping into a maiden-claiming race for the first time.

Like numerous others, Hemm began attending the races with his father. It was the late sixties, and the son became curious enough to search for books on the subject. He found none.

"For four or five years I just attended occasionally. It was something interesting to do, but I was not much of a participant. What I did mainly was look at the experts' picks in the *Daily Racing Form* and selected one to follow."

Then came 1973, and Secretariat.

"I loved Secretariat. He represented my first rooting interest in the sport. I followed racing more closely during his reign and felt a renewed interest in effective handicapping."

Secretariat notwithstanding, the dramatic change in Hemm as handicapper occurred in 1973 for another reason entirely. He made a fortunate acquaintance at the races.

"I met Bill Quirin, and he introduced me to his speed handicapping methods. The relationship changed me drastically.

"I began to get winners. As my understanding of speed handicapping techniques improved, so did I. I was amazed I could pick so many winners, where before I couldn't pick any. The motivation to succeed became immense.

"At the end of the 1973 season, for the first time, I felt confident I could succeed at the races. I am extremely grateful to Quirin for the positive impact he has had on my life. Bill has had a special and continuing influence on me as a handicapper."

For a time matters proceeded smoothly. Quirin was not yet in print, his horses won, as overlays, and many won again, as overlays. But soon Andrew Beyer burst into print, and the national surge to speed handicapping was under way. New York was a first frontier.

"The figures did not work as well once they became so popular," moans Hemm. "My handicapping entered a new phase, I guess. I started researching various angles. In short time I discovered a profitable angle on the Aqueduct inner-dirt course."

- Play was confined to sprints
- Bettable horses must have shown improved figures in each of their last two races
- If only one horse qualified, it deserved a bet

That's all.

"It got fantastic profits. But just for an intense, brief time. Then it lost its steam. I stopped using it."

When Quirin's *Winning at the Races* did arrive on bookshelves, in 1979, Hemm uncovered a second profitable angle.

It was Quirin's finding that the "bid and hung" move had a surprisingly positive impact value, and could be accepted as a strong indicator of peaking form. Handicappers had notoriously discounted horses that had "hung," meaning the horses had lost their acceleration and drive and were doing their best just to stay even. "Hangers," handicappers understood, never went by another horse nearing the wire.

But the facts proved more complex.

Where the flattening out followed a big move, on the far turn or into the upper stretch, Quirin demonstrated the next race was the time to bet.

Knowing horses that "hung" were dismissed by bigger bettors, thus elevating the odds, Hemm applied the angle in full detail:

- The horse must have bid and hung last out
- The horse must have beaten half the field
- The last race must have occurred within the past ten days
- The horse must have not failed previously in its next start following a similar pattern
- The horse must show at least one win in its past ten starts

"It was profitable for a few months," laments Hemm, sounding a familiar refrain about handicapping angles, "but then it began to lose money too. I quit looking for it. I've had only limited success with my favorite angles, but they are fun."

Next Hemm entered an intense track-bias phase. The sweet smell of success had never felt stronger.

"I felt this King of the World sensation at first. I took notes on biases every day. They were very profitable. But so did many others take the same notes. Biases in New York suffered a fate similar to speed figures. They just became too popular, and prices dropped."

Soon began a final temporary phase Hemm referred to as "the body-language phenomenon." He found himself visiting the paddock regularly.

"My first call strictly on body language I won, and the horse paid $22. It had the arched neck, was dancing on its toes, and its coat looked dappled."

What happened next? Déjà vu, of course. Body-language horses began to lose their dapple, and Hemm discounted them.

Hemm retains track bias and body language as staples in his handicapping process. He has evolved after twenty seasons, however, into an information manager. He subscribes to the proposition that primary methods must be supplemented by various types of information that might apply at different times, at different tracks.

"Other than Quirin's books, the one on *High-Tech Handicapping in the Information Age* [Quinn] has had the greatest lasting impact on me. It argues handicappers who have been strictly method players should become information managers instead. Collect unfamiliar types of pertinent information. Manage it. Learn how to interpret and use it. I believe it."

About this time, the mid-1980s, Quirin imposed upon his trackside friend to assist him in a handicapping project. The experience would have a stimulating, broadening effect on Hemm's development.

"He was writing his third book, *Handicapping by Example,* and he asked me to identify tricky handicapping situations where basic principles did not clearly apply. It turned out to be an intellectual challenge. Doing the research forced me to concentrate on races and situations I had not carefully attended to in the past. It helped me grow. I try to do that each season on my own now."

An evolving handicapper exploring new directions at various forks in a long testing journey, Hemm, as befits a banker, has remained relatively consistent as a bettor, though he began dividing win bets into win-place units as recently as 1987.

Hemm's advice on money management is terse, pointed, and widely applicable, whether handicappers are professional or recreational bettors.

"Percentage of bankroll is the wagering method I recommend. You do not go broke and it adheres to the single most important principle on betting: handicappers should bet more money when winning and less money when losing.

"Everybody knows that, it seems, but how many do it?

"I bet 5 percent of a $1000 bank each season to begin. I'm a recreational bettor. I make action bets, but I keep them small. When the local horses are in Florida, for instance, I consider my bets on them action bets. A big action bet is $20."

What constitutes winning? Is Hemm a consistent winner?

"A certified winner knows why—so he can repeat it—and has more winning years than losing years. By that standard I've become a consistent winner, but not so consistent I can win every year. I lost money in 1987, but have experienced only two losing years in the past seven.

"Recreational handicappers, I think, should evaluate themselves on an annual basis. They should simply win more money than they lose.

"I lost in the beginning and did not know why. To improve, you have to know why you win or lose. It took five years before I had a winning year.

"I tend to win in cycles. I want to win badly, so I will stop near the end of a year if I begin to lose. I want to finish in the black. I think that's important psychologically.

"During losing runs I simply cut back on the number of plays. If a losing run is extended and really bad, I stop. I make paper bets, and do not bet real money again until I sense I'm getting hot. I've never had to stop altogether for more than a month."

Even bankers relish risk-taking moments, and Hemm has been meticulously successful on the plunge.

In 1987 he fancied Bet Twice entering the three-year-old classics, and promptly lost $200 to win on the colt in the Kentucky Derby where Alysheba emerged. Hemm bet another $60 on Bet Twice in the Preakness. Alysheba's backers took that too.

"I had lost twice, but I did not feel defeated and I knew Bet Twice would be a terrific overlay in the Belmont. I love to bet against horses coming to New York and coming off Lasix for the first time. Alysheba was a perfect candidate for that kind of upset. I thought he might finish down the track, and I eliminated Alysheba entirely from my thinking."

Hemm bet another $200 to win on Bet Twice, and $20 exactas linking Bet Twice to Cryptoclearance and Gone West.

When Bet Twice romped by fifteen lengths, and Alysheba finished off the board, Hemm collected on all tickets. The win mutuel returned $18, the $2 exacta paid $70. Hemm's profit exceeded $2500.

"That's a score for a recreational bettor like me."

Five years before, Hemm had benefitted from another score, entirely different in kind. It was the daily double, and Hemm had bet the scheduled $100 to win on a selection he admired in the first half.

"I wanted to stab at the double that day," he recalls, "so I went to the monitors to see the probable payoffs on four horses I was considering.

"I don't stare at the monitors often, but this time I'm glad I did. One of my contenders was getting unreasonable action in the double pool.

"With six minutes to go this horse was paying $210 with my good thing in the first. I was astonished. It started gliding down wildly. With two minutes to bet it was paying $60. New York is an action town, but this was ridiculous.

"I forgot about my other contenders. I bet a $40 double, and another $60 to win on the action horse. I had never played tote action before.

"My horse in the first half won easily, and the action horse won just as easily. The double paid $50.

"I had never put much faith in charting betting trends, but if that kind of thing happens a couple of times a week, chartists can make good money.

"Since then I have charted many exactas from my key horse to win, but I have never again found anything unusual."

A nonconservative impulse Hemm obeys finds him doubling-down whenever his favorite horses get an unusual assist.

"My favorite bet has always been the lone frontrunner in a paceless field. If that kind of horse will be aided by an S+ bias, I alter my style. I double the bet size. It works. Profits are generous."

Hemm recounts an evening at the Meadowlands several seasons ago. He planned the occasion with his wife, in part to test a pet theory he had developed inadvertently after numerous seasons of observation.

"I had noticed for years that frontrunners did extra well the first and second days of each new Meadowlands season.

"Pat and I went the second night one year. I checked the charts for opening day, and sure enough, speed had won everything.

"We had dinner and wine at Trackside Restaurant upstairs. By the sixth race we had paid for dinner, the drinks, and still had a nice profit. I started making $100 flat bets on the speed. After expenses, we won $600 for the night. I had caught a speed bias. My wife was convinced after that."

Hemm is convinced he's at his best when playing along with positive speed biases. He's at his worst when playing exotics.

"The idea of risking $40 to win $1000 is enticing. It's something I wish I could do. But I have not been successful with exactas, and I do not play them often."

Friends of Anton Hemm, his social circle and business associates, are long-standing, card-carrying members of an eternal fraternity that believe horseplayers die broke. If they do not die broke, it's because they have consorted with shady characters.

It's a no-win situation for Anton.

"They do not appreciate how the standards of racetrack handicapping and betting have changed," Hemm notes. "They don't realize how many professionals and businessmen are playing regularly. To them, the negative image of racing, which means gambling on unpredictable horses, is still the truth.

"It's hurt me with a few professional associates—playing the horses. Some people just do not want to come too close to someone they perceive as a gambler."

Of his colleagues, naturally, Hemm singles out Quirin as an extraordinary handicapper.

"I know Quirin very well. His strengths are speed, pace, and grass.

"He analyzes the probable pace from start to finish, and can tell you which horses will be first, second, and third at the top of the stretch. He then can tell you how strongly each horse will finish. If the race features an honest pace, his key selections are first or second, almost without fail.

"Also, Bill's knowledge of grass sires must be unmatched. It is around here. I believe he could make a small fortune each season applying this specialty alone. I get a nice number of overlay winners myself each year on his grass sires. No matter how high the odds, I bet if he likes the horse the first time on the grass.

"I was also very impressed with Tom Brohamer, of Los Angeles, the brief time I spent with him in New York. You can just tell Tom's a solid citizen and a winner at the races.

"Actually, there are many top handicappers. I hear about them. I just don't know them. I'd like to. The association certainly spices a long day at the races.

"I shouldn't forget my father's influence on me either. It was positive. He taught me how to read the tote and to notice inside action. He told me to think about trainer intentions, which I do.

"Dad believed if a horse was well-meant, it would be well-backed. He was very selective, too, unusual for his generation, only playing the stakes and classified allowance races. He liked good horses."

Hemm sees the near future of handicapping emphasizing national or regional data bases that can download information to the personal computers of regular handicappers.

"The data base concept and service just has to be successful. There's so much information nowadays. No one can collect and manage it all, let alone do the data processing. Once they get on-line to a handicapping data base, full-time handicappers will have situational advantages they cannot imagine now, and without unreasonable effort, good players will be able to supplement their incomes by thousands of dollars a year.

"It's definitely the future."

What are Hemm's pet peeves about the sport and industry?

"My major peeve is the takeout. In New York it's still 17 percent, and 25 percent on trifectas, if you can believe that. It's too much to come out, and is the reason I began betting win and place last year.

"Many recreational bettors have just walked away from the game, and I can't blame them. The racing industry has done nothing for the betting public. They obviously don't care.

"If the take were reduced to 14 percent, many deserters would return to the races. New players would be attracted.

"If the take were reduced to 10 percent, NYRA tracks would probably get fifty thousand customers on weekends, and between the tracks and OTB the handles would top $15 million."

Ah, a banker's vision!

Hemm believes racetracks also miss the boat by not conferring special treatment on big bettors, as casinos do.

"I have a friend who bets big at the Jersey casinos. A limo picks him up at his home. He is driven to JFK. He flies free to Atlantic City. Another limo meets him there, takes him to the hotel. His lodging, food, drinks are on the house for his entire stay.

"There's no comparison between that and how racetracks treat their best customers."

Hemm suggests bigger bettors might be monitored at designated windows, unless they preferred privacy. Once the amounts wagered exceeded certain limits, for the day, week, month, or season, the special treatment, whatever it consisted of, would kick in.

Perpetual high rollers would receive special considerations automatically from season to season.

Hemm's prescriptions for novices revert to his characteristically conservative bent.

Before betting, novices should consult *Ainslie's Complete Guide*, Quirin's three books, and Quinn's books on eligibility conditions and high-tech handicapping.

Next, novices must make highly selective paper bets for six months. They must show a flat-bet paper profit.

For the next six months, betting small, novices should play *every race* and reflect on the outcomes, an intriguing, and I must say, incautious tactic. As much as possible, read other books concurrently. Hemm recommends Beyer, Davidowitz, Mitchell, Ledbetter, and Cramer. The idea is to identify strengths and weaknesses before serious action commences.

"Novices can learn in a year whether the game is suited to them or not. Many good handicappers are easily destroyed by greed, impatience, or both. This is an unforgiving game. It's a destructive combination, greed and impatience."

Handicappers dreaming of becoming professional, alternately, must understand it's far more demanding than a nine-to-five job.

"Professional handicapping is closer to a twelve-hour routine, and daily attendance is a must while playing for profit."

The professional's beginning bankroll should be $20,000, bets highly selective, and the standard of excellence at least 50 percent winners on key horses or best bets.

Bet size will be $1000 to begin, as 5 percent of $20,000 is $1000, and suddenly the bank seems to be taking the fun out of handicapping. In response, Hemm counters that in any worthwhile endeavor professionals get their pleasure from achieving results.

"For real professionals, I think a $100,000 income at the races is readily attainable."

Is that a banker's conservative estimate? Is that what Hemm expects to do on retiring from Park Avenue?

"Only if I'm financially independent already. I don't know if I could handle the nonstop pressure otherwise. My hat's off to the few who do."

CHAPTER NINE

Scott Finley

·

International Frequent Flyer

HE'S NOT MISSED A Breeder's Cup Event Day, and six weeks prior to the Fifth at Churchill Downs he could be overheard looking forward to the Sixth at Gulfstream Park.

He attends every Kentucky Derby, and if his business schedule has tied and roped him somewhere else in the nation, early in the morning of the Run for the Roses he jets to the Louisville scene.

Two weeks at Saratoga in August is de rigueur.

He's witnessed three Epsom Derbies, and since 1985 has not failed to land on time for the running of the world's premier horse race, at Longchamp, near Paris, the Prix de l'Arc de Triomphe.

He's bet the best races of Australia, South Africa, and New Zealand, in person, of course.

He's haunted the major tracks on the East Coast, regularly in New York, New Jersey, and New England, and more than occasionally almost everywhere else.

Three times he has flown across continents to go racing, as he puts it, with well-modulated English charm, on the West Coast.

In 1983 he flew from New York to Los Angeles for the first national conference on thoroughbred handicapping, and a week of play at Santa Anita.

In 1986 he flew from London to Los Angeles for the Third Breeders' Cup, and four more days at Santa Anita.

In 1987, midweek, he flew from London to Sydney on business; from Sydney to Los Angeles overnight Friday, arriving with hours to spare for the Fourth Breeders' Cup at Hollywood Park; left at seven P.M. that very night for New York; and again from New York, at noon, Sunday, for London, arriving on schedule to represent the firm with corporate clients at an international trade show Monday morning.

When Scott Finley refers to himself as a recreational handicapper, he virtually redefines the concept.

Finley performs on the world's stage, his handicapping an international tour de force. Finley goes where the action is. When good horses will be racing and titles will be decided, Finley will be there. No one else, not anyone, derives more pure pleasure from this sport, or from handicapping horses. In equal measure, he loves the racing and he loves the betting.

Now thirty-seven, a corporate executive earning six figures, the world on his rope, a jet-setter hopping to New York, to London, to Paris, to Cape Town, to Sydney, to Los Angeles, to Louisville, to Boston, to Washington, D.C., and back to New York, it's hard to imagine young Finley, age fifteen, his first day at the races, making a $2 bet to show on the favorite at Thistledown, in Cleveland, Ohio. When the animal won, Finley had to inquire of friends whether he would be getting $3.20 or $1.20.

When last spotted by me, over dinner, in Lexington, Kentucky, on the eve of the 1988 Bluegrass Stakes (Grade 1), Finley had entered the hotel only an hour before, from Florida, in town ostensibly to consult with one of the firm's publishing clients. Brother Bill Finley was there, on assignment from the New York *Daily News*, where he's a turf writer and handicapper. Another Finley client—a Texan, I believe—joined the animated after-dinner conversation, which only occasionally ventured from racing.

None of us liked the next day's Bluegrass. Finley met the firm's local client that noon, but dashed to Keeneland for the later races. Bill Finley had Thoro-Graph's speed figures for the card, but the three of us took a day-long lacing at the windows.

Scott Finley flew to Louisville that night. There he met a business client on Friday, and at Churchill Downs on the Saturday before the Kentucky Derby he won a splendid $4900.

Finley returned to Boston, his current corporate base.

He would reappear at Churchill in less than a week, to see the Kentucky Oaks (Grade 1), a gathering of the nation's leading 3YO fillies on Friday, and America's most popular horse race the next afternoon.

And so it came to pass that on Derby Day, Churchill Downs, 1988, Scott Finley would experience his single largest life-time score.

Again he had Thoro-Graph's speed figures, and this day, in the 5th race, they registered a killing. It was an allowance sprint for 2YOs, and on the "sheets" a 7–1 proposition stood apart by several points. Finley bet $300 to win. He added a $100 exacta, placing the 6–5 favorite on the underside. They finished one-two. Finley took $4995 from the race. He later triumphed in concert with Winning Colors. His profits on Derby Day surpassed $6400.

"I had my biggest score, and best day ever, on Derby Day," muses Finley, with an inflection intimating the connection fits. "The Saturday before at Churchill was prosperous, too. I hit several races and was just grinding it out. Two Saturdays at Churchill, and I take down $11,000.

"I can hardly wait for the Breeders' Cup."

It has not always been this way, but the two-trip plunder puts Scott Finley of 1988 in a timely perspective. His biggest score, and best day, coincide in the season that undoubtedly will be his best yet. With nine months gone, Finley stood $16,000 in front of the horses, striving for $20,000 in profits.

The money won has been refreshing, following losing campaigns in 1987 and 1986, and lends substance to a sharpening perception that Finley could someday emerge as the leading recreational handicapper of them all, assuming he can get his act together, as he has not in a turbulent past.

The romantic cross-country adventures aside, this is a very good handicapper—talented, knowledgeable, savvy, experienced, bright, but until 1988 a poor player and bettor, unstructured, impulsive, erratic, overly aggressive, too much a chaser, the positives and negatives coming together in a classically inconsistent game.

Recreational handicapping, of course, is characterized by a tendency toward losing, if only because information fronts cannot be updated, opportunities inevitably will be missed, the recreation includes playing numerous races that should be passed, and betting habits veer from uneven to awful.

In consequence, recreational handicappers, no matter how talented, no matter how knowledgeable, no matter how experienced, combat a tendency toward losing. Good recreational handicappers succeed in the struggle, normally cutting losses to tolerable amounts, occasionally winning. The tendency can be overcome entirely, but it's painstakingly difficult, normally encompassing time and energy demands that cannot be reconciled with other requirements of real life.

In practice, for recreational handicappers, the alternative to winning is scoring. Paradoxically, this intensifies the tendency toward losing.

Finley is practically the prototype of the paradox.

Finley's talent, know-how, and upscale style combine to arouse the suspicion he might develop into one of the biggest recreational winners ever, but his admitted faults magnify the deficiencies inherent in the recreational handicapper's game. He skips the homework, bets haphazardly, breaks his own money management rules, and chases lost dollars unintelligently.

Yet Finley's play in 1988 represents a definite break with the past, a hopeful promise that the most interesting of recreational handicappers may be ready to qualify as the best.

"The irony of my play is that I won consistently during the initial years, using $10 and $20 bets to win or place on solid low-priced horses.

"Even then I had an intuitive feel for biases and trips. My strength is visualizing how races will be run: which horses will be on the lead, which will be head to head, which are likely to be wide, which should shoot up the rail. I'm very good at that, and some of it goes back all the way. I can often eliminate false favorites because I know their trips will be too difficult to overcome.

"But somewhere along the way, I just went wrong. I'm not sure exactly what happened. I became erratic, I know, and didn't learn how to manage money. I began to chase the exotics, and have never had any real success with them.

"My main weakness today is breaking my own money management rules. I also become lazy as a handicapper, especially when I'm on a roll. I depend on the figures too much during those times, and don't do the other work that has to be done. There's no free lunch at the track, just as there isn't anywhere else.

"I've only been a consistent winner for a year. I've had other good seasons, but they resulted from big scores, or luck.

"It has taken me twenty years to achieve the consistency I'm now experiencing. I intend to remain consistent too."

Achieving consistency has required deliberate alterations in Finley's handicapping and money management habits.

Of money management, the new habits are now set in stone. Finley will not abandon them.

First, he sets aside $5000 of betting capital for each quarter year. He bets 5 percent of that bank, however it grows or shrinks, on each prime selection.

"My 5 percent of bank is a variation of Huey Mahl's optimal-betting idea, which I'm comfortable with. I bet to win, too, not to place anymore."

During losing runs, Finley lowers the bet size. Bad-run bets will be $80 or $100 to win, significantly below the base bet ($250), but not a bashful sum.

Regarding exactas, Finley amasses a separate betting pool. He bets $10 to $20 boxes as a rule, investing up to $200 to $250 by keying top choices to selected overlays.

The capital for exotics normally disintegrates. Finley describes his exacta play as "undisciplined."

"At Saratoga this year [1988]," says Finley, "I set aside $2000 for exactas only. I planned to invest 10 percent of that bank each time. It didn't work. I tapped out on exactas during the second week. I'm still undisciplined betting exactas."

Finley's handicapping methods at present are multifaceted and well-integrated, smoothed around the edges by a deeply intuitive knowledge as to how they should apply at the multivarious racetracks he visits.

His three emphases—professional speed figures, the performance class ratings promoted by William L. Scott, and body language—obtain greater emphasis or not, depending on the circumstances.

When Finley challenges Saratoga, or Belmont Park in the fall, he depends on the speed figures and class ratings as top priority, but at Suffolk Downs and Rockingham Park, the paddock inspection matters most.

"If the field contains eight to ten horses at Rockingham," he notes, "usually six to eight can be eliminated on body language.

"I used to sit in my seat. Now I go to the paddock every time. I've learned the importance of body language, especially at smaller tracks. Bonnie Ledbetter's book and video have helped me develop my skills at the paddock. So has Paul Mellos, who's helped me at the paddock in New York.

"No matter where I am, body language becomes a final separation factor for me now. If contenders are washy, listless, or hurting, and others are full of themselves, itching to run, I concentrate on the ready horses. I'll change my first choice."

Finley's step-by-step handicapping routine embraces these procedures:

1. Calculate speed points. The procedure identifies the frontrunners with amazing reliability.
2. Tabulate the performance class ratings, employing Scott's procedures. The procedure clarifies running styles and basic abilities.
3. Analyze the speed figures, or "sheets." Finley purchases the figures distributed by Jerry Brown's Thoro-Graph outfit, New York-based, but assembling figures for numerous major tracks nationwide.
4. If Thoro-Graph's figures are unavailable, Finley calculates horses' ability times, another method developed by William L. Scott.
5. Conduct the paddock inspection, primarily of paper contenders.

Finley lately has coveted having access to Thoro-Graph's figures for different tracks.

"It's hard to overstate how useful they can be to a guy like me, a recreational player who's traveling to so many tracks during the year.

"The figures take into account more than the daily variant. They reflect trips and biases, wind resistance and direction, and weight. They're dynamite this time of year [fall], with so many two-years-olds on the cards. And they're useful for grass races, comparing turf horses from several tracks."

After fifteen topsy-turvy seasons, Finley going nowhere, two experiences of the mid-eighties carved out the decisive differences.

"I attended the first national Expo on handicapping in 1983, and I was in awe of the professionals I met. Sharing meals and conversations with winning handicappers was incredible to me.

"I went away with a conviction the game could mean more to its practitioners than just cashing bets. That you could perfect your knowledge about a complicated game by taking a rational, even scientific, approach to playing it. I decided to learn all I could. It was inspiring."

If the '83 Expo gave Finley inspiration, it was a three-year tour in England that bestowed upon him the attribute he needed most: discipline.

Finley had prospered in sales for Atex, Inc., of New York, which markets computerized printing systems to publishers and newspapers. In 1985 Atex named Finley an international sales and marketing director and shipped him to the United Kingdom. He lived in Berkhamsted, Herts, near London.

Finley decamped on an English racing scene that was the best in the world, five pounds superior to racing in the States, at least, and dominated by the regal stables of Dubai's Sheik Maktoum al Maktoum and Britain's own soccer-pools magnate Robert Sangster.

A connoisseur of fine, elegant racing, Finley was enchanted. "The courses were beautiful, the races fantastic," he gushes. 'All that magnificent green, the rolling hills, the left-handed turns, the jump races in winter. Going racing was a treat. It was just wonderful.

"Though the purses are abysmal in comparison to the U.S., races are first-class every day." Among dozens, he admired the champions All Along, Pebbles, Miesque, and best of show, Dancing Brave, whose awesome 1986 Arc stands as the mightiest performance Scott Finley has ever witnessed.

"The first year, I was learning about the courses, the horses, the trainers, and the books. I bet modest amounts only, 20 to 40 pounds a race.

"You can't handicap properly, because you do not have the necessary data and information, but a few trainers tend to dominate, and trainer statistics are among the keys to success. This information is published extensively.

"I was so impressed with its usefulness, as soon as I returned to the States, I added trainer statistics to my routine."

By 1986 Finley felt sufficiently acclimated to assault the English racing scene. "My house and car were paid for by the company, and I had an excellent salary. I went hog wild, betting with the books."

The pound settled high above the dollar the majority of 1986, a circumstance Finley judged irresistible. English bookmakers were just as eager to oblige him.

"The main difference between England and the states," he observes, "is that in England you bet with the books, not on course. There is little action on course. You can bet early and get the odds on the day you bet.

"It's a betting-mad country. They'll bet on anything, from the American presidential race to the winner of the Eurovision sewing contest. They take dogs, horses, and sports.

"The bookmakers extend credit readily. If you look okay, and they come to know you as a bettor who pays weekly, or biweekly, on time, you can get as much credit as you want, anytime you want it. Two local books gave me credit as I pleased. The easy credit hurt me. I plunged, I chased. Some days, if I lost early races, I called and bet the late races, chasing my losses.

"I was sharing my income with the books. It turned out to be my worst year, 1986. I dropped 9400 pounds, approximately $17,000."

Early in 1986 Finley attempted a betting coup, potentially the biggest score of his life. In January his brother Bill called from New York to announce that the connections of the American jump-champion Flatterer were intending to run in the Cheltenham Jump Festival in March, the championship hurdles race of winter.

"I knew how good Flatterer was, and by this time I knew the English jump horses too. Flatterer would be a strong contender and a nice price, and I decided to go for it."

Finley began visiting the neighborhood books, betting in increments of 20, 30, and 40 pounds, at odds as high as 25–1. He stopped by regularly. By March he had bet 500 pounds to win and place, respectively, on Flatterer, at 20–1 or better.

"The bookmakers were surprised to see me, as English bettors normally wager 2 to 4 pounds. A 50- or 100-pound bet raises eyebrows.

"My brother and sister flew over to see the race. They had pounds down too. At post, Flatterer was 10–1 on course, and I sat there feeling smug, with my vouchers at 20–1 and up."

The race became an exciting, heart-palpitating experience for the Finleys.

"At the second to last jump, Flatterer lay third, but suddenly the field began to pass him. He wasn't finished. He rallied valiantly up the final hill but fell short by a length. The English champion See Then won, his third consecutive hurdles championship.

"I stood to make 20,000 pounds, or roughly $40,000. I saw my dreams of an English cottage by the seashore, and a leisurely life, go down the drain.

"Bottom line, I made about $2500 on the race, thanks to my

bets to place. It was my largest bet ever, approximately $2000, but the anticipation and excitement were great."

Throughout 1986–87 Finley journeyed to France, South Africa, New Zealand, Australia, Italy, Spain, and went racing in every port.

In 1987, anticipating glorious opportunities as thoroughbreds shipped to England from other countries, Finley began to compile fastidious records. At last a touch of discipline guided his betting. It would end as a losing effort, troubled in the main by the same demons that had pestered Finley for years. But with his detailed records and newborn discipline, as December approached, Finley abruptly formulated a short-term goal he ached to achieve.

"By December the pound was worth almost twice as much as the dollar. I set aside 2000 pounds on December first and determined to apply strict handicapping and betting procedures in an attempt to erase my losses.

"By the day before Christmas, December twenty-fourth, I had won 4900 pounds, almost $10,000. I was proud of that, the most pride I had ever felt in my handicapping and betting at the races. I decided to implement the same discipline in the future, and become the kind of winner I know I am capable of being."

On the brink of 1988 and consistency, Finley had globe-trotted quite a long ways from Thistledown and the summer of 1967.

That summer Scott could not land a summer job as a camp counselor, but a friend, a hot walker, got him a job at the racetrack.

"It was the summer of Dr. Fager versus Damascus," Finley remembers enthusiastically, "and I just got increasingly interested in the sport.

"I knew nothing about handicapping, and only bet on the horses that ran for the trainer I worked for.

"I looked for books on the subject, and my father gave me *Ainslie's Jockey Book*, which I must have read a hundred times. I still have it. It's dog-eared now, but it had a tremendous positive influence on enhancing my interest in the sport."

At age seventeen, Finley's family moved to Philadelphia and the first son's first taste of the big time, as he termed it. He soon would be showing up at Atlantic City, Garden State, Aqueduct, and Delaware Park.

"I saw Dr. Fager win the United Nations Handicap at Atlantic City.

"I saw Damascus win the Woodward at Belmont Park the same season. It was awesome. Handicapping was still a mystique, but I was hooked for good.

"As the years passed, my methods emphasized trips, class, and certain trainers, but nothing technical or professional.

"I always had a good aptitude for trips, but nothing was codified. I think I was ahead of the times on trips. I wrote copious notes on my program all the time, long before trip handicapping became fashionable. I would put stars alongside horses' names in the programs. Those were my trip horses, and I studied them the next three times they ran. It worked out okay."

Finley's breakthrough descended from his dad, a student of the game, who provided Scott with an intellectual perspective on winning.

"My father persuaded me handicappers had to be factual and systematic in their ideas and methods. He made me learn how to play smartly."

Eventually the standard books on handicapping edged their way into Finley's thinking, and he began to develop into a player.

"I credit the usual sources: Ainslie, Beyer, Scott, Davidowitz, Ledbetter, Quirin, Quinn—the leading authors. Ainslie's books are classics. I liked Beyer's *My $50,000 Year at the Races*, and Scott's three books have helped me a lot. His *Total Victory at the Races* brings it all together, and his finding in *How Will Your Horse Run Today?* that a five-furlong workout following a layoff is a positive tipoff of acceptable form has led me to many winners I would not have had previously.

"[Quinn's] book *The Best of Thoroughbred Handicapping* is an excellent reference that covers the entire field, and can lead you back to sensible money management ideas when you go astray."

The best bet at the races, according to Finley, is the horse "that looks good on everything, and is 4–1 or 5–1. The horse has the high figures, a good trainer, positive body language, fits the pace, and for some extenuating reason remains an overlay. That's my favorite bet.

"I also like to have an angle on a horse the public does not share, and then see it win. That's the greatest feeling at the races. You've put your money down, have won, and have earned the right to feel intellectually superior at the result."

Finley names family members as the best handicappers of his acquaintance, and means it.

"Bill Finley is number one on my list," he says. "He'a a pro.

He's consistently at the top, or near the top, among the New York public selectors—now with the *Daily News*, and before with the New York *Post*.

"My dad is a consistent winner, and always has been. And my sister Lucinda is quite a good recreational handicapper when she puts her mind to it.

"Paul Mellos, of New York City, is also an outstanding pro. He has insights I lack, and Paul is an excellent teacher. He's willing to help the helpless, and has assisted me each time I've been with him at the races. I see him occasionally at the Inside Track in the city, on Second Avenue, which I like because it attracts bigger players and there's no surcharge on winning bets."

Finley's goal in handicapping is to be consistent, to exercise in the future the discipline that characterized this game throughout 1988.

"I just want to win consistently from now on," he confides. "You can't make a fortune betting horses, but I admire anyone good enough to extract a living from this game. I know there are people who do this, and they have to be damn good."

Beyond handicapping, Finley admits to dreams of greater involvement in the racing industry.

"I would like to own racehorses. Good ones.

"Also, my background is in the publishing industry, and I would like to have an executive position with the *Daily Racing Form*. That was not possible when Triangle owned the paper, but maybe, with Murdoch, now it is."

What are Finley's pet peeves about the sport and industry? He responds sternly.

"The worst aspect of thoroughbred racing in the states, and New York is especially guilty, is drug abuse. Officials turn a blind eye to the problem. I get so upset I can't talk about it. . . .

"The differences between the U.S. and England on this issue are incredible.

"In New York, except at Saratoga and the Belmont fall meeting, you cannot bet seriously on claiming races. The claiming races of winter go to the horses getting the best chemistry.

"In England there are virtually no drugs. The officials there mean business. A trainer was suspended for sixty days and a horse disqualified from a $30,000 purse because a groom at Ascot fed the horse a Mars candy bar.

"The States just have to clean out this problem with better testing and stiffer penalties.

"In addition, track managers in general do not understand

the nuances of handicapping. So they don't do enough to inform the patrons. The $2 bettor is just cast to the winds; he has no chance. There should be a lower take, no OTB surcharge, and no featherbedding of jobs at the statehouse level.

"My third peeve regards the *Racing Form*. The paper has a virtual monopoly, and is statistically excellent, but editorially—in the writing, and on the production end—the *Form* is abysmal. It should be a much better paper. It could be a strong voice for the sport and consumers nationwide, which it is not now."

Finley's advice to novices is conventional—observe, study, listen, stay in a learning mode; read the good books two to three times; go racing with knowledgeable handicappers who are willing to teach; have a plan, methodology, and stick with it—until he delivers his final recommendation.

"At some point, take a part-time job at the track, preferably on the backstretch, working with the horses. Learn about horses and how to observe their body language."

The former hot walker from Thistledown is now regional director of sales and marketing for his company. The role necessitates extensive air travel, Finley's specialty.

"I go where the job takes me," he says, shrugging, meaning he frequents several racetracks along the eastern seaboard, and elsewhere, year in and year out. "I get to the races six to eight days a month, and some other days for the later races only. When I'm in Boston, I try to make it over for all the New York simulcasts."

Wherever Finley flies, if he bets to win on prime horses, and restricts exactas to duplications of his bet on the 6th race at Saratoga, August 28, 1988, he will be taking off and landing as one of the best, most consistent winners among the country's recreational handicappers.

That Sunday at Saratoga, before violent thunderstorms canceled the 8th and 9th races, Finley won the 2nd, 3rd, and 4th races, ahead then by $1,106.

In the 6th he confronted a 1–5 shot, and proceeded as only talented, knowledgeable handicappers can. He dutched $250 worth of $2 exactas, placing the odds-on standout on top of four overlays. A 36–1 shot finished second, and holding a negotiable $40 ticket, Finley converted a $75 exacta payoff in an otherwise unbettable race into a $1250 profit.

"It's the only kind of exotic success I've ever had," observes Finley. "Using exactas and trifectas instead of win bets when you have an overbet-but-legitimate favorite to win. I will bet $100 to $200 exactas straight, if I can get a 3–1 return or better. I have a 70 percent strike rate on that bet."

A handicapper of the world who knows how to win is not only the envy of his fellows, but he has no excuse for losing. Not in the States, at least.

CHAPTER TEN

Erika Holderith
·
Playing with Artificial Intelligence

A HARD BODY BLOW to all horseplayers who are male chauvinists—and there are thousands—hits flush with the notion that one of the most advanced, perhaps most intriguing, of the nation's high-tech handicappers is a woman.

She is Erika Holderith, of Los Angeles, and she mentions, rather casually, that she currently is developing three main data bases.

And that is the routine part.

The ambitious part is that the lady proceeds with a fascinating package of software that is neither an applications program nor a data base management system. It is a piece of artificial intelligence (AI).

AI software attempts to think intelligently, as humans do—or do not, of course. It endeavors to apply heuristics to a mass of uncorrelated data, create rules, solve problems, make decisions. The software thinks inductively, moving from specific instances to general conclusions. If it makes mistakes, the software struggles to learn from them and do better next time, a procedure it might teach numerous human thinkers to mimic, notably at the races.

The software is named BEAGLE, for Bionic Evolutionary Algorithm Generating Logical Expressions.

Say, what?

"Basically," explains Holderith, "BEAGLE uses an evolving induction strategy to create rules based on [the handicapper's] objectives, say, identifying positive and negative form guidelines. The objectives must be obtainable within the data base; the raw data must be stored.

"The software wanders around, if you will, in a portion of the data base, say half, trying to find the rules that satisfy the handicapper's interests and objectives."

Holderith describes an iterative process during which the player interacts with the software and data base, intending at first to reject irrational rules, such as always bet on Trainer A in turf routes. It's a search-and-destroy mission, so to speak. Muck around in a heap of disorganized data and generate some order there. But toss out stupid rules.

After rummaging through the data base for a time, BEAGLE generates a number of rational verifiable rules that might qualify as an effective approach to handicapping, such as do bet on Trainer B in allowance races when he switches from sprints to routes with nonclaiming three-year-olds, uses one of the following jockeys, and the odds are below 5–1.

"I'm searching for interesting patterns and correlations," says Erika. "Then these rules are tested against the other half of the data base. The successes and failures are analyzed. The more iterations, the more the system 'learns.' "

Large data bases yield more reliable patterns and correlations. The handicapper, the software, and the data base can interact more frequently. Productivity and reliability are simultaneously enhanced.

As mentioned, Holderith is developing three data bases concurrently.

In one, she enters the past performance lines of winners and of losing favorites. Two objectives are pursued. First, identify false favorites: identify the characteristics of. Second, identify long shots that are winners: identify the characteristics of. As Holderith notes, winning favorites and losing long shots seem to speak for themselves. Handicappers do not need a computer and artificial intelligence to spot them.

In another, from the results charts of the *Daily Racing Form*, she enters the running lines of all the contestants. Here she intends to analyze how races were run, digging for successful configurations of pace. She also sorts various relationships involving jockeys, trainers, and owners.

In a third, a file Erika has kept for years, she enters the exact conditions of the races and the running times, fractional and final. The software isolates the fastest and slowest races, especially at the same class level (class-within-a-class), and can uncover interesting horses to watch, notably on the rise.

Holderith has help with the data entry, a college student she hires. She wrestles with the most difficult operational decisions, such as whether the development of data bases should be a continuous activity or the raw material separated into convenient data sets and attended to once in a while.

Maybe BEAGLE could be instructed to generate a decision rule on that question?

Male-chauvinist handicappers unfamiliar with computers, and many that are, will relax with Holderith and her data bases once they learn she also prefers to bet on horses named Erika, or even Erica.

"Ericas have been kind to me. One of my favorite bets was a quarter horse named Go Erica Go, paying $40."

Erika Holderith did not come to thoroughbred handicapping from an interest either in computers or betting.

"I can remember a trip to Las Vegas when I was an engineering student. I spent much of my time studying a calculus text."

But she liked horses while growing up in central California, and even took formal equestrian training in Austria. Her father, who did enjoy betting, took her with him to Los Alamitos in the early 1970s. She found good fortune betting on well-muscled quarter horses.

A few years later Holderith inadvertently issued a bum check, signing for $40 when she possessed only $20. Before borrowing the difference, she reflected hastily on her good luck at the races and returned to Los Alamitos. Her boss had provided a lesson on reading the *Daily Racing Form*. She did not know how to read the tote. She bet $2 on each race.

"In the Seventh race I played a horse returning to a fast surface after a short series of dismal performances on an off track, which had been proceeded by good races on a fast track.

"The horse returned over $50. The check was covered, and I was eager to learn how to handicap."

Obviously, pattern recognition would never be a fundamental fault. Holderith, in fact, has been a pattern-recognition junkie ever since.

At first she followed quarter horses, even devising a method of calculating adjusted final times, modifying them by trips, but soon was graduated to the thoroughbreds. During the period she refers to as her initiation, the mid-seventies, Holderith persevered in handicapping and betting, all the while consulting what she euphemistically calls "the available literature."

In the early 1980s Holderith kept herself busy on two fronts as esoteric as handicappers will encounter. At nights she staffed an engineering survey crew engaged in "geodetic triangulation."

What's that? horseplayers might ask, but it is quite beside the point.

By day Erika engaged in handicapping tasks that were, at the time, every bit as unconventional.

She had met a few of the West Coast "Raggies," New York speed handicapper Len Ragozin's lieutenants, and the guys had recruited her to help them construct highly refined state-of-the-art speed figures.

"They enlisted me to keep track of how wide horses ran on the turns, who took up or checked, who had trouble at the start, and so forth.

"Also, weather was important to their calculations, and I found myself monitoring wind direction and wind speed for each race. I did it by watching the infield flag.

"Though I had studied Beyer's work with speed handicapping, this was my first experience using sophisticated figures. Variants were calculated using a cluster concept, by looking at the first four finishers, not just the winner's time."

The approach relied upon projected times as well, extrapolating from past figures how fast specific horses should run today. Holderith allows that the method entailed a lot of work, heady work, which it decidedly does.

From the Ragozin sheets, Holderith drew insights to other fundamental aspects of the handicapping process, notably form cycles. She alludes to her personal competitive experiences in athletics, understating them to a fault. Holderith was a member of the 1964 U.S. Olympic Swim Team, and a gold medalist and record holder, thank you, from the 1967 Pan American Games in the 100-meter freestyle.

"I know very well the relationship between ability and conditioning, and their respective impact on performance.

"I know better than to expect talent or desire to overcome fatigue or injury. Even Secretariat succumbed to fatigue and could not win every race."

Following years of practical experience with speed figures, Holderith concluded that their utility relates not so much to the accuracy of the numbers themselves, but to what the figures signify about other crucial factors, particularly current form.

"What I found important wasn't so much to try to make pre-

cise figures, although that is desirable, [but that] they were accurate enough to reflect *variations in performance.*

"What was important was, I was developing the ability to
perceive meaningful relationships within the data [figures],
to come up with a realistic picture of how that horse is going to do in the upcoming race."

When Andrew Beyer played at Santa Anita in 1983, his figures repeatedly alerted him to horses on the decline. Several
were young four-year-olds returning to competition against older
horses, following layoffs due to fatigue or injury. As three-year-
olds the horses had performed well, several in stakes. The crowd
expected repeat performances. Often Beyer's figures indicated
the horses had declined. They did not win.

Holderith would not be surprised. Multiple speed figures reveal declining and improving performance, no doubt of it.

Pace can have a dramatic effect on final figures as well. In a
greatly persuasive analogy, Holderith drew on her unique ath-
letic-training experiences to comprehend the effects of pace on
the outcomes of races.

"While training, my brothers and I could tell how fast we
were swimming during workouts to the tenth of a second. Years
later I had another training experience that taught me just how
sensitive to pace a physical specimen can be."

Holderith recounted a demonstration she gave to high school
swimmers in Japan during which she swam what she termed a
"descending series" of fifty-meter freestyles ten times in succession. Though not in competitive shape, her speed from swim to
swim amazed her.

"Each swim was exactly one-tenth second faster than the
previous."

She concluded that if her system could be supersensitive to
slight variations in speed, a horse's might be equally so.

"I am not saying that a horse judges time. But they are sensitive to the impact of subtle pace variations."

Holderith also leans on athletics to understand the peculiar
nature of the speed-class phenomenon in horse racing; that is,
the riddle as to why better horses beat cheaper horses in slower
time than the cheaper horses have previously run.

"I explain it as a function of competitive psychology.

"Before I had matured as a competitive athlete, I had been
known to drop back if I was up even with someone that I thought
should be better than I, for no other reason than feeling that I
was outclassed.

"As I learned how to compete successfully, I learned how to be on the dominant side of this difficult-to-define competitive relationship. While I don't know why this sense of superiority is generated, and whether or not it is communicated between racehorses, I sense similar processes are going on."

In a strangely agreeable way, Holderith even credits her avid interest in computer applications to racing's Pick 6.

Once, after staying up all night creating speed sheets for the next afternoon's races, she fixed on a $64 Pick 6 combination.

"I had the winning combination that day, but I didn't buy it, literally, because I was too tired to stand in a long line. The combination paid $26,000."

The discouraging experience convinced Holderith to automate her abundant handicapping data.

By that time the Ragozin team had returned to New York, postponing southern California as a market for the sheets. Deep into form cycles, Holderith began substituting William L. Scott's ability times for speed figures. Using the Ragozin formats, she coded a new set of sheets for ability times, adding additional information with color codes.

"I found myself staying up late again with my form sheets. For each horse I would project the figure I thought it should run. It was just too much labor."

Hence the commitment to computers; it's 1982.

Naturally Erika threw her energies into the computer project with the zest and regimen of an Olympian. She covered the waterfront for hardware and software. A DEC Rainbow computer and dBase II software (now updated to dBase III+) got her started.

She quickly slammed into the practical impediment and found the logical remedy.

"But there were no commercially available programs, so I learned programming."

Erika mastered the elementary language first, BASIC, but since has conquered Pascal, C, LISP, and "countless fourth-generation packages.

"I seem to have a knack for it," she says dismissively, eagerly adding that she craves creating her personal software applications in handicapping.

Referring to a significant career change as a side-effect, Holderith credits racing and subsequently computers for her new position as a Systems Specialist II for the City of Los Angeles

Planning Department. She has enrolled as well in an AI certification program at UCLA.

What does Holderith see as the role of computers in the handicapping process? She responds immediately, enthusiastically.

"Since I have started using computers for handicapping, they have played the role of a tool for managing, manipulating, researching, and formatting data. I have never liked the idea of a computer making selections when my own brain was smarter.

"I made an expert system of Scott's *How Will Your Horse Run Today?* I didn't use it, because by the time I wrote the program, I was so familiar with the concepts I could do everything faster in my head. But it was fun."

Holderith holds to a philosophy of handicapping not unlike her love of learning and doing throughout life itself.

"My philosophy is to learn everything I can and try to look at a race in as many ways as I can. I am interested in the practical applications of what I learn, and am not trying to come up with some Grand Unification Theory of the Pari-Mutuel Universe.

"I am an avid reader and have enjoyed the works of Quinn, Quirin, Mitchell, Davidowitz, Beyer, and Ziemba, to name the more prominent. I also like what I have learned about Sartin, Brohamer, and a few others whose names do not come to me now. I also pay attention to Ragozin and Scott, as I've described."

As expected, the years of effort and learning have resulted in consistent winning, though financially moderate and accomplished in streaks.

"I have enjoyed some very healthy streaks and cashed an occasional brilliant wager. I define 'brilliant wager' as having a strong opinion about a race where you've found value and the result is positive."

A memorable bet occurred at Santa Anita, in a conditioned allowance race on the turf. The favorite looked strong, had been running well in stakes. Holderith, however, had just finished reviewing Bill Quirin's studies on grass racing, and she spotted a Stage Door Johnny in its turf debut listed at 20–1. The colt had shown some ability initially, but its recent races had been poor, and the stable was switching to the turf.

Holderith bet $20 to win, plus $5 exacta boxes with the favorite and second choice. In textbook fashion the Stage Door

Johnny grass prospect upset the favorite, a one-two finish.

In the summer of 'eighty-four, the Olympic summer in Los Angeles, Holderith was recuperating from surgery on both knees and spent her convalescence creating and maintaining extensive files of horses' individual histories and race results. Back on her feet, she took the data to Hollywood Park nine days in a row.

"Eight times I cleared a profit on win and exacta wagering, ranging from 800 percent return one day to 8 percent on the smallest winning day. The mean return for the streak was 200 percent."

Conceding she next faced three losing days and returned home, Holderith said the experience taught her something crucial about herself.

"I learned I had developed the same mentality toward horse racing that I had had earlier toward competitive swimming. That is, if I felt I had properly prepared myself for the day's events, then I would approach the activity with the greatest of confidence and anticipation.

"I would experience success. And the converse was true."

The reality of losing is nonetheless painful for Holderith. Even as the majority of winners do not, she does not take losing lightly.

"I have never had fun at the racetrack while losing. And I never had the capacity to dismiss it, with, 'Oh, well . . .' I spend time thinking about how I won or lost each dollar.

"I've also had times when I wasn't cashing many bets, brilliant or dull.

"I have lost bets I thought I should have won by cutting the bet down too fine. I have made major bets on horses that I knew didn't really have that good a chance for a variety of irrational reasons.

"I would probably need the assistance of someone like Dr. Sartin to understand the mental processes that are going on when I'm not doing well.

"What I am improving at, though, is modifying my behavior during nonproductive times, to protect myself from losses. I've started focusing on Dr. Z place and show bets during such times."

As befits her rational persona, Holderith admits she does not enjoy winning as much—"though it's always fun to win"—if she feels she's benefitted from luck or just "taken a shot." She did not address the misfortune often experienced by excellent handicappers attaching to bad luck or unpredictable upset.

"It's as though I need to believe that I have to be able to identify patterns and follow a certain logic in order to be consistently successful . . . though sometimes just taking a shot may actually be the correct action—I realize that."

Ah, the complexities and ambiguities of playing the races; with real money, no less. Is there no refuge on earth?

Lining up solidly with many experts on handicapping, Holderith sees money management as her Achilles' heel.

For years she discounted money management, believing handicapping prowess counted most. The bitter lesson is that inappropriate bet size contributes to inconsistent results, lowering long-term profits. Holderith does not construct a handicapping line, but intends to.

"Only recently have I begun to keep wagering records. I'm eager to see what BEAGLE will tell me about myself that I can't see on my own.

"I do believe now that money management strategy is indispensable. I like the idea behind the Kelly technique, betting more when your chance to win is higher and your chance to get a higher return is there."

Holderith accepts herself as an amateur handicapper until her money management skills improve. "Like anyone else, I don't need much assistance when I'm on my game, but when I'm not, I can do some pretty silly things."

No matter what, it seems, brains notwithstanding, the random intuitive aspects of horse racing will be forever confounding to the brightest of handicappers. I can't figure it out, says the rational mind. That's just the way racing is, says the wise mind. Indeed, even though knowledge and skill can control events well enough to win the game, the best-prepared, most talented of handicappers will continue to lose more races than they win, to win less money than they should, and to muse about the circumstances ineffectively to the end.

Erika Holderith understands this paradox. Artificial intelligence, and the expert systems it generates, will help but not resolve the conflicts and contradictions inherent in the great game of handicapping. The ceiling on success, sad to say, is lower than most human experts care to imagine.

The final solution has come to Holderith, as in a miraculous vision, and I shall let her deliver it in her inimitable brilliant style to frustrated expert handicappers everywhere.

"One time when I was attending the track with the Ragozin guys, something unusual happened. I had a dream at night that I could see the next day's *Los Angeles Times*. For some reason, I had my wits about me, and I opened the sports section to view the race results. I was shown a specific race result. I saw Melscott with a win, and a payoff of $7.20. Bolger was shown as placing.

"The next day I checked the *Form* and saw that Melscott and Bolger were both entered in the seventh race. At the track I told Joe Santini and others about the dream. I predicted the outcome of the seventh race would be Melscott to Bolger. They scoffed.

"When the race arrived I bet half my money on Melscott to win and the other half on the Melscott-to-Bolger exacta, one way.

"That's how it came in.

"I can still see the race in my mind's eye. There's Bolger with the lead at the top of the stretch, drifting out. Here comes Melscott, on the inside. Nobody else makes any kind of move.

"The only difference between the outcome I saw that day and the dream was that Melscott actually paid $9.20 to win.

"This is the most accurate, and efficient, approach to successful handicapping I have run across yet.

"Since it has occurred only once, however, I don't think I can rely on the approach."

Back to reality, I suppose, and a less accurate, less efficient version of artificial intelligence.

CHAPTER ELEVEN

George Kaywood

·

Mensa Handicapper in the Midwest

THE LAST TIME I CHECKED the roster of the handicapping special-interest subgroup of American Mensa, the high IQ fraternity, I counted 150 members on the rolls. The roster does not identify the members as winners at the races or not, and curious minds do want to know.

Can aptitude beat the races? Do Mensa handicappers constitute a pool of winners significantly greater than the 5 percent in the general population?

The hypothesis must be null. Experiments from cognitive psychology demonstrate unequivocably that expertise consists of knowledge, information resources, and experience, but not intelligence. Ultra-bright horseplayers, the rest of us will be grateful to learn, have an equally convenient opportunity to squander their money at the nation's racetracks as do normal people and fools.

A well-documented exception is George Kaywood, of Omaha, Nebraska, a former editor of the witty *Mensacap*, the handicapping subgroup's quarterly newsletter, and a regular patron of Ak-Sar-Ben.

Given total control over content, Kaywood in 1988 delivered a ninety-second daily phone service to Ak-Sar-Ben customers. After thirteen weeks, and 200 race selections, Kaywood had tallied 85 winners, a splendid 43 percent. He had picked 152 horses that finished in the money; 76 percent. Average odds of Kaywood's winners was 2.2–1, for a ROI of 1.37.

Impressive numbers, yet for folks of normal mental acuity wanting added assurance, Kaywood in 1988 was a seventeen-year veteran, and by his own account did not become a certified winner until eight of those seasons had elapsed.

"I just started putting it all together, including money management," is how Kaywood succinctly summarizes the transition to the black. "My standard is simple. At the end of the racing season, have I made money?"

Obviously, factors other than intelligence have been hard at work throughout Kaywood's evolution. A review of Kaywood's current methods reveals a tactic all intelligent handicappers might apply, and presumably, the stronger the aptitude for it, the better.

Smart handicappers must adapt conventional ideas and methods to the peculiar circumstances characterizing their local racetracks and personal situations. Flexible thinking beats rigid rules. It also modifies convention.

To begin, Kaywood achieves a frame of reference on the daily program by means seldom practiced anywhere. The night before, he peruses the *Daily Racing Form*, noticing the types of races on the card and gathering a first sense of the quality of competition he confronts tomorrow. Kaywood wants to know whether the program will be cheap, average, or good. The survey informs George as to the amount of time he will need and the extra information he might be required to dig out during the study period.

"For instance, tomorrow's card at Ak-Sar-Ben has four maiden races; cheap races. It's a cheap day. I'll have more time and less homework."

Specific race analyses begin with close inspection of the conditions of eligibility. The objective is to form mental images of the kinds of horses best suited to specific kinds of races. Kaywood relies on the profiles of probable winners for each type of race outlined in *The Handicapper's Condition Book* (Quinn), but supplements those extensively with results of his own local research.

Some of his findings have proved provocative.

In Ak-Sar-Ben allowance sprints open to 3YO males and having purses between $11,000 and $17,000, the winner emerges from the four horses with the lowest odds 93 percent of the time. In routes, the percentage drops to 81. Kaywood allows that long shots do not often figure to win.

In open claiming races for fillies and mares, 4up, with selling prices from $6500 to $8500, data from the past three seasons show again the winners will likely be among the first four favorites.

Kaywood also studies how frequently Ak-Sar-Ben favorites win each race, 1st through 9th. Favorites win the 1st and 2nd about 47 percent of the time. They win the 5th a typical 31 to 33 percent. Ak-Sar-Ben provides exacta wagering on all races, and these data focus Kaywood on exotics where he can anticipate better statistical results.

As a rule, at this early phase of the handicapping Kaywood attempts to include horses with any reasonable chance, not eliminate contenders prematurely.

"I try to qualify as many horses as suited to the race as I can."

Kaywood has erected a claiming-class hierarchy for Ak-Sar-Ben, similar to the minor-track classification schemes Steve Davidowitz recommended in *Betting Thoroughbreds*. Kaywood's variation is to identify claiming races as cheap-average-good, and at the same selling prices identify the races that have actually been classier; that is, identify class within a class.

"My hierarchy reflects all the characteristics of winners I've found at the various class levels. Again, any horse that shares the characteristics of the winners of specific types of races, I leave them in."

Kaywood's contenders are evaluated using a number of esoteric pace ratings that have been formulated variously by John Meyer, Huey Mahl, and Howard Sartin. He currently produces a rating he calls "net acceleration," a measure of velocity that expresses in feet-per-second the difference between horses' acceleration during the early stages of races and deceleration during late stages. The method controls for distance.

As it must be, the method of rating pace utilizing velocity is computerized. Only a handheld hardware model is necessary. Kaywood obtains his printout from a Sharp 1360, and strongly recommends it for handheld computerized handicapping. Several rating methods can be stored. The data-processing requirements get shifted to computers, and will be accomplished more quickly, efficiently, and without error.

"After I get the ratings," says Kaywood, "I do an in-depth pace analysis, comparing what today's contenders can do with what recent winners have been doing at both the second call and the finish in my three main categories, cheap-average-better."

Sartin practitioners draw like comparisons on numerous pace intervals, and Kaywood has adapted the technique. Again, the thinking player's adaptation.

To obtain a more reliable indication of horses' running styles, Kaywood supplements his velocity ratings and pace comparisons with a technique promoted by William L. Scott in *Total Victory at the Races*. He adds each horse's running positions at the second call in each of its races listed in the *Daily Racing Form*. He then adds the running positions of each horse at the finish. He compares the totals.

"The technique shows clearly whether the horse is a pacesetter, even runner, or come-from-behind type."

Additional adaptations. Kaywood comments:

"The Scott technique forces you to use the whole record available in the *Form*, not just a single race. The full record represents a more reliable index of running style than a single recent race. Reliance on a single race for pace analysis is a flaw, in my opinion, of most speed and pace methods."

Kaywood notes his computer program does not rank the contenders from high to low, but in post position order.

"This forces the handicapper to examine all the data carefully. High to low rankings bias the handicapper toward the high-rated horses in a subtle way. The stress should be on the analysis, not the rankings. Final rankings should be done in the handicapper's mind."

Kaywood's adaptation on conventional thinking about money management is to form two small banks of $300, for straight wagers and exotics, respectively, and begin by betting 10 percent of each.

Half a season along, Kaywood takes inventory, and if he has been performing well enough, the percentage of bankroll bet size is raised to 16 percent. The 16 percent represents a realistic edge and a personal comfort zone, Kaywood stresses, but in the main equals greater flexibility for chasing bigger scores.

"The larger bets allow me to fashion plays on contentious races that are designed either to break even or to make a score. Usually I wind up somewhere in between."

Strategies for coping with exotics have become important to handicappers, Kaywood believes. Ak-Sar-Ben, for example, features exacta wagering on every race. Kaywood warns it's difficult for handicappers to isolate the most bettable exactas during the card, with the myriad distractions presented by horses, tote board, races, replays, program changes, and other bettors.

"I focus first on win betting," says Kaywood, "and my instinct is to avoid cheaper races in the exotics; less predictable results."

Kaywood prefers to take the rational overlays to win, at 10 percent of bank, if exotics look problematic, even during the second half of the season.

"On a spectacular horse, I will double-down."

It came together best for Kaywood during 1985, his most profitable season. After winning consistently the first half, Kaywood boosted his percentage bet to 16 percent. Twice, the larger bets paid off spectacularly, in particular on the afternoon of the Grade 2 Cornhusker Handicap, Ak-Sar-Ben's most prestigious race.

Kaywood collected the 17–1 exacta on numerous Cornhusker tickets that day, but an even larger windfall occurred on the 1st race.

A cheap claimer named Ilatan was entered in a sprint. Its past performances showed nine consecutive losses in routes, but the tenth race back was at six furlongs, a win.

"In all nine routes Ilatan had flashed speed to the second call," recalls Kaywood, "then tired. Three days before the start on Cornhusker day, Ilatan had worked a sharp three furlongs, not the five or six furlongs he usually worked."

Ilatan was 30–1 on the board. At the two-minute mark he plunged to 13–1 in one flash!

"The connections might as well have been waving signs. I bet heavily, and Ilatan won by eight. I hooked him with three horses in the second half of the double and caught that. The double paid $123.80. It was a great start to my biggest day ever."

That same memorable season, Kaywood settled easily on a shipper named Sefa's Beauty in Ak-Sar-Ben's $150,000-added Princess Stakes. In a six-horse field, Kaywood discovered an opportunity to apply an exacta betting strategy he likes.

"Sefa's Beauty was running against a top local campaigner named Bursid, a popular horse running the last stakes of its long career. It was billed as a two-horse race, though Sefa's Beauty was actually a standout at prohibitive odds, 3–5."

Kaywood examined the exacta probables. If exactas on the noncontenders warranted the bet, Kaywood would eliminate Bursid, an underlay to finish second. As the undersides of exactas from Sefa's Beauty, the four nondescript noncontenders became serious overlays.

Eliminating Bursid, Kaywood bought four $50 exactas. The strategy clicked, the winning combo paying $47.80, or 22–1. He had done the same in the Cornhusker, getting 17–1.

Eliminating overbet second choices in exactas, when faced with authentic odds-on stickouts to win, and then linking the superstar with the long-priced overlays that figure—or the field of random overlays, as the odds direct—is a productive exacta strategy first promoted by Davidowitz. Kaywood has learned to apply the strategy, as have numerous thoughtful handicappers.

The racetrack appeared for George Kaywood in Albany, New York, where he worked, as he does in Omaha, as a radio personality. A friend dragged him to the harness races in Saratoga. He liked the ambience of racing and betting, and George returned. Soon he concentrated on the running styles of horses, the styles of riders, and as he remembers the times, "got fairly good at picking winners."

The transition to thoroughbreds occurred when Kaywood moved to Erie, Pennsylvania, a town famous, of course, as the birthplace of Andrew Beyer. Beyer would not have been born if the local community had not contained a racetrack, but Erie boasted of Commodore Downs.

By now the mental stimulation of in-depth handicapping had possessed Kaywood like the devil. "Handicapping was the greatest detective game for amateurs I had experienced, and you got paid for solving the puzzles. I was charmed, and still am."

An early serendipity was a book on handicapping by Bernard Gould titled, *Smart Is Better than Lucky*. It delivered a mechanical system, based upon horses' average earnings for the past season or two. Kaywood applied the system at Commodore Downs, and it worked, for a time.

"Then it went sour. It was a good initial lesson. I have not touched a system since. This is a game of thought, not rules."

Kaywood liked the races enough to depart the radio station. He emerged as publicity director of Commodore Downs, no less, a three-year post.

"Now I could play the races three days a week and get a taste of the backside, frontside, horsemen, and bettors.

"At Commodore I learned how horsemen think, though not so much about how they train. To this day the cheaper races at smaller tracks are among my favorites."

Soon Kaywood graduated to the hometown hero's best-selling book on speed handicapping, *Picking Winners*. Instantly, Kaywood became a dedicated speed handicapper. Instantly, he began to prosper.

Next he devoured Davidowitz's *Betting Thoroughbreds*, where the author's explanation of the claiming-class hierarchies at smaller tracks was made to order for denizens of Commodore Downs.

"Understanding both class and speed improved my game tremendously. Once I got to that point at Commodore, I did well, and I lived well too. Those were good times."

All things change.

Commodore Downs closed. Kaywood returned to radio, now in Omaha. Ak-Sar-Ben was located there, Kaywood realized, before he signed.

By that time, speed figures had lost their glamour. More and more figure horses lost. Others that won paid less than they had.

"When the figures did not work at Ak-Sar-Ben," says Kaywood, "I asked why. I became enamored of local research on the various factors of handicapping.

"The books by Quirin and Quinn were out, and I decided winning handicappers must use various information for various races. That is, for me a kind of fine-tuning was under way. I wanted to know what worked best for particular kinds of races."

Once, in Las Vegas, during an early phase of his investigative period, Kaywood visited GBC Press and bought $100 worth of books on handicapping published in the 1930s and 1940s. He studied any chapter that treated a specific factor of handicapping, like class, weight, condition, or odds, to make comparisons with contemporary practice.

"There have been lots of changes, of course. Weight was highly regarded then. So was class. Speed was not. Form was not. The condition factor seemed to be the same mystery then as it remains today."

Kaywood obviously believes that studying handicapping books is a natural way to improve the skill, but he recommends an interesting twist when practitioners begin to apply what they have read.

"Beyond good books, the best thing serious handicappers can do is talk shop with other knowledgeable, experienced players.

"Don't ask who they like. Ask why they like the horses they

choose as best bets. My friend Dave Maycock at Ak-Sar-Ben has been a source of know-how and motivation to me. He's a top player, and keeps quiet about it, but will share his thoughts with peers.

"I've been fortunate to attend the two national expos on handicapping, and several Sartin seminars too. The best experiences are not the sessions themselves, though many have been first-rate, but the conversations among colleagues that go on around the sessions."

Kaywood attends Ak-Sar-Ben three days of five, but he scurries to advance wagering if he likes a horse on a day he cannot attend.

"I do watch the results on TV every night."

Following years of reading, playing, local research, and conversations with other skillful handicappers, Kaywood has crystallized his strengths and weaknesses, and he appreciates his pet plays.

"I have a couple of major weaknesses. Body language is one. Also, I rely too much on the numbers when I am tired or distracted. It's lazy handicapping. I also play too many races, and I tend to bet the same amount on each. That's poor money management.

"My strong point is using special information and research data that not many people have access to. I do not throw winning horses out too soon. I stick to my opinions and choices. Those are my major strengths."

Low-priced winners, of 3–1 and less, Kaywood considers standard fare at Ak-Sar-Ben. But he relentlessly looks for pet plays that pay better. A favorite is the overlay that last out ran fourth or fifth without threatening, perhaps versus better, or just against a fast field, and today is 5–1 or 6–1 and figures much stronger.

Another is the starter allowance race, or starter handicap.

"The crowd does not understand this type of race. The best horses win a lot, and pay well, but can be difficult to find. Last month I spotted just this kind of overlay. The horse won, paid $27.80."

Kaywood also prefers horses combining improving form and back class.

Handicapping aside, if Kaywood notices a "sharp and ready" horse on the track, and the odds become astronomical, he bets the sharpies to place. He points out these horses have run well, without winning, a surprising proportion of the time.

"My last body-language stab, I bet all of $5 to place and netted $103. The odds have to be huge. It's a kick, this kind of instant long shot."

A full shift on the radio weekdays sometimes interferes with Kaywood's playing the races, but not his daily handicapping routine.

"Hard-core handicapping off-track takes two hours a day," he says. "I normally find two or three plays on weekdays, but as many as six on Saturdays. Better races, better horses.

"Record-keeping takes another hour and a half, but I do that in bits and pieces much of the time."

Kaywood markets computer software in handicapping through Com-Cap, his company, but uses no personal computer himself while handicapping. He uses instead a three-ring manual he flips through quickly.

"Full-time handicappers need a PC for storage and retrieval," explains Kaywood, "but for part-time players a computer is not efficient while actually handicapping. If I want to see the exact conditions of a prior race, for example, I flip to the appropriate page in the notebook. It's quicker than searching computer files.

"I have no time to compile trainer and jockey records on a PC, so I purchase the products of others, and use them."

Mental fatigue rarely becomes a hardship for part-time handicappers, observes Kaywood, but when it does, he merely stops. Kaywood remains part-time, but identifies readily with the mental challenges full-time comrades confront.

"Three years ago I was abruptly fired from a local radio station, and I played the races full time, temporarily, for three months. I began to experience some problems with my eyesight. An optometrist diagnosed the condition as soreness resulting from too much concentration on the *Daily Racing Form*.

"I've learned if I don't push myself mentally, I handicap better."

About coping with normal losing runs, Kaywood understands the regular handicapper's burden. He gets visibly agitated, does not like losing streaks.

"Winning is very important," he states with emphasis. "Not only fiscally, but mentally. Losing runs that may be entirely normal can still destroy your spirit."

Kaywood recounted an abnormal experience at Erie when he lost 27 bets in a row. Abnormal or not, computer simulations show that normal proficiency levels are susceptible to losing runs of 22 or more, and 17 consecutive losses is not uncommon.

"I felt cursed. The last loss in the streak, the horse I bet was ten lengths in front, stepped on a rock, tossed the rider, and stopped cold. He just stood still.

"That losing streak had a lasting effect on me. When I begin to lose too often, I automatically think of it.

"The Sartin group deals best with normal win-loss patterns. They promote betting two horses, which cuts consecutive losses terrifically. It's a psychological cushion that saves tons of mental energy. I endorse that approach. Otherwise, when I am losing too many races, I just stay away for a few days. Abstinence is the short-term practical cure."

Broadly speaking, Kaywood believes negative events in life and relationships contribute to bad handicapping. During a marriage that ended, not due to racing alone, Kaywood's attitude that racing came first on Sundays was resented by his wife.

"She resented the time I allotted to handicapping, and I know it affected my play adversely."

A new lady has been bothered as well.

"She feels I put horse racing ahead of her, which is not true but has been experienced that way. Handicappers' wives can suffer as much as computer widows; the combination is deadly. Handicapping can become engrossing; it's a danger always.

"Life comes first. Handicapping should be handled like a faithful mistress. However long you're away, racing welcomes you back with open arms, a smile, and instant affection.

"If you are playing full time, you absolutely need undivided family support. Any personal problems you have, with time demands especially, they necessarily interfere with your success at handicapping."

Kaywood recommends developing other personal interests, and friends who do not care about racing.

"Years ago I tortured friends and associates at the radio station with my continual chitchat about horses and races, but I have changed all that. Now I keep my racing interests separate. It's much better that way. To people unfamiliar with the sport, besides, the social stigma that you are gambling is always there, or at least hovering in the background.

"Develop outside interests, and new friendships to share them. Say nothing about racing, or little. My outside interest is road-rallying. It's a game you win by outsmarting other people. Just like handicapping, I guess."

The best handicapper Kaywood has met is local colleague

Maycock. Like Kaywood, Maycock conducts extensive local research on effective handicapping factors and patterns at Ak-Sar-Ben, and he does his homework while analyzing the day's program.

Kaywood recalls:

"Years ago Dave fell headlong into the 'I can beat the favorite' trap, and it almost destroyed him. He was playing too many races he did not understand, trying to beat favorites he knew were false. But he bounced back, has put that kind of action behind him, and is now one of the strongest handicappers anywhere."

Kaywood admires Dick Quigley of Tampa for similar reasons.

"Dick is honest, hard-working, and plays no head games, either with himself or others. He's an excellent example of an older, veteran handicapper who has kept pace with the times and remains open to change and growth."

Kaywood's favorite dream, a goal even, is a farther move west, to southern California. He envies the off-track systems there and the evenness of the climate.

For the near future he wants additional time for identifying and collecting the special information that can make his handicapping more successful.

"And I wish like hell for OTB in Nebraska," he remarks wistfully.

Which brings us to the issue of pet peeves about the sport and industry.

"Mine are typical, I'm sure, of serious, more thoughtful handicappers," responds Kaywood. "The track managers do not promote the sport wisely or well. They should market two aspects of racing, the excitement of races, especially contentious stakes, and the mental fascination of handicapping. The latter is the only way to convert casual, occasional customers into loyal fans who will participate regularly.

"Also, the industry has given too much support to local breeders, at the expense of everyone else, surely trainers and bettors. Nebraska is an example. There are three or four maiden races a day. Very, very weak cards. State-breds run for $11,000 purses in these awful fields. Older open claimers often compete for purses of $5000, less than half. That's an incentive for cheap breeding, and a definite problem for horsemen and bettors.

"I would urge the racetracks as well to provide more solid handicapping information to the daily customers. Handicapping can be an arduous process. A helping hand would save the regular customer time and effort.

"Information centers are an appropriate start. The examples at Arlington Park, with Scott McMannis, and at Laurel's Palace, with Bill Quirin's computer handicapping application and the tapes customers can replay for trip handicapping purposes, are positive illustrations of the possibilities.

"The key is hiring outstanding handicappers to design and manage the information services."

While becoming effective handicappers, Kaywood cautions novices to take small money to the races to begin.

"While betting lightly, and observing what happens, new handicappers should be reading the good books. Read Beyer, Davidowitz, Quinn, and Quirin for sure."

Kaywood advises newcomers that the art of handicapping is highly dynamic, the emphases and priorities changing daily, weekly, monthly, seasonally, and year to year. It pays, he urges, to know as much about the game and local conditions as handicappers can comprehend, and use the knowledge variously, as circumstances dictate.

"Do personal research to validate what you read in the books at local tracks. Definitely do research to determine the effectiveness of pet angles before you bet too much on them."

Harking back to the beginning, and the stepwise system he implemented after digesting *Smart Is Better than Lucky*, Kaywood concludes on a wise warning note about the tools of the trade.

"Most important of all, keep an open mind. On finding a factor or angle you come to trust and believe in, don't say, 'That's the path to my fortune.' Say, 'That's one possible trick in a bag of tricks that can help me win a few bets.' "

CHAPTER TWELVE

Steve Klein

·

Angles, Angles . . .
Testing for Long Shots

THE WEEK OF March 15, six weeks before the deadline, handicapper Steve Klein drove from Los Angeles to Caliente Racetrack, in Mexico, to unload the largest bet of his life on the Future Book odds for the 1988 Kentucky Derby. He carried a roll of bills for himself, and another roll for twenty innocent friends he had touted.

The friends wagered from $20 to $200. Klein would not confide his bet size, conceding it was substantial. For discussion's sake, let's assume he bet $1000 on the nose.

Monday morning, March 15, Klein had called the Future Book hotline to check current odds on the filly Winning Colors, two days after she had destroyed the outstanding Goodbye Halo in the Grade 1 Santa Anita Oaks. The line was 50–1. Klein thought it would be 4–1, 9–2, 5–1, in that narrow gap.

"In the Oaks she had humiliated the best fillies in the country. I had followed her races carefully, and in my mind she changed that day from a good horse to a dominant horse, a brilliant horse.

"The prejudices in this country against fillies versus colts is the subtle kind of factor I look to exploit in the Future Books. Her Kentucky Derby odds were far out of line.

"The colt to beat, Forty Niner, had been winning and losing in ordinary time and style. He was no great shakes.

"I had had an interest in betting the Future Book for years, but had never found the horse I wanted. Winning Colors was my type, a brilliant horse, not yet well regarded for traditional reasons, available at very high odds."

As a teenager, thirteen years before, Steve had bet another horse in the Caliente Future Book for the Kentucky Derby. He had bet $50 on Foolish Pleasure, at 2–1. The colt won the Derby, all right, paid 9–5 on-track.

"It was a learning experience. The bet was silly, but the horse had won, and I had a good feeling about the Future Book that has never left me."

At thirty-one, Klein practices handicapping as a hobby. He gets to the races maybe once a week, more frequently at times. Yet he buys the *Daily Racing Form* every racing day and keeps tabs on a number of angles, winning angles, angles he has tested successfully across several seasons. So many angles, in fact, when he does arrive at the racetrack, Klein now can find as many as five or six solid bets, where before he found just one or two. Moreover, he now bets his angles with the confidence of a consistent winner, as he has been for the past four years.

If handicappers as a group will be individuals, Klein is a polemicist on the trait.

"I listen to everything I hear and read," says Klein, "but I believe in the efficacy of nothing until I've tested it." He means that, unremittingly.

When Klein's dad introduced young Steve to the sport of kings, the son benefitted in a way that became the sum and substance of his idiosyncratic practice.

"Dad was a pack rat," recalls Klein. "We always had a stack of *Racing Forms* around the house. I could use them to test many ideas."

He did.

An early question Steve tested, for example, asked whether horseplayers always lose by betting on favorites. He reinvented a wheel there, but that's not the point. The answer, Steve's answer, after completing extensive personal tests, was a resounding yes. So Klein does not bet on favorites.

Since the beginning, the constant of Klein's play has been a rigorous testing, **under local conditions,** of concepts and methods, basic or innovative, that sound intriguing or plausible. He's looking for a clear financial edge that stands the test of time. He discards all bromides or palliatives that look good—or harmless, at least, in the abstract—but have tested poorly.

A scary general conclusion is that even the most seemingly positive or neutral handicapping guideline can exert a subtle, and surprisingly fatal, long-time erosion on a bankroll. Factors such as days away, workout patterns, speed ratings, and the like, have to be checked empirically and monitored closely, for the negative long-term results can be debilitating. Cost effectiveness of single-factor studies is not encouraging; they almost invariably throw losses.

"Eight of nine of the factors and ideas I have tested yielded negative results. You just have to abandon them as not workable. The 'nuggets' you do find, factors that work well, are often more obscure. Not many people use them, but they provide a positive cash flow over time."

Klein regularly draws analogies between the racetrack and real life, several startling in their grim seriousness.

"Research on racing and handicapping has taught me crucial lessons about living. I found that many habits handicappers engage in reflexively actually have serious deleterious effects long haul. They eat away at a bankroll, or income, almost unknowingly.

"The deterioration that occurs might be compared to the slow deteriorating effects of consuming too much alcohol or too many drugs. Moderate levels of consumption feel acceptable, but as time goes by, an obvious deterioration begins to set in. The habits are really degenerative or self-destructive, but it's not easy to recognize that. At the track, you've lost a lot of your money, but are not even aware of what's happening."

Klein's uneasy analogy comes perilously near to throwing handicappers off balance. Is this a missive on the destructive effects of recreational gambling, or a brief on improving one's skill in handicapping?

Klein insists it's the latter, yet insists further that his horse-racing studies have alerted him as a handicapper to apparently harmless but potentially destructive personal habits.

"My tests of how accepted ideas actually work have given me a deep respect for the unknown, and for the improbable. Long shots do win. They have a better chance when certain conditions are present."

Here the uneasy analogy continues.

"I have one drink at a party. I wear seat belts. I realize the possibilities of long shots actually happening. Sometimes I feel horse racing has given me the mind-set of a fifty-year-old Republican."

An intriguing paradox, says Steve, is that most of his friends and associates perceive him differently as soon as they discover he plays the horses as a hobby. The hobby is judged abnormal, not an acceptable pattern of social behavior.

Yet Klein notes horse racing has provided him with important living skills and advantages most of his friendly critics lack.

"Most people work for somebody else. They rarely make important decisions about their own lives. They never learn to take favorable risks.

"Handicappers make important financial decisions all the time. Good handicappers become authentic experts on risk-taking. It amazes me how many real-life skills horse racing teaches."

The interplay of skills between the racetrack and life itself has become a dominant theme for Klein. He dismisses as nonsense the notion that gambling is a neurosis, that gamblers try to lose. People lose not because they like losing, but because they are ignorant about the games. Consider the complicated challenge of playing the odds-on horses intelligently. The implications include a useful carryover effect in daily living skills.

Klein cites the case of the traveler renting a car. Should he take the collision insurance?

At $10 a day, with the noninsured accident deductible at $500, Klein notes that a five-day rental costs $50 in insurance. Thus the natural odds of buying insurance against the deductible payment is 9–1.

"If I thought I had one chance in ten of having a collision, I wouldn't even be driving a car. People are terrible gamblers. They gamble, and take risks, every day of their lives, but haven't a clue as to how to do it smartly. They could learn lots from the racetrack."

In the beginning Klein was a traditional class handicapper, examining the *Form* to determine which horse had performed the best against the most talented horses.

He lost, but sustained himself with the thought he lost less than most horseplayers. He enjoyed a few winning streaks, but in the best of circumstances the gain on investment would be 5 to 6 percent, and only a scattering of attractive plays were found.

"Most people use class. There's no competitive edge. I can quantify anything, and had my numerical class ratings, but they were not enough. I had to look elsewhere for my edge."

In the next few years Klein's readings would be the biggest influence on his development. He called most of the instruction drivel, "90 percent of it," but 10 percent contained "nuggets" he would eventually transform into personal gold.

His modus operandi was always the same.

"Anytime I thought I recognized a worthwhile nugget, I would dive in headfirst. Not with money at the racetrack. Using money causes you to lose your objectivity. You second-guess yourself too much. I would instead research the idea for months. I use the past performances and results charts. I would find what works and discard the rest.

"I continued to do this for several seasons. I created my theories from readings, and tested them relentlessly under local conditions. The sport changes rapidly. The local racing is not the same as the national scene. The local testing is very important. I never skip it."

Klein mentions his replication of author William L. Scott's empirical studies of current form, inquiring about the relative advantages of recency vis-à-vis workouts.

Eureka! a golden nugget, Klein's to keep.

In a test he takes extra pride in discussing, Klein ventured to Hollywood Park for twenty consecutive racing days and charted the odds of every horse in every race.

Is tote action meaningful? he wanted to know. If so, what exactly constitutes a winning trend? He found a successful betting pattern on long shots, which has since stood a lengthy test of time.

"I only get a play a week, maybe, or one a month even, but it works and returns nice profits. I can scan the board for this trend easily."

Another golden nugget.

Regarding the 75 percent or more of his negative results, Klein says he has never looked back.

"For a hobbyist, time is a critical handicapping problem. You cannot lead a normal life and become a top handicapper too. A part-timer has to be clever about it. You find angles that work, and take them to the track when you go.

"Nowadays I don't even have the luxury of time for testing new ideas. I could never conduct the study of the tote I did years ago."

During the earliest testing periods, Klein devoured a pair of books on speed handicapping that influenced his handicapping strongly.

"*Gordon Jones to Win* probably had the most influence on me. I still use the speed charts Jones constructed. But the real impact was, he showed how long-term results could be categorized and reproducible.

"Jones is a good writer and teacher. He classified his results precisely. They could be replicated; tested. He showed what had not worked and what had worked well. He taught me to think scientifically as a handicapper."

The second book that counted was Andy Beyer's *My $50,000 Year at the Races*.

"I'll always be grateful to Beyer for opening my eyes to the importance of track bias. It has been a huge factor for me. I look for a bias constantly, either for a day or for a set of days.

"Breeders' Cup day of 1987, at Hollywood Park, I flew from Chicago to attend. I brought only $150 in betting money. I noticed a speed bias early in the program. I won $1800 that day. That's powerful."

Neither Jones nor Beyer escaped Klein's personal tests of their ideas, and the results proved provocative.

"I found that roughly 10 percent of the plays based upon speed handicapping were tossing 75 to 80 percent of the profits. I culled the plays that worked best and discarded the other figures. Even today I took for the types of speed figures I isolated in my tests."

What does Klein report on the efficacy of speed handicapping as method?

"Speed handicapping is a cost-effective way to start out as a handicapper. You can make long-term profits with speed figures, but not that much, unless you can eliminate the figures that don't work."

A couple of years after cross-examining Jones, Klein conducted a careful dissection of Beyer's $50,000 year. He wanted to know from where the profits actually came. So he scrutinized the book's contents closely.

"The findings were interesting," teases Klein, then comes clean. "In ballpark terms, and by his own account, 80 percent of Beyer's profits came from biases, only 20 percent from speed figures. That data really impressed me.

"I concluded speed handicapping simply is not that productive. I outgrew speed handicapping. My study of Beyer's results paralleled what I had learned studying Jones's ideas."

The initial rounds of testing concluded, Klein relaxed for a number of seasons, enjoying the handicapping hobby on weekends and occasional midweek outings. He carried a small bankroll, and bet in kind.

At major ovals like Santa Anita and Hollywood Park, Klein's original angles misfired enough, and he found few attractive overlays. It was disconcerting, to be sure. He recalls with savor the contrasting situation he encountered at tiny Portland Meadows, in Oregon, on excursions there with classmates at the University of Oregon, where Klein took a B.A. in journalism.

"My original angles worked well at Portland Meadows. We only went a few times a month, but my friends were impressed, and a few actually followed racing as a result. I liked that. I mainly tell friends I take to the races what *not* to do, because there's so much nonsense passed around every half hour, but in college at Portland my angles were working, and we bet on them. The guys won some money too."

Klein recalled a situation where the winner of Portland's Governor's Cup, a sprint, was stretching out next time after earning a huge figure. When Klein scanned the program, the stakes sprinter was listed at 20–1 on the morning line.

"This horse figured by ten to twelve lengths, at least. The morning line was irrational. I thought it must be because the horse was routing. But the bettors were not entirely fooled. The horse went off at 5–2, a mild favorite. I bet. The horse won easily, as it figured to win. Too bad we can't bet against the morning lines!"

Following what he called a nonproductive period of nontesting, Klein, back in southern California, renewed energetically his reexamination of several ideas and angles he had met in new books and from personal observations.

He eventually would identify six new angles that worked. Two isolated as many as two horses a day. A third found only one horse a month.

"By now I knew I was looking for long shots. Angle plays work roughly 14 to 15 percent of the time, so you need value, 10–1 and more. But angles provide value. Not many bettors know about them."

Not surprisingly, Klein's current methods represent a distillation of the sum of his tests across the seasons. His repertoire consists of six or seven angles that have been demonstrably effective and have withstood the longitudinal test of time.

"I now can get five strong plays on an average day," he asserts proudly. "That contributes to winning months, and the months turn to winning years. I have enough solid action anytime I go."

No longer surprised at positive results over a season, Klein remained modest about his financial goals until recently.

"I never thought I could win serious money at the races. My

goal at first was to break even; to play, in effect, for free. I accomplished that my fourth year."

Klein's bank in those years was small.

"I remember one season beginning with $200. I had $60 or $70 left at the end. I was betting $10 normally, as little as $2 when losing. My percentage loss was big, but the actual dollars nothing."

To newcomers, Klein passes along the wisdom of his early betting habits.

"I believe in small banks and in betting small amounts when learning this game. Learning to handicap includes a tuition cost. The roughest times occur when you're learning. If you begin by betting small, as I did, you avoid calamity. Guys that start out cold with big capital, like many thousands, could be in trouble. This is a difficult game. You should expect to lose, certainly at first."

In 1984 Klein transformed himself into a winner. His financial goals are not immodest now, but not ambitious either.

"I've done increasingly better for three straight years. I'm having my best season by far now [1988].

"The Great God of Horse Racing may punish me for saying this, but I think I have earned the right to say, I'm a winning handicapper.

"My profits are hardly enough to change my lifestyle in any way. I mean, Winning Colors guaranteed me a big 1988, and three months ago at Santa Anita a pet long-shot angle got me a $76 winner, but the annual haul until now has not exceeded $3000 to $5000.

"It's just a hobby, remember. The profit has not been much better than the minimum wage in relation to the time and effort."

On the topics of time and energy commitments, and notwithstanding the studies, Klein's hobby contrasts sharply with the practice of handicapping as an avocation or profession.

Off-track, when not attending, Klein merely scans the past performances for the presence of winning angles and keeps tabs of track biases. His homework consists of studying, intermittently, approximately two weeks' worth of *Racing Forms*, to determine how well his favorite angles have been getting along.

"I go once a week, but I keep on the lookout for track biases and will make special trips if a strong bias develops. That's my most productive time, I suppose.

"My four best days have been strong bias days."

Unlike hobbyists as a group, Klein holds strong opinions on money management and betting at the races. A mortgage broker, stock options trader, and licensed market-maker on the floor of the Chicago Board of Options Exchange—"my most exciting job; you're at the center of the action constantly; racing is nothing like that"—Klein sets forth the following betting guides:

1. Betting capital must be separate from all other cash flow.
2. The percentage of money allocated to betting on horses must be small in relation to income; extremely small.
3. The betting money must be expendable. If it's lost, the person, couple, or family will not miss it.
4. If betting capital has been lost, it must not be replaced until the next season.
5. When betting, the first rule is to cash your handicapping edge, whatever that may be.

"For instance, I practice flat betting. I bet on proven angles that pick the long shots most of the time. It's not prudent to bet a percentage of bankroll each time on long shots. You lose too much too often."

6. Exactas should be used as a substitute for betting to place.

In *Smart Money*, Gordon Jones showed that exacta keys of horses that win returned more profit by a bunch than comparable wagers to place. Klein's tests demonstrated the same.

7. There is no easy money at the track.

"My wife tells me I should give her more dividends from our gambling fund. I would, but I prefer to keep the fund intact. What if I experience a losing run?" Spoken like a fifty-year-old Republican, indeed.

Not many handicapping hobbyists operate in the finely structured world of a Steve Klein. His is a rarefied domain of angles, tests, rules, long shots, and directions for upsetting the Future Books of the racing universe.

Which brings us full circle to Klein's lifetime score.

"I was having a discussion on Future Book candidates this past Santa Anita with a representative of Thoro-Graph," muses Klein, shaking his head negatively.

"Thoro-Graph was high on the Kentucky Derby prospect named Buoy [1988]. The colt had been beaten regularly by other three-year-old candidates and was only 30–1 in the Future Book. They thought he was improving, and potentially a good one. That's not my kind of overlay. Not in the Future Book.

"When playing the Future Book, don't look for potentially good horses that have been roundly beaten, and do not bet on improving form. Handicappers should not be looking for horses 40–1 in the Future Book that might be 20–1 on race day.

"Look for the brilliant horse not recognized yet as brilliant. Look for something subtle that skillful handicappers understand as misleading but traditionalists do not appreciate, like fillies cannot defeat colts.

"That kind of hidden brilliance may be 50–1 or 100–1 in the Future Book [Winning Colors was 200–1, opening line], but go to the post at 5–1 or less.

"That's the kind of horse handicappers want in the Future Book!"

CHAPTER THIRTEEN

Dan McDevitt

•

Weekends in Boston

WHY DON'T YOU BET more money? trackside friends ask Dan McDevitt, a backhanded compliment to a potentially big winner.

"I would bet more if I won more," replies McDevitt.

This arouses the circular argument: which comes first, the chicken or the egg, the winning or the betting?

Successful handicappers concur on the matter. Winning precedes betting. What threshold of winning begets higher levels of betting?

Betting a fixed percentage of bankroll solves that dilemma, does it not? If McDevitt bets 5 percent of his bank each time, bet size will escalate as winnings accumulate, a perfect positive correlation.

"It's not that simple," counters McDevitt. "I'm a weekend player. I can understand the percentage of bankroll method for regulars, but not for weekends.

"I go out looking for perfectas and trifectas. That's the fun of it. That's where the value lies for weekenders. I like Beyer's 'crushing' concept. The best bet at the track risks a few dollars to win $1000. That's my twist on the 'crushing' idea. Bet a little, win a lot."

Dan McDevitt owns an advertising agency in Boston, and on weekends he plays the horses at Suffolk Downs. His style puts him in the company of tens of thousands, and he registers a point about the art of handicapping that applies, I suspect, to virtually all of them.

"It's hard to become a consistent winner playing on weekends. I have never played every day, followed them that closely, and I do not consider myself a consistent winner. I win and lose. If I win more money than I lose, that's an acceptable bottom line."

So McDevitt took justifiable pride in the bottom line for 1987, when he netted $53. The season swung to the black for keeps after he wagered $100 to win on a 9–1 shot that paid $20, a weekender's score. As this is composed, McDevitt has a chance to win ten times as much during 1988, and he's confident enough about it to up the ante.

Normally a $4 to $6 bettor, McDevitt will "step up to the plate," his metaphor, betting $10, $20, or $100, when the occasion warrants, which is not often.

"And my worst season ever, I lost $1000."

McDevitt's story reminds ardent handicappers how radically different the game of the weekend player who cherishes handicapping—or more broadly, the game of the casual occasional racegoer who cherishes handicapping—can be, perhaps must be.

McDevitt does no handicapping off-track. He usually does not buy the *Daily Racing Form* until arriving.

"I like to know which horses are actually running. There are so many scratches. Why waste time handicapping scratched horses? I also want to know the actual surface conditions. I need to see the first couple of races to know that."

McDevitt does not keep records, excepting financial records and track biases.

"You have to know whether you are winning or losing. And I like to know the post position biases at the track. Right now, for example, at Suffolk, I don't think the number-one post has won for a month. Number-two post has been rotten too. So there's a strong negative inside post bias; nice to know. But I do not use a PC, or any elaborate manual system, for tracking handicapping information."

Likewise, McDevitt does not depend upon speed figures.

"Speed methods are too complicated for an occasional player who does not have the time to keep the numbers current."

McDevitt does not take trip notes.

"I don't have the time for trip handicapping either. But I'm savvy enough to spot some live trip horses on the tote. I look for action on horses with seemingly dull races last out. If their prior races have been competitive, the last race probably can be excused due to a poor trip."

McDevitt does not study trainer patterns.

"There are just too many of them. And they conflict with one another in the same race so many times. It's too much bother for a part-time player."

McDevitt no longer even keeps tabs on successful turf sires, betting their progeny first time on grass, a tactic that has worked well for him in the past.

"Now if horses have no grass record, I throw them out. At Suffolk I look for class, money earned, and a come-from-behind running style on the turf. It works well enough."

McDevitt puts his pulse as well on the weakness that defeats the weekend player and the casual occasional racegoer who knows how to play.

"It's such a recreational and social experience for the weekend player," he notes. "I get easily distracted. I get lazy.

"You can't handicap at the track, see the horses, follow the tote, watch the replays, get set to bet, and so forth. All of that, throw in chatting idly with friends and associates, it's damn hard to be a consistent winner."

So McDevitt refuses to bet more money.

The adjustments of the weekend handicapper are oriented toward recreational play, methods of handicapping and wagering that accommodate a pastime, and McDevitt's habits reflect those realities.

"I've experimented with several methods," he comments, "but I have never won or lost much across the seasons with any of them.

"Recently I got William L. Scott's *Total Victory at the Races*, and that's my present approach. I am very impressed with it. I am doing better with Scott's techniques than anything I've tried. I don't use the performance class ratings. I use Scott's new ability times, modified by frequency of racing, and his detailed attention to the last running line."

Scott's ability times as method depends upon the past performances of the *Daily Racing Form*, a convenient outlet for occasional players. It facilitates cutting a field down to the size of its authentic contenders. McDevitt considers that skill essential and his best asset.

"I'm good at identifying contenders. I do it quickly. I can pare a ten- or 12-horse field to five very fast, without eliminating many winners. It's a reliable strength. I do not bet on many noncontenders."

Once the contenders have been identified utilizing ability

times, McDevitt scours the tote, checking for wagering patterns he knows to be relatively successful. He credits a Florida source for studies in Florida and New York that clarify effective interplays in exotics mixing favorites and long shots.

The studies, supported by Scott's, show that when one of the top three choices win, long shots regularly run second. McDevitt looks for long shots returning from layoffs, following claims, and switching distances or footing, handicapping angles having not only value, but also merit. He hastens to point out that long shots brandishing the best ability times should be bet to win.

The clever part, however, relates favorites and long shots to betting patterns.

"The studies show legitimate favorites should be bet below their morning lines. The morning-line favorite and second favorite should be cut in half. A 7–2 shot that's authentic should be 2–1. I try to exploit situations where favorites are not properly bet."

If the top two program favorites are bet properly—cut in half, that is—McDevitt looks for a long shot that has been bet enough, such that its public odds resemble its opening line. Presumably, inside action has kept the long shot afloat on the board. McDevitt hooks the favorites to the long shot.

If the top two favorites are not properly bet, McDevitt looks for overlays that figure. He now plays the overlays on top of the favorites, which finish second often in this reversal pattern.

McDevitt's favorite bet is a variation of the improperly bet favorites and depends upon Scott's concept of form defects.

"An odds-on favorite having a form defect will very likely lose. But it runs second. I look for a long shot or an overlay, preferably one having a jockey change to the leader, or to one of the top two riders in the standings. I play perfectas with the odds-on horse underneath. It's a winning play.

"I especially like a situation where the top one-two-three jockeys are on horses at 6–1 or higher and an underbet favorite figures to be second."

McDevitt knows the betting outfits at Suffolk. During his best season, 1986, "a good betting stable sent out a number of odds-on horses in the trifectas. I knew by the betting they had the right stuff.

"I bet $5 trifectas to two or three long shots each time. The stable's horses won and my long shots finished two-three repeatedly. The trifectas paid $300 to $350, in that range." McDevitt netted several thousand—a worthwhile year, to use his phrase.

On betting perfectas, McDevitt eschews multiple keys and multiple horses scrambled in numerous combinations.

"I bet one-way, or key one horse, not multiple horses. You need overlays in perfectas. Spreading increases the risk, and lowers the value of the return. Again, small risk and large reward is the key in perfectas."

While books on handicapping have not steered McDevitt to methods he can invoke to clobber the races on weekends, Scott possibly excepted, he has gathered tokens from several that he saves for special situations.

He credits *The Handicapper's Condition Book* for straightening his head about Graded stakes and nonwinners allowance races. McDevitt sets sails for Saratoga each August, takes ten-day vacations in Florida each winter, when Hialeah or Gulfstream runs, and receives simulcasts from New York to Suffolk all the time. He confronts the better horses enough so that he must come to grips with them.

"The book states that Grade 1 races are won by Grade 1 horses, and I've won a lot of money adhering to that guideline alone. I like Grade 1 or Grade 2 races where the favorites have shown speed but have no prior Grade 1 or 2 experience. I throw those favorites out, and they tend to lose. Classier horses handle them."

McDevitt also likes to back foreign horses of Europe exiting Grade 1 or Grade 2 stakes the first time they run in lesser races in either New York or southern California.

He also supports horses having Steve Roman's dosage indexes (4.0 and below) in the Kentucky Derby and Belmont Stakes each year, and has been amazed at the profits the angle has tossed.

"Almost no one mentioned that the second-place horse in the Belmont this year [1988] was a long shot with the correct dosage. I cashed the perfecta from Risen Star just by including the horse."

McDevitt began playing the races during his college days. His present routine has endured—astonishingly—for twenty years. Summer weekends he mixes a day of handicapping with interests in golf, tennis, and charity work. In winter he sometimes mixes handicapping with skiing. One of his generalizations strikes a melancholy chord.

"Handicapping for profit is a lonely, tiring business. I would not want to make a living at it. It's best as a diversion, for recreation."

None of McDevitt's goals or dreams involve the racetrack, yet he cherishes the friendships gained there.

"My friendships from the track have been extraordinarily good," he says. "And the experience has had a harmonious relationship with my family life. I take business calls at home Wednesday through Friday, so family members like to see me heading for the races on the weekends.

"I have taken my wife to the Kentucky Derby, to the Travers, and she likes to go to the Massachusetts Handicap each year at Suffolk. She enjoys those days."

Now fifty-three, McDevitt muses about playing the horses more frequently during his retirement from the advertising business.

"If I could make decent money at it, $40 to $50 a day on average, that's all, it might be a fun way to spend a portion of my retirement. But I'm not thinking about that these days."

McDevitt notes he would be forced to improve his handicapping skills if he played more often, and cites as his inspiration the best handicapper he knows, a gentleman named Scott Ruttan.

"Scott bets $6 a race and makes $3000 to $4000 in profits a year. I admire that kind of ability. He's comprehensive in his knowledge and skills, particularly strong at biases and dropdowns. But good at all the rest too.

"I admire another guy, Ted Lange. He's known as 'Trifecta City,' and he deserves the label. He picks two-three horses on top, buys $24 tickets, and gets lots of tri's in the $600 to $2400 range. I wish I could imitate him on that."

An evenhanded, complacent guy, McDevitt turns aggressive, hostile even, when nudged to air his pet peeves about the sport and industry.

"It's astonishing anyone can win at this game with the takeouts as they are. The take is 19 percent on all bets at Suffolk. Add one percent for breakage, and customers get an 80 percent payback.

"Rockingham Park is only thirty miles away, but I will never play there. Rockingham takes 26 percent on exotics, everything but win-place-show wagers. That's larceny. I'm not interested in supporting that."

McDevitt cites NYRA studies indicating the ideal takeout is 15 percent.

"Management here won't pay attention to it. They won't even talk about it. Fifty years ago the take at Suffolk was 8 percent. Have times changed!"

One phenomenon that has not changed, notes McDevitt, is modern handles and attendance. He blames unreasonable, irrational takeouts.

"Suffolk's handle today is $850,000. Ten to fifteen seasons ago Suffolk's handle was $850,000. With the inflation we've had in the interim, if I ran my business like that, I'd be gone, my employees would be gone; we'd be out of business.

"Racetracks have to give their customers a fighting chance to win. Younger people especially just lose interest. They find other pastimes and other forms of recreation. Racing has more appeal to certain personalities, because people can participate, physically and mentally, not just observe. But track managers sure have learned how to lose their best customers, and thousands of potential customers. The takeouts need to be cut."

McDevitt's advice to newcomers, and to casual occasional racegoers who want to become more effective handicappers and bettors, is far more sanguine.

"I would tell them to read the good books, especially *Total Victory at the Racetrack*." I really believe a novice who has mastered that method could get 30 to 40 percent winners on Scott's ability times alone.

"Also, the maximum bet should be no more than 5 percent of bankroll. Anything greater than that is too aggressive. They'll just lose, sooner or later.

"I also have developed a psychological ploy for coping with losing streaks.

"If things have been going from bad to worse, go to the races but get in the betting lines late. The idea is to get shut out. If you get shut out and the horses lose, you'll feel buoyed by it. It helps lift the spirits.

"I'm a master at this. After a few horses win, by the way, and you've been shut out, you'll feel you're back on the beam. You can start playing for keeps again."

On Saturday, July 9, 1988, following a brutish business week, McDevitt took himself to Suffolk Downs for the fun of it. He arrived at the 3rd race, and prepared to bet the 4th. Let's tag along for an interesting program:

4th Race. In a six-horse field the even-money favorite with the best ability times had no form defects. McDevitt hooked the favorite to two long shots in perfectas, and his 11–1 shot finished second. He had purchased $6 worth of perfectas, the winning combo twice, and netted $136.

5th Race. McDevitt felt three of nine maidens had a chance in the trifecta. The morning-line favorite was lowered to 9–5, a positive betting trend. The horse had shown early speed in a stakes race, besides, and McDevitt keyed it on top of the other horses he boxed. His combos ran 1–2–3, a winning trifecta. Another $6 bet was exchanged, this time for a $67 trifecta.

6th Race. A properly bet 3–5 favorite won. McDevitt missed with three long shots on the bottom side of perfectas. Minus $6.

7th Race. Another properly bet favorite won at 2–1, the race on the turf. The horse benefitted from a leading jockey-trainer combo, and McDevitt keyed it one-way in three trifectas. He won again. The $6 bet was returned as a $90 trifecta.

8th Race. This was a $3000 claiming route where the 4–5 favorite had a form defect, McDevitt's cup of tea.

"At Suffolk" he pointed out, "favorites tend to win approximately 20 percent of the lower-level claiming routes. Not even considering form defects, this horse confronted an 80 percent probability of losing."

A 9–1 shot that had been 8–1 on the program, the hidden overlay that McDevitt covets most, was also receiving a switch to the leading rider.

By McDevitt's own standards, here was the perfect setup, and the 9–1 horse won by three lengths handily. The 4–5 favorite with the form defect finished second, to complete the ideal perfecta.

Yet McDevitt purchased only one perfecta ticket, netting $62.50. He did not bet to win on the 9–1 shot.

He was miserable at the result.

"I knew it was the perfect betting situation. I should have bet $20 on the perfecta, or at least $10. I have no guts."

Collecting $62.50 when he might have—should have—collected $625, hung a dark cloud over McDevitt's prosperous day at the races.

To no one's surprise, I'm sure, things would not get any rosier.

9th Race. This was a simulcast of the Tidal Handicap (Grade 1), a turf route, from Belmont Park in New York.

McDevitt found a previous Grade 1 winner in the field, a foreign horse from France, but the import became a poorly bet favorite, and the second favorite was not bet as well as McDevitt insists either.

The correct trifecta wager, by McDevitt's standards, would have keyed one or two long shots McDevitt fancied to the pair of favorites boxed in the place and show holes. McDevitt liked an interesting long shot, Glaros, a 15–1 outsider in New York that was 17–1 at Suffolk.

"Glaros was also moving from an overnight handicap in New York to a Grade 1 stakes," advised McDevitt, "a positive pattern that I have observed is common for several New York stables." Ah, to be sure, a keen insight.

Nonetheless, McDevitt passed the race.

Glaros won, of course, and the two underbet favorites ran second and third. The $1 triple paid a healthy $197, or 197–1.

Need I go on?

In the final two races at Suffolk, McDevitt elevated the bets to $10 on two favorites he keyed to win, and each finished second.

McDevitt's handicapping was superlative this day. His profits totaled $235.

"It was a worthwhile day, I guess," he commented dryly and not altogether convincingly.

Head down, walking slowly, he exited the track.

CHAPTER FOURTEEN

Darryll Claussen

·

No Longer an Aeronautical Engineer; Not Yet a Professional Handicapper

THE WORST PLAY he never made, recalled Seattle's Darryll Claussen, happened opening day at Longacres, 1985. It was the 7th race.

A horse in the entries had won following a layoff on each of the two previous opening days. The horse had a minor trainer. It was 20–1 on the morning line.

Claussen was attracted as well to a trio of shippers from Portland Meadows. Sharp shippers from Portland that are not outclassed win frequently during the initial phase of the Longacres season. They often win as fat overlays. Claussen understood that.

Halfway through the betting the layoff-repeater was 40–1 on Longacres' board. The horse would go as a long shot.

When Claussen checked the probable exacta payoffs on the track's new projection system, which did not estimate beyond three figures to the left of the decimal, he felt nonplussed. All combinations with the layoff-repeater keyed top and bottom to the three Portland shippers showed $999.99.

Claussen decided not to bet.

One of the Portland shippers won at 9–1. The layoff-repeater finished second at 45–1. The $5 exacta paid $2506.

"I didn't bother to win," is how Claussen phrases the gaffe. "I felt bad, just terrible. It was a playable race, the odds practically demanded the bet, and I didn't make it."

The consequences of a botched wager can be overbearing, as veteran handicappers will admit. In 1985 Claussen netted roughly one third his normal take for the season. He attributes the slide to the opening-day blunder, which haunted him for half the season.

On a brighter note, Claussen's longest home run also involved a trainer pattern and the exacta.

"Anything moved up by Clint Roberts immediately following a claim," says Claussen, "has to be considered 'live.' "

On one delightful occasion a Roberts' claim up one level finished second to the 9–2 winner. Claussen had boxed the pair five times. The payoff was $865. The gross amounted to $4,325.

So the best and worst of times for Darryll Claussen featured trainers and exactas. The juxtaposition reflects the handicapper well.

Claussen's specialty is trainer patterns, not unlike that of numerous minor-track practitioners. It was not always so with Claussen, but he learned minor tracks can be hospitable to trainer patterns, as they often are not to conventional practices associated with the class, speed, and form factors.

"A lot of rules that apply well at major tracks do not apply as reliably at small tracks.

"But trainers at minor tracks tend to develop specialties. Purses are smaller. Stables have to supplement purses with winning patterns they can count on.

"Players at minor tracks need to know who's who and what's what among the trainers. It's important to know, for instance, that Larry Ross has not won with a first-starting three-year-old in three years."

That theme should be recognizable in this narrow survey by now. So should Claussen's next.

He dwells on exacta wagering, a strategy that wears well with handicappers of interloper status.

"I attend the races once on the weekends and another day during the week. Maybe a third day many weeks.

"Not a regular, I don't believe in grinding it out as a useful money management strategy. I believe in trying to 'crush' the races you really like; extract the most you can from certain spots.

"So I look for juicy exactas. I leave low-priced exactas alone, or use them as savers, and double-up on generous combinations I like.

"I'm not a big bettor. My flat bets vary from $20 to $40. But I will buy another $60 in exactas in those races. I use a key horse to others, maybe on top or bottom, or both.

"My only goal is to have a winning day. Enough of them adds up to a winning season."

Sounds like the recreational handicapper's manifesto, the part about winning applying to the few.

It's been that way for Claussen, the winning seasons, for twenty-two years. The results stay the same, but Claussen's ideas and methods have changed dramatically along the way. The odyssey of a consistent winner is invariably instructive to follow, and Claussen's journey crisscrosses some remarkable terrain.

Encamped comfortably at Boeing, in Seattle, in the mid-sixties, an aeronautical engineer on the Super-Sonic Transport (SST) team, Claussen lost job stability the day the project ended. He transferred to Vertol, in Philadelphia, where he conducted a series of wind-tunnel tests of automobile designs.

There, eastern chums introduced Darryll to the races. It began as a casual, though romantic, relationship.

"I used the last three races in the *Form* to obtain a speed rating. I averaged the best time and the average time for each horse, and modified the rating by lengths gained/lost in the stretch.

"My only goal even then was to have a winning day. I liked the races."

But handicapping is a data-based, numerically ordered pastime, and Claussen possesses the mathematical mind, so soon the relationship grew inexorably more serious.

An early project had Claussen plotting horses' odds and handicapping probabilities on graphs that might determine the optimal bets. They demonstrated that the optimal percentage bets declined from 7 percent to one percent, depending on the interaction of the odds and the horses chances of winning.

He also kept massive statistics on win-place-show wagering, looking for an edge in any hole having a payout.

Claussen in 1969 turned to Ainslie, the inevitable drift then of all budding handicappers.

"The rules seemed so conservative. I decided to study the *Form* to see if I could find more specific applications of the generalities."

Claussen analyzed a thousand races.

He identified the characteristics of current condition, class, distance, and form that won most frequently. He even attached impact values, or probabilities, to his results, five years in advance of Fred Davis's original probability studies of 1974 and a decade ahead of Quirin's monumental probability studies of 1979, conducted on national samples.

Claussen's earlier localized findings are worth specifying:

1. Maidens conformed to no discernible patterns.

On this point, the Davis and Quirin data overwhelmed Claussen, showing unmistakably that first-starting older maidens win half the rightful share of their starts, but experienced maidens 3up that finished second or third last out did twice to three times as well as might be expected.

2. Horses won equally well at the same or related distances, but not as frequently at new distances.

Later national data indicated sprinters do stretch out acceptably but routers do not shorten up so well, except when they have recorded high early speed to the second call of routes. Many students of handicapping would insist the national findings be replicated under local conditions. Claussen certainly would.

3. Weight changes correlated with nothing.

Everybody finds this, except horsemen, turf writers, and media commentators, to whom weight remains nothing if not everything.

4. A set of best criteria on the fundamental factors could identify contenders very reliably, but not the eventual winners.

Multiple regression studies of handicapping factors tend to toss modest profits to modest losses. Perhaps Claussen has explained why. Such studies isolate contenders, not winners.

5. The crucial separation factors were pace, early speed, and class.

Which is not the same as jockey-trainer-weight-post position. Recreational handicappers might take heed.

Adjusted speed ratings, optimal bet sizes, impact values, in the late sixties, no less! Darryll Claussen was a handicapper ahead of his times!

Soon Claussen became intrigued with the relations between running styles and post positions. Another series of personal studies focused on Delaware Park, Atlantic City, Garden State, and Liberty Bell.

The new round of results would guide Claussen's thinking for years. The findings will sound eerily familiar to numerous contemporary pace analysts.

Pace analysis should emphasize position and beaten lengths at the second call, distance notwithstanding. Winners regularly could be charted at designated positions near the second call, such as no worse than fourth and beaten by no more than a length and a half. Failing those qualifications, horses did not often win.

Claussen's data showed, too, that early speed horses won wire to wire in 25 percent of the races, regardless of racetrack. The finding held relatively constant for sprints and routes. Claussen could exploit these data, and did, getting overlays on speed horses that should be uncontested whenever they went postward at 5–1 or higher.

Post position biases varied with the track surfaces.

Inside lanes were favored at Garden State and Atlantic City, but became the kiss of death at Delaware Park and Liberty Bell. Regardless of racetrack, horses running behind the pace in holes one and two were "dead."

Days later, at Delaware Park, a maiden named Lematt, a first-starter having sharp workouts, drew the outside at five-and-a-half furlongs. Claussen implemented his post position findings with his inaugural large bet.

Lematt sped to the front, as if on cue, and went wire to wire easily, as Claussen watched with a sense of predestination. It paid $19, Claussen's first scientific betting coup.

"Funny," he comments, "I've liked the outside posts and speed horses ever since."

Back at Longacres, in the early seventies, persuaded the principles of class handicapping did not apply, Claussen turned to speed handicapping as the alternative.

First he summed the *Daily Racing Form* speed rating and track variant, which outperformed speed ratings alone. Years later, of course, Quirin demonstrated Claussen's perception statistically. Claussen relied upon parallel-time speed charts as well. He adjusted the times and figures "in idiosyncratic gimmicky ways," by what he derisively refers to as "diddle" factors.

In these years he also undertook a more studious consideration of equine body language, visiting the paddock every race. He still does. By coincidence, he began to notice repeated trainer patterns that won, a phenomenon he had not observed previously and a seminal influence that would strengthen with its repetition.

In 1975 a new book, *Picking Winners*, by Andrew Beyer, gripped Claussen's imagination with its innovative approach to speed handicapping. Beyer's speed charts embodied the principle of proportional time. This held that one fifth of a second possessed greater value at shorter distances, less value as distances lengthened. Beyer speed reflected a reality whereby horses that ran faster at six furlongs, for example, could be expected to run a 1¹⁄₁₆ miles relatively faster than slower horses at six furlongs. Final times, adjusted in relation to class and to track surface speeds, and the accompanying speed figures, were set proportional to distances.

"The concept that time was proportional to distance was the selling point to me. I did away with my gimmicks and practiced speed handicapping in a more professional way. The figures worked well for me from 1975 through 1978. As more handicappers collected figures, the odds dropped."

For a time Claussen applied Bill Quirin's method of making speed figures and liked the numbers, but the problem of diminishing odds had become a way of life.

"From speed handicapping I discovered my favorite racetrack bet. It's the lone frontrunner with improving figures. That's the best play at the racetrack. Because the horses are still improving, the odds can be fair to generous."

Claussen was influenced, too, by the work at Longacres of Jim Selvidge. "He emphasized body language and training patterns, unconventional ideas at the time, and I liked his money management approach, the base bet plus square root of the profit method." *

As has been true of most outstanding handicappers, Claussen's attention throughout an extended developmental period has been to the concepts and methods of handicapping. Much less attention is afforded to money management. That comes later.

Claussen cited 1984 as a typical season financially. He won approximately $3000. "If I netted even $1000 in a season, I considered that success. I knew I was beating a very challenging game."

In 1986, in his late forties now, Claussen lost to company layoffs a splendid-paying position in marketing and sales.

"I was very depressed. I didn't go to the races in that frame of mind, but I began to think about the possibility of handicapping for income."

Claussen held a bachelor's degree in aeronautical engineering and had completed graduate studies in mathematics, but the racetrack reared up as a definite lure.

*The bettor invests a minimum of $2 to begin betting, and adds to that amount the square root of any accumulated profits.

"My goal financially was clear. The income from handicapping would have to equal my income from the corporate sector. My wife is very understanding and supportive, but so far I had been a winner at the $5000 to $10,000 level.

"I'm uncertain I could make the professional leap. That would mean quite a change of pace for me."

A hobby becomes an avocation becomes a profession, the familiar procession. But we leave Darryll Claussen at stage two, uncertain he belongs at stage three, and undecided about attempting it.

About this time, as part of a new advertising and promotions budget for improving customer services, Longacres in the mid-eighties conducted a survey of its regular patrons, and Claussen was randomly selected to participate.

Track management might have benefitted from a serious, bright handicapper's point of view, but Claussen represented a minority opinion.

"I guess I was the scientist in the group. One guy was a ferocious gambler and the others were just racegoers. We sat at round tables and talked about our racetrack experiences. Managers observed us through a one-way glass.

"My main complaint was that bettors are not treated as customers. Customer services are not information-oriented at Longacres, and that's what bettors need most of all. Solid handicapping and betting information. Anything the track can do to help bettors win reinforces the inclination to attend more frequently and wager more money. An obvious point, but a point of view not understood and not appreciated by track managers.

"As matters stand now, only devotees of handicapping can cope financially with the races. Recreational bettors lose. That's why they do not come back as frequently, or bet as much, or tout the sport as much. The widespread losing is a large part of racing's negative-image problem with the general public.

"But I don't think track executives can identify with that. They have an underlying contempt for the bettors, and it shows. Whether it's the prices charged for parking and admission, the takes, or the lack of attention to basic information services their best customers need, it shows. Track managers really do not care how much money their regular customers lose.

"Why don't racetracks promote the challenge of playing a tough but exciting game well enough to win? It seems so simple, so obvious, doesn't it?"

Darryll Claussen enjoys trout fishing in lakes, streams, and rivers. He likes to listen quietly for hours to Mozart and Bach.

These are marvelous retreats from the stresses and noise of professional handicapping.

When losing runs happen, a handicapper can go fishing in a placid stream.

After bad luck at the races, a handicapper can rejuvenate the soul with a Bach concerto.

It's entirely feasible to earn that corporate salary at the races each year, playing professionally, and with calming diversions to fall back upon away from the din; why not give it an honest try?

Darryll Claussen says he's still thinking about it.

CHAPTER FIFTEEN

Tom Hambleton

·

Can a Loser Ever Win?

THE RACETRACK QUALIFIES as one of mankind's greatest levelers. It knocks the biggest trees down. Professionals, wealthy businessmen, corporate executives, effective managers, accomplished artists, brainy intellectuals, all fall back in the dust of horses that do not win.

People who have been successful in every other facet of their lives, the living legend holds, cannot cope with the peculiarities of the ponies. They lose their money, they lose their cool, and they know not why. So they chase, they complain, they cry, they invent excuses, and generally they make unabashed fools of themselves.

The track's capacity for turning winners into losers has contributed not a little to the much-cherished myth that you can't beat the races. No explanation for a successful person's demise could be more impenetrable.

Well, you can beat the races, and what unsuccessful cads at the racetrack do not understand is that otherwise-smart operators lose because they are competing in a complicated game they do not know how to play.

Less remarked is the racetrack's role as a lifter of poor souls. When small-time owners win the big stakes with the good horse at last, the trackside sentiment celebrating the achievement intimates that a place where the little guy can cop a small fortune at a rich man's expense cannot be altogether bad. The triumph of the underdog becomes the racetrack's redeeming social virtue.

Against all odds, another kind of racetrack triumph, much

135

more personal, is not similarly celebrated. To play a complex head game well enough to win money at it repeatedly is a feat worthy of social praise. Success in thoroughbred handicapping remains an infrequent, elusive, and therefore commendable goal. That purpose becomes a driving force, in fact, of loyal racetrack participation. Its accomplishment can alter an outlook on life. It can change its owner's mirror image.

"I'm a consistent winner," asserts handicapper Tom Hambleton, immediately, unequivocally, emphatically, "and it's been very gratifying."

Hambleton is a newly appointed teaching member of the national Sartin club of successful handicappers. He instructs the membership on how to apply the methodology and how to win.

An intriguing aspect of the Sartin experience for long-suffering practitioners is the psychological orientation of the founder. Howard Sartin believes the antidote to losing at the races is winning, not abstinence.

Learning how to win at the races, according to Sartin, includes the debunking of a number of social injunctions (playing the races is a vice, all gamblers crave to lose, the racetrack is a haunt for misfits) that contribute mightily, if subconsciously, to losing. The total cure involves learning how to win, actually winning, associating with winners, and feeling supremely good about the winning.

By his personal account, Sartin's cure was a perfect tonic for whatever it was that had been plaguing Tom Hambleton. In an eloquent testimonial to the power of the Sartin methodology for developing consistent winners, Hambleton stood in front of the membership at a Las Vegas seminar and told how the methodology did for him what he had so often failed to do for himself.

"I always had thought of myself as a loser," said Hambleton. "Even when I would do well at something, I would try to sabotage the results by saying I was lucky, or that I benefitted from circumstances. I could never give myself full credit for anything.

"I tried to do the same thing with Dr. Sartin's [computer] programs. When I first began to win, I told myself it wouldn't last. That I couldn't do it again. I tried to set up an expectation of losing. I fought my success all the way, because I felt I was supposed to lose.

"But Dr. Sartin and this group would not let me get away with it. Sartin told me I was a winner, and that my results proved it. He encouraged me to keep playing, and keep winning, and I did.

"Now I'm at the point where I know I am going to win. These methods are powerful. They do work. I'm not only confident, I'm certain. I've done it now for eighteen consecutive months. I'm even at the point where if I lose more than three days in a row, I know the races are not running to form. There's nothing wrong with the programs or printouts. Things will be back to normal soon and I'll be winning again, as usual."

Sartin practitioners play two horses a race, an expedient that facilitates a steady pattern of cashing. Hambleton has become a firm believer. Of money management, he asserts, "I am convinced the best road to profits with win wagering is betting two horses a race."

Sartin practitioners also evaluate themselves after twenty-race cycles. Betting two horses, Hambleton's records for the twelve months beginning in spring of 1987 (six separate meetings) show a win percentage of 69.5. He typically selected 13 to 14 winners during a twenty-race cycle. His best cycle had 20 of 22 winners, the worst 9 of 20. Amazingly, he began with a $200 bank, and invested 10 percent of bankroll each bettable race. Hambleton's twelve-month profit was $9,826.

"My weakness is a lack of courage for making larger bets," comments Hambleton. If he corrects the fault, someone might add, Hambleton will be poised to slaughter the races. At even-money on winners, a 70 percent win rate (two horses) amounts to an edge of .40, which is an ROI of 40 cents on each dollar invested. Forward, charge!

Hambleton currently uses *Energy*, a program developed jointly by Sartin and teaching member Jim Bradshaw of Texas. "I've had unbelievable success with it."

Energy produces a pace analysis that matches today's contenders with the pace of a mythical pacesetter at today's class, or the probable pacesetter in today's field. Horses are matched against the probable pace at each pace interval, or race segment. Bradshaw refers to the comparisons as "the match-ups."

The output ranks the contenders on several dimensions of pace, such as early pace, sustained pace, late pace, and the rankings are juxtaposed with the energy demands of the local track, as indicated by the energy distribution of recent winners at the distance.

The method is entirely empirical.

"Either the horses can handle the probable pace or they can't," explains Hambleton. "It's based strictly on past performance. Potential does not count, nor jockey, nor trainer. Does the horse measure up to today's probable pace or doesn't it? We support the two top-ranked horses on the pace interval that's been winning recently."

First, handicappers must qualify contenders and select pace lines to be evaluated. To find contenders, a number of guidelines are employed, not to mention comprehensive knowledge of handicapping, and Sartin provides a numerical class rating, as well as another program to determine APV (average purse value). Urged to reduce fields to five contenders, Sartin practitioners stumble about mysteriously in the effort. Proficient handicappers wrestle with the opposite condition, identifying contenders satisfactorily, sorting the winners unsatisfactorily. Hambleton finds as many as seven contenders.

The selection of current representative pace lines can be a trickier matter, and becomes an art form for experienced hands like Hambleton.

"It's a function of experience. I've been doing it so long, now I can take pace segments from various races and not distort the horse's performance. I really enjoy this part of it. It's an important part of my analysis."

Needless to say, Hambleton's cut-and-paste artistry with pace lines is not recommended for the general practice.

Beyond qualifying horses as contenders suited to the class or probable pace of today's race, Hambleton does not differentiate among nonmaiden races. In other words, races are treated interchangeably. The bottom line consists of the two horses ranked tops by Energy that fit the present energy demands of the track.

"Only the paceless race is difficult with this program," Hambleton attests.

Handicapping was hardly as cut-and-dried for Hambleton at the start, which was the Santa Anita winter meeting of 1970.

"I remember making a bet on the turf champion Cougar II, and he won easily, but that's the only winner I can recall. I attended the races occasionally then, because I liked the atmosphere. But I didn't know what I was doing."

For the next decade Hambleton attended the races occasionally still, and without knowing what he was doing. It can go on and on, he allows, the general ignorance.

Then he read a book that changed his outlook. It was *The Handicapper's Condition Book*, and suddenly the races began to make sense.

"That book gave the game credibility for me. The author [Quinn] had academic credentials, and the book presented an intelligent, organized plan the average guy could understand. There was a semblance of order to the races, after all.

"I reread the book often, even took it to the track with me. l would read it in the rest room, I'm embarrassed to admit, so that no one would see me and think I was some crazy egghead."

The book helped Hambleton pick contenders that frequently won, a new experience. He pursued other books.

"The next was Scott's *Investing at the Racetrack*. I was intrigued by the concept of making investments. I had always been taught gambling was evil, but investing was okay.

"I made profits with Scott's method for three consecutive weeks at Santa Anita, but the fourth week the method fell apart. I soon abandoned it."

Next Hambleton mastered Bert Norman's *Quick Figure Handicapping*, which produced additional contenders and winners, especially long-priced speed horses that had lasted to the stretch call last out. The rationale: those speed horses were rounding into peak form, to be demonstrated next race.

Soon Hambleton was experimenting with Gordon Jones's speed ratings and finding new types of winners.

"Mainly, these various methods cut my losses. They did not yield consistent profits.

"I kept experimenting, and on my own began adding the *Form's* speed rating and daily variant. I continued to improve.

"The first day I tried the Pick 6, I hit for $2100 on a $64 ticket."

That payday occurred in Las Vegas, where Hambleton was handicapping alongside a pro named Jerry Patterson. Patterson was impressed with Hambleton. Hambleton did not care to try the Pick 6 the day after he struck paydirt with it, but Patterson did. Patterson insisted he would ante up the money, and the two would rely on Hambleton's picks.

"The very next day at the Union Plaza we hit a $2600 Pick 5 three times. In two days I had accumulated $9900 worth of Pick 6 profits on an investment totaling $180.

"We played the Pick 6 the next ten days without cashing. I left town."

Now Hambleton was playing Oak Tree at Santa Anita during fall, looking for speed horses that could control the pace. Patterson perceived Hambleton's deep interest in handicapping and the pace factor, and referred him to Howard Sartin. It was October 1985, almost fifteen seasons past the casual bet on Cougar II. The rest, as they say, is history.

"I first used a Sartin program called *Ultrascan*. I was successful with it for six straight weeks. I began telling myself 'this shouldn't work,' but it did.

"I won with Sartin from the beginning, but not very much. I later switched to another Sartin program called *Phase 3*, which allowed me to enter daily track variants. I used Tom Brohamer's variants, and they're excellent. I began to win more money, still not thinking this computer stuff should be working successfully. But the programs continued to work, and I continued to win."

Playing to a small bank, making 10 percent investments on each bettable race, now utilizing advanced methods that tossed consistent winners, Hambleton's best scores occurred in the exotics. He has evolved into an armchair specialist on betting Pick 6's and triples (the serial-bet version by which bettors must select three consecutive winners).

Hambleton has tackled the Pick 6, for example, on 35 occasions lifetime, but has connected on 4, and has cashed the Pick 5 consolation 12 times. The accuracy rate in the racetrack's most difficult pool (the Pick 9 is a lottery) is an astonishing 44 percent. Hambleton's payoffs have been light, the largest at $7900 (Pick 5) on an $8 ticket, but the win percentage is uncanny.

Hambleton's Pick 6 procedure is to refrain from investing at all unless he can identify three singles. In addition, any maiden race in the sequence must not feature a short-priced favorite. Hambleton then covers the overlays that figure in the contentious maiden events, and the most logical contenders in the remaining races, typically two.

In July 1987, during twenty-two racing days, Hambleton cashed Hollywood Park's triple eleven times. His ticket always looked the same: 4 × 3 × 3, at $3 a parlay, a $108 investment. His net earnings for the bet during that July were $5500.

Naturally, a guy like Hambleton is eager to recount his biggest failures, too, and the pair he cites resulted from the tendency to cut back the appropriate bet size.

"The day after I had won $7900 in the Pick 5 consolation,

April fourteenth, 1987, I filled out a Pick 6 card that cost $1200. I quickly decided that was too much money to spend.

"I cut the ticket down to $120 and left the track.

"The original ticket hit. The Pick 6 paid $18,000 and counting the ten consolations I would have collected, the conservative impulse cost me approximately $26,000 gross."

Later that year, in the fall, at Pomona Fair—Fairplex Park now—Hambleton determined that all three favorites in the triple were destined to lose.

"When all three favorites lose," he explains, "the triple pays $1500 minimum. I liked the Sixth and Eighth races that day, but the middle race in the series, the Seventh, was an unpredictable mess."

Hambleton constructed his triple ticket carefully. It contained six horses in the 6th, three horses in the 8th, and seven horses in the unpredictable 7th. At $3 per parlay, the investment amounted to $378, a realistic sum. Again Hambleton resisted his logic, responded to the conservative impulse.

"I pared the ticket to my typical $4 \times 3 \times 3$ investment.

"I won the Sixth, and the horse paid $58.

"I lost the Seventh by a nose to a horse I had originally included.

"I won the Eighth.

"The triple that day paid $9800.

"I was sick about it. I couldn't deal with it, in fact. I never returned to Pomona that entire meeting."

In the bread-and-butter win pool, Hambleton avoids paceless fields and maiden races but relishes the rest, stakes especially, where he believes the public overbets horses' reputations and underbets improving form.

He especially covets races that bring together horses from different distances and different racetracks.

"I can take horses' records at different distances, and from different racetracks, and reconstruct the pace they will run today. It takes me more than an hour to analyze a race this way, taking sections of races, maybe from as far back in the record as ten races, but it's my favorite play. My specialty, so to speak.

"Because the field is so diverse, and the horses relatively unknown at today's distance or track, the public is often fooled. A top pace handicapper can get overlays that regularly pay $9 to $13 to win, and figure absolutely."

Beyond the horses the Sartin programs pick, Hambleton likes

the improving horses the public does not notice.

"I like reading between the lines to find the likeliest over-lays on form. I like a horse I think will be razor-sharp, if the crowd thinks it will be overmatched or outclassed. I look for those kinds of overlays all the time."

Hambleton's best season was 1987. He achieved the level of consistency that convinced him he had become a certified win-ner. At Hollywood Park, in the fall, during a 20-race cycle in which he won 10 races, Hambleton ran a starting bank of $200 to $1807, the bets graduating from $20 to $150. At one stage of the thirty-two-day meeting he won 12 races in a row (two horses).

"You have to understand, I'm a perfectionist," Hambleton notes. "Betting two horses a race, and using the powerful pace methods I do, more than three losses in a row is a losing streak to me.

"I really don't subscribe to the concept of a 'normal losing run' of 12 to 15 losses. I would stop long before that."

Hambleton points accusingly to the exacta as the wager he has struggled with unsuccessfully, and the resulting style re-flects his painstaking adjustments.

"I have never been a good exacta player. I'm improved now, but I will only play the exacta if the favorite can be eliminated. I only play about a dozen exactas a month. I try to maintain a 40 percent win ratio in exactas.

"I prefer to key a nonfavorite to two other nonfavorites. Or box two nonfavorites. Or even baseball three nonfavorites, de-pending on the way the race shapes up."

Hambleton sometimes doubles the standard bet size to 20 percent of bank, but never more than that, and only when all the circumstances of the race appear to be ideal.

He passes along the strategy to novices.

"My money management advice is to bet two horses a race, bet within your comfort zone, and never bet more than 20 per-cent of bank on any single race."

Hambleton singles out Howard Sartin and Tom Brohamer as handicapping models, but for vastly dissimilar reasons.

"Sartin is a free thinker, a creative thinker at the track or in the race books, where he prefers to play. He spots all the wagers available on the card, juggles bets smartly, and almost invari-ably makes it a profitable day.

"Brohamer is a model of uniformity. He dissects each race with a surgeon's skill. Each horse is evaluated on its own mer-its. Tom's not speculating. He's well-organized, like a businessman at the races, and performs consistently well, week in, week out. He's been an inspiration to me."

The paradox of Hambleton's handicapping career is that as success has increased, playing time has decreased. For instance, after playing 10 to 12 days a month during summers for years, in August 1988 Hambleton did not play at all. Instead he enrolled in college classes in chemistry and calculus.

His ambitious goal is a degree in chiropractic medicine.

"It's a worthwhile goal, I think," says Hambleton, in a characteristic understatement. "I was a small businessman for a time, but lost the business—and paid back an IRS debt of $9000 with racetrack profits, I might add—and have been a district manager in the maintenance field for the majority of the past twenty years.

"I'm forty-three years old, and now I look forward to my continuing schoolwork and to building a practice as a chiropractor."

Hambleton insists the racetrack in the near future will be visited only during breaks in his college class schedule, notwithstanding his recent winning ways.

"I think racing and handicapping hurt personal and family relations because the experience becomes so time-consuming. It's a total-energy effort to win. It can be harmful in that way. I feel closer to my wife and son when I'm not involved at the racetrack, no doubt of that. If it came to choice, racing, of course, would go."

Hambleton's dreams of professional handicapping remain faraway visions for now. They come wrapped in a surprisingly ironic twist.

"I would like to move out of southern California. Go somewhere where racing is not year-round, but seasonal. Then give my best to a full season of continuous play and see how well I could do. Maybe play at a minor track.

"But first I want to become a successful chiropractic doctor."

How about that?

Most would-be professional handicappers dream of leaving occupations and career tracks for full-time handicapping, and many of them dream of moving to southern California as a pro.

It's simpler moving in Hambleton's directions. Success at handicapping the races can contribute markedly to success in life at large, a nexus Hambleton has personified.

Unfortunately for the dreamers locked in so many small, confining worlds, the converse does not often come true.

CHAPTER SIXTEEN

Ron Cox
·
Captain Cover

SINCE 1978, following a score that provided the opportunity, Ron Cox has prospered as a professional handicapper on the northern California circuit. He calls his business a seven-day-a-week affair that he loves.

Shall we take a close look at the schedule Cox follows, the practices he promotes?

It's five A.M., and likely as not, Cox has awakened, freshened up, perked a pot of coffee, and settled in for four or five hours of consultation with the *Daily Racing Form* and assorted supplemental information resources.

The night before, Cox purchased the next afternoon's track program, available at the Pleasanton intertrack site, near the Cox residence, and a small advantage Cox has learned to exploit.

He begins the handicapping process by completing a ritual of mechanical steps intended to bring the day's racing program into sharper focus.

First Cox calculates the speed points (Quirin's technique for assessing the early speed of a race) for every horse on the card. It takes ten minutes. He records each horse's early-speed points next to its name on the track program. He strongly recommends recreational handicappers imitate him in the practice.

"It's amazing how often this simple technique clarifies the probable pace," notes Cox.

"I get a good sense as to whether the race will feature a solo pace or a duel. If a duel, how many horses will be fighting it out. Whether the early speed will come from the outside or inside. Whether one horse possesses superior speed."

Recorded on Cox's program as well are blinker changes and first-time Lasix horses.

Next, regardless of the race, Cox outlines with color-coded pens each horse's form cycles embedded in the past performances shown. He applies the technique promoted by William L. Scott in *How Will Your Horse Run Today?* with certain exceptions and additions.

"I take note of class drops, sprints and routes, distance changes, surface changes, the maiden win, if pertinent, and layoffs. Any layoff of two months or longer I underline with a green marker.

"The idea is to identify patterns that might be important.

"What's the horse's best distance? Best footing? Are any trainer patterns obvious? How has the horse performed following layoffs? Any clear class barriers? The underlining reflects these types of performance details. A sharper focus, if you will. You notice things you otherwise might miss or skip over."

Again Cox addresses the mechanics of recreational handicapping.

"The casual occasional racegoer can complete these preliminaries easily, and should."

Next Cox reads the conditions of eligibility carefully, as the handicapping differs in concert with the different types of races.

He consciously relates distance, footing, and posts to any track biases that might have been prevalent lately. Cox especially notes whether inside or outside lanes should be favored. He counsels himself as to speed biases, early or late, that might be advantaged at today's distance or on this surface.

Now the substance of full-dress handicapping gets under way, and it remains a comprehensive task.

"The emphases and priorities change according to the type of race, class of race, or other circumstances that may or may not count today, such as biases, official track conditions, hot trainers and cold jockeys, or whatever.

"There are no set methods that apply to every race all the time.

"In claiming races, however, the routine is to identify any key races and the most representative recent race, and calculate each horse's pace and speed figures. That part is standard.

"But the broader approach is comprehensive, and varies. It depends for its success on extensive knowledge, skill, and experience. No computer program, in my opinion, covers the variations that are possible."

As the handicapping proceeds, Cox refers continuously to an array of information products that shed bright light on dark questions not susceptible to resolution by analyzing the lines of the *Daily Racing Form*. He consults the following resources:

- Northern California Track Record
- The Northwest Track Review
- Handicapper's Report
- The Handicapper's Sire Reference
- Computerized printouts of trainer/jockey statistics, and of races, arranged from fast to slow by class, distance, sex, and age

The lead resource, the *Northern California Track Record*, is Cox's own weekly summary of the races at Golden Gate Fields or Bay Meadows. Cox sells the publication—at low and certainly cost-effective rates—to a steady, loyal base of subscribers who play the northern California circuit. He relies upon the publication to inform his personal betting as well.

When Cox suggests the process of professional handicapping at major tracks is comprehensive and varied, he is not kidding. Let's examine the information contained in the NCTR for the first race, June 15, 1988, at Golden Gate Fields.

WEDNESDAY JUNE 15 TRACK FAST	**Northern California** **TRACK RECORD**	WEDNESDAY JUNE 15 TRACK FAST

RACE/CONDITIONS/TIMES	NOTES

1st Race 1:12-0 SR=90
   Mdn Clmg 12,500 (6,500)
   6 Furlongs 3 M
 Cal Bred
 22-0 45-2 57-4 11-2
	OGLER (5/2)(Hess,Maple)(91-90)(A-A)(Field Strength=Average) On a day when early speed was winning all the sprints he got the best of DICK VAN PAT and PEACEFUL TIMES thru an early pace duel to draw clear on the turn and was ridden out to win by 2 lengths. SID'S GOLD broke slowly. ALISO BOY took-up at the break and closed ground vs bias. LAST FINAL FINAL(Lsx), FLECHE NOIR (Lsx), WHO'S STARRING (Lsx). Credit horses who closed ground today as the bias was very strong.

Under RACE/CONDITIONS/TIMES, handicappers learn this is a maiden-claiming 6F sprint, selling price of $12,500, for three-year-old males. The purse is $6500. The race is restricted to Cal-breds. The fractional times are provided, with the actual final time of 1:11 2/5 converted to an adjusted time of 1:12 flat. Thus the GG surface June 15 was Fast 3. The adjusted final time is equal to a speed rating (SR) of 90.

The NOTES indicate the winner was Ogler, odds at 5–2, the trainer was R.B Hess, the jockey Sam Maple. Ogler earned a pace figure of 91 and a speed figure of 90, which represents an average-average (A-A) pace configuration for the class and distance.

Handicappers are advised that early speed dominated in sprints June 15. Two horses in the first suffered troubled trips. Three received Lasix. Cox reminds handicappers to credit horses that closed ground against the strong positive speed bias.

Every race, every day, is recaptured in the same detail.

Below a day's recap, Cox provides a track bias note. For June 15 the note read: strong bias favoring the pace types in sprints today.

Other types of information in Cox's weekly alert subscribers to specific horses to watch in the near future.

Below are fifteen horses that benefitted from outstanding workouts or actual races at Golden Gate from June 10 through June 16. The horses represent fewer than one to 2 percent of the numbers that trained or raced during the period, a selective list.

"HOT WORKOUT HORSES"

MISS TANTOUL	6/10	59-1	This workout is third best of 58 at the distance.
ABSTRACT ENERGY	6/11	47-0	Four furlong drill ties as a "hidden bullet" of 41 at the distance.
RIO GRANDE	6/11	59-3	This workout is second best of 31 at the distance.
NAPA NATURAL	6/12	12-2g	This gate work is 2nd best of 9 to the Stakes winning filly MAGDELAINE.
GOLDEN PLEASURE	6/13	59-2	Big 5 furlong work is +3 Of 8 with the next 6 ticks faster than the rest
INDEXED	6/14	01-2	This work is 4 ticks best of 10 at the distance.
MAJESTIC FALCON	6/14	47-1	This 4 furlong work is 4 ticks best of 21 at the distance.
LUNAR BEAUTY	6/15	00-4g	This better than looks gate work is second best of 26.
RAKE EM IN	6/16	59-2	This workout is 3rd best of 21 to the 58-3 of ABSTRACT ENERGY (above)

"SOME HORSES TO FOLLOW"

ALISO BOY	Three year old in the Walter Greenman barn had been gelded since his last start back in November and was entered in a bottom level sprint on Wednesday June 15. He was forced to take-up at the start to be off very slowly and made up much ground while up against a strong bias favoring early speed types. With that prep under his belt he could be tough at the same level on a track more favorable to his closing style.
CODEX'S BRIDE	Came from off the pace to be beaten only 1½ lengths in recent sprint try over a track which was highly favoring the early speed types. She was also disadvantaged by a "race shape" which did not favor her style. The final time of the race was 1:10-1 with the variant applied, in a race for 32,000 Claimers which is good time for the class. She looks set for best and should be tough if can get a reasonable pace up front.
ESTRELLA BLANCA	Comes out of the same race as CODEX'S BRIDE above and had the same disadvantages while closing ground. They both should be followed.
L'COTTONTAIL	Closed versus a bias for frontrunners and a disadvantageous "race shape".
SYNCHRONOUS	No-fluke recent win at 16/1. She earned a 99 final rating and two races later that day CASA PETRONE won a NW3 Allowance race at 9/5 while registering a 96.
PROFESSOR SHANE	This 2 year old should win one soon. He closed for the place vs a strong bias favoring the frontrunners. The third horse was 7 lengths up on the rest as no one else closed.

Comments Cox: "My biggest personal scores often have resulted from following specific horses for three to four races. The horses develop a pattern of hidden form, then it's a go. It pays to know which horses to follow."

Golden Gate 1988

daily track variance

DATE	SPRT	RTE	COND		DATE	SPRT	RTE	COND
Tue. Jan. 26	+3	+3	Fast		Wed. Apr. 13	+7	+10	Fast
Wed. Jan. 27	+4	+4	Fast		Thur. Apr. 14	+4	+7	Fast
Thur. Jan. 28	+5	+8	Fast		Fri. Apr. 15	+8	+8	Fast
Fri. Jan. 29	+2	+3	Sloppy		Sat. Apr. 16	+6	+8	Fast
Sat. Jan. 30	+3	Ø	Muddy		Sun. Apr. 17	+7	+8	Fast
Tue. Feb. 2	+7	+10	Fast		Wed. Apr. 20	**	**	Muddy
Wed. Feb. 3	+7	+12	Fast		Thur. Apr. 21	-3	-5	Good
Thur. Feb. 4	+7	+12	Fast		Fri. Apr. 22	+5	+8	Fast
Fri. Feb. 5	+7	+10	Fast		Sat. Apr. 23	-1	-3	Good
Sat. Feb. 6	+7	+10	Fast		Sun. Apr. 24	+6	+8	Fast
Tue. Feb. 9	+7	+10	Fast		Wed. Apr. 27	+2	+3	Fast
Wed. Feb. 10	+4	+7	Fast		Thur. Apr. 28	Ø	Ø	Fast
Thur. Feb. 11	+7	+10	Fast		Fri. Apr. 29	-2	-2	Fast
Fri. Feb. 12	+3	+5	Fast		Sat. Apr. 30	Ø	Ø	Fast
Sat. Feb. 13	+5	+10	Fast		Sun. May 1	+2	+3	Fast
Mon. Feb. 15	+5	+10	Fast		Wed. May 4	-2	-2	Fast
Wed. Feb. 17	+7	+10	Fast		Thur. May 5	+2	+2	Fast
Thur. Feb. 18	+3	+6	Fast		Fri. May 6	+3	+5	Fast
Fri. Feb. 19	+6	+8	Fast		Sat. May 7	**	**	Sly/Gd
Sat. Feb. 20	+6	+10	Fast		Sun. May 8	+2	+2	Fast
Tue. Feb. 23	Ø	+3	Fast		Wed. May 11	+3	+5	Fast
Wed. Feb. 24	+2	+4	Fast		Thur. May 12	+6	+8	Fast
Thur. Feb. 25	+1	+3	Fast		Fri. May 13	+3	+5	Fast
Fri. Feb. 26	+2	+4	Fast		Sat. May 14	+5	+7	Fast
Sat. Feb. 27	Ø	+2	Fast		Sun. May 15	+3	+5	Fast
Tue. Mar. 1	Ø	+2	Fast		Wed. May 18	+1	+3	Fast
Wed. Mar. 2	+2	+4	Fast		Thur. May 19	+4	+6	Fast
Thur. Mar. 3	-1	-2	Fast		Fri. May 20	+2	+3	Fast
Fri. Mar. 4	-2	-4	Fast		Sat. May 21	+1	+3	Fast
Sat. Mar. 5	+1	+3	Fast		Sun. May 22	+6	+8	Fast
Tue. Mar. 8	**	**	Fast	** Changing track See race day	Wed. May 25	+5	+7	Fast
Wed. Mar. 9	+4	+6	Fast		Thur. May 26	+5	+7	Fast
Thur. Mar. 10	**	**	Fast		Fri. May 27	+3	+5	Fast
Fri. Mar. 11	+6	+8	Fast		Sat. May 28	+4	+5	Fast
Sat. Mar. 12	+8	+10	Fast		Sun. May 29	Ø	Ø	Fast
Tue. Mar. 15	+3	+5	Fast		5/30 +4 +6	6/3 +4 +5		
Wed. Mar. 16	+6	+8	Fast		6/1 +5 +7	6/4 +3 +5		
Thur. Mar. 17	+5	+8	Fast		6/2 +3 +5	6/5 +3 +5		
Fri. Mar. 18	+3	+5	Fast					
Sat. Mar. 19	+5	+8	Fast					
Tue. Mar. 22	**	**	Fast		6/8 ** **	6/11 +6 +8		
Wed. Mar. 23	+3	+3	Fast		6/9 +1 +1	6/12 +5 +7		
Thur. Mar. 24	+3	+3	Fast		6/10 +4 +5			
Fri. Mar. 25	+5	X	Fast	X No dirt routes today				
Sat. Mar. 26	+4	+5	Fast					
Tue. Mar. 29	+4	+5	Fast		6/15 +3 +5	6/18 -2 -2		
Wed. Mar. 30	+4	+5	Fast		6/16 +1 +1	6/19 Ø Ø		
Thur. Mar. 31	+4	+5	Fast		6/17 +1 +2			
Fri. Apr. 1	+6	+8	Fast					
Sat. Apr. 2	+5	+7	Fast					
Tue. Apr. 5	+4	+6	Fast					
Wed. Apr. 6	+2	+3	Fast					
Thur. Apr. 7	+3	+5	Fast					
Fri. Apr. 8	+7	+10	Fast					
Sat. Apr. 9	+10	+12	Fast					

Northern California **TRACK RECORD**

Cox's NCTR also supplies a cumulative log of daily track variants for the entire season, a service indispensable to handicappers who prefer to develop their own speed figures, pace ratings, or even class ratings. The issue of June 15–19, 1988, provided the daily variants for sprints and routes at GG since opening day, January 26. I present them below for the reader's edification: + means Fast, − Slow.

When Cox confronts shippers, which happens daily, he consults either *Handicapper's Report*, an informative biweekly that recaps the races of southern California, or *The Northwest Track Review*, which does the same for shippers from north of San Francisco, Longacres primarily.

The Handicapper's Sire Reference, which Cox has used only a year, provides previously unavailable perspectives on first starters, distance preferences, mud races, and turf races.

When a morning's handicapping marathon has ended, Cox has borrowed repeatedly from each of his information resources. He believes novices and recreational handicappers who wish to improve should not miss the point.

"To become competent, you must get the extra information handicappers need. Nobody can do it alone. The information load is too heavy. You need help. And nobody, no matter how smart, is good enough any longer to just analyze the past performances in the *Form* and beat this game, at least for any length of time."

On weekends Cox rushes from the morning handicapping routine to the seminars he delivers at restaurants near the tracks. Here he pores over the entire card again for the weekend customers. Other days he goes straight to the races. There he confronts the weak spots in his armor.

"I don't work hard enough at the track itself," says Cox. "My strengths are my experience, lots of energy, and an enduring love of the game, factors that should work well for me during the heat of the action, but at the races I am also a social butterfly. I get distracted. I do not concentrate enough on the board. I miss some possibilities."

Apparently, not many.

Cox's associates have labeled him "Captain Cover." Cox penetrates a race from several angles, recognizes the real possibilities, and covers each of them, at various levels of investment.

"I like the exotics. I go for the big score. Yet I cover myself as best I can. When I bet, I collect something most of the time. It keeps me in the ballgame, so to speak, until the big ones come along.

"In the last few years I've become a consistent winner, but not by the day, week, or even month. By the meeting, for the season. I really don't apply a systematic money management plan either. I let each race dictate the bets and amounts.

"I don't consider myself a big bettor. My neighborhoods are $200 to win, and $300 to $400 in the exotics. I never affect the board."

Does Cox's betting style lead to longer losing runs?

"Well, they call me 'Captain Cover.' I collect most times. When I don't collect for a time, it does hurt; it's a difficult period.

"The last few weeks at Golden Gate this season [1988], they resurfaced the strip. I lost a few consecutive prime bets, but immediately backed off.

"The important point about losing runs is to understand them. Know the reasons why you're losing. Try to correct any repetitive mistakes. That leads to improving your play. Normal losing runs do not bother me or lower my confidence, unless I don't understand them. That's the most difficult time of all.

"About five years ago at Bay Meadows the track surface went haywire. Severe biases appeared over all the track, and unpredictable horses were winning race after race. I was losing and couldn't correct it. I stopped; even stopped the seminars. It was my worst season as a pro."

At the track Cox watches the races and replays deliberately and closely. He's probing for subtle signals related to trips and biases.

"For instance, the Form might show a horse was fifth at the stretch call but gained six lengths to the finish and lost by a head.

"The customers reading the Form will assume the horse was flying by and just didn't get there. But after moving strongly, the horse might have hung, practically refused to win. It's crucial to know that. Otherwise, the player cannot interpret the horse's form properly."

For a professional searching for overlays in the exotics, the racing day becomes a lengthy, active afternoon. That handicapper is continually engaged in mental conflict. Thinking of the real possibilities to cover, juggling numerous alternatives

and plans, checking the probable payoffs on combinations repeatedly.

Cox chases exactas and triples relentlessly, but dips into the
Pick 6 only occasionally.

"My best scores have resulted from cashing exactas and triples multiple times. The greatest handicapping values are there.

"The triple [serial-bet version] is the best bet. It arrives later
in the card. You know today's track biases. You're dealing with
better races, better horses. Your concentration will be at its
keenest. And the payoffs for a reasonably predictable short series of outcomes can be astonishingly generous.

"The Pick 6 is another story. I'm sure I am far in arrears on
the bet. It's too tough, and not worth the money it takes to cover
the real possibilities, many of which will be short-priced.

"I and a few friends hit the Pick 6 this past season at Golden
Gate for $50,000, and I'm still far behind on the bet. I won't
even consider playing the Pick 6 now unless the carryover has
reached $100,000."

When the combat at the races has ended, Cox goes home and
relaxes. He does no handicapping or record-keeping until
the dawn.

"I relax at night," states Cox, revealing the secret of coping
effectively with the mental fatigue inherent in the professional
pursuit, a voracious day schedule he follows forty-four weeks
a year.

"I like to go out to dinner at night. I take a two-month vacation each July and August. I have a new love in my life I'm
enjoying. She works at the track, so that connection is convenient and our lives more easily shared.

"Mental fatigue is no problem for me. Never has been. I have
high energy, and I love the game."

Racing entered Cox's life while he attended college at the
University of San Francisco in 1958. A friend's father worked
in track management, and Cox began to accompany his pal to
the races. All-state at guard in high school basketball, and a
rabid football fan, Cox had stumbled upon a new game he liked
and could participate in as an adult.

In the beginning Cox observed the raw times horses ran. He
asked: which horse is fastest?

Cox did not know until much later that raw times do not
often supply the correct answer.

Soon he searched for patterns; winning performance patterns that repeated themselves frequently enough to make an impression.

It was the stuff of recreational handicapping.

"I liked the frontrunners from the beginning," recalls Cox. "I thought they won more than their share of the races. After a while, I played the speed all the time."

Cox remained a recreational handicapper for two decades. He had earned a teaching credential at Sonoma State College and was pursuing a relatively normal professional academic life. He had a marriage, and had entered the restaurant business with his wife, an avocation that lasted eleven years. His pleasure, and interest, in racing inevitably intensified.

Late in the 1970s Cox found himself entertaining what he perceived to be a potentially heavy racetrack score.

"Naturally, the horse was a frontrunner I had been waiting for. My four biggest scores have resulted from frontrunners, and the first was the best.

"A horse I had observed in its previous race, when it had broken poorly and rushed up, before fading, was entered in a large field with no early speed. The troubled race had been its first following a layoff.

"I knew the horse shaped up as the lone speed against this lackluster field. I knew the public would overlook the horse off a bad race following a layoff. I just figured the horse would go all the way. I couldn't sleep the night before the race. It was an eerie feeling, like knowing the future.

"I decided to go for it. I bet a lot of money.

"The horse went wire to wire, and paid $57."

Cox savored the experience and the sensibilities it had aroused in him. He abruptly decided to give professional handicapping a shot.

"It took a long time to become a consistent winner," Cox admits. "But that first season I noticed there were no information products or services for the regular customers."

Cox perceived a need, and he filled it, in 1979 creating the *Northern California Track Record*.

"No competing products were available for handicappers. I had been calculating my own variants and making speed figures. The figures worked in ways the unadjusted times never had. I thought others might want to buy solid technical information that would help them pick winners."

An enormous change in Cox and his product began to take

shape in the early 1980s, when the advantages attached to mak-ing modern speed figures began to erode.

"More and more players had the figures. Suddenly there were no more speed horses winning at 9–1. Instead, they were 9–5.

"I began to look for a new edge. Steve Davidowitz's book touting the significance of track biases and key races influenced me strongly at this time. I still use both concepts religiously.

"With a colleague, I also started compiling computerized trainer and jockey statistics.

"I also began to refine my skill at watching races, so I could identify troubled trips and subtle biases. I began to watch for horses that 'hang,' and still do."

The general growth pattern, which has continued uninter-rupted until now, reflected a dual purpose of expanding one's handicapping knowledge and skill, and collecting new sources of information that might constitute a vital edge in specific races.

Throughout layered stages of development as a handicapper and publisher, Cox contends the substantial literature on handicapping has wielded a strong positive influence on his success.

He has compiled a brief list of books-to-read for novices and others who take the pastime seriously enough to want to play it well.

"I believe novices should read the good books. But I also realize there are a number of books developing handicappers should avoid, and newcomers have a particularly hard time knowing what's good and what's bad.

"At first they should stick to a few books and authors.

"I already mentioned Davidowitz's *Betting Thoroughbreds* describing track biases, key races, and trainer patterns. It has a lot more that's excellent about trainers, speed, and class. Davi-dowitz was ahead of his time. He's one of the most compre-hensive, most practical authors on the subject. I wish he'd write more.

"Beyer's book should be read, of course. He shares his ex-periences particularly well. And he plays the game well. He puts his money down exactly as he recommends in his books.

"Quirin's books are loaded with solid information. I use his speed-points technique, pace and speed figures, and race shapes. He imparts a whole lot of basic knowledge besides.

"Quinn's book on eligibility conditions was a milestone for me. It taught me how to handle allowance races. It's a good treatment of class and of finding contenders suited to particular types of races.

"Scott's book on form cycles is a good treatment of form analysis. I don't care for Scott's treatment of speed and ability, but the material on form is first-rate."

The good books, as Cox characterizes them, form the centerpiece of a liberal in-depth education Cox believes must coordinate substance and practice. He cautions newcomers further to stay close, not only to the legitimate authors, but also to the following maxims:

1. Experience is ultimately the best teacher; play as frequently as you can.
2. Associate with winners, or at least with skillful players.
3. Pay the small expenses associated with obtaining the supplemental information handicappers need to evaluate the races intelligently.
4. Be vigilant for special information that few customers possess, and for the overlays the information is intended to uncover.
5. Keep records. No one should assume he or she can interpret *Daily Racing Form* data better than others, as no one can.
6. Remember that no one can do it alone. The game is too complex, the handicapper's information requirements too plentiful.

Among professionals he has met, Cox singles out Davidowitz, now of Minneapolis, and Paul Braseth of Seattle as tops.

"Paul is the best handicapper I've been personally associated with over time. He uses small money to make lots of profits better than anybody."

Cox notes as well that many of his local subscribers have been impressively astute. "A couple of local handicappers I respect keep their own tapes of races and compile extensive trip and bias notes. They operate with a precious edge and are probably winners."

Cox's best season has been his last, a circumstance he feels should be the trend among professionals.

"My only goal or dream is to beat the game. It's a feat a lot of people do not think can be done, and I take a lot of pride in doing it. I would like to win a little more each succeeding season."

On enhancing profits during any season, Cox imparts a piece of practical wisdom on money management not widely distributed. It's for talented handicappers only.

"Set up a separate savings account. Each day you win, put a portion of the winnings in the account. Set a specified date, perhaps the end of the meeting, and do not touch the savings until that date.

"Handicappers will be amazed how much of their winnings can be saved in that simple way. I've done this the past few seasons, and the amounts that grow from day to day have amazed me. It's a tidy form of profit-taking, and I strongly recommend it. Always put a portion of the winnings away."

Cox's pet peeves about the sport and industry are directed squarely toward track managers.

"Track managers do not provide the information resources the regular customers need. They provide the poorest service to their best customers. What other business or industry is guilty of that?

"Worse is the attitude held by many track managers that regular handicappers are losers. It's bothersome to me. It's contemptible."

Otherwise, seven days a week, early morning to early evening, forty-four weeks a year, relaxing at night, Ron Cox has no complaints. Captain Cover covers his familiar challenging beat rather well, like a pro.

CHAPTER SEVENTEEN

Frank Romano

•

High Roller

A PERFECTLY reliable index to the racetrack worldliness and personal maturity of everyday talented handicappers who profess the desire to succeed can be derived from the clarity or ambiguity of their responses to six questions about betting to win.

- What is a best estimate of your win percentage?
- What's the average odds on a season's worth of your winners?
- What is your edge, or the return on the invested dollar (ROI)?
- On average, how many prime bets do you get a day?
- What are your methods of money management and betting?
- How much money do you expect to win after a season's duration?

Handicappers motivated to succeed should know. Professionals motivated to pari-mutuel betting for income, or profit, must know.

Without knowing, handicappers do not comprehend their individual proficiency. They cannot determine how skillful they have become, or how much they need to improve, if they want to salute themselves as winners. They do not know, in fact, whether they are winners or losers, except as short-term bottom lines may suggest.

Without knowing, professionals cannot predict their income

or profits. They cannot determine their capital requirements, how much money they must set aside for racetrack betting. Unless they make flat bets, pros cannot determine the optimal bet size or the amounts best suited to individual proficiency levels. This risks underbetting, or betting too little in relation to personal skill, thereby minimizing profits. It also risks overbetting, or betting too much in relation to personal skill, thereby descending into eventual losses. The latter miscue guarantees that those professionals can anticipate something less than a long rewarding career at the races.

High rollers who are handicappers have the numbers at their fingertips.

Frank Romano's win percentage, based upon the entirety of his play in 1987, is 32 percent.

His average odds on winners is 2.84, relatively high because Romano will not take less than 2–1.

His edge, or ROI, is .23, meaning for each dollar Romano wagers he can expect to retrieve $1.23.

Romano finds one prime bet a day.

He bets a flat $2000 to win, no exceptions.

He can expect to win between $50,000 and $100,000, depending upon the number of racing days he attends.

In 1987 Romano won $60,000. Playing more frequently, he intended to net six figures in 1988.

Two numbers jump out, the winnings, and the bet size. At $2000 a pop, Romano is a high roller. The term is pejorative, intimating a gambler. When juxtaposed with proficient handicapping, however, the high roller turns fascinating. More than a big bettor, he becomes a big winner. That high roller qualifies as the envy of the rest of us, and for all the right reasons.

In my time, sixteen seasons, I have enjoyed the acquaintance of three high rollers who are good handicappers. A sample of three notwithstanding, certain similarities are worth pondering, for they differentiate high rollers from other regular/professional handicappers in unmistakable ways.

First, high rollers bet approximately ten times as much to win as the typical regular or professional handicapper.

The typical professional bets in the $200 neighborhood on prime horses, sometimes more, often less. High rollers bet in the $2000 neighborhood, sometimes more. The gap is hardly narrow; rather a great divide. Professional handicappers in the main are not high rollers.

Of my high-rolling acquaintances, two bet $2000 routinely, the third $3000. In that rarefied sense, Romano's flat bet is typical.

When regulars/professionals up the ante to the maximum, the richest wager of the season, they bet $500, or $1000, or maybe $2000. This occurs once, twice, three times a year, and an unexpected loss translates into a disincentive to reinvest the maximum. High rollers also invest a maximum a few times a year, but the bets are gigantic, such as 10 percent of an annual income, and a loss represents no disincentive for the future.

Independently, by sheer coincidence, ten years ago Frank Romano and I placed our largest bets of the season on the same horse. It was a Grade 2 grass stakes at Hollywood Park, at 1⅛M, on the 3–2 favorite Johnny's Image.

I bet $500.

Romano bet $10,000, his largest wager ever.

Johnny's Image won, rather handily, actually, despite being pushed by the fine turf horse Star-Spangled to a track-record time for the distance of 1:46 flat, which stood for eight seasons.

Romano recalled another gigantic bet, this one two years ago. It was a middling claiming sprint at Santa Anita, and Romano's selection had raced strongly its previous outing on the front against a strong negative rail bias. The horse was 2–1 on the comeback, and Frank began to salivate. He bet $6000. The horse broke badly and raced down the backstretch five lengths behind the field.

Swinging wide, and running gamely through the stretch, as Romano stared disbelievingly at the wire, the horse won by a lip. Two seasons later, amazingly, Romano had forgotten the $6000 horse's name.

> Second, for high rollers who are good handicappers the huge amounts are a matter neither for discussion nor interest.

Regular handicappers struggle consciously and persistently with betting practices and finances, and professionals debate money management strategies avidly, but high rollers rarely mention the topics. Comfort zone is not a relevant concept. Neither are actions bets, side bets, saver bets, angle bets, and the like, those types of recreational diversions. The cash has literally become currency, a means of exchange. It is targeted for racetrack speculation, period. Outside of that purposeful context, the money has no meaning, certainly not as principal for the cost of living, paying bills, or buying goods and services.

As curious as everyday handicappers might be about high rollers, and they are wildly curious, the big bettors themselves practically dismiss the subject as uninteresting. Large bets for them are merely a way of life at the races, like $20 bets have been for recreational handicappers.

> High rollers tend to share a long, tortuous history of betting big.

High rollers do not graduate to the big bucks, as if on a schedule. Betting big apparently is not a learned skill. The large bets do not grow in size with the passage of time, with age, or with experience. The first bets were relatively big ones. King-size bets become habitual early on. The ability to win is not a prerequisite either. Whether winning or losing, betting bigger is just part and parcel of the high roller's standard operating procedure. When losing, moreover, high rollers do not cut back, not dramatically.

"I always bet big, even in the beginning," says Romano, "when I was a gambler, not a handicapper.

"I've always made good money, so capital was not a problem. But winning was, and chasing was. I've had years, long ago, when I probably surrendered $60,000 too."

Alternately, professional handicappers who wager to win in the $200 to $250 range normally have advanced to those levels of investment, and not until acquiring the confidence that attaches to successive seasons of winning. The typical professional's bet size reflects a learned skill indeed. When losing, the typical professional does cut back, close to the bone.

> High rollers intend to win significant profits, and they can accept the risks associated with highly speculative investments.

High rollers are not afraid to lose. They do not like to lose—hate to lose, in fact—but do not mind taking rational chances. They possess the courage of conviction, among the rarest of all human virtues. Yet they are seldom fools, and seldom suffer fools. They understand the downside, but accentuate the upside. In any risk-benefit analysis, when the benefits clearly outweigh the risks, and the probabilities look favorable, high rollers are more than willing to take the plunge.

In addition, when high rollers lose, they lose bravely, if not like gentlemen. Unlike chasers, who toss temper tantrums or pout about the unfairness of it all because they do not know what they are doing and cannot accept responsibility for their actions, high rollers who are talented handicappers bounce back whole. They go to the next race, to the next positive betting opportunity. They do not alter their betting habits drastically. It's business as usual.

"The worst habit is chasing," states Romano. "You cannot chase, and beat this game.

"The only time I ever got in trouble at the racetrack is when I chased. That was years ago, my early days, and I paid for the habit. Now I just continue to play my game. I don't adjust up by chasing, and I don't adjust down. I just continue to play as best I know how."

> Another trait high rollers who are good handicappers have in common is a rabid interest in the art of handicapping well.

Frank Romano would rather talk about handicapping, which fascinates him endlessly, than betting, which bores him quickly. Now forty-seven, born in New York, this hard-bitten, high-rolling twenty-six-year veteran of the racetrack almost loses himself in soliloquy on the glories of thoroughbred handicapping.

"Other interests? Do I have other interests?

"With the amount of time I put into this game, most of my other interests have dwindled to family things. I find that my family and friends are all tired of hearing about handicapping. I never seem to tire of it. I am unbelievably distracted by it. I never run out of things to think about. I have got to the point of comparing life to this game, and I think it has helped me.

"This may seem strange to people, but I know a tennis player who once was on the tour, and he said that all the pros do is talk tennis and think about it even off the court. The ones that have several other interests are not on the tour long.

"I guess that also answers the question of relationships. It is my fantasy to try to start a club to see if I am the only crazy one. I am just afraid that if you run an ad, all you will get are people looking for a shortcut to big scores. I guess I would be interested in that also. I do have several people that are always willing to take advantage of my work. I don't mind it too much, but would prefer to exchange ideas. I love it when they tell you, after you give them a loser, that they had the winner until they talked to you."

It began for keeps just five years ago, the whole attitude change, as Romano characterizes it, the commitment to become professional, to be the best he can be.

"I had to come to terms with what that meant. It's easy to say you want to be a pro, but when you investigate what any professional athlete has to do, the parallels are undeniable, and you realize it will require a great deal of devotion and sweat. Professional handicapping is hard work, and instead of getting easier, it seems to get harder. The more you know, the more you see you have to learn."

Romano virtually dismissed all that came before, the entire twenty-one years leading up to his professional involvement at the track.

"I only know it was twenty-six years ago when I started, and I have little recollection of it, except that I lost a lot of money the first day I went."

Two years later Romano bought an Ainslie paperback, which imparted several insights his cronies had no knowledge of. He did not begin to win, but felt the material "put me in the game." He was a player, at least. For six years, approximately, Romano mixed Ainslie's guidelines and his own experiences, occasionally breaking even, or nearly breaking even, or even making a little.

"But I was a gambler, and gamblers have two strikes against them. They remember the good and block out the bad. I kept scarce records, if any."

He began calculating variants and keeping records about fifteen seasons ago. The ledger began to register profits more consistently, though looking back, concedes Romano, he cannot understand how.

Next on the scene came a spate of better books on handicapping, and Romano devoured them all. He seldom agreed wholly with the authors, but the books provided new perspectives on Frank's game, and some valuable information besides. More than anything, the books had an energizing effect on Romano's personal development. They motivated Romano to think critically about his handicapping, evaluate his results, and undertake an amazing series of individual studies that have not yet ended, and probably never will.

"As outside influences that have helped me, Ainslie comes to mind first, and I've gained something from many authors I have read.

"I especially like Quirin's Master Turf Sires lists, and [Quinn's] catalog of Graded and Listed stakes comparing imports' records to American race conditions. They are unusually helpful tools; they get overlays.

"The only thing I would tell people who read many handicapping authors is to keep an open mind. Try to fit what they are saying into your own style of handicapping. Remember, there are no simple solutions to this game."

All things considered, the formative years resulted in marginal, and not lasting, contributions to Romano's growth and development. The last five years tell the tale.

Romano's handicapping embraces all the pertinent factors, relating variously to horses, trainers, and jockeys. He singles out six integrating factors, and his perspectives on each are idiomatic and well worth presenting.

1. Consistency
2. Distance
3. Class, notably claiming class
4. Speed and pace
5. Patterns, meaning repetitive performance patterns embedded in horses' complete records or total performance histories
6. Trainers, notably positive patterns, or maneuvers

Romano is a stickler on consistency, and regardless of other factors, will not support horses to win that do not satisfy his standards. He adds an intriguing twist to the conventional guidelines on the factor.

Using the ten races displayed in the *Daily Racing Form*, Romano classifies horses into three main groups: likes to win (LW), doesn't like to win (DW), or likes to run (LR).

LW horses must win 25 percent of their starts, or at least 3 of 10, if the full complement shows. Two of 10 is acceptable, 1 of 10 is not acceptable.

LR horses are the intriguing kind, and Romano favors them

on the undersides of exactas only. Regardless of position, LR horses must have finished within two lengths of the winner in 6 of 10 starts, without winning. Failure to finish within two lengths in fewer than 3 of 10 starts earns horses a disputatious DR label, for does not like to run. These get Romano's boot.

Romano counsels that the crowd overbets LR types to win, which the horses do not do, yet LR horses regularly run their race and often represent fair to good value in the two hole.

Regarding LW horses, when confronted with the national probability data showing that inconsistency is no longer a reliable elimination factor in claiming races, Romano counters with abundant local data that indicate inconsistent horses do not win enough in southern California. He insists the local research deserves precedence, which it does.

"The LW designation I find especially effective at the lower claiming levels. You sometimes will find a LW $6000 claimer from Caliente or Fairplex Park entered against a DW field of $10,000 or $12,500 claimers at Del Mar, or even Santa Anita. The LW shippers have a strong edge, believe me."

Romano remains classical on the distance factor. A strict conservative. He expects horses 3up to have won at today's distance on today's surface, and is not lenient about wins at related distances. The reasoning is understandable at Romano's investment threshold. He does not care to squander two grand betting mature horses will do something today they have never done before.

Of class, Romano rates claiming horses carefully, jotting down for each horse the current claiming price he himself has assigned it. He logs his current values for every claimer on the grounds.

"It amazes me how many times you will find a $16,000 claiming race consisting of a single legitimate $16,000 horse and a bunch of others worth $10,000 tops, several less. That's a play."

If Romano displays a particular long suit, it's class handicapping, and his rating scheme for claimers clears a path to his favorite bet at the races. It's a claiming horse with a higher value dropping to a selling level where no other horses in the field actually belong. For instance, a solid $32,000 claiming horse dropping into $25,000 competition where no horse has been rated higher than $20,000, or perhaps $16,000. Romano cherishes these opportunities, and reports that it happens many times.

He does not feel as sanguine about allowance and stakes races, and bemoans certain changes of recent vintage, in the allowances especially.

"In relative terms, my strength is claiming races, and my weakness is allowance and stakes races. Allowance form especially seems to be difficult for me to get a firm handle on. My only explanation is that they are breeding so many horses now for year-round racing, they no longer can fill allowance fields with genuine allowance horses. Too many horses too often disappoint. I have never seen so many four-year-olds beat three-year-olds in preliminary nonwinners races.

"Also, since they now print the purse values of allowance races in the *Form*, record-keepers don't have the edge they once did.

"Also, better horses do not adhere as strictly to familiar patterns as claiming horses do. Take the 'bounce' pattern. I thought Super Diamond [a Grade 1 horse] would 'bounce' this year off an extraordinarily hard race at seven furlongs following a long layoff, but instead he won a Graded stakes next out handily. You have to be extra careful with better horses."

Romano employs speed and pace figures for every horse, but he uses them in unique applications, in tandem with his famous "patterns."

Romano's "patterns" are short-term performance patterns embedded in a thoroughbred's racing history. They come to life only as a result of extensive personal research, and they assume numerous shapes and forms.

What Romano does is gather together from two years of back *Forms* horses' entire racing records, and he smokes them over anew each successive time the horses compete. The practice has been continuing for three years, and Romano considers the patterns he discovers his professional signature, the information that sets his handicapping apart, with a telltale edge.

He emphasizes the advantage of accessing thirty races, or even twenty races, to evaluate horses' possibilities today. Although performance patterns are fantastically various among racehorses as a group, Romano swears they remain stubbornly consistent for individual horses. Even as horses grow from developing three-year-olds to the mature racing years, up to age seven, their "patterns" persevere.

Don't 2YOs differ from 3YOs, and 3YOs from 4up, in their "patterns"? I beg to know.

"It's not black and white," replies Romano, complicating the stew even further. "Some do, and some don't."

He added—smugly, I thought—it's nice to distinguish the horses that do and don't.

So, I pressed on, if a 3YO earns a suddenly gigantic figure as part of an improvement pattern, then "bounces," as many do, can handicappers expect the same up-and-down pattern of figures when the horse turns four or five?

"Some will, and some won't."

He does concede young horses should be regarded as developing horses, and handicappers must accept the "patterns" of lightly raced animals as tentative and inconclusive.

"My patterns will usually reflect the races in the younger years, but I do not rely on 'patterns' for younger horses often, until they have accumulated approximately twenty races. I must have confidence they have repeated themselves often enough in the past. I must admit I have often been fooled by young four-year-olds. They improve more dramatically than I think they will.

"Also, I am uncertain whether a horse seven or older can adhere to its past patterns, simply due to age. It's one of the many studies I promise myself I will do."

Patterns of individual horses, Romano advises, will often contradict the generally accepted principles of handicapping that apply to horses of a class. Romano offers a few provocative illustrations he finds recurring.

Among consistent horses, a large number will string together three good races but cannot add the fourth. On the fourth outing, the crowd overbets, but Romano looks elsewhere.

Regarding horses that "bounce," a number require two overexerting efforts after a rest, not one. Among claiming horses that return from lengthy layoffs and run two successive hard races, less than 10 percent can run strongly again the third race back.

Romano relishes the situation, as it contradicts the widely held conclusion promoted by Quirin's probability studies that the third race after layoffs will usually be the best. It ain't necessarily so, cautions Romano.

Horses that compete strongly against negative speed biases make sense on the comeback, all right, but not horses that have run "too strongly" against negative biases. If horses extend themselves for too long against a wicked bias, the exertion often knocks them out.

"If a bias is pronounced, I prefer horses run well to the top of the stretch, or the eighth pole perhaps, before tiring, but I don't trust them on the rebound if they lasted almost to the wire in an obvious exhausting effort. My data show these horses regularly suffer a temporary loss of form."

As a general rule, too, notes Romano, any horse that has accumulated thirty races should not be expected by handicappers to do something it has not yet done. Whether it's footing, distance, level of opposition, running well fresh, surviving a hotly contested pace, or whatever, retain a healthy respect for a past that suggests horses are likely to disappoint under today's circumstances.

"I'm convinced that understanding individual horse's patterns are the key to highly successful handicapping, the difference between 32 percent winners and 40 percent winners.

"My goal is to raise my win percentage to 40 percent, and only by understanding horses' specific patterns can I accomplish it. If I get there, I will make a small fortune at the races. So it's worth the time and effort I expend."

After horses have been filtered through Romano's performance screens, the handicapping process concludes only following a detailed attention to trainers and jockeys. Romano conducts studies of the positive performance patterns of each, updated daily. Here a microcomputer assists.

Of trainers, he determines which jockeys they employ when shooting, what types of races they win most frequently, indicators of hot and cold cycles, and effective maneuvers, the latter predicated on rate of profit. He describes a common maneuver that signals impending loss for a large majority of trainers who employ it, yet many handicappers are lulled into betting to win.

A claiming horse shows fast sharp regular workouts on returning from a layoff and is dropped noticeably in class. If the horse was competitive in its last race, even better. If it was claimed just prior to the layoff, even better. Such horses figure to lose, warns Romano. The public will be misled. Handicappers should not.

"What do players think these trainers are doing," wonders Romano, "giving away the store? There's a big hole. No one is giving the goods away, and there are very few gambling trainers and owners anymore, at least in southern California. I've got the records to prove it."

Romano's jockey studies are unusually fascinating. First, he

keeps close tabs on how jockeys do with horses that figure—by
his handicapping, that is.

"It gives you an excellent snapshot of what they do best and
what they don't do nearly as well. Jockeys really do differ in
their specialties and shortcomings. Some are much better in
sprints, others in routes. Some are better on turf, some with
fillies, some with two-year-olds, and so forth. I examine a large
number of categories. You'd be startled at the differences to be
found."

Most important, Romano attempts to identify when jockeys
have begun to tail off, presumably due to fatigue or a temporary
loss of vital conditioning. Romano argues, quite sensibly, that
even leading riders cannot be expected to stay in tip-top shape
twelve months a year, season after season.

He quotes a statement by Laffit Pincay, Jr., that when he's in
top shape he adds lengths to horses, but when slightly out of
condition he costs horses the same number of lengths.

I had not heard the argument, but its source is irrefutable.
Romano's research supports Pincay's claim. The handicapper
likes nothing more than catching a leading jockey turning sour.

"They all do," he snaps.

"I also keep detailed records of jockey switches, off horses I
like, onto horses I don't like.

"I record, too, which jockeys will follow horses down the
claiming ladder. Some do it effectively, others unsuccessfully.

"I particularly like to know what happens when top jockeys
get on stiffs, or horses that look like stiffs to me. Who wins with
them? Who doesn't? Again, there are surprising differences."

As part of a twelve-hour routine, Romano spends five hours
in the morning handicapping in a den furnished specifically for
that task. The repetitive poring over of patterns proves benefi-
cial in its unanticipated consequences, a serendipity Romano
did not envision but now respects as equally important to an-
swering specific questions about horses' abilities and preferences.

"I can't begin to tell you how much I have learned about
horses while looking for something else. It's a great added benefit, discovering these side-effects."

Ups and downs aside, it took fifteen seasons before Romano
pronounced himself a certified winner. He has not experienced
a losing meeting in three years. "I have losing days and losing
weeks, but no losing meetings anymore."

Oddly, Romano criticizes himself, unjustly perhaps, on money management.

"It's not a strong suit. I do like to use [bet] a figure that will force me to think seriously about what I am doing."

A mild understatement.

"As far as betting is concerned, I recommend handicappers track their bets as if they were $2 across the board.

"At the end of a hundred bets, find your win percentage. If it's below 30 percent, you cannot accept anything below 2–1. If it's 25 percent, you cannot take below 3–1.

"Determine where in the three holes [win-place-show] you are getting the best ROI. Stay in that hole until your records prove you can do better somewhere else. In 1987, for example, I spent almost the entire Hollywood Park meeting in the place hole. That was unusual.

"If after a hundred bets you show no profit in any hole, you should learn more about handicapping before you invest more money.

"Finally, to restate a critical point, don't chase lost money. Don't try to get it all back too fast. In fact, as preached by everyone, when losing, bet less."

Romano's dilemma is the exacta.

"I love exactas but seldom make a major bet in them. I usually box two horses, and often put each of them on top of a third horse."

Romano's practical solution to exactas has been to allocate 25 percent ($500) of his standard wager to each combination he supports.

"So far this year [1988] my biggest score has been in the exacta. I had a $500 box on Super Diamond and Epidaurus in a sprint at Santa Anita." The combination paid $162, and Romano cleared $16,200.

If Romano's highest score seems low for a $2000 win bettor, handicappers must realize high rollers do not find many legitimate opportunities beyond 8–1 or thereabouts. They spin no high tales about overlays they spotted at 25–1, thus collecting fifty grand by six lengths. High rollers confine themselves to low-priced overlays, almost exclusively. Romano reported no unforgettable scores when betting to win.

"I do play the Pick 6, but not frequently," says Romano. "I would guess I play it frequently enough, seventy times a year, or such. But I have a secret for beating the Pick 6. I never bet

more than $120 [60 parlays] on the series. I truly question guys
that put $2000 to $5000 into the Pick 6 all the time.

"Actually, until last year I had never cashed a Pick 6 in my
life, but last season I hit it five times. Nothing earth-shaking,
though. On consecutive days I hit the Pick 6 for $18,000. That's
my biggest score on that bet."

Romano took a B.S. in business administration from Pace
College in New York, and unlike his formative experiences at
the racetrack, he succeeded in business from the outset. With
partners, he started a profitable management consulting firm,
and later started an insurance division for the second-largest
executive-search firm in the world.

The affluence resulted from executive search. For a successful placement, Romano charged insurance companies 25 percent of the executive's first-year salary. A six-figure salary meant
Romano invoiced $25,000 minimum. He dug up many six-fig-
ure executives.

Why would Romano abandon a gravy train like that, not to
mention a thriving career he had spent an adult life erecting?

"The executive-search business nosedived during the 1981–
82 recession. It's bustling again, but I feel I am getting in on the
ground floor of the greatest economic opportunity I have ever
come across. I have a long ways to go, but the financial rewards
are there. There is no limit to where this game is going.

"All you have to do is look around. Five years ago, no more
than ten, handicappers had to go to a storefront to bet a horse
in Las Vegas. Now every hotel has a major race book. I believe
every major city will have one in the not-too-distant future.

"We have a society that now accepts social betting as a form
of recreation. Also, individual sports have become increasingly
popular, like golf, tennis, and racquet ball. Handicapping has
the same kind of individual appeal. Also, the public has developed a love affair with PC's. Racing accommodates that interest too.

"And any adult of any age or gender can play the game, and
with effort play it well."

Pointing to the tremendous successes of intertrack wagering
experiments around the nation, in California notably, Romano
anticipates pari-mutuel betting pools bulging with millions more
than anyone now imagines.

A high roller might not only bet hundreds or thousands more
on inviting horses, he would get paid better when he wins. Ro-

mano sees himself dipping into enormous pari-mutuel pools of the near future, a scenario he believes past due even now.

Which brings us to a high roller's pet peeves about the sport and industry. Romano does not mince words. His was the most severe, most impatient criticism of the status quo among respondents to this select survey. The irony should not be missed. The track's best customer is its harshest critic.

"With the usual few exceptions, they should round up the existing executives and managers and just clean house. The industry needs a total transfusion; fresh blood. With any vision and leadership whatsoever, this sport and industry should be soaring to new levels of success. Instead, it just crawls along, and not very impressively."

It's closing day, Del Mar, 1988. Romano regards two horses on the card as prime.

There's Eighty Below Zero in the 1st, a frontrunner that should go unmolested versus low-priced claimers from the No. 2 post.

In the Del Mar Futurity (Grade 1), for juveniles, at a mile, Romano much prefers the gelding Music Merci to the half-million-dollar Alydar colt Crown Collection, from the Lukas shedrow—heavily favored, overrated in Romano's view, and an unseasoned underlay in a Grade 1 mile, for sure.

"Music Merci has the stronger figures, has better seasoning, and is bred to route effectively. It has beaten much better runners too. The colt Crown Collection beat in a minor sprint stakes was exiting a maiden-claiming win, for God's sake."

My own pace ratings, quick and dirty variety, and based upon sprint performances, but track variants included, gave Music Merci a surprising ten-point advantage. Whether Music Merci got the mile impressively or not, Romano's case against Crown Collection as the day's glamorous underlay was undeniable.

At an acceptable 5–2, Eighty Below Zero sprinted clear early and lasted by a disappearing nose. It paid $7.

In the Grade 1 Futurity, Music Merci attended the pace in hand, and despite racing green while changing leads repeatedly through the lane, drew clear inside the eighth pole and won by open lengths. Racing far back, Crown Collection did not get a call, finishing up the course at 7–5.

Music Merci paid a splendid $14.80, absolutely an overlay, in particular to a high roller who rarely sees 6–1.

A pair of $2000 bets to win yielded profits of $17,800, a fine

day at the office. Romano tackled no other races. But it's difficult to dislodge a high roller from the moorings of reality.

"As I say, I'm a 32 percent handicapper. Three wins in a
row means that six losers are on the way," said Romano,
straightening me up.

I might have countered that six losers in a row would leave
a profit of $5,800 still, but did not.

Frank Romano's single-minded goal in handicapping is
achieving a consistent 40 percent win proficiency; ambitious,
laudable, and best of all, attainable.

"If I can reach that level of proficiency," he explains enthusiastically, and with a hint of his determination, "I can make
my fortune doing what I love to do. If there is a better game
than this, I have not found it."

Predicting the future is such good clean fun, as all wise
handicappers can agree. Let's gaze into Romano's crystal ball.

When he achieves the 40 percent win ratio—which he will,
I dare predict—let's assume Romano's average odds on winners
will drop to 2.5–1.

If he makes 250 prime bets a year, $2000 each, the total in-
vestment will be $500,000. Romano's edge, or ROI, will be .40,
producing $1.40 for each dollar wagered. Romano's annual profit,
not including exotics, will be $200,000. If he increases the bet
size, profits will be greater.

For the few outstanding handicappers who happen to be high
rollers, that's the reality, sports fans.

CHAPTER EIGHTEEN

Tom Brohamer
•
No.1 in My Book

EXTRAVAGANT CLAIMS will be laid bare quickly at the racetrack, so pundits best be restrained in their boasts and enthusiasms. I probably should not assert that Tom Brohamer is the best pace analyst in the United States. But I do. After little more than two seasons in his company, I should not call Brohamer the best handicapper I have met. Yet I do.

Masterful with figures and numerical relations, the guy's as dependable in their interpretation as a jurist instructing jurors.

Brohamer has never felt the sting of a losing season. I have not known him to record a losing month. He absorbs few losing weeks. On the point of consistency, virtually no one stays with him.

Nor is Brohamer overly selective, but finds winners regularly, low-priced overlays mainly, but not exclusively, with 4–1 to 7–1 payoffs weekly occurrences.

On Gold Cup day at Hollywood Park, 1988, in a seminar on the afternoon's program, incredibly, Brohamer swept the card. The well-hidden winner of the 9th was switching from dirt to turf and moving ahead in class, but with a late-pace advantage against an early-pace scenario, an obscure situation that Brohamer detected. The horse paid $52.80. In the big event, Brohamer called Cutlass Reality, improving impressively at the time, a pace standout today versus champions Alysheba and Ferdinand. At 9–2 Cutlass Reality won by fifteen lengths.

Brohamer confesses, a bit apologetically, to no debilitating losing runs that are entirely normal for handicappers—even excellent ones—with an explanation I can readily accept.

"I'm conservative and consistent," he says. "I know that normal losing runs turn around, and that mine have always been short. A losing day, or losing week, doesn't fluster me. I've learned to cope with losses by learning about myself.

"If there is a success pattern you've experienced for years, you become comfortable with that. It may happen, but I do not anticipate streaks—winning or losing—now or in the future, longer than what I've become accustomed to in the past.

"On the other hand, there is a price to pay, a downside. I'm not a crusher. I'd like to, but I don't clean the table from one race, or a few, the way some others do. My style emphasizes consistency. I know what to expect and what not to expect."

Beyond its consistency, Brohamer's story weaves an elegant paradigm for handicappers of many stations—serious hobbyists, regulars engaged in an avocation, even professionals. Brohamer, forty-seven, turned professional in 1988, leaving a career position in sales management after twenty-two years with Pacific Bell of southern California via an early retirement program he barely qualified to join.

Before that, not unlike many winners, he had experimented with several methodologies and implemented each successfully. As noted, his methods today emphasize pace handicapping, embracing innovative powerful concepts such as early energy, turn time, and track modeling.

It's instructive to return to the beginning and consider the professional development of this extraordinary individual. Part-time handicappers by the thousands flirt continuously with the notion of becoming professional. Rightly so, they contemplate the pitfalls and are suspect of their readiness. Specifics aside, the most reliable path to success resembles Brohamer's personal odyssey.

Though Brohamer's parents were avid handicappers and introduced Tom to the races soon enough, the important transition began in 1968, and at a not unfamiliar point of departure. That year he digested the formally constructed selection-elimination guidelines in Tom Ainslie's *The Complete Handicapper*. Brohamer adapted the material to a usable format and applied it for two seasons.

"I began to make more of a commitment to handicapping," he recalls. "The game had started to become more than a hobby."

Novices, journeymen, those who care, should understand the point. The change demands commitment. The transition from hobby to avocation is characterized by greater degrees of active participation and a conscious regard for producing positive results. A deeper sense of personal responsibility toward the racetrack experience will be necessary.

No longer is it enough to arrive at the racetrack, purchase the *Daily Racing Form*, and commence handicapping. It's insufficient as well to imitate the methods promoted by others for a couple of hours a night in your den.

A deliberate subjective style of work and study now makes the difference.

The approach takes on the shine of the artisan or craftsman, the crafting of ideas, techniques, and procedures into personal methods. As the new tools are implemented, handicappers monitor the outcomes carefully, and the continuous development and refinement of the methods is under way.

This second crucial stage will normally be succeeded at regular short-term intervals by an assortment of methods, as with Brohamer.

In 1970 Brohamer experimented with the Taulbot method of rating pace, using the pace calculator. Since the calculator depended upon a set of universal pars for one track, in effect the data, and resulting ratings, for all other tracks were off, or out of balance.

So Brohamer tinkered with the pars, adjusting them to local conditions.

The experience taught him valuable lessons about pace and pars. They were extremely sensitive to track class and surface.

In 1972 Brohamer bought the Kelco calculator, with which he rated the horses in a field from high to low on Average Purse Value (APV). To the higher-rated horses he applied the Ainslie form and class guidelines. Now Brohamer began intermingling distinct methods, forming, if you will, a methodology.

"It worked best early during the winter season at Santa Anita, and for several successive seasons," says Brohamer, "because the horses arrived there from different tracks.

"Once the horses had been racing at Santa Anita for a time, APV became worthless."

The personal journey ebbed and flowed.

In 1975 Brohamer absorbed Beyer's *Picking Winners* and immediately undertook a phase of advanced speed handicapping that would endure into the early 1980s.

He constructed speed charts reflecting Beyer's proportional times at the regularly run distances for the southern California tracks. Pars, variants, adjusted times, speed figures, projected times, and new figures were elaborated daily, simulating Beyer.

"I'm a numbers man," stresses Brohamer, quite succinctly.

Eventually, speed figures became their own source of dissatisfaction to Brohamer, and inexorably created a void in his thinking.

"The high-figure horses got beat as often as they won. I became increasingly dissatisfied with them."

As his experience with speed figures intensified, Brohamer arrived at the great conclusion of his career. The high-figure horses lost too often, not because of class and form factors the figures did not represent, or due to other non-numerical differences, but due to the influences of pace.

In the next five years Brohamer would develop into one of the most influential practitioners of pace handicapping the game has ever known.

But the background here is important, and it's a mistake to depart the formative scenes too abruptly. Regarding professional development, Brohamer's career has been prototypical, greatly similar to other pros in this short compendium, but greatly dissimilar from method players as a group, far too many of whom seek professional status by ill-timed, ill-considered means.

In seven years, from 1968 to 1975, Brohamer had veered from fundamental Ainslie to advanced Beyer, with predictable weigh stations in between. He internalized two standard texts, applied two practical rating instruments. He dealt studiously and empirically with class-form, earnings, speed, and pace. He mixed elements of each into new wholes which he implemented, monitored, and evaluated. He mastered each theory. He adapted each method. He tossed out what did not work, retained what did. He kept plugging away, striving to improve his performance, his results.

The process of development becomes one of playing, studying, implementing, evaluating, adapting, relearning, and recycling, until demonstrably effective methods nicely suited to personal temperament and local conditions have been forged. Nothing very meaningful happens passively, as from the passage of time. Thoughtful, active participation becomes mandatory. Progress goes hand in hand with continuous personal development.

This contrasts sharply with the conventional wisdom and general practice.

The hobbyist longs to become the pro. The deep instinct, in

part a cultural value of the racetrack, is to search for clear-cut answers. To find the final solution. To identify the best methods. To learn the tricks of the trade. To gain entry to the inside information. To learn the truth, so to speak.

The personification of this folk wisdom is the method player. This handicapper applies a comfortable rational method centered on fundamentals—speed, class, pace, trips, trainers—and attempts to perfect it. This is fair play, to be sure, but a process something less than professional, for reliance on method play contains its own fatal flaw.

Method players cling to their methods. In its essentials the broader process of personal development is subverted prematurely. New ideas, contemporary developments, radical change, even subtle alterations, are not easily assimilated. The further outside of the method's parameters important new ideas, new practices, fall, the less likely they will be perceived as meaningful and incorporated.

The bottom line is depressing. No comprehensive understanding of the game as a whole can be achieved. Little chance to be a pro.

Handicapping authorities unite, for instance, on the proposition that practitioners shaped by the classical Ainslie ideas of two decades past are outmoded now, unless they have found new contexts for those guidelines.

Less sympathy has been accorded the enthusiastic modern speed handicappers of the late seventies who have remained virtually the same practitioners today, yet a similar pattern of obsolescence has been calcifying for years. Focused forever on speed, these practitioners strive for better figures, extending themselves to trips and biases, perhaps, but their understanding of a changing game and of themselves as complete handicappers has not much improved.

All systematic methods will be susceptible to the same process of erosion and obsolescence but not the handicappers that apply them. Humans can change, and grow, with the times.

So handicapping practices that reflect years of personal development and encompass a diverse array of ideas, techniques, and practical applications are the professional's methods of choice. The resulting methodologies have proved demonstrably effective to users in several complementary ways. The methods (a) salute the fundamentals of the game, (b) reflect the tastes and realities of the times, and (c) remain nicely suited to the personality and temperament of the individual.

In 1982 Tom Brohamer began the final passage from hobbyist, to man-with-an-avocation, to professional, when he responded to an intriguing *Racing Form* ad promoting a modern approach to pace handicapping.

The ad had been placed by Howard Sartin, creator of the now-famous Sartin Methodology, an innovative computerized strategy predicated upon the energy distribution of racehorses and utilizing velocity ratings in preference to seconds and fifths of seconds. Velocity ratings express a thoroughbred's rate of speed at any point in a race. The ratings are expressed in feet per second, a function of distance divided by time.

Brohamer was attracted to the method's basic concepts at first sight. Within a few years he would be widely recognized as the club's foremost practitioner.

A basic idea was to match the running styles and pace preferences of horses to the energy profiles of winners and track surfaces. A sprinting frontrunner that expended 52.45 percent of its energy to the second call at Belmont Park would likely finish up the track there, but could become a romping winner if shipped to Hollywood Park.

Since Brohamer's initiation, Sartin's ideas and methods have been refined and enhanced by club disciples who become teaching members. Brohamer has been a major contributor, prized by the national membership for delivering the Brohamer Model, and again by the members from California for the continuing success of his track variant/horses-to-watch service.

Properly developed and implemented, the Brohamer Model shows Sartin practitioners anywhere whether today's races will likely be won by horses ranked one-two on early pace, sustained pace, late pace, average pace, or any other interval of pace handicappers care to analyze. A model of how the track surface has been affecting race outcomes as recently as today and yesterday, Brohamer's tool can be extremely sensitive, not only to the gross-energy demands of tracks, but to subtle variations in track bias.

Brohamer's ultimate claim to fame, however, is as the quintessential Sartin practitioner. He's a consistent winner, and everybody in the club knows it. What fewer members understand is that Brohamer wins consistently not because he implements the methodology faultlessly or unfailingly, which he does not, but because he had evolved into an outstanding handicapper before meeting Sartin. Brohamer would win big with any set of power tools, though admittedly not as much.

While crediting Sartin for influencing his career as has nobody else, Brohamer cites several authors as playing formative roles besides. Agreeing that excellent, comprehensive handicappers will also become the most successful method players, he recommends the following resources to new Sartin members, as well as novices and aspiring journeymen everywhere:

1. *Ainslie's Encyclopedia of Thoroughbred Handicapping* (Tom Ainslie)
2. *Picking Winners* and *My $50,000 Year at the Races* (Andrew Beyer)
3. *Winning at the Races* and *Thoroughbred Handicapping: State of the Art* (William L. Quirin)
4. *The Handicapper's Condition Book* (James Quinn)
5. *Percentages and Probabilities* (Fred Davis)
6. *How Will Your Horse Run Today?* (William L. Scott)

"But it was Howard Sartin that made the ultimate difference in my career. He's first. He also gave me a forum for creating and writing, and I've valued that terrifically. It's made me a much better, far more concentrated player."

With the Sartin programs in hand, and his daily variants calculated from the projected times of specific races, Brohamer attacks his favorite races, and arrives at the racetrack with a set of figures not surpassed in this country. Add to that a highly experienced, highly refined analytical skill, and Brohamer's consistency becomes palpable. It's figure handicapping at its best.

"My strength has always been an understanding of how races will be run. I can visualize the probable pace very well. The Sartin tools, like early energy, turn time, and the track model, put real teeth into that skill. Pace analysis is the method, or approach, I'm most effective with.

"I also have a keen understanding of class, and I spend lots of time with the charts, coming up with angles I think will work in special situations. Those are my strengths. I have real weaknesses as well, but I've learned to minimize them by skipping races where my weaknesses apply."

Weaknesses?

"Sure. Certain higher-class races trouble me. Nonwinners three times allowances. Nonwinners four times. Competitive feature races.

"I'm not particularly strong on the turf. I pass many grass races.

"And though I thrive on middling claiming races in general, races limited to cheaper three-year-old claimers can be a weak spot. They have been this season to date, definitely. My data reveals that."

When the conversation shifts to results, Brohamer has shined from the start as few handicappers do.

"I've been a consistent winner for years," he states matter-of-factly.

"I won only small money at first, but began to win bigger about 1980, while using the Beyer figures."

A catastrophe in the world outside contributed to a quantum leap in Brohamer's financial output at the races. He lost a family business to the hard times of 1982. He owed tens of thousands to a pair of banks, the IRS, and the California Franchise Tax Board, respectively.

Equipped with the Sartin programs and years of successful experience, he began to rely upon track profits to repay a portion of the debts.

In 1984 the IRS formalized Brohamer's repayment schedule. He now faced a monthly nut, to be cracked with racetrack winnings.

"Most of the year I paid the bulk of the debt with track profits, but each month, besides, was forced to dip into savings. So a good year at the track was also a worst year financially."

Then it happened. Atypical for Brohamer, a win-bettor deluxe, he managed a heavy score.

At the Pomona Fair bull ring, on a Friday in September, Brohamer filled out a $20 Pick 6 ticket on a day featuring a tempting carryover pool. With a friend as partner, Brohamer won the pot, the lone live ticket, a $66,000 kill.

"The key was a shipper from Sacramento [a minor track on the northern California fair circuit]. It ranked high using Sartin's *Phase 3* program, and it fit the Pomona track profile well. I singled the horse. It paid $75 and we were fortunate enough to sweep the whole pot.

"The truly ironic part is, I had been ill all week with a virus. My friend happened to call, suggesting a day at Pomona. My wife was there, and urged me to go. I would not have been there without the call, or my wife's encouragement, for that matter."

Brohamer settled the remaining debts comfortably. As a

kicker, he won thousands more at the races in the final quarter of 1984, to date a best-ever season.

"I was playing relaxed for the first time in three years. I got hot, and couldn't lose. So 1984 was both the worst of years and the best of years.

"I'll be forever grateful to Howard Sartin, and to racing, and to handicapping."

Press Brohamer about additional scores and he waves you away.

"I'm not a big-score player. I'm a win bettor, basically, and at times will try to take more from a race by keying exactas in conjunction with the win bet. But I'm conservative and dull-consistent as a bettor."

Pushed, he acknowledged two additional Pick 6 triumphs, one he split for roughly $13,000, and another, a consolation, for $4000.

Brohamer's natural progression in handicapping reached its climax in November 1987, the month he retired. That early retirement fulfilled an adult dream, and he was on to full-time handicapping. The new issues were greater attention to money management and betting strategy.

Brohamer advocates percentage-of-bankroll wagering, at 4, 5 percent tops. It's prudent to underbet, he cautions, if handicappers do not know their proficiency, foolish to overbet regardless.

In theory, Sartin disciples support two horses a bettable race, a tactic Brohamer engages approximately one third of the time. Otherwise, he bets one unit to win, two units to place, same horse, because his style gets a high proportion of runners to place (or win), and the wagering strategy minimizes losing runs. Numerous handicappers do the same for the same reasons, though review of financial records usually shows they would net more by betting strictly to win.

Brohamer invests $200 to $300 on prime selections, as little as $10 to $20 on side bets. He issues a strong opinion on bet size.

"Side bets cannot cancel prime bets. It's one of the main faults of many handicappers. I see it repeatedly with the Sartin players.

"They bet $30 on the prime horse and $15 on side bets. That's bad money management."

In Brohamer's illustration, the ratio of prime- to side-money is 2–1. It should be 5–1 or 10–1, as great as 20–1.

The awful money management habit suggests most handicappers cannot distinguish their prime bets and side bets. Brohamer speaks firmly on the point.

"Prime bets are to be found in the kinds of races handicappers know from past experiences they can beat. Not always, of course, but the betting approach should be consistent. My own prime bets most frequently are placed in middle-range claiming races. I know these are the races I can beat best. When I like a horse strongly in one of these races, that's a prime bet."

Brohamer extends the argument cleverly to the exactas. He prefers exactas not as side bets, but as exotics that supplement a prime bet to win.

"It's my way of trying to take more money from a single race. I like to key my prime selections in exactas as well. I do less shopping in exactas of races I do not understand as well."

Brohamer distinguishes this exotic-betting pattern from exotics that are strictly a rear action.

"The triple for me is a side bet. So I do not invest more than $24 to $36 a day. If I have to bet more to cover the real possibilities, I realize I do not understand the races very well and will be fishing. Fishing costs too much long haul."

Other fundamental money management advice comes tripping off Brohamer's tongue.

"It goes without saying, or should, the betting bankroll must be uncontaminated. It's capital, not income. If you need it to pay the bills, that's sacred money. I know.

"The choke point is also a real concept. I have mine, and so do most players.

"I once got involved in an investment strategy where we were betting $1600–$1700 in a short time. I got uncomfortable and didn't like it. I was glad to stop.

"I recommend a starting bank of $10,000. A $200 bet will be 2 percent of the bank. That's comfortable. It works for just about everybody.

"Percentage of bankroll is an effective basic strategy. You bet more when winning, less when losing, and handicappers have little chance of losing the entire bank. I've never lost mine, and that contributes over the years to a strong feeling of confidence."

Brohamer's pet plays can serve as inside tips to everyone.

"I love horses moving ahead in class by two levels or more

after a win showing a clearly improved figure, especially if a good trainer engineers the move. I look for these types all the time.

"I also like the 'bounce' pattern which has been particularly rewarding this year but which I've liked for a long time. The key race is the third following a long layoff. The first is a strong performance, but an overexertion. The second, at low odds usually, the horse regresses. It 'bounces.' The third start, at higher odds following the disappointing second out, is the bounce-back effort. This is where the prime bet belongs."

Brohamer accentuates that the time and energy requirements of dead-serious handicapping can be great and are often underestimated by hobbyists wanting to stretch themselves.

"I spend two-and-a-half to three hours handicapping off-track. With travel, I'm at the track six, seven hours. I spend another one-and-a-half hours record-keeping. That's a twelve-hour day, high end. I provide a variant service to others, so I have special demands on my time. But serious handicappers are looking at a ten-hour day. The time and energy requirements are enormous, no getting around it.

"I spend about two hundred days a year on this regimen. You have to love it. You really do."

Mental fatigue sets in, as if on schedule, for Brohamer. When it does, he flees.

"I usually play well the first six, seven weeks of Santa Anita, then in mid-February I, like, hit a wall. I go on a vacation, or stay away for a week. I like camping and fly-fishing, and those are nice antidotes.

"I used to try to play through the mental fatigue, but learned it's a mistake. I would drop a nice portion of my profits. Now the problem is under control."

Brohamer also employs a personal computer to cope with the record-keeping, not to mention to obtain pace ratings.

"I put my variants on a spread-sheet program. I also use a handheld Sharp PC to implement the Sartin programs. Those require computer processing. Any writing or record-keeping, like notes, I do plan to store on the PC as well."

Another tactic Brohamer promotes to cope more efficiently with time-energy demands is to tackle the daily cards in programmed fashion. He handicaps the races he prefers first.

"Using the Hollywood card of May twenty-sixth [1988] as an illustration, I went first to the Fifth. It was an open claimer,

for $32,000 fillies and mares, four and up. I had recognized one
of my horses-to-watch in the entries. She figured best, and won,
paid $6.40. I made a prime bet.

"I next went to the First, a similar claiming race, but for
cheaper. I found nothing.

"I next scanned the two maiden-claiming fields for the horses
I like in those races. One was a stickout, but odds-on and
no play.

"I skipped by a low-level claiming route limited to three-
year-olds. I also passed by a turf race.

"That's my preferred cycle. Proceed to the races you generally like, and go from there. It's efficient."

To a considerable extent, Brohamer brings it all together at
the races as he has in real-time outside the tracks. Not only
have his personal life and family relations not suffered from his
involvement in a greatly participative sport, both have benefitted significantly.

"Racing has had a very positive influence on my life. I have
made lots of new friends from the sport.

"Other friends and associates have been fully supportive from
the start. They know I'm not a gambler, and have just envied
me for doing what I want to do.

"My wife Shirley has been extra supportive. We came through
the family-business loss together. That was the test, not the track,
and as it happened, the handicapping rewards helped ease our
financial burdens appreciably.

"Still, I'm neither a gambler nor a big bettor. I love to go to
the race books in Vegas, but can be there for a week and not
touch a casino game. Gambling has no appeal for me. If I lost
my edge with the horses, I would pack it in."

Since taking a B.A. in political science from California State
University at Long Beach years ago, Brohamer, father of three,
has combined a full family life and corporate career with avid
pursuits of golf, chess, fishing, camping, and thoroughbred
handicapping.

A scratch golfer until four years ago, when he quit cold turkey, Brohamer could have golfed for a living as a club pro, but
instead joined Pacific Bell. With money up, he has beaten tour
professionals at golf, a convenient backdrop for coping with the
crises of handicapping.

"I've been rather one-dimensional since turning professional
in handicapping," admits Brohamer. "But I still get to the

camping and fishing on my occasional departures from the races."

Only two dreams beckon.

"I'd love to write the book on pace handicapping. Get it published. Have the recognition. It would be a long-lasting contribution. The kind of accomplishment you can show your grandchildren, tangibly. That kind of conceit.

"I also dream of moving to Las Vegas in a few more years. I like the race books. Several tracks at once, and more prime horses a day. I have a daughter in college still, but should be free to make the move soon enough."

Of the numerous good handicappers Brohamer's path has crossed, he cites Andy Beyer as most impressive, and for interesting reasons.

"I only met him briefly, and admired his knowledge and style immensely, but what's really impressive about Beyer is his courage. He has tremendous courage of conviction, and can clean the table with it in ways I cannot. He's a crusher, and for the right reasons. I envy that skill and would like to develop it in myself.

"Beyer also accepts the positives and negatives with equanimity. He has the psychological makeup of the most successful players. It's a skill he's developed, not a natural talent. You can't help but admire him.

"I also like Lee Rousso. Not only is he witty, friendly, and sincere, he's a very good player and a creative handicapper. Lee can clean the table, too, and he's particularly good at coming back from losing runs. He's streaky, but in touch with his play, knows his strong points and how to play to them.

"I also like your [Quinn's] play," says Brohamer. "You're an authentic expert on class, just as your reputation had suggested, and you're very consistent.

"I see a lot of myself in you. You don't chase or overextend. You do not have extensive losing periods. Like me, you don't crush or clean the table with a bet. We've talked about that deficiency. Both of us would like to correct that. I'm not certain it's really all that bad a shortcoming. Winning consistently is the bottom line.

"Consistency, and lack of panic, they are very important to the psychological makeup of a successful handicapper. Lee [Rousso] has that talent also. Come to think of it, Lee has a lot going for him, doesn't he?"

Brohamer is characteristically thoughtful, frank, and direct on his pet peeves about the sport and racing industry.

"I worked for a large corporation for twenty-two years. The Bell system, by definition of its size, is lethargic, slow to move, but they are nothing compared to the racing industry.

"I gotta tell you, racing's executives just fail to move, even when they clearly should.

"Intertrack wagering, for example, which has just started [1988 in southern California], was called for years ago. It's here, on a limited basis, but the economic climate had to become far too serious before anything was done.

"A broader OTB model is what's actually needed, but the industry can't bring themselves to move on that yet.

"The racing industry, I'm afraid, lacks courage. Whether it's the *Form*, the local tracks, or the industry as a whole, decisions are not made, appropriate stances are not taken. Nothing that should be done gets done."

Peculiarities notwithstanding, Brohamer muses that racing might benefit from a commissioner having national stature and clout, a Peter Ueberroth or Pete Rozelle.

"He would get things done that need to be done."

Brohamer is just as demanding of handicappers, notably newcomers who want to be successful handicappers and make important money at it.

"To begin, [newcomers] have to read the right books. They must construct their own par charts. They have to do some personal research. They have to keep records. They have to understand themselves as handicappers and bettors.

"But actual experience is the ultimate teacher. Handicappers need to go through the trial-and-error phase, experiment a lot, and come to recognize the success patterns within their personal play.

"No one can give you that but you.

"Until you've actually done it, and done it over a period of time, there's no way you can become what we refer to as a competent handicapper, let alone think about becoming a pro, doing it for a living."

And when the preliminaries have been exhausted and the raw recruit has been graduated at last to serious journeyman— or to pro—how much money can the professional expect to win?

"That's a math concept and depends upon your edge, how much you bet, how frequently; those variables.

"One thing many newcomers, or even veteran handicappers

who want to do better, overlook is their financial comfort zones.

"Expectations become so unrealistic. That may be the single biggest weakness of most handicappers.

"I bet $200 to $300 on prime horses, and I play some two hundred days a year. At my edge, I can expect to make $25,000 to $30,000 a year from handicapping profits. And that's what I generally will do.

"To make more, I'd have to escalate the bets significantly, and that would take me out of my comfort zone. I would not play as well.

"People just do not realize the bet sizes necessary to make a decent living at this. Go to a computer. Enter your win-loss percents, number of bets, bet size, and money management procedures. Simulate your expectations. You'll be surprised.

"To make the money they want to make, most handicappers are probably taking themselves out of their comfort zone."

The sober reflections of one of the nation's most consistently successful professional handicappers.

How many want to hear it, really?

CHAPTER NINETEEN

Winning Time

•

Brohamer, Quinn, and Rousso at Santa Anita

91 DAYS/WINTER SEASON/1988

THE WINTER SEASON at Santa Anita, 1988, survives among the most exhilarating of the author's handicapping career. I shared a season box at the sixteenth pole with two of the finest professionals in southern California. You are about to be entertained by the results and participate in a reprise of the most interesting races.

One colleague was Lee Rousso, at thirty, as solid and complete a handicapper as can be found anywhere. With handicapping tools as varied as a bag of golf clubs, Lee suffers no deadly flaws.

Rousso's versatility had impressed me since I met him five years ago in the California Thoroughbred Breeders' Association library a few days prior to the Kentucky Derby. I was researching a writing project. Rousso was calculating dosage indexes. This was two seasons before dosage became known to handicappers as a group, let alone the hottest controversy of Derby week. A deep instinct told me this young man had to be taken seriously. He promptly won two handicapping tournaments in Nevada, banking $147,000.

Until the Santa Anita experience, I did not appreciate Rousso's particular strengths, but now I do. His comprehension of early speed, notably in low-to-middling claiming routes, is uncanny. He's a virtuoso with track biases. He finds overlays that can be provocative, even to other expert handicappers.

The other colleague was Tom Brohamer, the most dependable winner of my acquaintance, and a premier figure handicapper. Brohamer uses projected times to calculate daily variants, an esoteric art he has refined to almost perfect pitch. Brohamer's specialty is pace analysis, and he brings to the endeavor a number of original empirically validated concepts that afford him an enviable edge.

With few exceptions, for example, by examining their early-energy distribution in relation to the early-energy distribution of recent winners at the distance, Brohamer determines whether sprinters can stretch out successfully. If he says they cannot, they do not. I never fail to ask him. Brohamer slaughters the mid-to-high-level claiming races. At any track he's a valuable resource, and a definite threat to win any race he plays.

With some claims to versatility, my own strengths tend toward class appraisal in the nonclaiming races and in turf races. I emphasize speed-pace figures, in combination, in the claiming races, the variants calculated as deviations from par.

Individual strengths and weaknesses aside, all three professionals can display a diverse repertoire of handicapping skills and techniques, as circumstances require. All three rely on multiple sources of information, meticulously updated. All three depend upon handicapping results for a portion of their annual income.

At Santa Anita, 1988, the three of us united as first-time practitioners of the speed and pace methods promoted by Bill Quirin. These set the $10,000 claiming pars for older horses equal to 100. Other pars are equal to 100 plus or minus a point for each one fifth of a second faster or slower than races for older $10,000 claiming horses. Standard adjustments are applied, for fillies and mares, for maiden-claiming races, and for three-year-olds at various stages of the calendar year.

For routes, Quirin promotes two pace figures, one at six furlongs, the second at four furlongs. The pair of pace figures and the final speed figure, in combination, provide handicappers with a vivid mental picture of how fast races were run at three points of call.

We were skeptical of the four-furlong pace figure in routes to begin, but soon changed our minds. Early pace stickouts won repeatedly, and impressively. A few examples to be presented here should dramatize the case with figure handicappers everywhere.

Our threesome arrived at Santa Anita that season from divergent circumstances.

Brohamer had recently taken early retirement from Pacific Bell. Santa Anita would be his first full continuous meeting as a professional handicapper.

I had not played since the end of the previous Santa Anita winter season, a few recreational sessions excepted—my habit of several years now.

Rousso had recently returned to full-scale handicapping following a year's sabbatical. Burnt-out at the racetrack, he had labored as a stock broker as an interim alternative. Suffice to say, Rousso was back where he belonged.

Financial goals went unstated to begin, though Brohamer expected to win between $25,000 and $30,000 for the whole of 1988, and I hoped to win $15,000 during Santa Anita, roughly $1000 a week. These projections were hinged to past experience and personal investment levels.

Rousso held a vastly different set of expectations and aspirations. He expected to crush the races, on no particular schedule, but clearing six figures before the year was up sounded just fine, a not unreasonable objective.

As Magic Johnson likes to say, it was winning time.

OPENERS

Opening day at Santa Anita, a tradition, always the day after Christmas, has surrendered a glimmer of its glamour for handicappers since southern California has scheduled year-round racing. The sense of a new beginning has been blurred.

For me, a seasonal player, the charm remains intact, and of our noble trio it was I who sped to the front. I took the 1st, 3rd, 8th, and 9th, none of them prime shots, plus a generous 5th-race exacta. Four $50 win bets netted $900.

The featured 8th proved fascinating. It was the Grade 2, seven-furlong Malibu Stakes, limited to 3YOs, to be new 4YOs in five days. Three of the entrants were exiting the most definitive stakes on the 3YO calendar. Each was ranked a leader of the division. A fourth horse figured rugged at today's distance.

Examine the records of the four.

8th Santa Anita

OUT OF CHUTE ▶
7 FURLONGS
SANTA ANITA
◆ FINISH

7 FURLONGS. (1.20) 36th Running of THE MALIBU STAKES (Grade II). $100,000 Added. 3-year-olds. (Allowance.) By subscription of $100 each to accompany the nomination, $250 to pass the entry box and $750 additional to start, with $100,000 added, of which $20,000 to second, $15,000 to third, $7,500 to fourth and $2,500 to fifth. Weight, 126 lbs. Non-winners of two races of $100,000 in 1987 allowed 3 lbs.; of a race of $30,000 or two of $50,000 in 1987, 6 lbs.; of a race of $30,000 since October 6, $40,000 in 1987, or a race of $100,000 in 1986, 9 lbs.; of a race of $30,000 in 1986–87, 12 lbs. Starters to be named through the entry box by the closing time of entries. A trophy will be presented to the owner of the winner. Closed Wednesday, December 16, 1987, with 18 nominations.

Temperate Sil — Ro. c. 3, by Temperence Hill—Rukann, by Ruken

SHOEMAKER W 126 — Br.—Frankfurt Stable (Ky) — 1987 9 2 1 1 $519,900

Tr.—Whittingham Charles — 1986 5 3 0 0 $549,625

Own.—Frankfurt Stb &Whittingham — Lifetime 14 5 1 1 $1,063,525 — Turf 2 0 1 0 $21,750

21Nov87-4Hol 1 ①:453 1:09 1:324fm 5½e 123 21 21½ 86¼ 87 ShmrW13 Br Cp Mile 96 — Miesque, Show Dancer, SonicLady 14
21Nov87—Grade I

18Oct87-8SA 1⅛①:454 1:102 1:474fm 3¼ 122 13 1½ 11 2hd DlhossyE3 Volante H 88-15 TheMedic,TmprtSil,HotAndSmoggy 9
18Oct87—Grade III

27Sep87-10LaD 1¼:47 1:362 2:031ft 2¼ 126 54½ 43 42½ 45¼ ShmkrW6 Super Dby 80-19 Alysheba, Candi's Gold, Parochial 8
27Sep87—Grade I

22Aug87-8Sar 1¼:461 1:362 2:02 sy 5¼ 126 1½ 55 715 829¾ ShomkrW7 Travers 60-16 JavaGold,Cryptoclearnce,PolishNvy 9
22Aug87—Grade I

26Jly87-9Hol 1¼:45 1:342 2:021ft *6-5 123 1hd 12½ 13½ 11 ShomkrW4 Swaps 81-12 TemperteSil,Cndi'sGold,PledgeCrd 6
26Jly87—Grade I

3Jly87-8Hol 1⅛:46 1:094 1:473ft *3-5 124 2½ 2hd 47½ 516¼ ShmkrW2 Slvr Scrn H 83-09 Candi's Gold, OnTheLine,TheMedic 6
3Jly87—Grade II

4Apr87-5SA 1⅛:464 1:104 1:49 ft 3¾ 122 2½ 2½ 12½ 15½ ShmkrW4 S A Dby 84-17 TmprtSl,MstrflAdvoct,SmthngLcky 6
4Apr87—Grade I

22Mar87-8SA 1$\frac{1}{16}$:462 1:104 1:43 gd *8-5 122 2½ 2½ 1hd 33½ ShmkrW7 Sn Flpe H 82-23 ChartTheStrs,Alysheb,TemperteSil 8
22Mar87—Grade I

7Mar87-8SA 1 :452 1:10 1:354gd 8-5 122 52 55 49 516¾ ShomkrW7 Sn Rfl 72-19 MstrflAdct,ChrtThStrs,HtAndSmgg 7
7Mar87—Grade II; Broke slowly; lugged in, wide 3/8 turn

14Dec86-8Hol 1 :444 1:093 1:361ft 5¼ 121 63¼ 55 32 1nk ShomkrW3 Hol Fut'y 82-18 TempertSil,Alyshb,MstrfulAdvoct 12
14Dec86—Grade I

●Dec 23 SA 5f ft :583 h Dec 19 Hol 7f m 1:294 h Dec 13 Hol 6f ft 1:134 h Dec 8 Hol 5f gd 1:013 h

On The Line — Ch. c. 3, by Mehmet—Male Strike, by Speak John

CORDERO A JR 117 — Br.—Intrntl Tb Brdrs Inc (Fla) — 1987 15 3 4 0 $182,980

Tr.—Lukas D Wayne — 1986 4 1 1 0 $19,400

Own.—Klein E V — Lifetime 19 4 5 0 $202,380 — Turf 4 0 0 0 $10,625

21Nov87-1Hol 6f :211 :44 1:084ft 26 124 98¾ 1012 1111 1011¼ RomrRP 4 Br Cp Sprnt 87-12 VerySubtl,Groovy,ExclusivEnough 13
21Nov87—Grade I; Bobbled start

4Nov87-8SA 6f :214 :44 1:09 sy 2¾ 116 2½ 2½ 21½ 2½ StvnsGL 2 Anct Title H 92-26 Zany Tactics, On The Line, Carload 3
4Nov87—Bumped start

23Oct87-8SA 7f :22 :442 1:214sy 8-5 114 22 1hd 12 2¾ Stevens G L 1 Aw48000 90-21 Skywalker,OnTheLine,HotSuceBby 5

12Oct87-8SA 1$\frac{1}{16}$:454 1:092 1:404ft 5¼ 113 2½ 2hd 31½ 43½ McCrrCJ 5 Ynkee VlrH 93-15 SuprDimond,StopThFightng,Infndd 5

27Sep87-9Cby 1 :46 1:091 1:351ft *1 116 11½ 1½ 2½ 2½ Perret C 2 Bd Br Cp H 104-09 Minneapple,OnTheLine,ArcticDrem 9

9Aug87-8Dmr 1$\frac{1}{16}$①:472 1:111 1:421fm 10 117 51¼ 31½ 42½ 62¾ VlnzlPA 10 La Jolla H 86-12 ThMdic,SomthingLucky,SvonTowr 11
9Aug87—Grade III; Rank, took up 6 1/2, 3/4

26Jly87-9Hol 1¼:45 1:342 2:021ft 5 120 2hd 22½ 23½ 46 VlnzulPA 3 Swaps 75-12 TemperteSil,Cndi'sGold,PledgeCrd 6
26Jly87—Grade I

3Jly87-8Hol 1⅛:46 1:094 1:473ft 6¾ 116 1½ 1hd 11½ 2nk VlnzulPA 1 Slvr Scrn H 99-09 Candi's Gold, OnTheLine,TheMedic 6
3Jly87—Grade II; Lugged out

21Jun87-8Hol 1⅛①:444 1:09 1:464fm 7½ 118 17 15 32 56 VlnzlPA 1 Cinema H 88-06 SomethingLucky,ThMdic,SvonTowr 6
21Jun87—Grade II; Bumped at 3/16

7Jun87-3Hol 1$\frac{1}{16}$:461 1:104 1:434ft *6-5 117 12 13 13 12½ Stevens G L 1 HcpO 90-17 On The Line,TheMedic,DavidsSmile 5
7Jun87—Lugged out 1st 5/8

Dec 20 SA 4f ft :513 h Nov 17 Hol 4f ft :482 h

Masterful Advocate — B. c. 3, by Tersion—Miss Satin Doll, by Grey Dawn II

PINCAY L JR 123 — Br.—Houston J W (Ky) — 1987 5 3 1 0 $365,500

Tr.—Manzi Joseph — 1986 5 2 1 1 $170,925

Own.—Belles (Lessee) & Leveton — Lifetime 10 5 2 1 $536,425

2May87-8CD 1¼:462 1:364 2:032ft 6¼ 126 76 137¾ 1113 1216¼ PincyLJr7 Ky Dby 64-09 Alysheba, Bet Twice, Avies Copy 17
2May87—Grade I; Crowded 1st turn

4Apr87-5SA 1⅛:464 1:104 1:49 ft *2-5 122 43 42½ 44½ 25½ PincyLJr1 S A Dby 78-17 TmprtSl,MstrflAdvoct,SmthngLcky 6
4Apr87—Grade I; Bumped start; rank, steadied 7/8, lugged out 3/8

7Mar87-8SA 1 :452 1:10 1:354gd *1 122 11 12½ 13 15 Pincay LJr5 Sn Rfl 89-19 MstrflAdct,ChrtThStrs,HtAndSmgg 7
7Mar87—Grade II

1Feb87-8BM 1$\frac{1}{16}$:464 1:112 1:422ft *3-5 120 11 1½ 13 16 PncyLJr7 Cm Rl Dby 80-25 MstrflAdvct,FstDlvry,HtAndSmgg 11
1Feb87—Grade III

14Jan87-8SA 1 :462 1:103 1:362ft *2-3 117 11 12 12½ 14½ PincyLJr6 Ⓡ Los Feliz 86-20 MsterfulAdvocte,RdAndBlu,Tlinum 6

14Dec86-8Hol 1 :444 1:093 1:361ft 6¾ 121 106 65½ 42 3½ PincayLJr1 Hol Fut'y 81-18 TempertSil,Alyshb,MstrfulAdvoct 12
14Dec86—Grade I; Broke slowly, wide stretch

15Nov86-8Hol 7f :22 :444 1:23 ft *6-5 117 42½ 32 42¼ 44 PincyLJr7 Hol Prvu 85-14 ExclusivEnough,Prsvrd,GoldOnGrn 8
15Nov86—Grade III; Wide backstretch

30Oct86-7SA 6f :214 :451 1:102ft *4-5 118 62½ 31½ 11 17½ Pincay L Jr2 Aw25000 86-18 MstrflAdvoct,HostnBrgg,SprmStnd 8
30Oct86—Broke slowly

18Jun86-8GG 5½f :213 :452 1:043ft *3-5 117 54 31 2½ 21 CastanedaM6 Kndrgtn 87-14 Nujc,MsterfulAdvoct,HmiltonHous 8

21May86-5Hol 5f :22 :452 :58 ft *6-5 118 33 3½ 1hd 1½ Pincay L Jr1 Mdn 96-13 MstrflAdvct,BrdyPnt,HnkTnkDncr 10

●Dec 20 SA 7f ft 1:232 h ●Dec 14 Hol 6f ft 1:112 h Dec 9 Hol 5f ft :591 h ●Dec 4 Hol 1 ft 1:392 h

Candi's Gold *
STEVENS G L 123
Own.—Royal Lines (Lessee)

B. c. 3, by Yukon—Holmgirl, by Captain Nash
Br.—Whelan D & Elizabeth (Fla)
Tr.—Gregson Edwin
Lifetime 13 4 5 2 $688,840

1987 12 4 5 1 $686,290
1986 1 M 0 1 $2,550

21Nov87-7Hol	1¼ :46² 1:35² 2:01²ft	27	122	2hd 2hd 2hd 42¾	Black CA ½	Br Cp Clsc	82-12	Ferdinnd,Alysheb,JudgeAngelucci	12
21Nov87—Grade I									
7Nov87-8SA	1⅛ :48³ 1:13¹ 1:50⁴m	2½	117	42½ 2½ 31½ 21	StvnsGL³	Gdwd H	74-26	Ferdinand, Candi's Gold,Skywalker	5
7Nov87—Grade III									
27Sep87-10LaD	1¼ :47 1:36² 2:03¹ft	9	126	32½ 1¹ 1¹ 2½	StvnsGL¹	Super Dby	84-19	Alysheba, Candi's Gold, Parochial	8
27Sep87—Grade I; Bumped start									
12Sep87-8Dmr	1 :45 1:09¹ 1:34⁴ft	4	113	3² 52¼ 41 32¾	ShmkrW¹	Bd Br Cp H	91-14	GodCmmnd,StpThFghtng,Cnd'sGld	6
26Jly87-9Hol	1¼ :45 1:34² 2:02¹ft	3	123	56 45½ 35 21	StevnsGL¹	Swaps	80-12	TemperteSil,Cndi'sGold,PledgeCrd	6
26Jly87—Grade I									
3Jly87-8Hol	1⅛ :46 1:09⁴ 1:47³ft	3½	116	31 3½ 21½ 1nk	StvnsGL⁶	Slvr Scrn H	99-09	Candi's Gold, OnTheLine,TheMedic	6
3Jly87—Grade II									
31May87-9Hol	1 :44⁴ 1:09³ 1:34³ft	*3-2	114	31½ 2hd 11 12½	Stevens G L⁶	Aw27000	90-18	Candi's Gold, Pewter, No Marker	7
2May87-8CD	1¼ :46² 1:36⁴ 2:03²ft	49	126	34 84¾ 89 89¾	HawleyS¹²	Ky Dby	70-09	Alysheba, Bet Twice, Avies Copy	17
2May87—Grade I									
11Apr87-7Kee	1 1/16 :47² 1:11³ 1:44²ft	6½	115	1½ 2hd 22½ 22½	ShmkrW⁴	Lexington	81-25	War, Candi's Gold, Momentus	6
11Apr87—Grade III									
21Mar87-7SA	1 1/16 :47 1:11⁴ 1:48⁴sy	*2	114	1½ 1½ 1½ 12	Stevens G L³	Aw31000	82-16	Candi's Gold, Reland, Rakaposhi	6

●Dec 21 Hol 5f ft :58¹ h ●Dec 15 Hol 6f ft 1:12¹ h ●Dec 9 Hol 5f ft :58³ h Dec 4 Hol 4f ft :48² h

Temperate Sil had not earned even a single impressive speed figure, had not sprinted in two seasons, and had been pummeled in its lone try versus older horses, in the November 21 Breeders' Cup Classic, no less. I judged Temperate Sil overrated, with little chance in this rapid sprint.

Masterful Advocate was returning against vicious competition following a serious knee injury and eight months on the shelf.

My contenders were Candi's Gold and On The Line.

On The Line not only had been sprinting well against older horses lately, but its runner-up efforts to the stakes stars Zany Tactics and Skywalker (Breeders' Cup Classic winner of 1986) had resulted in superb pace ratings and speed figures. It also would enjoy an early speed advantage on a day when five of six dirt races would be won on the front.

Candi's Gold had not sprinted the entire season, but otherwise looked ferocious, and its trainer assured the racing public that seven furlongs was the colt's best distance. Its fourth-place finish in the Breeders' Cup Classic behind Ferdinand, Alysheba, and Judge Angelucci, beaten just 2¾ lengths after fighting the fast pace throughout, was the single most impressive line in the field.

The odds at post were:

Temperate Sil	3–1
On The Line	8–1
Candi's Gold	5–2
Masterful Advocate	5–2

With advantageous early speed, strong speed and pace ratings, recent sprints versus top older runners, and splendid odds, On The Line warranted the bet. As the result chart shows, On The Line darted to the front and became the easiest winner of the afternoon.

The outcome proved bittersweet for me nonetheless. In line to play the triple before the 6th race, I changed my mind and omitted the favorite in the 7th race, adding an overlay in the 6th because it had flashed early speed and would be on Lasix for the first time. Using three horses in the 6th, two in the 7th, and two in the 8th, a $36 ticket, I cheered when the Lasix front-runner took the 6th, but cringed when the 5–2 favorite I had abandoned won the 7th.

EIGHTH RACE
Santa Anita
DECEMBER 26, 1987

7 FURLONGS. (1.20) 36th Running of THE MALIBU STAKES (Grade II). $100,000 Added. 3-year-olds. (Allowance.) By subscription of $100 each to accompany the nomination. $250 to pass the entry box and $750 additional to start, with $100,000 added, of which $20,000 to second, $15,000 to third, $7,500 to fourth and $2,500 to fifth. Weight, 126 lbs. Non-winners of two races of $100,000 in 1987 allowed 3 lbs.; of a race of $90,000 or two of $50,000 in 1987, 6 lbs.; of a race of $30,000 since October 6, $40,000 in 1987, or a race of $160,000 in 1986, 9 lbs.; of a race of $30,000 in 1986–87, 12 lbs. Starters to be named through the entry box by the closing time of entries. A trophy will be presented to the owner of the winner. Closed Wednesday, December 16, 1987, with 18 nominations.
Value of race $111,550; value to winner $66,550; second $20,000; third $15,000; fourth $7,500; fifth $2,500. Mutuel pool $1,140,554.

Last Raced	Horse	Eqt.	A	Wt	PP	St	¼	½	Str	Fin	Jockey	Odds $1
21Nov87 ^{1}Hol^{10}	On The Line	b	3	117	4	2	1^{1}	$1^{1\frac{1}{2}}$	1^{5}	$1^{7\frac{1}{2}}$	Cordero A Jr	8.00
21Nov87 ^{4}Hol^{8}	Temperate Sil		3	126	2	9	9	$6^{\frac{1}{2}}$	$3^{1\frac{1}{2}}$	$2^{\frac{3}{4}}$	Shoemaker W	3.40
21Nov87 ^{7}Hol^{4}	Candi's Gold	b	3	123	7	4	6^{hd}	4^{hd}	$5^{1\frac{1}{2}}$	$3^{\frac{1}{2}}$	Stevens G L	2.60
12Dec87 ^{9}Hol^{2}	Reconnoitering		3	114	1	8	$4^{\frac{1}{2}}$	$2^{\frac{1}{2}}$	2^{1}	$4^{2\frac{1}{2}}$	Gryder A T	18.40
21Nov87 ^{9}Hol^{1}	W. D. Jacks		3	120	6	3	2^{1}	$3^{\frac{1}{2}}$	4^{1}	5^{1}	Delahoussaye E	5.40
21Nov87 ^{9}Hol^{2}	Wayne's Crane		3	117	3	6	7^{hd}	8^{1}	6^{1}	6^{hd}	Day P	15.00
2May87 ^{8}CD^{12}	Masterful Advocate		3	123	8	5	5^{1}	$5^{1\frac{1}{2}}$	$7^{3\frac{1}{2}}$	7^{7}	Pincay L Jr	2.90
28Nov87 ^{8}BM^{1}	Hot And Smoggy	b	3	120	5	7	3^{hd}	7^{1}	8^{2}	$8^{2\frac{3}{4}}$	Valenzuela P A	24.00
13Dec87 ^{7}Hol^{2}	Magic Door		3	114	9	1	8^{1}	9	9	9	Velasquez J	115.30

OFF AT 4:16. Start good. Won ridden out. Time, :22⅕, :44⅖, 1:08⅕, 1:21 Track fast.

$2 Mutuel Prices:				
	5-ON THE LINE	18.00	7.00	4.20
	2-TEMPERATE SIL		5.60	4.00
	8-CANDI'S GOLD			2.80

Ch. c, by Mehmet—Male Strike, by Speak John. Trainer Lukas D Wayne. Bred by Intrntl Tb Brdrs Inc (Fla).

ON THE LINE sprinted to the front early, drew away to a commanding lead in the upper stretch and gradually extended his advantage in the final furlong. TEMPERATE SIL, devoid of early speed after breaking a bit slowly, steadily worked his way forward after a quarter, was never a threat to the winner in the drive but gained the place. CANDI'S GOLD dropped back a bit after getting away in good order, was bumped at intervals approaching the half mile pole, advanced to menace going into the far turn but lacked the needed further response in the last three furlongs. RECONNOITERING broke a bit slowly, moved up to get into close contention before going a quarter, prompted the pace on the far turn and weakened in the drive. W. D. JACKS forced the early pace and gave way. MASTERFUL ADVOCATE, in close contention early after bobbling at the break and wide down the backstretch, drifted out turning into the stretch to come into the stretch five wide and gave way. HOT AND SMOGGY, in close contention early and bumped at intervals approaching the half mile pole, lugged out in the stretch and faltered. MAGIC DOOR, bumped at intervals approaching the half mile pole, lugged out in the final quarter and was six wide into the stretch. GRAND VIZIER (3), TEMPRANERO (9) AND BROADWAY POINTE (10) WERE WITHDRAWN. ALL WAGERS ON THEM IN THE REGULAR POOLS WERE ORDERED REFUNDED AND ALL OF THEIR PICK SIX, PICK NINE AND TRIPLE SELECTIONS WERE SWITCHED TO THE FAVORITE, CANDI'S GOLD (8).

Owners— 1, Klein E V; 2, Frankfurt Stb & Whittingham; 3, Royal Lines (Lessee); 4, G Arakelian Fm Inc-Kayian-Kradjian; 5, Warren W K Jr; 6, Di Palma J; 7, Belles (Lessee) & Leveton; 8, Magee & Stute; 9, Buse-Goodman-Odom.

Trainers— 1, Lukas D Wayne; 2, Whittingham Charles; 3, Gregson Edwin; 4, Marikian Charles M; 5, Drysdale Neil; 6, Chiasson Steve; 7, Manzi Joseph; 8, Stute Melvin F; 9, Odom Ray.

Scratched—Grand Vizier (12Dec87 ^{8}Hol^{6}); Tempranero (21Nov87 ^{9}Hol^{6}); Broadway Pointe (13Dec87 ^{7}Hol^{3})

$3 Triple (2-1 or 2-5) Paid $1,593.90. Triple Pool $459,398.

Note. The circles mean the horses won their next start. Professionals use the technique to identify "key races," the most productive races of the season.

When On The Line triumphed, the triple returned $1593.90. Brohamer and Rousso chided me for the gaffe. It was the kind of agonizing blunder that turns a winning day sour. I walked out with approximately $800 in profits when it should have been $2400 and change.

When the day's variants were constructed, they looked a bit unusual:

Sprints	F1	F1	
Routes	F3	S5	
Turf	S8	S6	(short)
	S4	S6	(long)

Sprints had been fast by one length, both at the pace call and final time. Routes had been fast three for six furlongs, but slow by five lengths at the finish. The turf races had been extra slow, sprint and route, both at the pace call and final call.

The track bias was S+, meaning an extra-strong speed bias favoring frontrunners.

When speed and pace figures were tabulated, two horses, the winners of the 3rd and 8th races, made the horses-to-watch list of the three professionals. Each returned to win. The figures looked as follows for the two horses:

3rd	102/	126	111	116	FF	In Toto
8th	110/		108	114	AF	On The Line

The figure in front of the slash represents the par figure for the class-distance. The 3rd race was a route, and gets three figures; the 8th was a sprint, and gets two figures.

Look at In Toto's four-furlong pace figure, a 126. At the 4F call, 4 points equals a length.

Setting a blistering early pace, In Toto ran the first four furlongs six lengths faster than par.

At the second pace call in routes, after six furlongs, 2 points equals a length.

In Toto (111) ran to the second call roughly five lengths faster than par.

At the final call, or finish, 1 point equals a length. At 116, In Toto finished an amazing fourteen lengths faster than the class-distance par, an extraordinary figure, in this case abetted by an extra-strong speed bias.

The letters FF and AF indicate the race shapes, or configurations of pace. FF means fast-fast, or fast in relation to par at both the fractional call and final call. AF means average-fast, or average in relation to par at the fractional call, but fast in relation to par at the final call.

In routes, a fast shape requires a figure three lengths faster than par at the finish and three lengths (6 points) faster than par at the second call. In Toto's performance qualified at both calls, thus the FF shape.

In sprints, a fast shape requires a figure two lengths faster than par at the finish, two lengths (4 points) faster than par at the fractional call. On The Line earned the F designation at the finish only.

Alternatively, a slow-slow shape (SS) means Slow 6 (fractional) and Slow 3 (finish) in routes, Slow 4 (fractional) and Slow 2 (finish) in sprints. At 108, On The Line ran Slow 2 (one length) to the fractional call, an average performance.

Experience has persuaded me an FF shape in claiming races can be telltale, notably when a single horse in the field has exited a fast-fast pace. With a four-furlong figure of 126 besides, In Toto's performance looks devastating. At 114, On The Line had finished four lengths faster than Santa Anita's stakes sprint par, a very powerful performance. That both horses won their next start was hardly surprising, not to any of us.

As the meeting proceeded, I experienced a hot run of winning overlays during the first fifteen days. The horses figured considerably better than the odds suggested. Here are a few of the highlights.

December 27, 2nd Race

Savio ($21.40) was jumped two class levels by a sharp trainer after earning improving pace ratings in its last pair. On December 12 it clobbered $12,500 claimers, earning a pace rating equal to any horse in today's lineup. When a clever trainer executes this double-jump, and the figures support it, handicappers get prices. Watch for it!

Savio — B. g. 5, by Foolish Pleasure—Naples, by Graustark
CASTANON A L — 114 — Br.—duPont R C (Md) — Tr.—Ippolito Steve — $18,000
Own.—Laiacono Carol — Lifetime 22 4 4 2 $74,420
1987 7 1 2 0 $17,350
1986 14 3 2 1 $54,220
Turf 1 0 0 0

12Dec87-1Hol	6½f	:21^{3}	:44^{2}	1:17^{3}ft	*6-5	111^{5}	2^{1} 2$^{1\frac{1}{2}}$ 1^{3} 1^{4}	Gryder A T 9	12500	90-18	Savio, Classic Quickie, BuenChico	11
29Nov87-2Hol	6f	:21^{4}	:45	1:10^{2}ft	6	116	2$^{1\frac{1}{2}}$ 3$^{\frac{1}{2}}$ 2$^{\frac{1}{2}}$ 2$^{2\frac{1}{4}}$	Gryder A T 3	12500	88-12	Move Free, Savio, ElectricMoment	12
18Nov87-2Hol	6f	:22^{1}	:45^{2}	1:10^{2}ft	51	114	1$^{1\frac{1}{2}}$ 1^{hd} 1^{hd} 2^{hd}	Rivera H Jr 1	10500	90-12	Move Free, Savio, Zac K.	12
12Nov87-1SA	6f	:21^{4}	:45	1:11 ft	32	116	4$^{1\frac{1}{2}}$ 4^{3} 7$^{6\frac{1}{4}}$ 7$^{11\frac{1}{4}}$	Rivera H Jr 9	12500	72-21	Star Of America,Shantin,MoveFree	8
12Nov87—Broke poorly												
7May87-1Hol	6f	:22^{2}	:45^{4}	1:11^{1}ft	3	115	1^{hd} 4$^{3\frac{3}{4}}$ 4$^{6\frac{1}{2}}$ 4^{10}	Ortega L E 4	12500	77-13	PowerfullPul,RmonRod,John'sJove	8
25Apr87-7Hol	6½f	:22	:44^{3}	1:16 ft	12	116	4$^{1\frac{3}{4}}$ 3$^{3\frac{1}{2}}$ 5$^{8\frac{1}{4}}$ 8$^{14\frac{1}{4}}$	Pedroza M A 11	25000	86-13	Pilor,MischievousMtt,ForbesReply	12
11Apr87-1SA	6f	:21^{3}	:45^{1}	1:10^{4}ft	18	116	8$^{2\frac{1}{4}}$ 9$^{8\frac{1}{4}}$ 7$^{2\frac{3}{4}}$ 4^{6}	Ortega L E 5	25000	78-16	Pegus,FollowTheDancer,HighNturl	9
11Apr87—Broke in a tangle, steadied 3/8												
20Sep86-9Pom	6½f	:21^{4}	:45	1:16^{3}ft	5½	116	2^{hd} 4$^{2\frac{1}{2}}$ 6^{10} 8$^{18\frac{1}{2}}$	Sibille R 7	25000	78-09	Yukon's Star, Slugfest, Calabonga	8
16Sep86-11Pom	6f	:21^{4}	:44^{2}	1:09^{2}ft	85	112	3$^{\frac{1}{2}}$ 3^{5} 7^{14} 9^{15}	Garrido O L 1	Aprisa H	89-05	BundlOfIron,Mtronomc,ProdstHor	10
17Aug86-3Dmr	6f	:22	:45	1:09^{2}ft	31	116	1^{1} 1^{hd} 3$^{2\frac{1}{2}}$ 7$^{7\frac{1}{2}}$	Kaenel J L 3	55000	83-16	Infntrymn,Frnch'sLck,UrbnCowboy	8
17Aug86—Bumped early drive												

Dec 20 Hol 4f ft :48^{2} h Nov 26 Hol 4f ft :47^{3} h Nov 7 SA 5f m 1:01^{4} h Nov 1 SA 5f sy 1:03 h

December 29, 9th Race

Lyphard Chimes ($20.20) should have been 5–2 from the 12 post versus $12,500 platers in the slop. See if you don't agree.

With the high mud figure in the field, comfortably, the five-year-old gelding was dropping off a deceptively poor effort from the outside, where he had been mishandled by jockey Sibille. Too close to the front while wide, Lyphard Chimes tired. But he liked the slop this day, making a huge middle move and drawing off to win by three.

Lyphard Chimes * — B. g. 5, by Lyphard—Four Bells, by Quadrangle
BANDERAS A L — 111^{5} — Br.—Pillar Stud Inc (Ky) — Tr.—Tinsley J E Jr — $12,500
Own.—Hirmez-Sittu-Valpredo — Lifetime 39 6 1 5 $59,622
1987 23 2 0 2 $32,975
1986 8 1 0 2 $14,922
Turf 10 3 1 1 $11,725

20Dec87-9Hol	1$\frac{1}{16}$	:48^{3}	1:13	1:44 ft	15	115	4$^{\frac{3}{4}}$ 1^{hd} 5$^{2\frac{1}{2}}$ 7$^{8\frac{3}{4}}$	Sibille R 2	14000	74-08	Rvolutionry,Bruli'sAnt,ForvrBluJns	8
13Dec87-1Hol	1$\frac{1}{16}$	:47	1:12^{2}	1:44^{4}ft	22	119	5$^{4\frac{1}{2}}$ 5$^{3\frac{1}{2}}$ 3^{3} 4$^{3\frac{3}{4}}$	Sibille R 10	12500	75-13	Bruli'sAnte,PrsonJohn,GnuinJohn	12
5Dec87-1Hol	1$\frac{1}{16}$	:46^{3}	1:12^{3}	1:46^{1}sy	7½	115	4$^{5\frac{1}{2}}$ 1^{1} 1$^{3\frac{1}{2}}$ 1$^{3\frac{1}{2}}$	Sibille R 1	10000	72-17	LyphrdChims,BoldSintPt,Yippyyo	10
26Nov87-1Hol	6½f	:22^{1}	:45^{2}	1:17^{4}ft	43	115	10$^{7\frac{1}{4}}$ 8$^{8\frac{1}{2}}$ 5$^{4\frac{1}{2}}$ 5^{5}	Sibille R 1	10000	84-18	Inquisitive, Classic Quickie,Ayaabi	10
26Nov87—Steadied 5/8												
18Nov87-2Hol	6f	:22^{1}	:45^{2}	1:10^{2}ft	46	115	11^{11} 10$^{9\frac{1}{4}}$ 10^{10} 10$^{11\frac{1}{2}}$	Ortega L E 4	12500	78-12	Move Free, Savio, Zac K.	12
18Nov87—Bumped start												
24Aug87-9Dmr	1⅛	:45^{3}	1:10^{4}	1:49^{2}ft	43	114	8$^{9\frac{1}{2}}$ 12^{12} 12^{18} 11^{22}	Ortega L E 12	10500	61-17	L.A.Fire,WonderPlum,BronzTudor	12
22Jly87-2Hol	6½f	:22^{1}	:45^{1}	1:17^{1}ft	9	116	7^{7} 7^{7} 8$^{9\frac{1}{2}}$ 7$^{10\frac{1}{2}}$	Pedroza M A 7	12500	83-15	Bride'sAdvice,Doodlesck,HighNturl	8
12Jly87-4Hol	6½f	:22^{1}	:45^{1}	1:16 ft	31	109^{5}	8$^{5\frac{1}{4}}$ 7^{5} 6$^{4\frac{3}{4}}$ 6$^{7\frac{3}{4}}$	Patton D B 8	14000	92-09	MightyBuck,BlzeFlme,Bruli'sAnte	11
5Jly87-2Hol	1$\frac{1}{16}$	:45^{2}	1:10^{4}	1:44^{3}ft	46	114	5^{7} 4$^{3\frac{1}{2}}$ 5^{5} 6$^{6\frac{1}{2}}$	Pedroza M A 9	14000	79-11	GlcilStrem,PowrfullPul,PinpplJck	10
28Jun87-1Hol	1$\frac{1}{16}$	:45^{4}	1:11^{1}	1:43^{4}ft	42	114	7$^{8\frac{1}{2}}$ 7$^{5\frac{3}{4}}$ 5$^{8\frac{1}{2}}$ 6$^{10\frac{1}{2}}$	Pedroza M A 5	18000	80-12	Power Forward,Chagrining,OhDad	10

Dec 28 SA 3f ft :36^{3} h Nov 14 SA 3f gd :37^{3} h ●Nov 7 SA 6f m 1:15 hg Nov 1 SA 5f sy 1:01^{1} h

December 30, 5th Race

Consider the 2–1 favorite and 35–1 longshot in this $40,000 claiming sprint for two-year-old fillies. Which do you prefer?

5th Santa Anita

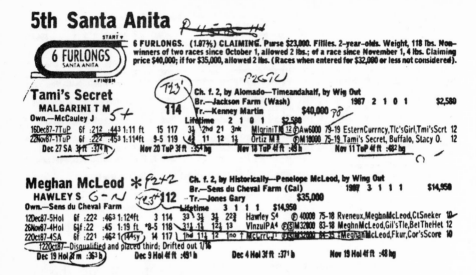

The favorite Meghan McLeod can be dumped immediately. Exiting a slow race at every call, it lost too much ground in the stretch. It beat state-bred maiden claimers previously, in milk-wagon time.

Now examine the shipper from Turf Paradise.

After barely surviving the lowest maiden-claiming conditions to break its maiden, Tami's Secret is not only entered under nonwinners allowance conditions, it almost wins, after breaking from hole 12. On blistering fractions, the filly fought gamely at every call, still digging in near the finish. Its pace rating (unadjusted) for the Turf Paradise allowance sprint is 25 points superior to Meghan McLeod's Hollywood pace rating, nothing to sneeze upon.

Drawn inside on a wet, muddy surface, Tami's Secret can be expected to show early speed in this field, and might get loose. Importantly, two-year-olds are either improving or deteriorating, often markedly, and the shipper looks like the improving sort, moving impressively from lowly maiden competition to solid allowance competition. At 35–1, who can resist?

Tami's Secret did show speed, did draw clear, was two on top at the quarter pole, and romped home uncontested. She paid $77. The favorite finished eighth of ten.

I got the win, but missed a $1760.50 exacta, linking the shipper to the wrong overlays.

January 2, daily double

By linking three overlays in the first half to the favorite and two overlays in the second half, multiple times, I cashed three tickets on a contentious daily double that clicked. The double returned a sweet $477.00, my largest double ever, I believe. The net was $1162.50.

The second-half winner, at 8–1, was dropping off a fast turn-time from $32,000 claiming to $25,000 claiming; in my judgment, the most significant price drop in the southern California claiming division. All circuits have similar dividing lines in the claiming hierarchy. Handicappers savvy on the point can take advantage of the overlays when the drops occur, as they regularly do.

Brohamer and Rousso limped through the holiday season in search of handicapping gifts, but sprang to life on New Year's Day. For the timeliest of reasons, the two collared a long shot their colleague should be embarrassed to have overlooked. It was a six-furlong $16,000 claiming race, limited to newborn four-year-olds.

Consider the past performances below:

Snappy Band
SOLIS A — Own.—Koosa C — 114
Dk. b. or br. c. 4, by Exalted Rullah—Lita's Rising Star, by Rising Market
Br.—Scofield L L (Cal)
Tr.—Stein Roger $14,000
1987 15 4 3 4 $21,625
1986 8 3 2 1 $10,178
Lifetime 23 7 5 5 $31,803

An improving horse, Snappy Band jumps up two class levels after finishing in sluggish time a week ago at Hollywood Park.

Or does it?

As all appreciate, except the responsible editors, the western edition of the *Daily Racing Form* does not print horses' ages in the past performances.

As Rousso noticed: "Snappy Band finished a fast-closing second against older horses last week. The rise in class is entirely misleading. In effect, this race has been restricted to three-year-olds. Older horses have such an advantage in three-and-up claiming races, Snappy Band is not really moving up at all today."

At 22–1, Snappy Band was certainly an overlay. Brohamer and Rousso bet. The one-day-old 4YO won, paid $47.40.

The next day, 1st race, Rousso nailed a $16,000 claiming filly at six furlongs for $41.40, a bet below prime, because she was the single horse that qualified on his form standards—an improving horse. He notched two exactas that afternoon as well.

Five days later Rousso got the first opportunity to display his specialty. This was another $16,000 claiming event, a route. The favorite at 5–2 was an off-pace horse, the type that closes gradually, dropping from $20,000 to $16,000. Two horses possessed the early speed of the field. I present both.

Rousso sizes up the early pace of route races exceedingly well. He was not deceived by the presence of a sprinter here. Trus T. Danus, a gelding of authentic route speed when in form, was Rousso's second choice to the favorite. Up two levels, and breaking from the outside, it was forsaken by the crowd, a 25–1 shot. Rousso boxed Trus T. Danus and the favorite in $5 exactas.

Both speed horses broke alertly. Trus T. Danus angled to the front from the outside. When Numpkins (9–2) faltered quickly, Trus T. Danus went all the way, the favorite Vinegarone getting only a steady-finishing second, a highly predictable place outcome.

The exacta paid $911.50.

January 9, 9th Race

Two days later Rousso repeated the trick, picking a horse he later called the best 5–1 shot of the season. Knowing now what to look for, examine the entries.

Pettrax — B. g. 10, by Petrone—Roman Dame, by British Roman
BLACK C A 118 — Br.—Charlton B (Cal) — 1987 14 2 2 1 $43,950
Tr.—Charlton Wayne $20,000 — 1986 12 4 2 1 $91,700
Own.—Charlton B W — Lifetime 79 17 14 5 $541,036 — Turf 36 6 5 2 $209,325
19Dec87-5Hol 1 1/16 :47 1:112 1:424gd 4¼ 116 56 911 1013 1014¼ Cordero A Jr2 25000 75-10 Centenary,TahoeTango,FlyingLord 10
29Nov87-3Hol 1⅛ :481 1:124 1:513ft 7¾ 116 31½ 32½ 2½ 13 Cordero A Jr5 20000 79-12 Pettrax, Bold Decree, Palestiglio 7
7Nov87-5SA 1 1/16 :481 1:131 1:452m 5 114 21 4¾ 41¾ 44 Black C A5 22500 65-26 Dennis D., Bruli's Ante, BoldDecree 7
24Oct87-10SA 1 1/16 :464 1:113 1:444gd *2½ 116 42½ 42¾ 45½ 58 Black C A2 25000 69-17 Dennis D., Dr. Daly, Tahoe Tango 7
24Oct87—Wide final 3/8
5Sep87-9Dmr 1 1/16 :453 1:101 1:432ft 4½ 116 42 33½ 44 2½ Black C A9 25000 82-13 Rampour, Pettrax, Passer II 11
16Aug87-9Dmr 1 1/16 :452 1:101 1:424ft 5 116 67½ 66½ 510 410 Kaenel J L7 32000 76-11 Convncng,PowrForwrd,NorthrnVlor 8
16Aug87—Wide 3/8
1Aug87-9Dmr 1 1/16 :471 1:113 1:431ft 5½ 116 2½ 2½ 33½ 33¾ Kaenel J L4 32000 80-15 Video Kid, Incluso, Pettrax 6
1Aug87—Lugged out 7/8
27Jun87-10GG 1 ⓣ:4711:1141:371fm 31 116 21 31 43½ 76¾ Hamilton M11 40000 74-21 FlklndsRulr,SonnyBrch,NorthOfLk 12
13Jun87-10GG 1 1/16 ⓣ:4721:1121:433fm 10 116 62½ 107¾ 117½ 116¾ Lambert J7 40000 77-12 GllntHwk,TellFloHello,NorthOfLk 11
20Apr87-3SA 1 1/16 :461 1:103 1:441ft 7¾ 116 44 65¾ 67½ 610½ Stevens S A3 50000 70-17 Fracoza, Poley, Double Sheng 6
20Apr87—Wide 3/8 turn
Jan 3 SA 4f ft :481 h — Dec 14 SA 4f ft :50 h — Nov 23 SA 5f ft 1:042 h

Bang Bang Bang — B. g. 8, by Ack Ack—Became a Lark, by T V Lark
DELAHOUSSAYE E 116 — Br.—Whittingham-Wynne-Bradley (Ky) — 1988 1 0 0 0
Tr.—Luby Donn $20,000 — 1987 6 1 0 1 $18,675
Own.—Miramar Stable — Lifetime 43 7 5 4 $136,100 — Turf 13 0 2 0 $33,250
2Jan88-9SA 1 1/16 :481 1:12 1:43 ft 6½ 116 3½ 42½ 79 911 Solis A9 25000 75-15 L. A. Fire, John Vigors, Tio Nino 10
2Jan88—Wide 7/8 turn
9Dec87-5Hol 1⅛ :462 1:112 1:501ft 5 116 815 89 56½ 46¾ DelahoussayeE7 32000 79-16 Rampour, Valiant Cougar, Air Alert 8
8Nov87-3SA 1 :473 1:114 1:391gd 3½ 116 711 611 610 512½ DelahoussayeE2 50000 59-25 SiberinHero,Centenry,SpdyShnnon 7
18Oct87-3SA 1 1/16 :471 1:113 1:423ft 2¾ 116 56½ 55½ 56½ 59¾ DelahoussayeE2 50000 79-15 Power Forward, Sidersell, Le Cid 5
26Aug87-5Dmr 1 1/16 :452 1:101 1:421ft *2¾ 116 914 79½ 56½ 34 DelahoussayeE3 60000 85-15 ForignLgion,SibrinHro,BngBngBng 9
26Aug87—Broke in a tangle
9Aug87-9Dmr 1 1/16 :462 1:104 1:431ft *9-5 116 99 76½ 41¾ 1hd DelahoussyeE12 40000 84-14 BngBngBng,Tourismo,VlintGeorge 12
29Jly87-7Dmr 6½f :22 :45 1:162ft 8¾ 116 1214 1111 77½ 54½ DelahoussayeE2 40000 85-17 Pialor, Mondanite, Lo Card 12
29Jly87—Pinched at start
20Nov86-5Hol 1⅛ :464 1:114 1:512ft 5½ 119 88¾ 78½ 95½ 75½ DelahoussyeE11 32000 75-16 Oak TreeII,Bedouin,ValiantGeorge 11
20Nov86—Wide on turns
26Oct86-9SA 1 1/16 :463 1:111 1:434ft 9¾ 118 913 88 34½ 1hd DelahoussayeE9 32000 82-16 BngBngBng,TooMchFrT.V.,ItmTw 10
3Oct86-9SA 1 1/16 :454 1:102 1:432ft 6 122 913 99¼ 88½ 65 Kaenel J L6 c25000 79-17 MrkInThSky,HrrcnHc,ForgtThRng 12
Dec 20 SA 5f ft 1:001 h — Dec 1 SA 5f ft 1:004 h — Nov 17 SA 5f ft 1:002 h

Predominance — Ch. h. 5, by Affirmed—Heatherglow, by The Axe II
CASTANON A L 116 — Br.—Harbor View Farm (Ky) — 1987 9 2 1 3 $32,925
Tr.—Bellasis Richard L $20,000 — 1986 7 M 0 1 $5,135
Own.—Olson L — Lifetime 20 2 1 5 $42,890 — Turf 6 0 0 1 $6,430
6Dec87-1Hol 1 1/16 :48 1:13 1:454gd 4½ 1145 63 33 42½ 1½ Gryder A T6 c16000 74-17 Predominnce,GumFleet,PrsonJohn 8
29Nov87-3Hol 1⅛ :481 1:124 1:513ft 3½ 118 44½ 55 53½ 54½ Pincay L Jr1 20000 75-12 Pettrax, Bold Decree, Palestiglio 7
11Nov87-4SA 1 1/16 :47 1:122 1:451ft *3½ 119 54 31 12 13 Pincay L Jr12 M28000 75-18 Predominnc,RoylRingr,BoobrsTim 12
11Nov87—4-wide 7/8
31Oct87-4SA 1 1/16 :474 1:133 1:47 sy 4¾ 119 1½ 12 1hd 32½ Solis A5 M28000 64-25 Versing,RoyalRinger,Predominnce 10
31Oct87—Four wide 7/8 turn; checked final strides
17Oct87-4SA 7f :23 :462 1:234ft *3½ 121 117½ 810 68½ 48¾ Vergara O5 M32000 72-16 TimesEscping,Erosion,Tht'sBlrney 12
17Oct87—Very wide into, through stretch
8Oct87-2SA 6½f :214 :444 1:171ft 5 121 78½ 911 911 56½ Vergara O6 M32000 78-19 SharpPort,TizStealin,SummerKing 11
8Oct87—Wide into stretch
22Mar87-4SA 1 1/16 :471 1:131 1:471gd *9-5 118 53½ 42 21½ 21 ValenzuelaPA2 M45000 64-23 Patrick O., Predominance,Yippyayo 9
17Mar87-6SA 6½f :22 :452 1:163ft 3¾ 118 63½ 34 34½ 36 ValenzuelaPA5 M45000 81-16 Hapigrin,SuperHigh,Predominnce 12
22Jan87-6SA 6½f :214 :451 1:17 ft 6 120 107¾ 79 68½ 38½ Simpson B H2 Mdn 76-23 Rufjan, Starshield, Predominance 11
28Dec86-4SA 1 1/16 :46 1:102 1:424ft 7 117 48½ 49½ 515 515 Vergara O2 Mdn 72-14 Valiant Cougar,Vysotsky,Centenary 8
Jan 5 SA tr.t 6f ft 1:171 h — Jan 2 SA 3f gd :364 h — Dec 27 SA 5f ft 1:014 h — Dec 22 SA 4f ft :483 h

Move Free — Ch. h. 6, by Sadair—Fast Freedom, by Vertex
VALENZUELA P A 116 — Br.—Meadowbrook Farms Inc (Fla) — 1987 13 3 4 2 $37,190
Tr.—Stute Melvin F $20,000 — 1986 5 2 0 0 $9,675
Own.—Hughes Brothers Ranch — Lifetime 31 8 5 4 $83,455 — Turf 1 0 0 0
23Dec87-2Hol 6f :222 :461 1:114ft 2¾ 117 53½ 53½ 55 84½ ValenzuelaPA1 c16000 79-19 ElDiamonte,GranTerresto,Melchip 11
29Nov87-2Hol 6f :214 :45 1:102ft 4 118 31½ 2hd 1½ 12½ Cordero A Jr4 12500 90-12 Move Free, Savio,ElectricMoment 12
18Nov87-2Hol 6f :221 :452 1:102ft *2½ 115 21½ 2hd 2hd 1no Cordero A Jr8 12500 90-12 Move Free, Savio, Zac K. 12
12Nov87-1SA 6f :214 :45 1:11 ft 2¾ 116 31½ 31½ 2hd 33½ Hawley S2 12500 79-21 Star Of America,Shantin,MoveFree 8
17Oct87-2SA 7f :221 :451 1:243ft 2½ 116 4nk 3½ 1hd 41½ Hawley S11 12500 76-16 SilverStrike,Vingron,TuscnKnight 12
17Oct87—Jumped mirror reflection at finish line
7Oct87-1SA 6½f :213 :442 1:16 ft 13 116 32 31 22 2½ Hawley S5 12500 89-10 Jimed, Move Free, Tigerillo 10
27Sep87-12Fpx 6f :22 :453 1:112ft *2½ 1145 66½ 44½ 54 84½ Patton D B6 12500 86-13 QuickRoundtrip,Witching,JulioNMe 9
27Sep87—Wide into stretch
21Sep87-8Fpx 6f :223 :462 1:111ft *9-5 1115 31½ 2hd 11 13¾ Patton D B5 10000 91-15 Move Free, Buen Chico, Tigerillo 8
9Sep87-5Dmr 6f :22 :45 1:092ft 8½ 116 41 41 43 46½ Black C A7 12500 84-13 FbulousPrtndr,Inquisitiv,PlsntPowr 9
3Apr87-1GG 6f :22 :45 1:10 ft *6-5 117 32½ 32 11 22½ Baze R A6 c10000 86-13 StreetsmrtNtive,MoveFree,Cheroot 8
Jan 6 SA 4f ft :493 h — Dec 31 SA 4f m :472 h — Dec 19 Hol 4f m :483 h — Dec 12 Hol 4f ft :473 h

Loverue
BANDERAS A L 1115
Own.—Banche Mr-Mrs N C
Dk. b. or br. h. 6, by Ruffinal—I'm Affectionate, by Turk's Delight
Br.—Westerly Stud Farms (Cal)
Tr.—Arena Joseph $20,000
Lifetime 28 3 4 5 $65,065
1987 3 0 0 0
1986 7 1 2 1 $35,975
Turf 10 1 3 2 $42,365

26Dec87-7SA 1⅛Ⓣ:4631:1121:494fm 3¾ 117 21½ 32 920 — Hawley S5 Aw38000 — — GeorgiaRiver,Euphrates,Eliminante 9
26Dec87—Eased
25Nov87-7Hol 6½f :212 :434 1:153ft 37 116 57 79¼ 77¼ 78¾ Hawley S1 Aw28000 91-13 Reconnoitering,Fracoz,OrchrdSong 7
13Nov87-7SA a6½f Ⓣ:214 :4431:16 fm 18 117 86½ 1016 1015 1018¾ Meza R Q1 Aw31000 60-21 MohmedAbdu,ChiefPl,SuprmStnd 10
16May86-5Hol 1⅛Ⓣ:4831:1321:484fm 4 116 11½ 1½ 21 41¾ DelhoussyeE7 Aw25000 86-07 Quintillon, Nonno, Kingsbury 7
17Apr86-8SA 1⅛Ⓣ:4731:12 1:481fm 5½ 116 12 1½ 2hd 21 DelhoussyeE5 Aw30000 85-14 Corridor Key, Loverue, Faridpour 11
27Mar86-5SA 1⅛Ⓣ:4541:1021:474fm 14 117 2½ 2hd 3nk 31 DelhoussyeE6 Aw35000 87-12 Prime Assett,LordGrundy,Loverue 10
16Mar86-5SA 1 1/16 :47 1:122 1:47 sy 5¾ 118 33½ 22 54½ 611½ ValenzuelPA7 Aw35000 54-24 JonO.,ExclusiveCpde,Vigor'sPrince 9
23Feb86-7SA 1⅛Ⓣ:4711:12 1:504fm *2¾ 118 3½ 31½ 42 43½ DelhoussyeE1 Aw34000 69-24 Soldat Bleu, Kala Dancer, Solstein 9
23Feb86—Crowded stretch
26Jan86-5SA 1⅛Ⓣ:4641:1111:49 fm 6 120 89 52½ 21 23½ DelhoussyeE4 Aw30000 78-17 LouisLeGrnd,Loverue,PrimeAssett 10
26Jan86—Rank, checked off heels 1/8, 1st time around, wide 3/8
4Jan86-5SA 1¼Ⓣ:47 1:3712:023fm 7¾ 116 32½ 31½ 1hd 13 DelhoussyeE9 Aw26000 74-23 Loverue, Star Formation, Witan 12
Jan 3 SA 5f ft 1:003 h Dec 20 SA 5f ft 1:003 h ●Dec 4 SA 4f ft :471 h Nov 21 SA 5f ft 1:014 h

***Passer II**
PATTON D B 116
Own.—Buck-Cain-Rionda
Dk. b. or br. h. 5, by Irish Conn—Curious Carolyn, by Wig Out
Br.—Navarro J S (Mex)
Tr.—Stute Melvin F $20,000
Lifetime 32 3 3 2 $145,989
1987 18 1 0 1 $24,987
1986 11 0 2 1 $37,325
Turf 3 0 0 0

19Dec87-5Hol 1 1/16 :47 1:112 1:424gd 17 116 21 1hd 32½ 67¼ Valenzuela P A 8 25000 82-10 Centenary,TahoeTango,FlyingLord 10
29Nov87-3Hol 1⅛ :481 1:124 1:513ft 9½ 1135 2hd 2½ 3½ 43 Banderas A L 7 20000 76-12 Pettrax, Bold Decree, Palestiglio 7
7Nov87-5SA 1 1/16 :481 1:131 1:462m 5¾ 1115 11 3nk 53¾ 57 Banderas A L 7 25000 62-26 Dennis D., Bruli's Ante, BoldDecree 7
31Oct87-10SA 1 1/16 :474 1:121 1:443sy 15 1115 2½ 1hd 1hd 1hd Banderas A L 10 20000 78-25 Passer II, Bruli's Ante, Tio Nino 10
4Oct87-12Fpx 1⅜ :484 1:39 2:172ft 29 115 32 31 65½ 65½ Kaenel J L 9 H25000 82-12 Siraluoval, Rampour, Dennis D. 9
25Sep87-8Fpx a1⅛ :462 1:112 1:492ft 5½ 113 14 12 44½ 610 Black C A 1 A25000 86-13 Fond O'Green,Rampour,SpiceTrade 6
5Sep87-9Dmr 1 1/16 :453 1:101 1:432ft 30 116 65 43½ 33½ 31 Sibille R 5 25000 82-13 Rampour, Pettrax, Passer II 11
18Aug87-9AC 1 1/16 :47 1:11 1:421ft 4¼ 1055 31 31½ 55¾ 46½ Gryder A T 5 Aw8000 87-11 Trouble T., Sasebo, Forio 5
4Aug87-9AC 1 1/16 :463 1:10 1:411ft 23 114 31½ 31 55 56½ Martinez JC1 Summer 92-12 Benemerito, Bugarian, Sasebo 7
18Jly87-9AC 6f :224 :452 1:101ft 4 108 81¼ 72 51¼ 54 Barsallo E5 Aw5000 84-17 Step Son, Jockey Up, Throw Home 7
Jan 3 SA 4f ft :472 h Dec 29 SA 4f ft :48 h Dec 12 Hol 4f ft :483 h Nov 27 Hol 4f ft :482 h

Forever Blue Jeans
SHERMAN A B 1095
Own.—McCracken C W
Dk. b. or br. g. 5, by Advocator—Mink and Jeans, by Cornish Prince
Br.—Northwest Farms (Ky)
Tr.—Sena Peter E $18,000
Lifetime 31 3 5 5 $51,590
1987 20 2 3 3 $30,965
1986 7 0 2 1 $11,800
Turf 2 0 0 0

20Dec87-9Hol 1 1/16 :483 1:13 1:44 ft 36 1115 1hd 2hd 1½ 32½ Sherman A B4 16000 80-08 Rvolutionry,Bruli'sAnt,ForvrBluJns 8
8Nov87-10SA 1 1/16 :484 1:14 1:481gd 20 115 52 63¼ 78 610½ Sibille R4 14000 59-25 Revolutionry,OlimpicBingo,BlzeFlm 9
23Oct87-9SA 1 1/16 :474 1:13 1:452sy 20 115 31 52 33½ 34 Sibille R6 13000 70-21 Bruli'sAnt,GlicKnight,ForvrBluJns 10
17Oct87-2SA 7f :221 :451 1:243ft 36 116 88¼ 1012 1116¾ 96½ Stevens S A5 12500 70-16 SilverStrike,Vingron,TuscnKnight 12
17Oct87—Bobbled start
2Oct87-9Fpx 1 1/16 :463 1:121 1:45 ft 14 116 31 31½ 32½ 34¼ Warren R J Jr5 12500 82-13 OlimpicBingo,Mjstuso,ForvrBluJns 9
2Oct87— Blocked 1st turn
27Sep87-12Fpx 6f :22 :453 1:112ft 31 116 79 77½ 86¼ 74 Warren R J Jr4 12500 86-13 QuickRoundtrip,Witching,JulioNMe 9
5Aug87-9Dmr 1 1/16 :461 1:112 1:441ft 96 1115 46½ 78 89½ 813 Cisneros J E4 16000 66-20 Convincing,Crowning,GreyGuntlet 10
5Aug87—Bumped 1/2; lugged out
27Jly87-4Hol 6f :22 :451 1:094ft 28 115 66½ 67½ 68½ 612¾ Fernandez A L5 16000 81-11 Bride'sAdvice,RosesArRb,SndDiggr 6
4Jly87-1Hol 1 :453 1:103 1:362ft 11 1115 54½ 46½ 48½ 512¾ Gryder A T 2 c12500 68-09 StretsmrtNtiv,MightyBuck,ItmTwo 8
4Jly87—Bumped start
20Jun87-9Hol 1 1/16 Ⓣ:4631:1041:412fm 73 117 21 43½ 812 821 McHrgueDG 4 Aw24000 66-13 FvDddyFv,Istorto,BooBoo'sBckroo 9
20Jun87—Bumped 7/8 turn
Jan 2 Hol 5f ft 1:02 h Dec 16 Hol 4f ft :474 h Dec 10 Hol 6f ft 1:174 h Dec 5 Hol 6f sy 1:144 h

I backed Good Thought Willy, exiting the FF pace of December 26, and boxed Good Thought Willy and Bang Bang Bang, which had been mishandled from the outside on January 2, another rapid race.

Brohamer abstained.

Rousso salivated over Move Free, a six-year-old stretching out following the claim by astute Mel Stute. He predicted the kind of sluggish route pace an inveterate sprinter would find irresistibly comfortable. I present the result chart on the point.

NINTH RACE
Santa Anita
JANUARY 9, 1988

$1\frac{1}{8}$ MILES. ($1.45\frac{4}{5}$) CLAIMING. Purse $21,000. 4-year-olds and upward. Weights, 4-year-olds, 120 lbs.; older, 121 lbs. Non-winners of two such races at one mile or over since November 16, allowed 3 lbs.; of such a race since then, 5 lbs. Claiming price $20,000; if for $18,000, allowed 2 lbs. (Claiming and starter races for $16,000 or less not considered.)
Value of race $21,000; value to winner $11,550; second $4,200; third $3,150; fourth $1,575; fifth $525. Mutuel pool $358,314. Exacta pool $554,037.

Last Raced	Horse	Eqt.	A.	Wt	PP	St	¼	½	¾	Str	Fin	Jockey	Cl'g Pr	Odds $1
23Dec87 ^{2}Hol^{8}	Move Free		6	116	6	1	1^{1}	$1^{3\frac{1}{2}}$	$1^{3\frac{1}{2}}$	1^{8}	1^{8}	Valenzuela P A	20000	5.10
2Jan88 ^{9}SA^{3}	Bang Bang Bang		8	116	4	8	8^{6}	8^{5}	8^{7}	$3^{1\frac{1}{2}}$	$2^{\frac{1}{2}}$	Delahoussaye E	20000	3.30
26Dec87 ^{3}SA^{3}	Good Thought Willy	b	6	116	1	3	$5^{\frac{1}{2}}$	$6^{1\frac{1}{2}}$	2^{hd}	$2^{3\frac{1}{2}}$	$3^{4\frac{1}{2}}$	Toro F	20000	7.40
19Dec87 ^{5}Hol^{6}	Passer II	b	5	116	8	6	$6^{1\frac{1}{2}}$	$5^{\frac{1}{2}}$	$6^{1\frac{1}{2}}$	$4^{\frac{1}{2}}$	$4^{2\frac{1}{2}}$	Hawley S	20000	10.20
20Dec87 ^{9}Hol^{1}	Revolutionary	b	7	116	2	9	7^{4}	7^{5}	7^{2}	5^{3}	5^{3}	Shoemaker W	20000	2.20
20Dec87 ^{9}Hol^{3}	Forever Blue Jeans		5	109	9	5	4^{hd}	3^{hd}	$5^{\frac{1}{2}}$	6^{hd}	6^{3}	Sherman A B^{5}	18000	42.30
19Dec87 ^{5}Hol^{10}	Pettrax		10	118	3	2	2^{1}	4^{1}	$3^{\frac{1}{2}}$	$7^{2\frac{1}{2}}$	7^{nk}	Black C A	20000	9.50
6Dec87 ^{1}Hol^{1}	Predominance		5	116	5	7	9	9	9	9	$8^{2\frac{3}{4}}$	Castanon A L	20000	11.40
26Dec87 ^{7}SA	Loverue		6	111	7	4	3^{1}	2^{hd}	4^{hd}	8^{2}	9	Banderas A L^{5}	20000	12.00

OFF AT 4:57. Start good. Won ridden out. Time, $:23\frac{1}{5}$, :47, $1:11\frac{3}{5}$, $1:36\frac{1}{5}$, $1:49\frac{1}{5}$ Track fast.

$2 Mutuel Prices:			
6-MOVE FREE	12.20	7.40	4.80
4-BANG BANG BANG		5.40	3.60
1-GOOD THOUGHT WILLY			4.60

$5 EXACTA 6-4 PAID $148.50.

Ch. h, by Sadair—Fast Freedom, by Vertex. Trainer Stute Melvin F. Bred by Meadowbrook Farms Inc (Fla).

MOVE FREE, in front throughout, drew out to a commanding lead after six furlongs and remained far in front through the strech. BANG BANG BANG, devoid of early speed, was never a threat to the winner but got up for the place. GOOD THOUGHT WILLY, in contention early, lacked the needed response in the last quarter. PASSER II, four wide into the cloubhouse turn and wide down the backstretch, was five wide into the far turn. REVOLUTIONARY, patiently handled while being outrun early after breaking slowly, lacked a sufficient response when called upon. FOREVER BLUE JEANS, in close contention early and four wide into the far turn, came into the stretch four wide and faltered. PETTRAX, prominent early, faltered. LOVERUE, prominent early, was through after six furlongs.

Owners— 1, Hughes Brothers Ranch; 2, Miramar Stable; 3, Koosa C; 4, Buck-Cain-Rionda; 5, Goldman-Goldman-Rosoff; 6, McCracken C W; 7, Charlton B W; 8, Olson L; 9, Banche Mr-Mrs N C.

Trainer Stute kept Move Free running long, and the six-year-old possessed arguably the keenest route speed in the mid-claiming class at the meeting. Move Free completed four consecutive wire jobs. As handicappers understand, sprinters win their fair share of routes. When a competent trainer makes the move—following a claim, especially—handicappers can imitate Rousso. Prices will frequently be hard to resist.

After taking a thin slice of the pool returned to backers of Snappy Band on January 1, Brohamer continued an early struggle with his assorted figures. A Sartin pace analyst, now using Quirin-style speed and pace figures, he was juggling velocity ratings with fractional final times, as well as daily variants associated with each set of numbers. This applied to the races at Bay Meadows, near San Francisco, as well as Santa Anita. Lots of numbers floating about, day to day.

Brohamer became preoccupied, too, with ironing out certain baffling differences reflected on three par-time charts for Santa Anita's new season: the chart from the 1987 winter season, which I used; the chart for the recent Oak Tree at Santa Anita season, thirty-two racing days of fall; and Quirin's chart, a national computerized study of final times at all major tracks.

For the first two weeks, Brohamer kept his head above water with a set of Bay Meadows' figures he used to evaluate shippers, notably in lower-level claiming races, where northern California horses often ship successfully to Santa Anita. The most interesting of several occurred January 8, the 2nd race, a $16,000 claiming sprint for 4YO fillies. It gave Brohamer the daily double on top of a prime bet to win.

Examine the records of Brohamer's shipper and of the most appealing local contender.

Lady Kell — B. f. 4, by Mike Fogarty—K O Kelly, by Big Jess
VALENZUELA P A — 116 — Br.—Abrams S (Cal) — 1987 8 1 4 0 $22,265
Own.—Ansara N J — Tr.—West Ted — $16,000 — 1986 0 M 0 0
Lifetime 8 1 4 0 $22,265
11Dec87-1Hol 1 :452 1:111 1:383ft *3¾ 115 54½ 53½ 23 2nk Cordero A Jr1 (F) 20000 70-18 Scarlet Lake, Lady Kell,WildDrive 12
18Nov87-1Hol 6f :22 :453 1:112ft 3¾ 115 55½ 33½ 32½ 21 VlenzulPA11 (F) c16000 84-12 Un Bel Di, Lady Kell, Tableland 12
4Nov87-5SA 6f :22 :451 1:122sy 4 118 85¾ 97 74¾ 42½ VlenzulPA10 (F)[S] 20000 73-26 SweetExpcttions,Eghlnd,HvyWthr 12
4Nov87—Rough trip
20ct87-10Fpx 6½f :213 :443 1:172ft 2¼ 115 58 66 68 610½ Castanon AL4 (F) 32000 79-13 AliasNin,DncersOrbit,FelisConcolor 8
25Sep87-11Fpx 1116 :46 1:112 1:45 ft 4 114 1½ 31½ 44½ 44¼ PttDB3 (F)[S]C TBAMrn 82-13 QuickMssngr,Tmtul,John'sLdyLuck 8
25Sep87—Wide into stretch 1st time around
18Sep87-10Fpx 1116 :46 1:121 1:461ft 7½ 115 21 1hd 1½ 2nk KaenelJL10 (F)Aw27000 80-18 ProfitIsland,LadyKell,LyricalPirte 10
2Sep87-4Dmr 6f :22 :45 1:102ft *1 1125 1½ 1hd 11½ 13½ PattonDB1 (F)[S]M32000 86-17 LdyKell,TimeToSweep,ChicMoren 11
2Sep87—Bumped start; lugged out down backstretch
21Aug87-4Dmr 6½f :22 :45 1:17 ft 5½ 1125 2½ 11 12½ 2hd Patton D B7 (F)M32000 87-15 Reiterate, Lady Kell, Interpretress 12
Dec 21 SA 3f ft :354 h — Dec 4 SA 6f ft 1:153 h — Nov 27 SA 4f ft :50 h

Holy Smokes — B. f. 4, by Holy War—Summershine, by Olympiad King
SOLIS A — 114 — Br.—Weigel M J (Cal) — 1987 20 7 5 1 $33,980
Own.—Fanning B — Tr.—Stein Roger — $14,000 — 1986 5 M 2 2 $4,850
Lifetime 25 7 7 3 $38,830
26Dec87-4BM 6f :22 :452 1:11 ft *2½ 118 43½ 43½ 3nk 12 Long B6 (F)[S] c10000 84-14 HolySmoks,Sm'tmGyps,Tmmy'sTx 10
28Nov87-3BM 6f :22 :444 1:10 ft *3-2 118 22 22 22 21½ Long B1 (F)[S] 10000 87-11 FltBrgin,HolySmoks,HighTchniqu 10
13Nov87-3BM 6f :223 :461 1:12 m *2½ 115 2½ 2½ 12 12½ Long B5 (F) 10000 79-25 Holy Smokes, FunnyFacts,Rubeth 10
4Nov87-1BM 6f :224 :464 1:113ft 9 116 42¼ 41½ 12 17 Long B2 (F) 8000 81-25 Holy Smokes, SatansTouch,KeeliH. 9
24Oct87-1BM 6f :222 :462 1:13 gd *9-5 1115 86½ 87¾ 78 66¾ IammrinoMP7 (F) c6250 67-20 StnsToch,LdyExclsv,ErtArtstProf 11
8Oct87-6BM 6f :22 :45 1:104ft 6½ 1115 54½ 55½ 36 22½ ImmrinoMP3 (F)[S] 8000 82-23 FleetBargin,HolySmokes,DrsHope 10
11Sep87-4Bmf 6f :23 :462 1:12 ft 2¼ 1095 1½ 1½ 2hd 1½ IammarinoMP3 (F) 6250 79-21 Holy Smokes, Lucky Par, HitALulu 6
20Aug87-5Stk 6f :221 :453 1:104ft 2½ 1105 22 42 36 25 IammarinoMP5 (F) 6500 91-04 R.Pursntcher,HolySmoks,GoldSpcil 6
27Jly87-10SR 6f :221 :454 1:103ft *2½ 1085 2½ 1hd 2hd 1½ ImmrinoMP4 (F)[S] 6250 88-14 HolySmokes,FlyingJeni,Ick'sNigh 10
14Jly87-4Sol 6f :214 :452 1:101ft 4½ 1095 66 44 46 55 Medero F9 (F) 8250 87-13 CstlyFclft,IfNtNwWhn,MssJmyJn 10
Dec 19 BM 4f gd :501 h — ●Dec 8 BM 4f sy :493 h (d) — Nov 24 BM 4f ft :504 h

Notwithstanding the apparent class differences, and the rise and drop, respectively, Holy Smokes had earned the stronger figures consistently. Brohamer had no hesitation.

Alert class handicappers might have arrived at the same conclusion but by a different, just-as-reliable method of analysis. Consider the conditions of eligibility.

2nd Santa Anita

6 FURLONGS. (1.07⅗) **CLAIMING.** Purse $14,000. Fillies. 4-year-olds. Non-winners of three races. Weight, 121 lbs. Non-winners of two races since October 1 allowed 3 lbs.; of a race since then, 5 lbs. Claiming price $16,000; if for $14,000 allowed 2 lbs. (Races when entered for $12,500 or less not considered.)

Santa Anita cards restricted claiming races infrequently, but this was one. Handicappers that noticed the race was limited to 4YOs which had not won three races lifetime could hardly have missed a filly boasting 7 wins in 20 starts.

Holy Smokes had remained eligible only because it had raced consistently below today's exemption price of $12,500. Victories at cheaper levels would not count against the shipper's eligibility.

Whenever a consistent winner at a slightly lower selling level confronts chronic nonwinners at the presumptively higher level, class evaluation takes the curves easily. The winning horses moving up frequently enjoy a pronounced edge and deserve the handicapper's favoritism, notably when the crowd disagrees. Moreover, chronic nonwinners notoriously lack speed. When the horse moving up also sports the high speed figure, it's prime-bet time.

Holy Smokes won again, paid $10.20. The daily double gave Brohamer $64.20 multiple times.

During week three, Brohamer got in gear. He caught Good Taste ($7), Savor Faire ($10.40), Bright and Right ($8.20), Annoconnor ($13.40), Fond o' Green ($6.80), and Aspirate ($10), six prime bets. He missed three too.

Just prior to the breakout, on January 7, Brohamer suffered a near-miss that stung, losing an apparent 7–1 winner named Valiant Cougar by a disqualification. It was a 1 1/16M allowance route, 4up, for nonwinners two times other than maiden or claiming. Valiant Cougar was exiting a $40,000 claiming route it had won by eight, earning a sizable figure that exceeded today's allowance par. High-figure horses exiting classier claiming races can rule the preliminary nonwinners allowances during winter, when these fields are regularly stocked with older runners still seeking the first, or second, allowance win.

I preferred Lucky Harold H., a shipper from the stakes division at Bay Meadows. A restricted stakes winner October 25, Lucky Harold H. had earned a superior pace rating in an open stakes last out. The horse was a 4YO, with just 14 starts, and fit these nonwinners conditions snugly.

As their records reveal, the pair reflect two real-time models of the horses speed handicappers and class handicappers can prefer under these allowances.

Lucky Harold H. B. g. 4, by Coulee Man—Kahala, by Pia Star
STEVENS G L 116 Br.—Hinch Nan Barich (Cal) 1987 14 2 1 4 $78,575
Own.—Hinch Racing Stable Tr.—Threewitt Noble Turf 5 1 0 2 $27,325
Lifetime 14 2 1 4 $78,575

13Dec87-9BM	1 1/16 :45³ 1:09³ 1:41²ft	7½	115	2hd	53	32	54¼	JudiceJC¹	Lnd Stfd H	81-22	NicklBnd,NoTimFlt,H'sADncngMn	10
13Dec87—Steadied 3/8												
28Nov87-8BM	a1⅛ Ⓣ 1:48³fm	17	115	74¾	85½	59	310½	CstndM⁶	B M Dby H	81-08	HotAndSmoggy,Wolsy,LckyHroldH.	9
28Nov87—Grade III												
14Nov87-8BM	1 1/16 Ⓣ:47⁴1:13 1:46²gd	12	115	77½	75½	86¾	86¼	CastnedM⁶	Rnd Tbl H	65-31	NicklBnd,HotAndSmoggy,CrosLov	10
14Nov87—Ducked out start												
25Oct87-10BM	1 1/16 :46³ 1:10³ 1:41³ft	6½	115	21½	2½	11	1nk	CstdM¹	ⓈSn Jqn Iv H	84-20	LcHrldH,CndctnChrgr,HsADncnMn	6
9Oct87-8BM	1 :45¹ 1:09⁴ 1:35⁴ft	6¼	115	76	52½	21½	31½	Castaneda M⁴	HcpO	87-16	CndctnChrgr,HsADncnMn,LcHrldH	9
1Oct87-8BM	1 :46 1:10³ 1:35²ft	9½	116	42½	41½	21½	21½	Maple S⁸	Aw20000	89-19	AckLikeMe,LuckyHroldH.,HotMtl	10
26Aug87-7Dmr	1 :45⁴ 1:10³ 1:36¹ft	11	116	4¾	51¼	52	44	Baze R A²	Aw24000	83-15	LordTurk,SludYPests,CirclViwDriv	8
26Aug87—Bumped hard 3/8												
12Aug87-7Dmr	1⅛ Ⓣ:47⁴1:12²1:50 fm	8½	118	84½	84¾	53	32	Baze R A⁸	Aw23000	81-17	PoltclAmbtn,CntctGm,LckyHrldH.	10
12Aug87—5 wide into drive												
30Jly87-5Dmr	1 1/16 Ⓣ:48⁴1:13³1:45 fm	48	120	52½	73¾	62¼	41¼	Baze R A⁸	Aw23000	74-17	Just Bobby, Jonleat,ContactGame	10
17Jly87-11Sol	1 :46³ 1:10² 1:36²ft	17	114	32	31	31½	33½	Judice J C⁷	Aw14000	88-16	ExclusvPtrot,Dm'Rff,LuckyHroldH.	9

●Dec 29 BM 6f sy 1:14¹ h (d) Dec 22 BM 5f ft 1:01² h Dec 11 BM 4f m :48 h Dec 5 BM 1 sy 1:38⁴ h

The contest was fought savagely by the two throughout the second half, Valiant Cougar prevailing, but tiring and bumping its rival late. Speed-class handicappers who boxed the pair got $204 for each $5 exacta. With par at 103, Valiant Cougar's figures were 114–109–110. The shape was FF, and the impressive figures would pay dividends for our deserving trio soon enough.

January 10, 9th Race

Brohamer and I had narrowed the field to three contenders. Brohamer liked a filly moving up one level escorted by the high figure and a hot trainer, one of his favorite plays. I preferred a filly down one level, with a good figure, and a good trainer too. Odds on the three at post were:

Romantic Jet	6–1	(Brohamer)
Tamtulia	2–1	(Public)
Profit Island	8–1	(Quinn)

Consider the past performances:

9th Santa Anita

1 MILE
SANTA ANITA

1 MILE. (1.33⅗) CLAIMING. Purse $30,000. Fillies and mares. 4-year-olds and upward. Weights, 4-year-olds, 120 lbs.; older, 121 lbs. Non-winners of two races at one mile or over since November 16 allowed 3 lbs.; of such a race since then, 5 lbs. Claiming price $40,000; if for $35,000 allowed 2 lbs. (Claiming and starter races for $32,000 or less not considered.)

Romantic Jet — B. f. 4, by Tri Jet—Goddess Roman, by Chieftain
MEZA R Q — 115 — Br.—Hooper F W (Fla) — 1988 1 1 0 0 $12,100
Tr.—Spawr William $40,000 — 1987 16 1 2 3 $20,825
Own.—Mngy-O'Connor-Ptrsn Etal — Lifetime 19 2 2 3 $33,695 — Turf 1 0 0 0

1Jan88-9SA 1 :472 1:114 1:38 gd 10 114 3½ 1hd 11 14 Meza R Q 3 Ⓕ 28000 78-22 RomntcJt,EgyptinVrdict,DoublDnt 9
1Jan88—Bumped hard 7 1/2
2Dec87-8Hol 1⅛ Ⓣ:4711:1031:481fm 20 113 55 77½ 1012 911¾ Meza R Q 10 ⒻAw31000 75-13 StylishLass,LadyAnnabelle,Maidee 10
26Nov87-7Hol 1 1/16 :47 1:112 1:443ft 4½ 116 76½ 87¾ 57½ 43¾ Meza R Q 5 Ⓕ 32000 76-18 FirstSilverHwk,Divest,DoubleDent 10
12Nov87-5SA 1 1/16 :472 1:121 1:452ft 31 115 53½ 21½ 2hd 11¾ Meza R Q 4 Ⓕ 25000 74-21 Romantic Jet, Divest, DoubleDent 10
12Nov87—Disqualified from purse money
28Oct87-1SA 1 1/16 :474 1:121 1:452ft 6 116 87 98¾ 911 89 Stevens G L 1 Ⓕ c20000 65-16 ZackyFashion,Encroch,PetiteZoot 11
28Oct87—Jumped reflection
3Sep87-9Dmr 1 1/16 :464 1:114 1:45 ft *3¾ 118 76½ 77¾ 55 43¾ Baze R A 6 Ⓕ 25000 71-18 ProfitIslnd,FirstSilverHwk,Believbl 8
3Sep87—Broke in, bumped
19Aug87-2Dmr 1 :454 1:114 1:373ft 7½ 118 77 74 43 57¾ McCarron CJ 9 Ⓕ 32000 72-14 BehindTheScens,CIticLdy,‡Unssilbl 9

Tamtulia — Dk. b. or br. f. 4, by Tamtoul—Top One, by Envoy
STEVENS G L — 115 — Br.—Wackeen C (Cal) — 1987 10 3 1 2 $49,300
Tr.—Canani Julio C $40,000 — 1986 6 1 1 1 $14,100
Own.—Sofro D I — Lifetime 16 4 2 3 $63,400 — Turf 2 0 0 0 $3,600

18Dec87-8Hol 1 1/16 :473 1:13 1:464m 2½ 114 3½ 32 31½ 33¾ CordroAJr7 ⒻAw36000 65-22 Table Frolic, Cee's Vigor, Tamtulia 7
18Dec87—Wide throughout
21Oct87-7SA 1 :46 1:111 1:371ft 3½ 116 78 77½ 67 79 StevensGL5 ⒻAw29000 73-20 GoldenGlxy,CrossedArrows,Develop 8
15Oct87-9SA 1 :463 1:112 1:372ft *1 116 21 11 12 12 Stevens G L2 Ⓕ 40000 81-19 Tamtulia, Profit Island,CelticLady 10
25Sep87-11Fpx 1 1/16 :46 1:112 1:45 ft 4½ 114 3½ 1hd 12 2hd PdrMA2 ⒻⓈCTBAMrn 86-13 QuickMssngr,Tmtul,John'sLdyLuck 8
11Sep87-7Dmr 1 Ⓣ:4731:1221:381fm*8-5 117 2½ 21½ 24 63¾ StevnsGL10 ⒻAw24000 76-20 DerMorgn,TimeForHrt,SlyChrmer 10
25May87-7Hol 1 1/16 :462 1:113 1:451ft *9-5 114 — — — — StevensGL8 ⒻAw24000 — — PlayingTaps,AmericanDrama,LSierr 8
25May87—Lost rider, Reared start
6May87-5Hol 1 1/16 Ⓣ:4641:1121:413fm 2½ 114 54½ 53½ 32½ 33 StevensGL4 ⒻAw24000 85-11 Quadrada, Silken Light, Tamtulia 9
20Apr87-2SA 1 :463 1:12 1:381ft 3½ 116 32 12 13½ 14½ Stevens G L3 Ⓕ 32000 77-17 Tamtulia, Beseya, Divest 9
11Apr87-3SA 6f :214 :45 1:104ft 7 118 68½ 613 615 617½ Pedroza M A3 Ⓕ 40000 66-16 CoronMiss,FoxiesEgo,LefkdinSrnd 6
11Apr87—Lugged out
7Jan87-6SA 1 :474 1:131 1:392m 2¾ 115 13 14 12 11 Stevens G L4 Ⓕ 40000 71-21 Tamtulia, Abrojo, Most Dramatic 8
Jan 2 SA 4f gd :472 h Dec 27 SA 3f ft :36 h Dec 16 SA 3f ft :361 h ●Dec 10 SA 4f ft :461 h

Profit Island — B. f. 4, by Ack Ack—Raw Sugar, by Judger
VELASQUEZ J — 115 — Br.—Loblolly Stable (Ky) — 1987 13 3 3 1 $44,475
Tr.—Lewis Craig A $40,000 — 1986 0 M 0 0
Own.—Glazer Lauren — Lifetime 13 3 3 1 $44,475

31Dec87-9SA 1 :484 1:133 1:40 gd 12 1085 2½ 2hd 3½ 73¾ Gryder A T 4 Ⓕ 50000 64-19 Thai Dye,HerRoyalGrace,Missadoon 9
17Dec87-5Hol 1 :453 1:11 1:372sy 5 114 78¾ 55¼ 58½ 510 Velasquez J 2 Ⓕ 50000 66-22 FlyingHigher,PlyingTps,Blke'sDncr 7
28Nov87-4Hol 7f :221 :451 1:23 ft 8 116 78 67 34 2½ DelhoussyeE 7 Ⓕ 50000 88-12 Alias Nina,ProfitIsland,Linguistical 7
28Nov87—Wide backstretch
15Oct87-9SA 1 :463 1:112 1:372ft 15 1125 77½ 54½ 22 22 Gryder A T 10 Ⓕ 40000 79-19 Tamtulia, Profit Island,CelticLady 10
15Oct87—Wide throughout
18Sep87-10Fpx 1 1/16 :46 1:121 1:461ft 6½ 1075 65½ 45 32 1nk Patton DB 5 ⒻAw27000 80-18 ProfitIsland,LadyKell,LyricalPirte 10
3Sep87-9Dmr 1 1/16 :464 1:114 1:45 ft 5 116 41½ 1hd 1hd 1hd Stevens G L 8 Ⓕ 25000 75-18 ProfitIslnd,FirstSilverHwk,Believbl 8
3Sep87—Bumped 1/16
7Aug87-3Dmr 1 :461 1:12 1:39 ft 7¼ 116 53 74 43 3½ Stevens G L 7 Ⓕ 25000 72-15 Unassailable,CelticLady,ProfitIslnd 8
30Jly87-7Dmr 1 :464 1:122 1:381ft 13 1115 52 97½ 914 925¼ Gryder A T 3 Ⓕ 25000 52-21 Rhinbcky,FirstSilvrHwk,PrincssKll 10
30Jly87—Bumped start; broke stride 3/8
25Jun87-9Hol 1 :452 1:104 1:373ft 3½ 119 84¾ 73½ 62½ 63¼ Pincay L Jr 4 Ⓕ 32000 72-14 Green Isar, Flying Up, Rhinebecky 8
12Jun87-9Hol 1 :451 1:111 1:381ft 15 118 45½ 32½ 2hd 22¼ Ortega L E 6 Ⓕ c25000 70-16 TimeForHrt,ProfitIslnd,PrincssKll 10
Dec 6 Hol 4f gd :482 h Nov 13 SA 6f ft 1:161 h

Brohamer supported Romantic Jet strongly to win, and boxed her in exactas with Profit Island.

I took Profit Island to win, boxed Romantic Jet and Profit Island in exactas, and played each filly on top in additional exactas, with the race favorite on the bottom.

The three fillies challenged one another throughout the long stretch drive, Profit Island overtaking a pacesetting Tamtulia nearing the sixteenth pole, seeming to draw away enough to win. After a troubled stretch run on the inside, Romantic Jet took up sharply at the sixteenth pole, swung quickly to the outside, and overhauled Profit Island near the wire with a final burst.

Romantic Jet returned $15.60, to Brohamer only. All three in the box cashed the juicy exacta, collecting $509 per ticket.

After fifteen days the three pros were comfortably in front of the meeting.

A pair of tickets on the Romantic Jet–Profit Island exacta pushed me ahead by $1533 that day and climaxed what would prove to be my best winning run of the meeting. I was $4625 ahead, the victim of only three losing afternoons so far.

Following a brief mild case of the holiday blues, Rousso finished the three weeks in the black at $2500, and Brohamer was heating up, too, $2000 on top.

THE CASE FOR VALIANT COUGAR

The boldest imprint of the first fifteen days, shared by three, was that Quirin's speed and pace figures packed more dynamite than any of us had realized. The paired figures permitted the visualization of a race that speed figures by themselves never had.

The trio of figures for routes proved especially intriguing. High pace figures in addition to a high final figure had so far whipped horses showing comparable final figures but inferior pace figures. Where the four-furlong figure of routes had been abnormally high, and the other two figures similar, the four-furlong standouts had delivered the goods.

The new-style numbers also invigorated a renewed spirit of figure handicapping.

Brohamer had long since deserted conventional speed figures for Sartin-style pace ratings. He now was willing to come full circle for another trial, hoping the combined speed-pace figures might arouse the same mental images at less toil.

Rousso had used Beyer-style figures for years, more sparingly as the seasons drifted by. He liked the new numbers too. I had supplemented Beyer-style final figures with race shapes for four seasons. The new figures did not embody the principle of proportional time, but I felt the pace figures overcompensated nicely.

Come January 20, we arrived in unanimous spirit. A horse in the 7th race looked a walkover on figures, and we "knew" it unequivocally.

As the program progressed, each of us advised acquaintances and inquisitors that Valiant Cougar represented the best bet of the day, perhaps of the young meeting.

Brohamer consulted daily with Sartin colleagues and former

associates at Pacific Bell (conveniently on hand while working collaboratively with Santa Anita executives on the development and expansion of southern California's spanking-new intertrack wagering network), Rousso with seminar patrons and assorted companions, and I with friends in the turf club and season boxes.

Of my companions, the most interesting of 1988 would be thoroughbred owner Ben Bollinger, a savvy veteran handicapper with inside connections to the stables of trainers Darrel Vienna and Mel Stute. Bollinger was campaigning four horses he had purchased from Europe in a package, including the stakes contender Santella Mac, placed to Swink in the Grade 2 Del Mar Invitational, on turf in 1987. But the Bollinger connection of interest to us were the speed figures he had begun to buy daily from Thoro-Graph, the well-respected "sheets" originating in New York but under distribution for the first time on the West Coast, compliments of a handicapper named Julian Weinberg.

The sheets supply customers with a career's array of speed figures for every horse on the program. By tracing patterns of improving and declining figures, season to season, month to month, handicappers can predict whether horses should outrun their recent figures today, or regress (bounce), as they have in the past. By this strategy, blind ambition with speed figures is resisted. Interpreting horses' cycles and patterns matters most. Handicappers who purchase Thoro-Graph's figures can attend for free a weekly users' seminar where experienced hands explain their appropriate use, a helpful service. Bollinger went weekly.

When I sighted Bollinger January 20, I inquired as to which horse in the 7th had Thoro-Graph's top figure. This kind of exchange occurred daily, or almost. Bollinger answered Valiant Cougar, but immediately cautioned the horse was expected to "bounce," meaning no play.

The warning sign was out because Thoro-Graph's sheets showed Valiant Cougar had regressed in the past after earning the high figure it had at Santa Anita on January 3, a 110 by our methods. Par today would be 105 for allowance horses at 1 1/16M, nonwinners twice other than maiden or claiming. Valiant Cougar's pace figures January 3 had been clearly superior to par as well, at 114 (4F) and 109 (6F). Bollinger and I disagreed as to whether Valiant Cougar should bounce today, which makes it a horse race, I guess.

Our final authority, Brohamer, was adamant that Valiant

Cougar would not bounce. He commented: "The horse was in different hands last season, sore, and out of shape much of the time. He was very inconsistent. Valiant Cougar has since been claimed, and looks to be in the sharpest form of its career."

To extend the argument to its logical conclusion, as a group four-year-olds cannot be expected to perform in cycles or patterns they demonstrated at three, while still maturing; three-year-olds, likewise, cannot be expected to perform in cycles or patterns they demonstrated at two. Horses older than four may repeat past patterns more frequently, or may not, as circumstances dictate, such as the substantial changes in Valiant Cougar and his surroundings.

Past performances for the horses in the 7th race can be found below. Here are the pars, speed and pace figures, and race shapes of their latest lines. Which do handicappers prefer?

Boo Boo Buckaroo	104/		102	105	AF
Red and Blue	104/		98	103	AF
Midnight Ice	not available				
Fancy Oats	104		101	103	AF
Fiction	not available				
Valiant Cougar	103/	114	109	110	FF
Syrian Wind	103/	126	103	104	AA
Glory Forever	106/		100	105	AA

Of the two with figures unavailable, Midnight Ice might be dismissed, but Fiction could not. It fit the eligibility conditions snugly, but lightly raced four-year-olds are not as talented (normally) or reliable as their three-year-old counterparts which dominate these races during spring and summer. Fiction should not jump up and win here, but might be included in the two-holes of exactas.

7th Santa Anita

1 1-16 MILES
SANTA ANITA
START · FINISH

1 1/16 MILES. (1.40⅘) ALLOWANCE. Purse $38,000. 4-year-olds and upward which are non-winners of $3,000 twice other than maiden, claiming or starter. Weights, 4-year-olds, 120 lbs.; older, 121. Non-winners of two races other than claiming at one mile or over since November 16 allowed 2 lbs.; of such a race other than maiden or claiming since then, 4 lbs.

Boo Boo's Buckaroo — B. g. 4, by Kris S—Merry Graustark, by Graustark
HAWLEY S — 116 — Br.—Meadowbrook Farms Inc (Fla) — Tr.—Palma Hector O
Own.—Vicki-Beth Stables Inc
Lifetime 28 4 1 7 $86,050

1988	2	0	0	0		$2,625
1987	20	4	0	5		$74,100
Turf	10	1	0	3		$33,750

10Jan88-5SA	7f	$:22^2$	$:44^4$	$1:22^1$ft	22	115	75¼	53½	54	43	Pedroza MA 1	Aw35000	86-15	ReEnter,Fanticola,Buckland'sHalo	10
3Jan88-9SA	1 1/16	$:46^3$	$1:10^4$	1:43 ft	8½	111^5	60	—	—	—	Banderas AL 6	Aw38000	— —	‡VlntCougr,LckyHroldH.,Incndktor	8
3Jan88—Lost rider; Hit rail 3 1/2															
20Dec87-5Hol	7f	$:22^1$	$:45^1$	$1:22^3$ft	12	110^5	52½	31	21	32½	Gryder A T 1	62500	88-08	J.R.Johnson,Spccpt,BooBoo'sBckro	8
6Dec87-9Hol	1⅛Ⓣ	$:49^1$	$1:13^2$	1:52 yl	12	113	54½	43	43	43½	Hawley S 2	Aw40000	64-29	FivDddyFiv,L'Empir,CrtivFinncing	12
6Dec87—Steadied start															
16Nov87-5SA	1⅛Ⓣ	$:47^2$	1:12	$1:50^4$fm	19	113	31½	2½	1hd	44½	Hawley S 8	Aw33000	68-34	Chess Set, L'Empire, Feraud	12
18Oct87-5SA	1⅛Ⓣ	$:46^4$	$1:11^2$	$1:49^1$fm	16	113	55	95¼	75½	66¾	Pedroza MA 5	Aw33000	74-15	GoodThoughtWlly,Ephrts,L'Empr	10
18Oct87—Wide into stretch															
26Sep87-11Fpx	1 1/16	$:45^2$	$1:10^3$	$1:43^1$ft	7¾	119	89	88¼	811	812¼	SornsnD 4	ⓇDerby Trl	83-11	DistntPl,TemptationTime,Nourishd	10
5Sep87-5Dmr	1 1/16Ⓣ	$:47^1$	$1:12^1$	1:43 fm	3¼	116	813	86½	77½	46¾	DelahoussayeE 5	70000	78-13	CrosLove,ContctGme,PrcDesPrincs	9
27Aug87-7Dmr	1 Ⓣ	$:47^1$	$1:11^1$	1:37 fm	19	116	77	74½	63¼	4½	DelhoussyeE 3	Aw26000	85-14	DarkPromise,GeorgiaRiver Delpre	10
22Aug87-7Dmr	1 1/16Ⓣ	:48	$1:11^3$	1:43 fm	16	113^5	76¾	87¼	88¾	88¾	Gryder A T 5	Aw26000	76-15	JustBobby,MagnaPlus,Uptothehilt	10

Dec 31 SA 4f m $:51^1$ h ●Dec 18 Hol 4f sy $:47^1$ h Nov 25 SA 4f ft $:47^1$ h

Red And Blue
Ch. c. 4, by Vigors—Greenbriar Girl, by Nearctic
VALENZUELA P A 116
Br.—Hawn W R (Ky) 1988 1 0 0 0
Tr.—Lewis Craig A 1987 15 0 2 1 $47,550
Own.—Glazer Lauren Lifetime 21 2 2 1 $74,125 Turf 2 0 0 0

10Jan88-5SA 7f :222 :444 1:221ft 10 115 89½ 87½ 87 74¾ ValenzuelPA5 Aw35000 84-15 ReEnter,Fanticola,Buckland'sHalo 10
10Jan88—Bumped, stumbled start; wide 3/8 turn
27Dec87-5SA 6½f :214 :444 1:163ft 24 116 76½ 76 75½ 31¾ ValenzuelPA9 Aw35000 85-17 WndwoodLn,TmForSkrt,RdAndBl 10
27Dec87—Wide into stretch
19Dec87-10Hol 1⅛ :463 1:10 1:40 gd 6½ 114 42½ 42¾ 614 622½ Cordero AJr4 Aw40000 80-10 Power Forward, Rupperto, Bananas 7
19Dec87—Hit gate at start
13Dec87-5Hol 7f :22 :45 1:223ft 14 114 86 64½ 45½ 46¾ Santos J A8 Aw36000 84-13 TddyBrHug,OrchrdSong,LoclsOnly 10
13Dec87—Crowded start
28Nov87-8Hol 1⅛ :47 1:112 1:432ft 3½ 116 54½ 43 54½ 41¾ DelhoussyeE2 Aw35000 84-12 Captain Valid, Be Scenic, Rupperto 7
6Nov87-8SA 7f :231 :46 1:233m 8½ 116 54½ 59 55½ 44½ DelahoussayeE3 ⓇTell 78-24 NoMrkr,HotAndSmoggy,SludYPsts 5
25Oct87-5SA 1⅛ :46 1:102 1:423gd 9 114 67½ 33 44 44½ Stevens G L1 Aw32000 84-19 Light Sabre, Midnight Ice, Fracoza 8
11Oct87-7SA 1⅛ :451 1:093 1:422ft 14 114 912 710 55½ 46½ Stevens G L9 Aw33000 82-14 No Marker, Valiant Cougar,Fracoza 9
31May87-9Hol 1 :444 1:093 1:343ft 8¾ 117 74¾ 79½ 721 — Pincay L Jr3 Aw27000 — — Candi's Gold, Pewter, No Marker 7
31May87—Eased; Stumbled start
23May87-8Hol 1⅛Ⓣ:463 1:111 1:43 fm 83 113 87 98½ 924 — PdrzMA1 Wl Rgrs H — — SomethingLucky,TheMedic,Persvrd 9
23May87—Grade III; Eased
Jan 7 SA 4f ft :48 h Dec 7 Hol 4f m :474 h Nov 23 Hol 5f ft 1:014 h

Midnight Ice
Gr. g. 5, by Zamboni—Je Reviens, by Beloved
GRYDER A T 112⁵
Br.—Longden E J (Cal) 1987 12 1 4 2 $52,450
Tr.—Longden Eric J 1986 6 1 1 0 $17,365
Own.—Longden E J Lifetime 18 2 5 2 $69,815 Turf 8 1 3 1 $39,375

26Nov87-8Hol 1 :451 1:092 1:352ft 13 112 21 44½ 610 612 MezRQ4 ⓈOn Trust H 74-18 CrosLove,MrkChip,TommyTheHwk 6
16Nov87-5SA 1¼Ⓣ:472 1:12 1:504fm *2 117 11 1½ 3½ 55¾ Pincay L Jr9 Aw33000 67-34 Chess Set, L'Empire, Feraud 12
25Oct87-5SA 1⅛ :46 1:102 1:423gd 7¾ 117 46½ 44 21 2nk Pincay L Jr6 Aw32000 88-19 Light Sabre, Midnight Ice, Fracoza 8
9Oct87-8SA 1 Ⓣ:464 1:11 1:363fm 6½ 117 21 31 2hd 31½ Solis A2 Aw36000 90-08 Putting, Dark Promise,MidnightIce 8
9Oct87—Steadied 3/8
5Sep87-8Dmr 1⅛Ⓣ:462 1:104 1:421fm 33 112 46½ 44 53½ 53 SolsA4 ⓇEscondido H 86-13 CptinVigors,ConquringHro,RchErth 8
5Sep87—Crowded stretch; took up 1/8
27Aug87-7Dmr 1 Ⓣ:471 1:111 1:37 fm 5½ 117 31½ 42 41½ 51½ Pedroza MA9 Aw26000 85-14 DarkPromise,GeorgiaRiver,Delpre 10
6Aug87-5Dmr 1⅛Ⓣ:481 1:114 1:431fm 4 117 1½ 11½ 1hd 2½ Pedroza MA2 Aw25000 83-16 WrDbt,MdnghtIc,BooBoo'sBuckroo 9
23May87-10GG 1⅛Ⓣ:473 1:112 1:432fm *1 122 31½ 31 1½ 2½ Solis A1 Aw19000 84-20 GallantHawk,MidnightIce,DrbyBoss 8
6May87-8Hol 1⅛Ⓣ:464 1:101 1:403fm 11 121 52 31½ 1½ 21 Pedroza MA3 Aw27000 90-11 ArcticBlastII,MidnightIce,Starsalot 9
17Apr87-5SA 1⅛Ⓣ:454 1:102 1:472fm 21 117 42 21 1hd 11 Pedroza MA2 Aw31000 90-14 MidnightIce,ThreshItOut,HloHtch 10
Jan 14 SA Ⓣ 1 fm 1:453 h (d) Jan 8 SA 7f ft 1:262 h Jan 2 SA 5f gd 1:013 h Dec 28 SA 5f ft 1:031 h

Fancy Oats
Ch. g. 4, by Properantes—Gold Chain, by King's Balcony
MCCARRON C J 116
Br.—Headley & Pegram (Cal) 1988 1 0 0 0
Tr.—Headley Bruce 1987 5 2 2 0 $38,650
Own.—Headley & Rancho RioHondo Lifetime 6 2 2 0 $38,650

10Jan88-5SA 7f :222 :444 1:221ft *2½ 117 65 64½ 65½ 64½ DelhoussyE10 Aw35000 84-15 ReEnter,Fanticola,Buckland'sHalo 10
10Jan88—Fanned 6 wide into drive
2Dec87-3Hol 6½f :22 :45 1:162ft 3 108⁵ 63¾ 44½ 23 1hd Gryder A T7 Aw29000 96-16 FancyOats,Athlone,GoldenGauntlet 7
4Sep87-5Dmr 7f :22 :444 1:221ft *2½ 114 89½ 75½ 63 43½ ShoemkerW5 Aw22000 88-16 KingOfBazar,Athlone,Bride'sAdvice 8
4Sep87—Wide into stretch
14Aug87-3Dmr 6½f :22 :451 1:163ft *4-5 113 53½ 44 43 2¾ ShoemkrW3 ⓈAw21000 88-17 IrishRobbery,FancyOats,TahoeTngo 6
14Aug87—Crowded backstretch
31Jly87-3Dmr 6f :214 :443 1:102ft 5¾ 114 79 78 45 2nk ShoemkrW1 ⓈAw21000 86-17 AsInEagles,FancyOts,IrishRobbery 8
5Apr87-6SA 6½f :214 :45 1:171ft 8½ 117 1011 75½ 32½ 11½ Shoemaker W1 Mdn 84-16 Fancy Oats, Acquired, Social Man 10
5Apr87—Broke slowly; wide 3/8
●Jan 5 SA tr.t 5f ft :593 h Dec 31 SA 5f m 1:032 h Dec 26 SA 5f ft 1:002 h Nov 28 SA 5f ft 1:01 h

Fiction
Ch. c. 4, by Perrault—Fact, by Dancing Moss
SHOEMAKER W 118
Br.—Brdly-Chndlr-Whittngham (Ky) 1987 3 2 1 0 $40,500
Tr.—Whittingham Charles 1986 2 M 0 1 $3,300
Own.—Bradley-Chndlr-Whttngham Lifetime 5 2 1 1 $43,800

24Dec87-9Hol 1⅛ :47 1:113 1:49 ft 2 118 12 1hd 2½ 12½ ShoemkerW3 Aw36000 92-10 Fiction, The Great Prize, Sinforoso 7
24Dec87—Very wide into drive
9Dec87-4Hol 1 :46 1:112 1:364ft *2-3 118 62½ 52½ 3nk 1¾ Shoemaker W4 Mdn 79-16 Fiction, FortyGrand,FortunateHour 9
19Nov87-6Hol 6f :222 :453 1:10 ft 4½ 118 41½ 41½ 43 23½ Shoemaker W3 Mdn 88-14 Dance For Lee, Fiction, Diarmaid 7
19Nov87—Boxed in 3/8 turn
25Oct86-6SA 1⅛ :464 1:112 1:442ft 6 117 75¾ 46 46 34½ Kaenel J L7 Mdn 75-17 On The Line, Thunder Cat, Fiction 8
25Oct86—Lugged in stretch
11Oct86-6SA 6½f :214 :444 1:172ft 18 117 1014 1015 712 710½ Kaenel J L12 Mdn 73-17 JustBobby,Brb'sRls,ExclusvEnogh 12
Jan 19 SA 3f gd :364 h Jan 16 SA 3f ft :352 h ●Jan 11 SA 1 ft 1:38 h Jan 6 SA 5f ft 1:002 h

Valiant Cougar
B. g. 5, by Naskra—Valiente, by Cougar II
STEVENS G L 117
Br.—Hancock III & Peters (Ky) 1988 1 0 1 0 $7,600
Tr.—Mitchell Mike 1987 13 3 2 0 $62,975
Own.—Alxndr-Blmonte-Popvichetal Lifetime 19 4 4 0 $87,625 Turf 2 0 0 0

3Jan88-9SA 1⅛ :463 1:104 1:43 ft 7 112⁵ 1hd 1hd 1½ 1¾ †Gryder A T3 Aw38000 86-17 ‡VlntCougr,LckyHroldH.,Incndrkor 8
3Jan88—Drifted in, bumped late; †Disqualified and placed second
18Dec87-3Hol 1⅛ :472 1:121 1:444m *8-5 111⁵ 1hd 1½ 13 18½ Gryder A T3 40000 79-22 ValiantCougar,Hrrison'sTurn,LeCid 5
9Dec87-5Hol 1¼ :462 1:112 1:501ft *2½ 111⁵ 31½ 11½ 1hd 22 Gryder A T3 32000 84-16 Rampour, Valiant Cougar, Air Alert 8
27Nov87-6Hol 1⅛ :462 1:11 1:434ft 3 116 2½ 1hd 31 46½ Vasquez J3 40000 78-18 PassPassPassed,Bedouin,ThoeTngo 7

25Oct87-5SA 1 1/16 :46 1:10² 1:42³gd 6¾ 117 11½ 11 33 810¼ McCarronCJ 4 Aw32000 78-19 Light Sabre, Midnight Ice, Fracoza 8
11Oct87-7SA 1 1/16 :45¹ 1:09³ 1:42²ft 5¾ 117 2hd 1½ 22½ 25½ McCarronCJ 4 Aw33000 83-14 No Marker, Valiant Couga ,Fracoza 9
18Jly87-6Hol 1 1/16 :46 1:10² 1:42¹ft *3 117 1hd 2hd 69½ 716½ Pincay L Jr 1 50000 81-07 He's A Saros, Breu, PowerForward 8
9Jly87-9Hol 1 1/16 :45¹ 1:09³ 1:43²ft 4½ 116 22½ 68½ 812 719¾ Meza R Q 4 62500 72-15 Mschfnmnd,PnstrpII,EghtyBlowZr 8
30May87-5Hol 1⅛ :46² 1:11 1:50 ft 4¾ 117 11 11 13 13 Pincay L Jr 7 50000 87-14 ValiantCougar,ForeignLegion,Poley 9
15May87-9Hol 1⅛ Ⓣ:47 1:10² 1:47 fm 7 117 3½ 21½ 78 720¾ Pincay L Jr 6 62500 72-12 Sherkin, Shanaar, Snowcreek 7
Jan 13 Hol 5f ft 1:00³ h

Syrian Wind
VELASQUEZ J **118**
Own.—Hibbert R E
B. c. 4, by Damascus—Wind Spirit, by Round Table
Br.—Hibbert R E (Ky) 1987 5 2 1 1 $39,875
Tr.—Manzi Joseph 1986 0 [illegible] 0 0
Lifetime 5 2 1 1 $39,875
26Dec87-9SA 1 :45⁴ 1:11¹ 1:38¹ft 4 118 1½ 1½ 1½ 1no Cordero A Jr 2 Aw34000 77-16 Syrian Wind,LuckyAdvance,BooW. 10
6Dec87-7Hol 1 :45 1:10¹ 1:37¹gd *2¼ 119 46 57½ 56½ 55¾ DelhoussyeE 5 Aw35000 71-17 Fanticola, Barnhart, Shigamba 7
14Nov87-4SA 1 1/16 :48 1:12⁴ 1:45²ft *8-5 117 1½ 1hd 1½ 11¾ Delahoussaye E 7 Mdn 74-22 Syrian Wind, Silver Dude, Vysotsky 9
11Oct87-6SA 6f :21² :44² 1:09²ft 5½ 117 32½ 21½ 22½ 21¾ Delahoussaye E 7 Mdn 89-14 JustIdeas,SyrianWind,Man'sIntent 10
14Sep87-2Dmr 6½f :22 :45 1:16⁴ft 7½ 117 65½ 55¾ 65 33 Delahoussaye E 8 Mdn 85-19 Chinati, Price, Syrian Wind 9
Jan 16 SA 5f ft 1:00³ h Jan 10 SA 7f ft 1:26³ h Jan 3 SA 4f ft :50 h Dec 16 Hol 1 ft 1:41² h

Glory Forever
DELAHOUSSAYE E **116**
Own.—Brdtt-Coutts-Lskr-Psce Etal
Gr. c. 4, by Forever Casting—Fager's Glory, by Mr Prospector
Br.—Peskoff S D (Ky) 1988 1 0 0 1 $5,250
Tr.—Drysdale Neil 1987 5 0 1 1 $38,181
Lifetime 12 2 1 2 $79,505 Turf 12 2 1 2 $79,505
3Jan88-5SA a6½f Ⓣ:22 :45 1:15⁴fm *9-5 116 106¾ 86¼ 66 36 DelhoussyeE 8 Aw35000 74-23 Crystal Run,KingHill,GloryForever 12
3Jan88—Broke slowly
16Aug87 ♦ 3Deauville(Fra) a1 1:35 gd 57 121 Ⓣ 819 RndB PxJacqsLeMrois(Gr1) Miesque, Nashmeel, Hadeer 9
16Jun87 ♦ 3Ascot(Eng) 1 1:43²gd 28 126 Ⓣ 59½ AsssC StJames'sPalace(Gr2) Half aYear, Soviet Star, Risk Me 5
31May87 ♦ 5Longchamp(Eng) a1⅛ 1:56²yl 6 128 Ⓣ 67 EddryP Px Jean Prat(Gr1) Risk Me, Soviet Star, Bengal Fire 9
10May87 ♦ 5Longchamp(Fra) a1 1:36¹gd 41 128 Ⓣ 31¼ EddrP PleEssaiPoulns(Gr1) SovietStr,NobleMinstrl,GloryForvr 14
18Apr87 ♦ 5Kempton(Eng) 1 1:43²gd 14 129 Ⓣ 24 EddryP BonusprintEaster ShdyHghts,GloryForvr,MntnKngdm 7
18Nov86 ♦ 6StCloud(Fra) a1¼ 2:23⁴sf 29 126 Ⓣ 54 VlszJ Criterium deStCloud(Gr2) Magistros, SirDavid,GroomDancer 15
17Oct86 ♦ 5StCloud(Fra) a7½f 1:36¹gd 12 119 Ⓣ 1nk VlszJ Px Thomas Byron(Gr3) GloryForever,Libertine,HrlmShuffl 7
29Aug86 ♦ 4Sandown(Eng) 7f 1:29²gd 8½ 126 Ⓣ 75 Lowe J Solario (Gr3) Shining Water, Sanam, Lockton 11
8Jly86 ♦ 1Newmarket(Eng) 7f 1:28³gd 3½ 126 Ⓣ 1nk Lowe J JoStewart(Mdn) GloryForever,Nordavano,SntellSm 10
Jan 13 Hol 5f ft 1:01³ h Jan 8 Hol 3f ft :36¹ h ●Dec 30 Hol 5f gd :59³ h Dec 24 Hol 5f ft 1:00¹ h

If Syrian Wind had sustained its four-furlong figure at the second pace call, that colt could become a problem, but its par figure of 103 at the second call put it securely in arrears of Valiant Cougar at that junction, with scarcely a chance to catch up.

On speed and pace figures, Valiant Cougar looked unbeatable here, and he might inherit an early speed advantage besides.

Convinced they were staring the sweetest bet of the young season in the face, our three heroes decided upon prime bets to win. Valiant Cougar entered the gate at 5–1 in a race the public judged wide open. I took Valiant Cougar on top of Fiction in multiple exactas as well, which did me no good.

But Valiant Cougar won in a breeze, by 7½ official lengths. The result chart documents just how airtight the case for Valiant Cougar would be.

SEVENTH RACE
Santa Anita
JANUARY 20, 1988

1 1/16 MILES. (1.40⅗) ALLOWANCE. Purse $38,000. 4-year-olds and upward which are non-winners of $3,000 twice other than maiden, claiming or starter. Weights, 4-year-olds, 120 lbs.; older, 121. Non-winners of two races other than claiming at one mile or over since November 16 allowed 2 lbs.; of such a race other than maiden or claiming since then, 4 lbs.
Value of race $38,000; value to winner $20,900; second $7,600; third $5,700; fourth $2,850; fifth $950. Mutuel pool $322,538. Exacta pool $395,312.

Last Raced	Horse	Eqt.A.Wt	PP	St	¼	½	¾	Str	Fin	Jockey	Odds $1
3Jan88 9SA1	Valiant Cougar	b 5 117	6	2	1¹	1¹	1³	1⁵	17½	Stevens G L	5 60
10Jan88 5SA7	Red And Blue	4 116	2	7	8	7hd	71½	4½	21½	Sibille R	[illegible]
26Nov87 8Hol6	Midnight Ice	b 5 112	3	3	41½	3¹	22½	21½	3nk	Gryder A T5	13 70
24Dec87 9Hol1	Fiction	4 118	5	8	7²	8	8	61½	41½	Shoemaker W	5 60
10Jan88 5SA4	Boo Boo's Buckaroo	b 4 116	1	4	6½	61½	6½	7⁵	5nk	Hawley S	13 00
10Jan88 5SA6	Fancy Oats	4 116	4	6	53½	52½	51½	31½	61¾	Meza R Q	7 60
26Dec87 9SA1	Syrian Wind	4 118	7	1	2hd	41½	4½	5½	7⁹	Velasquez J	24 60
3Jan88 5SA3	Glory Forever	4 116	8	5	3½	2¹	3½	8	8	Delahoussaye E	3 80

OFF AT 3:52. Start good. Won ridden out. Time, :23¼, :46¾, 1:11, 1:36¼, 1:42¾. Track fast.

$2 Mutuel Prices:

6–VALIANT COUGAR	13.20 7.00	5.00
2–RED AND BLUE	16.00	11.00
3–MIDNIGHT ICE		8.20

$5 EXACTA 6–2 PAID $453.00.

B. g, by Naskra—Valiente, by Cougar II. Trainer Mitchell Mike. Bred by Hancock III & Peters (Ky).

VALIANT COUGAR, a pace factor from the outset, drew off in the final three furlongs RED AND BLUE far back early, was along for the place. MIDNIGHT ICE, close up early, weakened in the drive FICTION, devoid of early speed after breaking a bit awkwardly, failed to threaten. BOO BOO'S BUCKAROO was four wide into the stretch FANCY OATS had no apparent mishap. SYRIAN WIND, prominent early, gave way GLORY FOREVER, prominent early faltered.

Owners— 1, Alxndr-Blmonte-Popvich et al. 2. Glazer Lauren. 3. Longden E J. 4. Bradley-Chndlr-Whttngham 5. Vicki-Beth Stables Inc; 6. Headley & Rancho Rio Hondo. 7. Hibbert R E. 8. Brdtt-Coutts-Lsar-Pice Et al

Trainers— 1, Mitchell Mike; 2. Lewis Craig A. 3, Longden Eric J. 4. Whittingham Charles. 5 Pajma Hector

O: 6, Headley Bruce; 7. Manzi Joseph; 8. Drysdale Neil

Postscript. Valiant Cougar's winning figures and race shape looked like this: 105/ 104 111 107 FA.

ROUSSO'S RUN

Lee Rousso began to perform his cleverest handicapping tricks on January 24. Two days before, he had failed to cash a $4000 exacta three times by a photo.

He awakened on a Sunday. Rousso caught a moderate double ten times, the second-half winner having a tiny one-point figure edge but also a repeater sent forth from Mel Stute's barn, up a notch in claiming class. Rousso explained that Stute shines with claiming-class repeaters.

He took the 3rd and 5th races, coupling other logical contenders for a $290 exacta twice in the 5th, when the favorite appeared sore in the post parade.

Next Rousso focused on the triple, serial-bet variety, and the 6th through 8th races at Santa Anita.

The 7th offered a simulcast from Bay Meadows, the rich El Camino Real Derby for three-year-olds. The winner was a stick-out shipper from southern California, Ruhlmann ($7.20), and so was the exacta combination Rousso cashed six times, at $185 each. The place horse had earned a competitive figure down south.

On exchanging the tickets, Rousso revealed with justifiable pride that he had cashed seven consecutive simulcast bets at Santa Anita.

In the 6th Rousso used a strongly backed first starter against a slow field of maidens. It paid $6.80.

Alive in the triple, a $100 bet, to 6–5 favorite Sam Who in the feature, Rousso watched sorrowfully as the horse finished second to 13–1 outsider Prospector's Gamble. Happily, he had purchased a $3 saver to the long shot, and the triple, as it so often does, yielded a generous $1313.90. Payoffs of this degree have persuaded regular handicappers of southern California the triple has become the best bet on the program. Introduced by Santa Anita in 1987, the wager offers the small and moderate bettors an opportunity for a kill, as the syndicates have no incentive to dominate the pool. The odds returning Rousso's $1313.90 were 5–2, 2–1, and 13–1. A $3 win parlay yields $441, in contrast. One long shot amounts to a minor kill. Two means a bonanza. Three hits the jackpot, as much as $20,000, or odds of 6666–1!

Rousso cleared $3000 for the afternoon. He remarked, idly, that by using a hot trainer's horse in the 4th, a winner at 12–1, in the Pick 9, he would have had eight winners. No one picked eight winners that day. The payout would have amounted to $23,555.

Rousso picked up additional steam the next racing day, January 27. He again zeroed in on the triple.

The 8th race seven-furlong sprint stakes featured the return to competition of Laz Barrera's Mi Preferido, Hollywood Juvenile (Grade 2) winner, and considered by Rousso and Brohamer as Santa Anita opened, the leading West Coast candidate for local Derby laurels. A statistical improbable on dosage for the classics, his figures were undoubtedly best of the West. Rousso singled Mi Preferido.

He used four horses in the 7th, a nonwinners-once allowance sprint, 4up, and benefitted when a 5–1 shot overtook the 3–5 underlay near the wire.

The 6th was the interesting heat. Rousso singled a horse his companions bet to win. It was a mile for maidens, and a lesson in handicapping that will pay hefty dividends is contained in the past performances. Examine the six contenders' records below, and make a choice.

6th Santa Anita

1 MILE. (1.33⅗) **MAIDEN. Purse $27,000. 4-year-olds and upward. Fillies and mares. Weights, 4-year-olds, 119 lbs.; older, 120 lbs. (Non-starters for a claiming price of $32,000 or less in their last three starts preferred).**

Cat Call		Dk. b. or br. f. 4, by Cougar II—Cal Suite, by Native Charger	
GRYDER A T		Br.—Hancock III & Bradley Mary (Ky)	1988 1 M 0 1 $4,050
Own.—Bradley & Hancock III	1145	Tr.—Whittingham Charles	1987 1 M 0 0
		Lifetime 2 0 0 1 $4,050	

1Jan88-6SA 1 :472 1:123 1:384gd 3⅛ 1145 32 42 41 33 Gryder A T⁸ ⑤Mdn 71-22 Fleur De Lune, Elvia, Cat Call 8
13Dec87-4Hol 6f :222 :454 1:10¼ft 2⅛e1135 10¹⁰ 9⁷¼ 9¹⁵ 6¹⁴¾ Sherman A B⁴ ⑤Mdn 76-13 PrsonProft,Art'sProspctor,FncySc 10
13Dec87—Hesitated start, wide
Jan 20 SA 4f ft 1:15³h   Jan 13 Hol 5f ft 1:01⁴h   ●Jan 8 Hol 3f ft :35²h   Dec 28 Hol 5f ft 1:03h

Elvia
MCCARRON C J **119**
Own.—Taylor Mrs Shirley H
B. f. 4, by Roberto—Chain Bracelet, by Lyphard
Br.—W Lazy T Limited (Ky)
Tr.—Gosden John H M
Lifetime 8 0 4 1 $22,625
1988 2 M 1 1 $9,450
1987 5 M 3 0 $13,175

13Jan88-6SA 1 1/16 :464 1:12 1:453ft *2-3 119 44 44 43½ 33½ McCarron C J11 ⒻMdn 69-20 Alisha's Favorite, Fluttery, Elvia 12
1Jan88-6SA 1 :472 1:123 1:384gd *1 119 53½ 1½ 2½ 2¾ Meza R Q2 ⒻMdn 73-22 Fleur De Lune, Elvia, Cat Call 8
16Sep87-6Dmr 1 :461 1:11 1:354ft 2½ 116 21 1hd 1½ 2½ Meza R Q4 ⒻMdn 88-15 Legislative Dance, Elvia, HeartLock 9
16Sep87—Broke out, bumped
20Aug87-6Dmr 1 1/16 :461 1:104 1:432ft 3½ 116 31½ 2hd 21 2¾ Meza R Q5 ⒻMdn 82-19 Boldly Driven, Elvia, Catfish Lady 9
6Aug87-6Dmr 1 :461 1:111 1:362ft 5¼ 116 21 22½ 24 29 Toro F8 ⒻMdn 77-15 Oueee Bebe, Elvia, Fleur De Lune 10
12Jly87-3Hol 1 :442 1:091 1:351ft 3¾ 115 55½ 58 46½ 46 McCarron C J6 ⒻMdn 81-09 GoldenGlxy,OueeeBeb,Annoconnor 8
12Jly87—Stumbled start; wide 3/8 turn
27Jun87-6Hol 6f :22 :444 1:092ft 13 115 63¾ 64½ 56 57½ McCarron C J4 ⒻMdn 89-09 SummrDrss,Annoconnor,SonicDrm 8
9Oct86-4Bel 6f :223 :461 1:104ft 23 117 910 89¾ 713 812¾ Vasquez J13 ⒻMdn 75-18 Fold theFlag,SubtleBlend,Tchaika 13
Dec 28 Hol 5f ft 1:003 h Dec 23 Hol 5f ft 1:014 h Dec 14 Hol 1 ft 1:412 h ●Dec 8 Hol 7f gd 1:284 h

Slew Of Fortune
STEVENS G L **119**
Own.—Post & Spendthrift Fm Inc
B. f. 4, by Seattle Slew—Whydidju, by Tom Rolfe
Br.—Spendthrift Thbd Brdng No 1 (Ky)
Tr.—Barrera Lazaro S
Lifetime 8 0 3 1 $22,850
1988 2 M 1 1 $8,750
1987 6 M 2 0 $14,100

16Jan88-2SA 6f :211 :443 1.111ft *6-5 119 911 59½ 47 33¾ Stevens G L 6 ⒻMdn 78-20 QuenForbs,PutThCs,SlwOfFortun 11
16Jan88—Bumped start
8Jan88-6SA 6f :214 :453 1:113ft 4½ 119 77 64¾ 52¾ 2no Stevens G L 4 ⒻMdn 80-19 RpAtThDr,SlwOfFrtn,Art'sPrspctr 12
26Dec87-4SA 6½f :221 :46 1:18 ft 5½ 118 82¾ 75¼ 45 45½ Stevens G L 5 ⒻMdn 74-16 Suspiciously,FancySuce,BrbrAllen 11
26Dec87—Steadied at 3/8
13Dec87-4Hol 6f :222 :454 1:101ft 3½ 118 96¾ 86½ 813 715 Pincay L Jr 10 ⒻMdn 76-13 PrsonProft,Art'sProspctor,FncySc 10
5Dec87-4Hol 6½f :22 :452 1:181sy 2¾ 118 63½ 66½ 55½ 44¾ Cordero A Jr 1 ⒻMdn 82-17 ShyLight,StarOfLove,BarbarAllen 10
27Nov87-4Hol 1 1/16 :463 1:122 1:454ft *2 117 23 31½ 32 21¼ Pincay L Jr2 ⒻMdn 73-18 DncAllSummr,SlwOfFortun,Fluttry 7
20Nov87-4Hol 6f :221 :452 1:114ft *1-2 119 44 56½ 57 44¾ Santos J A1 ⒻMdn 78-13 Olympia's Spy, Our Amy,Mogadora 6
11Nov87-6SA 6f :22 :443 1:102ft 4½ 118 97¼ 86½ 65 27½ ♦Stevens G L11 ⒻMdn 78-18 TblFrolc,GypsyDncng,SlwOfFortn 11
11Nov87—Broke slowly, took up sharply 5/16, wide into stretch; ♦Dead heat
Dec 24 SA 3f ft :354 h

Fancy Sauce
VELASQUEZ J **119**
Own.—Yellow Ribbon Ranch
B. f. 4, by Sauce Boat—High Renaissance, by Acroterion
Br.—Jones B C (Ky)
Tr.—Marti Pedro Jr
Lifetime 8 0 3 3 $26,200
1987 4 M 3 1 $16,000
1986 4 M 0 2 $10,200

26Dec87-4SA 6½f :221 :46 1:18 ft 3 118 52 11 12 21 Pincay L Jr1 ⒻMdn 79-16 Suspiciously,FancySuce,BrbrAllen 11
13Dec87-4Hol 6f :222 :454 1:101ft 3¾ 118 4¾ 42½ 35 38 Cordero A Jr2 ⒻMdn 83-13 PrsonProft,Art'sProspctor FncySc 10
2Dec87-6Hol 6½f :221 :452 1:181ft *1 118 2½ 2½ 1hd 21¾ CordroAJr3 ⒻMc50000 85-16 Antoinetta, Fancy Sauce, Our Amy 8
20Feb87-6SA 6f :213 :443 1:093ft *3-2 117 2½ 21½ 23 27 VlenzulPA3 ⒻMc50000 83-16 FrostyFreeze,FncySuc,ThirdDown 12
20Feb87—Bobbled start
28Dec86-6SA 6f :214 :444 1:102ft 14 1125 55 55½ 56 45¾ Patton D B9 ⒻMdn 80-14 Aflot,TimelyReserve,Crol'sWonder 12
13Dec86-5Hol 6f :221 :454 1:104ft 5¾ 118 51½ 4¾ 34 37½ Vergara O11 ⒻMdn 82-09 Buryyourblf,Crol'sWondr,FncySuc 12
13Dec86—Wide stretch
30Nov86-6Hol 6f :213 :452 1:104ft 16 118 1hd 21 23½ 48½ Black C A 12 ⒻMdn 80-16 Dvl'sBrd,SmmrSonds,DncAllSmmr 12
30Nov86—Drifted out late
21Jly86-10LA 6f :221 :453 1:113ft 2e115 52½ 1hd 11½ 22¾ †CastnonAL5 ⒻSdlebck 82-12 ShrpMovinKris,‡FncySuce,Jon'sBu 6
†21Jly86—Disqualified and placed third
Jan 21 Hol 7f ft 1:283 h Jan 3 Hol 5f ft 1:024 h Dec 21 Hol 5f ft 1:001 h Dec 8 Hol 4f gd :494 h

Art's Prospector
HAWLEY S **119**
Own.—Paulson A E
B. f. 4, by Mr Prospector—No Duplicate, by Arts and Letters
Br.—King Ranch Inc (Ky)
Tr.—Scott George W
Lifetime 7 0 1 1 $9,350
1988 1 M 0 1 $3,750
1987 1 M 1 0 $5,600

8Jan88-6SA 6f :214 :453 1:113ft *3-5 119 21 3nk 2hd 3½ Hawley S1 ⒻMdn 79-19 RpAtThDr,SlwOfFrtn,Art'sPrspctr 12
13Dec87-4Hol 6f :222 :454 1:101ft 8¾ 118 1hd 2hd 1hd 2hd Hawley S6 ⒻMdn 91-13 PrsonProft,Art'sProspctor FncySc 10
15Nov86-6Hol 6f :22 :462 1:114ft 8-5e118 2hd 2hd 44 910¾ Meza R Q 1 ⒻMdn 73-14 TimelyAssertion,HiloBb,LivlyMiss 11
29Oct86-4SA 6f :212 :443 1:121ft 15 117 55 58 1011 1012¼ Pincay L Jr 2 ⒻMdn 65-17 Infringe, Folia,YouMakeMeHappy 12
1Sep86-4Dmr 1 :463 1:114 1:372ft 15 116 52½ 812 921 — DelahoussyeE 5 ⒻMdn — — TipASou,Rose'sCntin,AlwysAWomn 9
1Sep86—Eased
4Aug86-6Dmr 1 :46 1:123 1:384ft 3¾ 116 12 1hd 43½ 915½ Valenzuela PA 8 ⒻMdn 58-13 Picene, FlowerChain,KeepOnFlying 9
26Jly86-6Dmr 5½f :22 :46 1:044ft *9-5 116 84½ 64¾ 76¾ 99 Valenzuela PA 8 ⒻMdn 78-13 Moraima, Picene, Call Bock 11
26Jly86—Bumped, pinched back start
Jan 22 SLR tr.t 6f ft 1:154 h Jan 16 SLR tr.t 4f ft :50 h Dec 29 SLR tr.t 5f ft :593 h Dec 23 SLR tr.t 4f ft :48 h

```
*Daloma U-N T                    Gr. f. 4, by Bellypha—Ricabie, by Baldric
 SHOEMAKER W              119     Br.—Asterus S A & Resk (Fra)            1987  8 M  4 2    $31,735
 Own.—Enemy Stbs&MandyslandFm      Tr.—Whittingham Charles                 1986  2 M  0 2     $5,595
                                  Lifetime  10  0  4  4   $37,331          Turf 10  0  4  4    $37,331
30ct87♦6Longchamp(Fra) a1¼ 2:08²gd  12 117  ① 3½   DSm⑰M      ⑤Px Chas Lffit  Tortosa, MissEvans, Daloma       11
20Sep87♦2Longchamp(Fra) a1 1:43 gd  14 118  ① 7½   Legrix ℃   ⑤Px d Liancourt LouiseALaPlage,SilverArmd,Miny⑤K13
26Aug87♦2Deauville(Fra) a1¼ 2:14³sf *6-5 128 ① 4½  Head F     ⑤Px de Chmieres ArcticRiver, Halutz, SilverArch    9
2Aug87♦6Deauville(Fra) a1¼ 2:06⁴yl  3½ 123  ① 2½   Head F     ⑤Px de Dives   Rakisa, Daloma, Ruffle            13
27Jun87♦2Longchamp(Fra) a1¼ 2:11 yl 2½ 119  ① 2½   Head F     ⑤Px de Meudon  Karmiska, Daloma, Enlightened      9
8Jun87♦6StCloud(Fra) a1½ 2:19²gd   *3 121  ① 2ⁿᵈ   Head F     ⑤Px Seria     Enlightened, Daloma, Fille d'Eve   14
7May87♦7Longchamp(Fra) a1½ 2:34⁸gd  2½ 128  ① 3⁴   DSm⑰     ⑤Px d Neuilly(Mdn) Lutive, Crivjica, Daloma         8
17Apr87♦2StCloud(Fra) a1½ 2:16¹gd  14 126  ① 22   DStrM     ⑤Px Dushka(Mdn) Khariyda, Daloma, Crivjica         13
 Jan 26 SA 3f ft :35³h     Jan 21 SA 5f ft :59h    ●Jan 5 SLR tr4 7f ft 1:26³h    Dec 31 SLR tr4 6f ft 1:42h
```

Par was 98, and no horse's latest figure equaled par. An unreliable race? Only apparently so.

One horse actually stands apart.

First, handicappers must disregard Slew of Fortune, a not atypical unreliable low-priced also-ran. Daloma received heavy action (5–2), but its record insists it be forgotten. If she wins, she wins, but why bet on it? Daloma finished a strong second.

Now look closely again at Art's Prospector, which not only won by 3½ lengths, but earned a figure of 102, four lengths better than par.

The outcome was predictable.

Art's Prospector personifies the "bounce pattern," a tricky aspect of form analysis not to be confused with Thoro-Graph's "bounce-back" from high speed figures to lower figures.

The bounce pattern of form analysis embraces these characteristics:

1. A lengthy layoff, often of four months or longer
2. A good race, but overexerting effort, the first race back
3. A disappointing performance the second race back, usually dispensed at low odds following the comeback race, and occurring within four weeks of the comeback race
4. A resurgence to top form in the third race following the layoff.

The second race in the series represents the "bounce," the third race the "bounce-back." The inviting aspect of the pattern finds low odds in the second race, when the horse loses, and significantly better odds in the third race, when the horse bounces back and wins.

Art's Prospector illustrates the pattern perfectly. Off since November 15, 1986, some thirteen months, the filly earned a splendid figure against a nice opponent December 13. The effort proved too taxing, however, and Art's Prospector "bounced" at 3–5 January 8, earning a figure of 94 in a slow-slow race. If this filly reverted to its sharp form today, at 5–1, thank you, Art's

Prospector should romp against this below-average field.

When Art's Prospector did romp, she triggered a $267 triple, which Rousso multiplied by 8½ tickets, collecting $2269.50.

For dessert, Rousso invested $200 in a predictable two-horse exacta box in the 9th, $140 worth supporting his top choice on top. It came that way. He cashed a $68 payoff 28 times, collecting $1904.

Bottom line for the day: $4300 net.

Trickles of profits spiced Rousso's run for the next nine racing days, until February 10, when another thunderstorm struck.

Rousso likes older claiming horses with early speed entered under nonwinners-once allowances limited to 4up. It's often a smart play, the aging nonwinners lacking real ability, and the public suspecting the claiming horses are moving into the allowance division too ambitiously, when they are not.

Under exactly those allowances February 10, Rousso spotted a 16–1 shot with high early speed, and on Lasix for the first time following a poor mud effort. Its final figures looked dull but not dismal. Named Threegees, Rousso keyed the claiming horse in exacta boxes with a 3–2 favorite that figured to win on cold dope, and on top of a generous second choice (5–1) which might regress off a winning race—not overly strenuous—and ten-month layoff.

When the 3–2 favorite Torres Vedras, in front wraps, stumbled badly out of the gate, Threegees sped to the front uncontested. It coasted for five-eighths, and lasted by a half length over the late-running second favorite. The exacta paid $425, and Rousso exchanged four tickets. Luck played a role here, an influence that often propels a red-hot run.

The next afternoon, 9th race, Rousso pieced together a three-horse exacta box in a $16,000 ten-furlong claiming marathon, and pocketed another $612.

The next afternoon, February 12, day thirty-seven, Rousso's dad joined him from Seattle for a day at the races, and Lee announced he expected good things to happen.

"My father played different horses all afternoon," said Rousso later, shaking his head regrettably. The father recalled the races not so fondly, as the son slaughtered the card, recording his biggest earnings of the season.

Nothing happened until the 5th. It was a $32,000 claiming race at six furlongs, and Rousso hooked two horses exiting the fastest race versus similar in multiple exactas. They finished one-two, the exacta paying $142, Rousso cashing six tickets.

In the 6th Rousso backed a maiden with strong figures dropping into a maiden-claiming route, and the good thing waltzed home by ten. Late betting on the horse lowered fancier odds to 7–2.

As the odds to win dropped, Rousso coupled the maiden dropdown and another horse in the 6th with singles in the 7th and 8th in the triple. He risked a prime amount, $200.

"You have to play aggressively in the exotics you like," is how he boiled down the wagering philosophy. "That's the chance you're waiting for, the chance for the sudden kill."

His filly in the 7th, a 5–2 co-favorite that had stopped near the wire twice on tiring surfaces, today stayed in front easily.

In the 8th, a downhill turf specialist returning from a seven-month absence in a highly restricted classified allowance grass sprint outran a listless band as the 8–5 favorite.

The triple was meager, at $78. Rousso had hammered it 33⅓ times, however, and collected $2613.

He saved the best for last, in the 9th catching a speed horse on a stretchout while moving ahead in claiming class, a typical Rousso maneuver. Since Rousso's mare was changing distance following one sprint and a seven-month layoff, would be breaking from the far outside at a flat mile, and worst of all, would steal the bacon from the filly I liked at 32–1, I demanded of Rousso a detailed explanation.

"This was my trip horse of the year," he exaggerated, on purpose, to rub my nose in it. "Since Del Mar she had changed hands for the better, too, going to trainer Jacque Fulton."

That was no exaggeration.

We had already agreed Ms. Fulton had been impressive with everything she had sent forth. She had become an underrated, unknown training commodity we wanted to support whenever plausible.

Jacque Fulton had sprinted Irish Kristen for a $25,000 tag in her comeback race, and today raised her to a $32,000 route, a tough double-jump up and confident maneuver.

"Irish Kristen was five wide all the way in the sprint," continued Rousso, long after I cared to hear no more, "and was bumped hard at the gate. I think she should have won that race."

The crowd concurred, I guess, making Irish Kristen its lukewarm 3–1 choice in the route. Rousso risked $280 to win, plus $40 exacta boxes coupling my long shot. He needed Fulton's mare as well for five of six winners in the Pick 6 parlay, a consolation prize.

Irish Kristen broke sharply, tracked a frontrunner on the inside for six furlongs, and breezed to the wire to win by 5½. She paid $9.80 to win, the exacta paid $90, and the Pick 5 consolation paid $951. Rousso raped the race for $3043.

Escorting Dad to the airport that Sunday in mid-afternoon, Rousso mentioned he had won $7300 on Friday, and although horses had been a battle of wits between the two for years, suggested it was too bad he, Dad, did not use the same horses and action. Lou Rousso endured a long flight home, as the vanquished do.

The next afternoon, Saturday, the 3rd and 5th races were preliminary nonwinners allowances for 4up, the 3rd at a 1¼M on grass, the 5th at 6½ furlongs on dirt. In each, Rousso preferred horses exiting $40,000 claiming races. Both won. Payoffs on the seemingly class-climbing claiming horses were splendid, as usual, the first winner returning $12.60, the second $11.80.

Where winter racing occurs, handicappers can keep an eye peeled for the same clever maneuver. If the claiming upstarts possess the high figures, and the races are limited to older horses that have not yet won an allowance race, perhaps two, chances are the allowance types will be dull and the claiming horses sharp. Some seasons the angle fires repeatedly, as it would at Santa Anita 1988 for Lee Rousso.

Rousso did not win a dime on Valentine's Day, but returned for an encore performance Monday, February 15, the fortieth day of racing.

He notched a small double, in the first half betting to win as well, a 2–1 shot exiting the fastest $10,000 claiming race of the season.

He bet $100 to win on a horse that barely survived in the 4th, a tough call, paying $11.80.

He caught a $50 exacta in the 5th ten times.

Soon came the feature and my biggest bet of the half season.

It was the Grade 2 San Luis Obispo Stakes, 4up, at 1½M on the turf. I had been awaiting Trokhos ever since he had set the blazing pace January 13 in the fastest turf route of a season when the grass had been playing five to six lengths slow every day, at times still slower.

When the crowd gave me 5–2, my $500 investment looked much grander already. Below are the records and latest figures for the main contenders.

8th Santa Anita

1½ MILES. (Turf). (2.23) 21st Running of THE SAN LUIS OBISPO HANDICAP (Grade II). $200,000 added. 4-year-olds and upward. By subscription of $200 each to accompany the nomination, $2,000 additional to start, with $200,000 added, of which $40,000 to second, $30,000 to third, $15,000 to fourth and $5,000 to fifth. Weights Wednesday, February 10. High weights preferred. Starters to be named through the entry box by the closing time of entries. A trophy will be presented to the owner of the winner. Closed Wednesday, February 3, 1988 with 19 nominations.

Trokhos
TORO F — 116
Own.—Kanowsky V
B. h. 5, by Tromos—Lusaka, by Tom Rolfe
Br.—McMakin & Snyder (Ky)
Tr.—Anderson Laurie N
Lifetime 16 5 5 3 $140,364
1988 2 0 1 1 $22,000
1987 7 3 2 0 $75,614
Turf 16 5 5 3 $140,364

30Jan88-11TuP 1⅛Ⓣ:4711:1111:482fm*3-2 117 53½ 1½ 12½ 31 Toro F10 Tu P H 97-06 Ifrad, Forkintheroad, Trokhos 10
13Jan88-7SA 1⅛Ⓣ:4541:1021:474fm*9-5 115 12½ 11½ 2½ 24 Toro F5 Aw60000 84-12 PoliticlAmbition,Trokhos,RichErth 5
27Sep87◆3Longchamp(Fra) a1⁵⁄₁₆ 2:043gd 8 123 Ⓣ 42 LequuxA Px Dollar(Gr2) TkfYmed,PortEtienne,HighstHonor 8
17Sep87◆3MLaffitte(Fra) a1⅛ 2:003gd 4½ 126 Ⓣ 21½ BrxJM LaCp dMLa(Gr3) Tabayaan, Trokhos, Mill Native 7
3Sep87◆4Bordeaux(Fra) a1⅛ : yl *9-5 130 Ⓣ 12 BruxJM G P D LaTeste Trokhos, Vigorine, Mapocho 9
3Sep87—No time taken
5Jly87◆6StCloud(Fra) a1⁵⁄₁₆ 2:09 gd 6-5 130 Ⓣ 11 Eddery P Px Fourire Trokhos, Manndesh, Family Friend 4
16May87◆4StCloud(Fra) a1½ 2:411sf 3½ 128 Ⓣ 615 VlsqzJ Px J d Chdny (Gr2) Lascaux, Village Star, Productive 9
14Apr87◆5StCloud(Fra) a1⁵⁄₁₆ 2:164yl *1 130 Ⓣ 12½ VelsquezJ Px Altipan Trokhos, Star Rose, Roi Normand 10
27Mar87◆5MLaffitte(Fra) a1⅞ 3:171sf *2½ 123 Ⓣ 21½ RegnardD Px Quicko Floma, Trokhos, Farid 14
●Feb 8 SA Ⓣ1 fm 1:384 h (d) Jan 27 SA 5f ft 1:002 h Jan 21 SA 4f ft :481 h Jan 10 SA 5f ft :594 h

***Forlitano**
SHOEMAKER W — 121
Own.—Evergreen Farm Thds Inc
B. h. 7, by Good Manners—Forlita, by Pardallo
Br.—Haras Ojo de Agua (Arg)
Tr.—Whittingham Charles
Lifetime 38 10 6 2 $596,995
1988 1 0 0 0 $11,250
1987 12 4 3 1 $431,850
Turf 22 6 6 1 $563,721

24Jan88-9SA 1¼Ⓣ:4731:3722:023fm 3 122 35 43½ 75 44½ VelsquzJ3 Sn Mrcs H 69-21 GrtCommnctor,Schllr,BlloHorzont 10
24Jan88—Grade III
13Dec87-8Hol 1½Ⓣ:4832:0222:27 fm 13 126 31½ 3nk 1hd 2nk VlnzulPA7 Trf Cp Iv 86-16 Vilzak,Forlitano,PoliticalAmbition 14
13Dec87—Grade I
29Nov87-8Hol 1⅛Ⓣ:4741:11 1:472fm 2½e 120 52 2½ 1hd 1½ VlnzulPA2 Citation H 91-11 Forlitano, Conquering Hero, Ifrad 12
29Nov87—Grade II
11Oct87-8SA 1¼Ⓣ:4821:3742:031fm 3½ 121 11 1hd 31½ 53½ Baze G1 C F Brk H 67-23 Rivlia, CaptainVigors,CircusPrince 10
11Oct87—Grade I
6Sep87-8AP 1¼Ⓣ:4821:3832:022fm 22 126 1½ 21 811 815½ Baze G1 Bud Arl Mil 66-27 Manila, Sharrood, Theatrical 8
6Sep87—Grade I
27Jly87-8Hol 1½Ⓣ:4641:5942:25 fm 7½ 122 44 1½ 1hd 22 Baze G8 Sunset H 95-08 Swink, Forlitano, Rivlia 10
27Jly87—Grade I
13Jun87-8GG 1½Ⓣ:4832:0312:28 fm *2 119 1½ 11 13 14 Baze G8 Rllng Grn H 97-12 Forlitano, Lord Grundy, Wylfa 9
13Jun87—Grade III
24May87-8GG 1⅜Ⓣ:4631:3632:141fm *2½ 120 2hd 32 43½ 46½ Baze G7 G G H 80-12 Rivlia, Air Display, Reco 8
24May87—Grade II
20Apr87-8SA 1¼Ⓣ:46 1:3411:591fm 3½ 120 1½ 1hd 1½ 1½ Baze G1 ⓇSn Jcnto H 91-06 Forlitano, Bello Horizonte, Reco 11
20Apr87—Broke out, bumped
4Apr87-8SA 1¼Ⓣ:4641:3532:002fm *2½ 120 42½ 52½ 43 32½ Baze G7 ⓇSt Grtrs H 83-16 Schiller, Wylfa, Forlitano 9
Feb 11 SA 5f ft 1:02 b Feb 5 SA 6f ft 1:134 h Jan 21 SA 5f ft 1:013 b Jan 16 SA 1 ft 1:374 h

Great Communicator
SIBILLE R — 117
Own.—Class Act Stable
B. g. 5, by Key to the Kingdom—Blaheen, by Beekeeper
Br.—Waitress James R (Ky)
Tr.—Ackel Thad D
Lifetime 32 6 6 6 $493,490
1988 1 1 0 0 $100,400
1987 14 2 4 4 $365,430
Turf 21 5 4 4 $479,360

24Jan88-9SA 1¼Ⓣ:4731:3722:023fm 12 115 21 21 1½ 1hd SibilleR 10 Sn Mrcs H 74-21 GrtCommnctor,Schllr,BlloHorzont 10
24Jan88—Grade III
13Dec87-8Hol 1½Ⓣ:4832:0222.27 fm 86 126 2hd 2hd 3½ 42½ Sibille R 8 Trf Cp Iv 83-16 Vilzak,Forlitano,PoliticalAmbition 14
13Dec87—Grade I
21Nov87-6Hol 1½Ⓣ:4712:0012.242fm 26 126 14 74 1215 1213½ CordrAJr 4 Br Cp Trf 86 — Theatrical,Trempolino,VillageStrII 14
21Nov87—Grade I
31Oct87-8Lrl 1¼Ⓣ:4631:3722:024fm 17 126 1hd 12½ 12 2nk DsrmxKJ 8 D C Intrnl 83-20 LeGloriux,GrtCommunictor,Motly 14
31Oct87—Grade I
18Oct87-10Lrl 1¼Ⓣ:4811:3712:002fm 4½ 113 24 22 31½ 31½ DsrmKJ 5 Turf Cup H 93-09 YnkAffr,MyBgBoy,GrtCommnctor 10
18Oct87—Grade III
26Sep87-10LaD 1⅜Ⓣ:4821:38 2:134fm 16 113 32½ 21 32 35½ TroschrAJ 1 La D H 91-10 Iades, Ifrad, Great Communicator 12
26Sep87—Grade III
7Sep87-8Dmr 1⅜Ⓣ:4921:38 2.134fm 27 115 1hd 2hd 64½ 76½ StvnsSA 3 Dmr Inv H 94-10 Swink, SantellaMac,SkipOutFront 12
7Sep87—Grade II
27Jly87-8Hol 1½Ⓣ:4641:5942:25 fm 19 112 33 62½ 42½ 43½ StevnsSA 4 Sunset H 94-08 Swink, Forlitano, Rivlia 10
27Jly87—Grade I; Shuffled back turn
12Jly87-9Hol 1⅟₁₆Ⓣ:4621:1021:412fm*6-5 118 1½ 1½ 11½ 1nk Stevens S A 1 Aw30000 87-13 GrtCommunctor,WorldCort,Cntnry 7
14Jun87-8Hol 1½Ⓣ:47 1:5942:241fm 12 112 1½ 1½ 21½ 24 StevnsSA 4 Hol Inv H 97-03 Rivlia, GreatCommunicator,Schiller 6
14Jun87—Grade I
Feb 12 Hol 5f ft 1:03 b Feb 7 Hol 6f ft 1:172 h Jan 21 Hol 5f ft 1:032 h Jan 16 Hol 5f ft 1:042 h

Trokhos	109/	134	125	115	FF	5–2
Forlitano	109/	101	110	106	AA	5–2
Great Communicator	109/	105	113	111	AA	11–1

Which did Rousso prefer, if any?

"I liked Trokhos best, but at the distance I thought Great Communicator a strong second choice, and a play at the odds."

With its full record in France just satisfactory, Trokhos's loss in the Turf Paradise Handicap might have scuttled thoughts of a prime bet, except for two excuses. The horse had bled in Phoenix, and would be medicated with Lasix first time today. Trokhos might have "bounced" legitimately as well, the out-of-town race its second following a four-month vacation and strenuous comeback race.

Moreover, and conclusively, Trokhos would control a leisurely pace today, a much slower pace than it had carved out January 13 against the multiple Grade 1 winner Political Ambition.

When bets were placed, Rousso split his money, putting half on his second choice, Great Communicator, an 11–1 overlay, who did show the second-highest figures. When you're hot, you're not only hot, you make the right decisions.

After being slightly headstrong early, Trokhos assumed the lead and relaxed. Great Communicator challenged ruggedly at the top of the stretch. Trokhos responded but could not hold his challenger at bay.

To my dismay, but Rousso's hurrah, Great Communicator drew away late, paid $24.20.

Rousso's booty for this day was $1500, but he seemed strangely detached from the scene.

"I'm not certain why, but I didn't bring a winning attitude to the races today," he remarked. "This could have been a huge day for me. It was good, but nothing like it might have been."

During the spree of winning, January 24 through February 15, or sixteen racing days, Rousso netted $14,000. Handicappers might notice the diverse factors that accompanied the procession of winners. From the top:

Jan. 24   trainer-body language-speed figures
Jan. 27   speed figures-form analysis
Feb. 10   early speed-Lasix-eligibility conditions
Feb. 12   speed figures-maiden dropdown-early speed plus distance switch-trips

Feb. 13   eligibility conditions, claiming to allowance
Feb. 15   improving form-overlay, second choice

With less than half the season gone, Rousso was ahead of Santa Anita's horses by $16,000.

BROHAMER'S RUN

An artistic handicapper in possession of state-of-the-art figures can be an inspiration when the horses have circled the course a time or two and his game begins to jell. ,

State-of-the-art figures depend upon projected times, in preference to pars, and these require an in-depth familiarity with the population of horses on the grounds. Reliance on pars, which are averages, renders the speed handicapper susceptible to errors, possibly gross, when final times are above or below par by several lengths; not because the track surface was fast or slow, but because a specific field was strong or weak. Using projected times, or predictions of how fast particular horses should run, as bases for calculating track variants, Brohamer avoids the grossest errors of figure handicapping. His figures can thus distinguish class-within-a-class and complete the enviable chore of identifying the very best runners at each class level. Recreational handicappers cannot reproduce the figures, and neither can speed handicappers relying on pars.

On January 31, the twenty-ninth day, Brohamer's figures began to cook and boil.

The 5th that day was carded at seven furlongs, a $62,500 claiming sprint, 4up, which brought together the fastest high-priced claiming sprinters in the barns. Par was 108.

Brohamer narrowed a large field quickly to four runners. Here are the speed and pace figures, race shapes, and class levels of their recent lines.

J. R. Johnson	109/	105	109	AA	$62,500
Bright and Right	109/	108	109	AA	$62,500
Quip Star	107/	109	109	AF	$50,000
Buckland's Halo	104/	104	106	AF	Alw, NW × MC

Pace figures separate the four cleanly, identifying the main contention as Bright and Right and Quip Star. I hope handicappers can track that reasoning.

In its last, Quip Star's turn time (fractional time between first and second calls of sprints, adjusted by lengths gained or lost between calls), was a remarkable 22 flat. Santa Anita's par, said Brohamer, was 23 flat. Bright and Right normally went 22 2/5 around the turn, an excellent pace.

At six furlongs, maybe 6½, Quip Star would have deserved the nod, even though Bright and Right has the classiest figures at $62,500 on the circuit. But its peaked form notwithstanding, Quip Star weakens at seven furlongs slightly. Bright and Right finds that extra gear.

The odds near post were: J. R. Johnson (3–1), Bright and Right (6–1), Quip Star (9–2), and Buckland's Halo (6–1).

Brohamer invested a prime wager of $200 to win on Bright and Right, and boxed that horse and Quip Star in multiple exactas.

Quip Star attended a rapid pace and surged to the front approaching the second call, completing the turn in 22 2/5 seconds, which is blazing.

Bright and Right chased the leader into the stretch and began to close the gap approaching the sixteenth pole. Quip Star finished evenly today, without tiring. But Bright and Right found extra energy and prevailed by three-quarters. The two left the others three lengths back, J. R. Johnson finishing third.

Bright and Right returned $14.20, the exacta $149.50. Brohamer grabbed $1500 from the race.

Same day, the 9th, a $25,000 claiming route, 4up, offered a tantalizing opportunity to prosper from speed and pace figures that towered over the field.

Examine the past performances below. Then review the latest figures of the four main contenders.

Kenai Dancer B. g. 5, by Marshua's Dancer—Misty Clarion, by Proud Clarion

HAWLEY S 116 Br.—Harris W C (Ky) 1988 1 0 1 0 $4,800

Own.—Moonshadow Stable Tr.—Lewis Craig A $25,000 1987 7 0 1 2 $8,955

Lifetime 20 2 5 2 $28,520

16Jan88-9SA 1 1/16 :46 1:111 1:434ft 16 116 21½ 21½ 25 26½ Hawley S7 25000 75-20 MoveFree,KenaiDancer,FstDelivery 9

27Dec87-2SA 6f :214 :444 1:10 ft 19 1115 64 55 46 48½ Banderas A L11 c20000 81-17 Savio, Courage Ruler,IdealQuality 11

4Dec87-5Hol 6f :221 :451 1:103ft 5½ 1115 108¼ 108¾ 107¾ 109¾ Banderas A L7 25000 79-21 RdwoodBoy,BolgrMgic,CuttingLin 11

4Dec87—Reared at start

22Nov87-1Hol 6f :22 :444 1:101ft 14 1125 75¼ 78½ 56½ 35¼ Banderas A L10 32000 86-14 MeYouAndQ.,NtiveRelity,KniDncr 10

7Nov87-1SA 6f :213 :442 1:112m 4½ 115 45 33½ 32 21¼ Valenzuela P A2 20000 79-26 And Justice,KenaiDancer,Dr.Reality 6

10Oct87-9AC 6f :221 :441 1:081ft 3½ 114 31 42½ 33 32¾ Martinez J C2 Aw6000 95-11 Fill Up, Starshield, Kenai Dancer 6

26Sep87-9AC 6f :23 :451 1:092ft 2¼ 114 51¾ 43½ 42 41 Lopez A D1 Aw6000 91-19 Fill Up, Cutting Line, Starshield 5

22Aug87-9AC 6f :221 :44 1:084ft 5 114 31 54½ 31½ — Enriquez H F1 Aw6000 — — Tomari, Maso Blue, Fill Up 6

22Aug87—Fell

8Nov86-4Hol 6f :22 :453 1:104ft 21 119 54½ 1118 — — Valenzuela P A6 25000 — — SprbMmnt,GrdnsCmmnd,FrrBlJns 11

8Nov86—Pulled up

29Oct86-1SA 6½f :214 :443 1:17 ft 11 118 41¾ 31 31½ 22¾ Valenzuela P A3 20000 82-17 LansManus,KeniDncer,PecefulImge 8

Jan 10 SA 5f ft :594 h Dec 24 SA 4f ft :47 h Dec 17 Hol 4f sy :482 h

Subito B. g. 4, by To the Quick—Zimbaba, by Bravest Roman

BLACK C A 115 Br.—Carl W A (Ky) 1988 3 1 0 0 $11,875

Own.—Richmond-Sears-Walsh Tr.—Richmond A B $25,000 1987 13 4 2 0 $40,525

Lifetime 16 5 2 0 $52,400

24Jan88-2SA 6½f :213 :442 1:164ft 7½ 115 — — — — Stevens G L3 25000 — — GrowlerSndue,Ssebo,RedwoodBoy 12

24Jan88—Lost rider; Bumped, clipped heels

16Jan88-1SA 6f :212 :442 1:11 ft 3½ 1105 21½ 21½ 1hd 12 Gryder A T1 c20000 83-20 Subito, Rising Pine, Agua Russo 10

3Jan88-2SA 6f :212 :442 1:11 ft 5 116 75 57 55 42¾ DelahoussyeE10 25000 80-17 Cliff'sPlc,SundncSqur,SuprmStnd 12

3Jan88—Bumped start

14Nov87-2SA 6f :212 :443 1:112ft 7¾ 1095 21½ 24 24 55 Banderas A L6 c22500 76-22 SwtwtrSprings,HighRgrds,Shrwdy 11

14Nov87—Bumped start

4Nov87-3SA 6f :22 :451 1:121sy *2½ 1115 3nk 2½ 2hd 2nk Banderas A L9 20000 77-26 Sharp Port, Subito, Royal Agori 9

18Oct87-1SA 6f :214 :45 1:104ft 5¼ 1115 1½ 11 12½ 14½ Banderas A L3 16000 84-15 Subito, Punch Bowl, Jazz Player 12

11Oct87-2SA 6½f :214 :45 1:171ft 3½ 1135 51¼ 2½ 3½ 64¾ Banderas A L7 20000 79-14 ColdNHrd,RoylAgori,Mr.Edelweiss 10

14Sep87-5Dmr 6f :22 :452 1:103ft *2¾ 118 2hd 2hd 2½ 65¾ Meza R Q4 20000 79-19 DelJunco,CminoBmbino,Gl'ntThot 12

14Sep87—Broke in a tangle; lugged out final 1/8

29Aug87-2Dmr 6f :213 :442 1:092ft 6¾ 116 31 32½ 55½ 79¾ Olivares F7 40000 81-12 GoldnGntlt,SwtwtrSprngs,NrthYrd 10

13Aug87-7Dmr 6f :22 :451 1:10 ft 9¾ 116 11 11 11½ 13½ Olivares F2 25000 88-20 Subito, Del Junco,ImpressiveResult 8

Jan 1 SA 3f gd :35 h Dec 19 SA 5f ft 1:004 h Dec 11 SA 5f ft 1:011 h

Jazz Player * B. g. 4, by Pianist—Fancys Pride, by Sir Khalito

DELAHOUSSAYE E 115 Br.—Weiss Mr-Mrs C F (Cal) 1987 13 3 1 1 $31,375

Own.—Banche Mr-Mrs N C Tr.—Arena Joseph $25,000 1986 3 1 0 0 $6,750

Lifetime 16 4 1 1 $38,125

30Dec87-2SA 1 1/16 :464 1:113 1:442m 4 116 1½ 12 12 15½ DelahoussayeE3 20000 79-23 Jazz Player, Precedence, Amatar 11

15Nov87-2SA 1 :463 1:114 1:383ft 4¾ 116 108½ 88¼ 67¼ 46 DelahoussayeE8 20000 69-18 John Vigors,NomadBoi,SavorFaire 10

15Nov87—Wide into, through stretch

5Nov87-5SA 1 1/16 :473 1:122 1:452sy 3½ 116 11 1hd 2hd 1½ DelahoussayeE7 16000 74-23 JzzPlyer,Tibon'sTk,Bnny'sBoldBid 11

18Oct87-1SA 6f :214 :45 1:104ft 4½ 116 1111 911 97½ 36½ DelahoussayeE9 16000 77-15 Subito, Punch Bowl, Jazz Player 12

18Oct87—Hopped in air

10Oct87-1SA 6½f :214 :45 1:164ft 15 116 911 89¾ 65½ 23½ DelahoussayeE3 20000 82-17 PddyMldoon,JzzPlyr,StndByYorMn 9

10Oct87—Bobbled start

10Sep87-1Dmr 6f :214 :444 1:102ft 6¾ 1155 79 55½ 66½ 44¼ Cisneros J E8 12500 82-14 WellLaDeDa,RreTyson,SuperAdios 10

27Aug87-5Dmr 6f :214 :451 1:101ft 10 1105 119¼ 108½ 85¼ 55¼ Cisneros J E8 13000 82-17 HoustonBragg,RreTyson,RzeBook 11

27Aug87—Wide 3/8 turn

19Aug87-1Dmr 6f :221 :453 1:112ft 49 1095 87½ 75¼ 42 1½ Cisneros J E2 14000 81-14 Jazz Player,Forcefully,BoldRoyale 10

19Aug87—Bumped start; steadied near 1/8

30Jly87-3Dmr 1 1/16 :464 1:114 1:44 ft 61 114 73¾ 1115 1119 1125¼ Solis A1 18000 55-21 PlyngForKps,BornToRc,WtL'Ost 11

2Jly87-9Hol 1 :453 1:11 1:373ft 12 116 76¾ 85¼ 75¼ 79½ Solis A7 16000 65-15 Glory Quest, Amatar, Terrefying 9

Jan 23 SA 6f ft 1:143 h Jan 21 SA 5f ft 1:013 h Jan 11 SA 5f ft 1:014 h Dec 22 SA 5f ft 1:014 h

Nomad Boi	102/	109	110	104	FF
Kenai Dancer	103/	104	100	97	AS
Subito	102/		109	103	FA
Jazz Player	102/	130	114	109	FF

Jazz Player stood so far apart on the figures, it seemed a cinch. As a Julio Canani claim (hot trainer) out of a fast-fast race, Nomad Boi looked best of the rest.

Brohamer sat silently, as the prognosis favoring Jazz Player was almost violently contradicted by a regular handicapper visiting the box.

"How can you like Jazz Player?" began the oaf. "He won in the mud on the lead. From the twelve spot today, he'll have to be used early, and he won't see the front regardless."

Jazz Player, in fact, had rolled on a muddy-wet surface December 30, but previously had won from far behind as well. On January 31, prior to the nitecap, sprints had been running Slow 3 and routes Slow 5, variants for a surface that had been assisting off-pace styles all day.

Brohamer deposited his second prime bet of the afternoon.

Following a terrible break and worse trip, Jazz Player would need his tremendous figure advantage to complete the assigned task. The running line of the official chart captured his sparkling performance well.

> "Jazz Player, devoid of early speed, and wide down the backstretch, came into the stretch four wide, battled for command through the final furlong, and prevailed by a narrow margin in a stiff drive."

Examine the winner's figures:103/ 114 99 98 AS

After a fast four furlongs the pace fell apart, setting up the closers. Jazz Player's dominating figures proved barely enough to overcompensate for a lousy break, the wide trip, a collapsing pace, and the stiff stretch drive.

Most amazing, Jazz Player went to the post at 10–1. It paid $23.40 to win. Brohamer departed with a few thousand in profits.

The next day, 5th race again, Brohamer fancied Royal Blue Eyes, a 15–1 shot on the morning line. My figures had placed Royal Blue Eyes two lengths behind a pair of sprinters moving up from $25,000 to $32,000 claiming, in my opinion the stiffest rise on the southern California circuit.

Brohamer mentioned his reliance on projected times, pointing out that the use of pars would mistake Royal Blue Eyes's figures last out by four lengths. Note the differences:

Horses	Pars			Projected times		
Royal Blue Eyes	103/	105	102	103/	109	106
Sasebo	103/	103	104	103/	103	104

Speed handicappers who calculated variants and figures utilizing class-distance pars would have preferred Sasebo in the 5th on February 3. Experts realized that Royal Blue Eyes was lengths superior, both at the fractional call and final call.

At 6–1, Royal Blue Eyes won handily, paid $14.40. At 5–2, Sasebo finished third.

Brohamer quickly annexed the 6th and 7th.

The winner of the 6th was a first starter in a maiden-claiming race. No experienced runner had earned a figure as high as a length below par. The debuting winner was sent out by a trainer having an attractive percentage with first starters in these awful processions.

The 7th race winner merely had Brohamer's top figure.

On February 5 Brohamer liked a 9–2 shot named Alabama Roger. The three-year-old was exiting a maiden-claiming route limited to Cal-breds, which it had won by four, and was entering a mile open to $32,000 winners. It won by four again.

I'm not sure I've ever supported this kind of winner, so let's pursue Brohamer's analysis. Below are the latest figures and class levels for Alabama Roger and the two horses I preferred.

Alabama Roger	94/	87	96	96	AA	M32,000	Won by 4
Out of Full	101/		95	92	AS	$25,000	Won by 3
Tricky Lad	101/		100	92	FS	$40,000	5th, beaten 5

Proposed: maiden-claiming graduates entered against winners at the same selling price, or higher, normally falter badly. Instead, the selling price should drop, by as much as half.

Here Alabama Roger, the figure horse, beat winners at the same claiming price, drawing out in the stretch, after leading all the way.

Brohamer comments: "Maiden-claiming grads should have a significant edge in the figures. I mean, three to four lengths at least, as did Alabama Roger. I also want them to show a turn time of par or faster. The second-quarter pace will defeat a great proportion of slow horses. And, ideally, the final figure should equal or exceed today's par."

Alabama Roger did not qualify on the last criterion, I protested. Par for an open $32,000 mile, 3YOs, was 100.

"If he had," replied Brohamer, "I would have bet more," and left to exchange the tickets.

Brohamer and Rousso, as a routine, will support maiden-claiming graduates against winners when they possess the top figures, class aside. Yet the two agree the horses are not as reliable as are high-figure horses in open events. In particular, an unfamiliar rapid pace that is contested can crush their spirit. No wonder Brohamer insists on a decent turn time.

Can handicappers earn substantial profits on this play? Or do they lose money in the long run? An interesting study, not yet on record.

In the 5th on February 5, again relying on projected times to obtain variants and figures, Brohamer found a prime bet on a 3YO dropping from nonwinners-once allowance competition to a $50,000 claiming race restricted to 3YOs. Overtaking a sluggish start, Temper T. won straight, at 3–1.

This dropdown, by all means, extends excellent opportunities whenever the figures support the drop. The horses win, and win repeatedly, since the three-year-old claiming class, especially during winter, remains significantly slower than three-year-old allowance competition.

Two days later, February 7, Brohamer liked a six-year-old stretching out following one sprint and a fourteen-month layoff. It was a $32,000 claiming race, 4up, at 1 1/16M. Just as strongly, I preferred a four-year-old gelding named Savor Faire.

Ono Gummo *
B. h. 6, by Gummo—Dancing Alone, by Whodunit
MCCARRON C J 116 Br.—Thurman S M (Cal) 1988 1 0 0 0 $2,100
Tr.—Truman Eddie $32,000 1986 13 2 1 6 $55,510
Own.—Davies-Fisher-Slusher Lifetime 42 7 6 14 $173,840 Turf 6 0 0 3 $11,810
27Jan88-9SA 6f :213 :443 1:094ft 12 114 84¼ 86½ 55 43 McCarron C J10 35000 86-19 Savio, Raise APound,SocietyRoad 11
7Dec86-3Hol 1 :453 1:10 1:354gd 3½ 116 21½ 31½ 31 33¼ Valenzuela P A5 57500 81-18 Olajuwon, RisingChum,OnoGummo 6
5Nov86-7Hol 1⅛ Ⓣ:4731:1131:483fm 4½ 116 22 33 33 42½ Toro F4 50000 82-14 Too Much For T. V.,Massera,Tarver 8
4Oct86-9SA 1 1/16 :472 1:112 1:43 ft *3 115 31 31½ 42 53¾ Stevens G L2 62500 82-18 GoSwiftly,SilverHro,AutoCommndr 8
4Oct86—Steadied, altered course 1/16; took up
20Sep86-5BM 1 Ⓣ:4611:10 1:351fm *2½ 115 65 34½ 33½ 34½ Baze R A4 65000 99 — JackTr,Position'sBest,OnoGummo 10
20Sep86—Steadied 3/4
6Sep86-5Dmr 1⅛ Ⓣ:4631:11 1:492fm 7 117 44 41½ 63¾ 31¾ Stevens G L9 62500 85-09 Aviator II, Keyala, Ono Gummo 10
24Aug86-9Dmr 1 1/16 :452 1:093 1:412ft 14 116 1hd 12½ 18 15½ Baze R A7 50000 93-12 OnoGummo,TimeForSilenc,Oljuwon 9
7Jun86-7Hol 1 :453 1:10 1:37 ft 7½ 116 43 52½ 42½ 1hd Stevens G L8 50000 78-17 Ono Gummo, Menswear, Paskanell 8
16May86-9Hol 1⅛ :453 1:11 1:493ft 4 116 35½ 23½ 68¼ 610¼ Kaenel J L4 50000 79-19 Bedouin, Vigorous Vigors, Tio Nino 7
4May86-9Hol 1 :453 1:103 1:362ft 5½ 116 1hd 21 21½ 23½ Valenzuela P A9 50000 77-18 Silver Hero, Ono Gummo, Juntura 9
●Jan 26 SA 3f ft :351 h Jan 21 SA 7f ft 1:302 h Jan 7 SA 6f ft 1:152 h Jan 2 SA 6f gd 1:16 h

Savor Faire
Dk. b. or br. g. 4, by Steve's Friend—By the Hand, by Intentionally
PEDROZA M A 117 Br.—Steinbrenner G M III (Fla) 1988 2 1 0 0 $12,100
Tr.—Canani Julio C $32,000 1987 15 2 1 5 $36,239
Own.—Gleason L Lifetime 20 3 3 5 $55,139 Turf 2 0 0 0 $678
17Jan88-3SA 1 1/16 :461 1:104 1:43 sy 3½ 115 1hd 2½ 66 614½ Valenzuela P A 2 35000 72-17 Rakaposhi,Bananas,Dncellthednces 7
7Jan88-5SA 1 :454 1:11 1:37 ft 4½ 114 33½ 21½ 1hd 12¾ Pedroza M A 3 28000 83-23 SavorFaire,BoldBargin,FstDelivery 10
27Dec87-5SA 6½f :214 :444 1:163ft 29 115 63¾ 65 65 87½ Pedroza M A 2 Aw35000 79-17 WndwoodLn,TmForSkrt,RdAndBl 10
15Nov87-2SA 1 :463 1:114 1:383ft 3½ 116 31½ 31½ 33½ 33¼ Solis A 10 c20000 72-18 John Vigors,NomadBoi,SavorFaire 10
15Nov87—Fanned wide 7/8
21Oct87-9SA 1 1/16 :461 1:113 1:444ft 9½ 116 3nk 2hd 1½ 21¾ Solis A 8 20000 75-20 Dncellthdncs,SvorFir,StrdustFolly 10
10Sep87-8Cby 6f :224 :454 1:10 ft 3½ 115 52½ 53¾ 47 410¾ Martinez F III 5 35000 85-17 Texas Trio, Que Me In,Buxinmytux 6
29Aug87-9Cby 1 1/16 :472 1:133 1:451ft *6-5 112 31½ 31 22 3¾ Kutz D6 Aw10300 84-13 Goatville, Kapalua, Savor Faire 6
29Jly87-8Cby 1 :464 1:112 1:37 ft 9-5 117 21 41½ 42 33¼ Kutz D 3 Aw11300 93-16 CaptainSkiff,BlindDestiny,SvorFire 6
12Jly87-9Cby 1 :463 1:113 1:391gd 4¾ 120 2hd 1hd 31½ 32¾ MrtFIII 1 Ⓡ MnnBrdDb 82-17 TelephonCnyon,Momsfurrri,SvorFir 5
6Jun87-9Cby 7½f Ⓣ:231 :4541:292fm 6½ 117 67½ 57 44 42 CervantesED 1 Aw11300 96-02 Arrow Sport, Feudal, Desperate 9
Jan 31 SA 4f ft :474 h Jan 25 SA 4f ft :481 h Jan 15 SA 3f ft :362 h ●Jan 5 SA tr.t 3f ft :353 h

Here are the records and figures for handicappers to review.

Ono Gummo	104/		98	103	AF	5–2
Savor Faire	105/	106	108	108	AF	6–1

Knowing that handicapping probabilities discount the one-sprint stretchout following a long layoff, and considering the impressive figures of Savor Faire, the decision appears clear-cut.

Not in Brohamer's opinion.

Look at the pace figure Ono Gummo recorded in its comeback sprint. Six points, or three lengths, below par. Not altogether encouraging, correct?

Brohamer's interpretation focused instead on Ono Gummo's early-energy distribution, a novel concept. By that analysis, Ono Gummo's low pace figure is entirely misleading.

"The horse's early energy was exactly right for routes at Santa Anita at the time. Usually it takes two sprints until the early energy looks appropriate for the route. The first sprint, horses coming back from long rests use too much energy early. But for this specific pattern [Ono Gummo] was just right."

Ono Gummo boasted back class, and when ready to show its best, a few faster figures than Savor Faire, though the comparison remained close.

Brohamer bet Ono Gummo. I bet Savor Faire. Each of us protected the prime amounts with exacta boxes.

Immediately following the break, the two horses engaged in a ding-dong pace duel that never faltered. As the pair approached the eighth pole, I felt extremely confident the current conditioning of Savor Faire would prevail.

The chart presents the result.

NINTH RACE
Santa Anita
FEBRUARY 7, 1988

1 1/16 MILES. (1.40⅗) CLAIMING. Purse $27,000. 4-year-olds and upward. Weights, 4-year-olds, 120 lbs.; older, 121 lbs. Non-winners of two races at one mile or over since December 1 allowed 3 lbs.; of such a race since then, 5 lbs.; Claiming price $32,000; for each $2,000 to $28,000, allowed 1 lb. (Claiming and starter races for $25,000 or less not considered.)

Value of race $27,000; value to winner $14,850; second $5,400; third $4,050; fourth $2,025; fifth $675. Mutuel pool $516,007. Exacta pool $960,002.

Last Raced	Horse	Eqt.	A.	Wt	PP	St	¼	½	¾	Str	Fin	Jockey	Cl'g Pr	Odds $1
27Jan88 9SA4	Ono Gummo		6	116	4	3	2½	1hd	21	1½	1¾	McCarron C J	32000	2.60
17Jan88 3SA6	Savor Faire	b	4	117	11	2	1½	21½	1hd	23	23½	Pedroza M A	32000	6.90
10Jan88 7SA	Super Punk		5	116	9	12	12	9½	6½	41½	31	Black C A	32000	24.50
21Jan88 5SA5	Breu		7	116	12	5	3½	3½	3½	3½	41¾	Solis A	32000	7.00
10Jan88 2SA3	Centenary	b	6	116	3	10	9½	101	9hd	5½	5½	Delahoussaye E	28000	3.60
31Jan88 4SA9	Dennis D.	b	5	109	1	4	61	7hd	103	61½	62	Valenzuela F H5	28000	26.90
18Jan88 1SA6	Lemmon Juice		5	116	5	8	81	81	71½	93	71¼	Castanon A L	32000	14.50

2May87 9Hol4	Imperial Palace		5 111	10	7	52½	4½	42	71½	8nk	Gryder A T5	32000	18.90
16Jan88 9SA3	Fast Delivery	b	4 115	2	1	41	53½	5½	8hd	92¾	Stevens G L	32000	6.60
31Jan88 5SA11	Midnight Steel		4 115	8	11	11½	11hd	115	101½	103	Steiner J J	32000	72.90
26Dec87 2SA7	Sky Warrior	b	4 115	7	9	72	61	8½	116	119	Shoemaker W	32000	9.50
1Feb88 10TuP3	Most Gallant		4 110	6	6	101	12	12	12	12	Sherman A B5	32000	85.50

OFF AT 5:17. Start good. Won driving. Time, :23⅕, :47, 1:11⅘, 1:37, 1:43⅘ Track fast.

$2 Mutuel Prices:

4-ONO GUMMO	7.20	4.80	4.00
11-SAVOR FAIRE		7.40	5.80
9-SUPER PUNK			9.40

$5 EXACTA 4–11 PAID $128.00.

B. h, by Gummo—Dancing Alone, by Whodunit. Trainer Truman Eddie. Bred by Thurman S M (Cal).

ONO GUMMO, a pace factor from the beginning while inside SAVOR FAIRE, proved best in a hard drive. SAVOR FAIRE, a pace factor from the start while outside ONO GUMMO, had to settle for the place. SUPER PUNK, devoid of early speed after being bumped in the initial strides, came into the stretch four wide while in the process of improving his position and could not gain the needed ground in the drive. BREU, close up from the outset, weakened

On February 11 trainer John Sadler lowered Mischievous Matt from $20,000 to $12,500 at six furlongs. The horse's figures of January 9 indicated it could humble the $12,500 field. Trusting horse and trainer, Brohamer wagered confidently, taking 8–5.

When Mischievous Matt galloped by eight, Brohamer did not realize the maneuver would set up perhaps his most impressive play of the season six days later. He merely cashed the tickets en route to another winning day.

Mischievous Matt — Dk. b. or br. h. 5, by Run of Luck—Classic Caper, by Pilot John
Br.—Waller H E (Wash) — 1988 2 0 0 0 $1,025
PINCAY L JR 116 — Tr.—Sadler John W — $12,500 — 1987 20 2 5 1 $48,950
Own.—Sanger E or Fae — Lifetime 41 8 8 2 $119,285

31Jan88-1SA	6f	:22	:453	1:11 ft	*4	116	85	95¾	64¼	54¾	Valenzuela P A 2	20000	78-21	Melchip, Bum Bee Ray, Crack'n It	12
31Jan88—Bobbled at start															
9Jan88-3SA	6f	:212	:441	1:094ft	5¾	116	75½	86	74¾	55	Valenzuela P A8	25000	84-17	Savio, IdealQuality,RoyalB'ueEyes	11
27Dec87-2SA	6f	:214	:444	1:10 ft	6½	116	76	66½	78¼	77¾	Sibille R2	c20000	80-17	Savio, Courage Ruler,IdealQuality	11
4Dec87-5Hol	6f	:221	:451	1:103ft	6¾	116	41¼	42	21½	41½	Sibille R5	25000	87-21	RdwoodBoy,BolgrMgic,CuttingLin	11
22Nov87-1Hol	6f	:22	:444	1:101ft	4	117	65	811	78½	66¾	Sibille R5	32000	84-14	MeYouAndQ.,NtiveRelity,KniDncr	10
28Oct87-2SA	6½f	:214	:444	1:161ft	4¼	116	64¾	41½	2hd	2½	Sibille R8	25000	88-16	AirAlert,MischivousMtt,WstBoyII	10
28Oct87—4 wide into drive															
23Sep87-10Fpx	6½f	:213	:451	1:16 ft	4	114	33	44½	57½	58¼	Sorenson D1	35000	88-12	IdelQulity,MgicLeder,LuckyBuccnr	7
31Aug87-7Dmr	6½f	:22	:443	1:153ft	6¾	116	41½	41	1hd	2hd	Sibille R7	32000	94-14	DshonorblGst,MschvosMtt,LoCrd	11
16Aug87-2Dmr	6½f	:221	:451	1:153ft	6¼	116	22	22	21	2½	Sibille R3	c20000	93-11	FollwThDncr,MschvsMtt,B-l'sAnt	11
2Aug87-2Dmr	6f	:221	:453	1:103ft	5½	116	84	51¼	21½	2½	Sibille R7	20000	84-12	WildPursut,MschvousMtt,Brul'sAnt	9
2Aug87—Wide 3/8 turn															

Jan 26 Hol 5f ft 1:012 h — Jan 20 SA 4f ft :504 h — Jan 6 SA 4f ft :464 h — Dec 22 Fpx 4f ft :50 h

Next day, February 12, 5th race, Brohamer hammered the exacta. Two contenders were exiting a "tandem" race, or a race whose graduates present figures superior to anything else in the field. Examine the speed-pace figures below and try to spot the predictable exacta. It paid $142.

Rabuccola	102/	97	95	AS	$50,000
Rich Tiger	101/	106	94	FA	$40,000
Do Right By Dudley	101/	105	95	FS	$40,000
Le Tache	100/	95	93	AS	$25,000
M' Lord Andrew	100/	99	93	AA	$25,000
Cremona	101/	98	96	FS	$50,000

With comparable final figures but clearly superior pace figures, Do Right By Dudley won and Rich Tiger finished second. A numerical pace analyst could hardly miss this boat race.

Brohamer captured the $139 triple this day—as did his seat-

mates—and enjoyed a prosperous afternoon. His winnings totaled $1200.

The next morning Brohamer made his debut on radio, at host
Lee Rousso's invitation, and told horseplayers in southern California to bet Time To Sweep would upset favorite Alias Nina
in the afternoon's 5th race.

The race was a sprint for nonwinners of an allowance race,
4up. Par was 101. Here are the figures for the two contenders,
post-time odds at the right.

Time To Sweep	102/	102	104	AF	9–2
Alias Nina	103/	102	101	AA	8–5

Time To Sweep triumphed by 4½ lengths in hand, and despite Brohamer's tip citywide, paid $11.80. An obvious exacta,
favorite in the two-hole, paid $72.40.

In the land of fantasy and celebrity, yet another media star
had been born.

At the track that afternoon Brohamer collared the 6th and
7th as well, and stood to collect another bundle if Carload could
annex the stakes sprint in the feature. Carload lost by a head in
the last stride to Sylvan Express, benefitting from a sensational
courageous ride under Eddie Delahoussaye.

Delahoussaye's daring stopped Brohamer cold for twenty-four
hours, but he roared back on February 15 with the pièce de
résistance, a virtuoso performance. He swept the 1st, 2nd, daily
double, 3rd, and 4th; passed the 5th; hit the 6th; passed the 7th
and 8th; hit the 9th.

The 9th would be quintessential Brohamer. It was for older
fillies and mares, $16,000 claimers, going a route, and was taken
by a Golden Gate shipper jumping two levels in class and
stretching out after a series of sprints.

Brohamer knew Tabula Rosa not only had the high figure,
but its early energy was perfect for going a middle distance at
Santa Anita. By now I had learned to ask Brohamer about the
early-energy distribution of sprinters stretching out. I wondered
out loud about Tabula Rosa's chances.

"She has the correct energy and top figure," came the pointed
response.

A lone frontrunner, Tabula Rosa did not escape the attention
of Santa Anita speed handicappers. She won, all right, and paid
$11.40, but might have returned twice the price. On the other
hand, the exacta, to the second-high figure horse, paid nicely,
at $249.50.

Catching six winners and two exotics, Brohamer took $2600 out of the handle.

Following an unscheduled day off, Brohamer returned February 17 to find his recent benefactor, Mischievous Matt, entered at the route in the 9th. He anticipated one of his best bets of the season.

This was a $20,000 claiming event, 4up, at 1 1/16M. Rousso liked Maui Melody a bunch, and I thought Siberian Hero stood out. It was unusual for the three of us to disagree so vehemently. Below are the records and latest figures for the three horses. Which do handicappers prefer, and why?

Siberian Hero — B. h. 6, by Nasty and Bold—Tundra Queen, by Le Fabuleux
TORO F — 116 — Br.—Tartan Farm Corp (Fla) — Tr.—Cross Richard J — $20,000
Own.—Paulson A E
1988 2 0 0 1 $4,050
1987 12 4 3 1 $82,700
Lifetime 41 7 11 8 $167,859 — Turf 21 1 5 6 $48,247

24Jan88-10SA 1 1/16 :471 1:114 1:434ft 4 1/2 1115 32 42 32 1/2 34 Gryder A T2 32000 78-18 ExoticMotion,L.A.Fire,SibernHro 10
24Jan88—Broke out, bumped
6Jan88-7SA 1 :461 1:104 1:353ft 4 3/4 1135 42 32 1/2 55 1/2 610 3/4 Gryder A T2 50000 79-19 GoodTste,LstCommnd,HisHighness 8
13Dec87-9Hol 1 1/16 (T):4711:1111:422fm 7 1/2 116 11 1hd 2 1/2 99 Santos J A5 62500 73-16 Pinstripe II, Kensof, Centenary 12
8Nov87-3SA 1 :473 1:114 1:391gd 4 1/2 1095 33 32 1/2 31 11 1/2 Gryder A T3 45000 72-25 SiberinHero,Centenry,SpdyShnnon 7
10Oct87-10SA 1 1/16 :48 1:121 1:44 ft *2 1/2 118 31 31 2hd 1hd Meza R Q6 25000 81-17 SiberianHero,L.A.Fire,MightyBuck 11
7Sep87-9Dmr 1 :444 1:093 1:35 ft 4 1/2 117 45 22 33 1/2 47 Pincay L Jr9 62500 86-14 He'sASaros,IdelQulity,LstCommnd 9
7Sep87—Bumped start
26Aug87-5Dmr 1 1/16 :452 1:101 1:421ft 3 1/4 117 57 43 1/2 33 24 Pincay L Jr9 62500 85-15 ForignLgion,SibrinHro,BngBngBng 9
2Aug87-9Dmr 1 :451 1:103 1:363ft *2 3/4 117 45 1/2 31 1/2 2hd 1nk Pincay L Jr6 50000 85-12 SbrnHro,ForgnLgon,GodThghtWlly 8
9Jly87-9Hol 1 1/16 :451 1:093 1:432ft *2 1/4 116 66 1/2 57 1/2 65 3/4 55 1/4 Toro F2 62500 87-15 Mschfnmnd,PnstrpII,EghtyBlowZr 8
9Jly87—Bumped start, wide 3/8 turn
17Jun87-5Hol 1 :451 1:101 1:354ft *2 1/4 116 41 1/2 21 2 1/2 2no Toro F4 62500 84-15 SocietyRod,SibrinHro,RomnMgstrit 7
17Jun87—Wide 3/8 turn
Jan 2 SA 5f gd 1:033 h — Dec 28 SA 5f ft 1:004 h — Dec 24 SA 3f ft :354 h

Maui Melody * — B. g. 6, by Messenger of Song—Maui, by Hawaii
STEVENS G L — 116 — Br.—Carver Stable (Cal) — Tr.—French Neil — $20,000
Own.—Walker Bonnie J
1988 1 0 0 0 $625
1987 4 1 1 0 $11,546
Lifetime 24 11 2 1 $63,555 — Turf 8 4 0 0 $20,690

3Feb88-5SA 6 1/2f :213 :442 1:163ft 16 116 52 1/2 52 1/2 64 1/2 55 1/2 Sibille R8 32000 81-20 RoyalBlueEyes,Cliff'sPlace,Ssebo 10
3Feb88—Wide into stretch
1Mar87-9TuP 1 (T):4641:1131:372fm *3-5 112 21 1/2 2hd 21 1/2 46 1/2 Powell J P2 Aw8100 88-09 StandingGood,Ruffgatter,Ablemint 6
15Feb87-8TuP 7 1/2f (T):243 :4831:30 gd *6-5 115 11 1/2 1 1/2 2hd 1 1/2 Bergsrud S A2 Aw8000 104 — MauiMelody,Apeldoorn,KuhioKing 12
1Feb87-11TuP 1 1/8 (T):4631:1121:48 fm 36 113 12 1 1/2 42 1/2 87 1/2 Licata F2 Tu P H 100 — Narghile,SirNaskra,‡SkipOutFront 14
1Feb87—Placed seventh through disqualification
4Jan87-10TuP 1 1/16 :46 1:094 1:412ft 9 1/2 118 2 1/2 21 1/2 22 1/2 2no Licata F7 Mrcpa Fr H 91-12 SonoitBlu,MuiMlody,ChuckNLuck 12
7Dec86-9TuP a7 1/2f (T):254 :5011:343gd 5 113 13 1 1/2 12 12 1/2 Licata F1 Aw8000 90-10 Maui Melody, Pinstripe,GrandEcart 9
9Aug86-8Cby 7 1/2f (T):242 :4741:311fm 6 1/2 123 12 1/2 2hd 13 11 1/2 Lidberg D W1 50000 — — MauiMelody,NickelBack,Numchuek 9
20Jly86-8Cby 6f :222 :452 1:102ft 5 1/2 120 41 3nk 1hd 14 1/2 Hawley S7 Aw12000 95-14 MuiMelody,SilentRg,Portr'sBroom 7
28Jun86-8Cby 1 :47 1:121 1:393ft 4 123 35 34 1/2 56 1/2 610 1/4 Hansen R D3 Aw13300 73-17 Cowboy Bill, Dr.ChoCho,IReallyDid 8
4Jun86-7Cby 1 :481 1:13 1:394ft 2 1/2 118 1hd 2hd 11 13 Hansen R D1 Aw12300 82-24 Maui Melody, Allatime,HeatedFury 6
Feb 12 SA 4f ft :484 h — Jan 26 SA 5f ft 1:003 h — Jan 21 SA 5f ft 1:003 h — Jan 15 SA 4f ft :49 h

Mischievous Matt — Dk. b. or br. h. 5, by Run of Luck—Classic Caper, by Pilot John
HAWLEY S — 116 — Br.—Waller H E (Wash) — Tr.—Sadler John W — $20,000
Own.—Sanger E or Fae
1988 3 1 0 0 $9,275
1987 20 2 5 1 $48,950
Lifetime 42 9 8 2 $127,535

11Feb88-1SA 7f :222 :452 1:233ft *8-5 117 31 41 1/2 1 1/2 18 Pincay L Jr1 12500 82-23 MschvsMtt,PrvngSprk,LrdDckwrth 7
31Jan88-1SA 6f :22 :453 1:11 ft *4 116 85 95 3/4 64 1/4 54 3/4 Valenzuela P A2 20000 78-21 Melchip, Bum Bee Ray, Crack'n It 12
31Jan88—Bobbled at start
9Jan88-3SA 6f :212 :441 1:094ft 5 3/4 116 75 1/2 86 74 3/4 55 Valenzuela P A8 25000 84-17 Savio, IdealQuality,RoyalBlueEyes 11
27Dec87-2SA 6f :214 :444 1:10 ft 6 1/2 116 76 66 1/2 78 1/4 77 3/4 Sibille R2 c20000 80-17 Savio, Courage Ruler,IdealQuality 11
4Dec87-5Hol 6f :221 :451 1:103ft 6 3/4 116 41 1/4 42 21 1/2 41 1/2 Sibille R5 25000 87-21 RdwoodBoy,BolgrMgic,CuttingLin 11
22Nov87-1Hol 6f :22 :444 1:101ft 4 117 65 811 78 1/2 66 3/4 Sibille R5 32000 84-14 MeYouAndQ.,NtiveRelity,KniDncr 10
28Oct87-2SA 6 1/2f :214 :444 1:161ft 4 1/2 116 64 3/4 41 1/2 2hd 2 1/2 Sibille R8 25000 88-16 AirAlert,MischivousMtt,WstBoyII 10
28Oct87—4 wide into drive
23Sep87-10Fpx 6 1/2f :213 :451 1:16 ft 4 114 33 44 1/2 57 1/2 58 1/2 Sorenson D1 35000 88-12 IdelQulity,MgicLeder,LuckyBuccnr 7
31Aug87-7Dmr 6 1/2f :22 :443 1:153ft 6 3/4 116 41 1/2 41 1hd 2hd Sibille R7 32000 94-14 DshonorblGst,MschvosMtt,LoCrd 11
16Aug87-2Dmr 6 1/2f :221 :451 1:153ft 6 1/2 116 22 22 21 2 1/2 Sibille R3 c20000 93-11 FollwThDncr,MschvsMtt,Brl'sAnt 11
Jan 26 Hol 5f ft 1:012 h — Jan 20 SA 4f ft :504 h — Jan 6 SA 4f ft :464 h — Dec 22 Fpx 4f ft :50 h

Siberian Hero	104/	104	101	103	AF
Maui Melody	104/		108	102	FS
Mischievous Matt	100/		98	104	AF

Dropped two levels six days ago, to win by eight, Mischievous Matt now is returned to former heights, and stretched out besides. Did the horse figure to repeat with this double-jump and distance change? According to the track's leading pace analyst, it did.

With fine tactical route speed, and superior class credentials, I felt Siberian Hero would be too much hombre once the probable pace duel weakened the pair of sprinters on the stretchout.

Rousso believed Maui Melody would own the early pace, discourage Mischievous Matt, and get home safely, before Siberian Hero could catch up.

The essential analysis belonged to Brohamer, however, and—again—it rested upon the early-energy distribution of the two sprinters. Here are the critical indicators:

Maui Melody	53.30 feet per second
Mischievous Matt	52.20 feet per second
WIN ENERGY	52.20 feet per second
(at Santa Anita)	

The win-energy line shows that recent route winners at Santa Anita were dispensing approximately 52.20 percent of their energy to the second call. A length equals roughly .15 fps.

Mischievous Matt is perfect on early energy.

Maui Melody, however, goes almost seven lengths too fast to the second call. When routing at Santa Anita, that kind of sprinter will collapse, at least by Brohamer's standards.

Mischievous Matt should have lots in reserve at the second call, and if the final figures tell the tale, should outrun Siberian Hero to the wire by a length, or less.

By conventional pace analysis, pace handicappers pondering the speed-pace figures alone would certainly have preferred Maui Melody's 108 to Mischievous Matt's 98. No contest. Applying energy concepts, that analysis is backwards. The slower pace of Mischievous Matt fit the win-energy pars of Santa Anita route winners of late.

Brohamer felt supremely confident on the point, and scored again, this time at 7–1.

Siberian Hero, as the chart reveals, actually forged in front by half a length at the stretch call, but the sprinter came on again, and won in a long hard drive. What's a conventional pace analyst to do? Very impressive handicapping here!

The exacta returned $167.50, which I had carefully included a few times among my tickets.

NINTH RACE
Santa Anita
FEBRUARY 17, 1988

1 $\frac{1}{16}$ MILES. (1.40$\frac{1}{5}$) CLAIMING. Purse $21,000. 4-year-olds and upward. Weights, 4-year-olds, 120 lbs.; older, 121 lbs. Non-winners of two races at one mile or over since December 25, allowed 3 lbs.; of such a race since then, 5 lbs. Claiming price $20,000; if for $18,000, allowed 2 lbs. (Claiming and starter races for $16,000 or less not considered).

Value of race $21,000; value to winner $11,550; second $4,200; third $3,150; fourth $1,575; fifth $525. Mutuel pool $302,552. Exacta pool $489,397.

Last Raced	Horse	Eqt.	A.	Wt	PP	St	¼	½	¾	Str	Fin	Jockey	Cl'g Pr	Odds $1
11Feb88 ^{1}SA^{1}	Mischievous Matt		5	116	6	2	2^{hd}	2^{2}	$2\frac{1}{2}$	$2^{3\frac{1}{2}}$	1^{nk}	Hawley S	20000	7.00
24Jan88 ^{10}SA^{3}	Siberian Hero	b	6	116	3	4	4^{1}	$4^{1\frac{1}{2}}$	$3^{2\frac{1}{2}}$	$1\frac{1}{2}$	$2^{2\frac{3}{4}}$	Toro F	20000	4.60
6Feb88 ^{9}SA^{4}	High Regards	b	4	116	11	11	$6^{3\frac{1}{2}}$	$6^{1\frac{1}{2}}$	4^{1}	3^{1}	3^{hd}	Delahoussaye E	20000	21.50
6Feb88 ^{9}SA^{3}	Bronze Tudor	b	5	116	4	7	$8\frac{1}{2}$	9^{5}	$9^{1\frac{1}{2}}$	$5^{1\frac{1}{2}}$	$4\frac{3}{4}$	Meza R Q	20000	4.80
7Feb88 ^{9}SA^{7}	Lemmon Juice		5	116	7	9	11	10^{hd}	10^{hd}	$8^{1\frac{1}{2}}$	5^{1}	Castanon A L	20000	12.50
11Feb88 ^{9}SA^{3}	Silver Surfer		7	116	10	5	$5\frac{1}{2}$	5^{1}	5^{2}	4^{1}	6^{nk}	Velasquez J	20000	12.20
30Jan88 ^{7}SA^{5}	Amatar		4	110	2	8	9^{6}	$8\frac{1}{2}$	$6^{1\frac{1}{2}}$	$7\frac{1}{2}$	$7^{3\frac{1}{2}}$	Gryder A T5	20000	20.40
3Feb88 ^{5}SA^{5}	Maui Melody	b	6	116	5	1	$1\frac{1}{2}$	1^{hd}	1^{hd}	6^{1}	8^{hd}	Stevens G L	20000	2.80
16Jan88 ^{9}SA^{4}	Tio Nino		7	117	9	10	$10\frac{1}{2}$	11	11	$9^{3\frac{1}{2}}$	9^{6}	Pincay L Jr	20000	7.30
7Feb88 ^{9}SA^{6}	Dennis D.	b	5	116	8	6	7^{4}	7^{3}	7^{1}	$10^{2\frac{1}{2}}$	$10^{3\frac{1}{2}}$	Cordero A Jr	20000	18.30
24Jan88 ^{2}SA^{10}	Mondanite		6	116	1	3	3^{3}	3^{2}	$8\frac{1}{2}$	11	11	Shoemaker W	20000	27.90

OFF AT 5:23. Start good. Won driving. Time, :22$\frac{3}{5}$, :46$\frac{2}{5}$, 1:11$\frac{4}{5}$, 1:37$\frac{4}{5}$, 1:44$\frac{4}{5}$ Track fast.

$2 Mutuel Prices:

6–MISCHIEVOUS MATT	16.00	6.60	6.60
3–SIBERIAN HERO		5.80	3.80
11–HIGH REGARDS			7.80

$5 EXACTA 6–3 PAID $167.50

Dk. b. or br. h, by Run of Luck—Classic Caper, by Pilot John. Trainer Sadler John W. Bred by Waller H E (Wash).

MISCHIEVOUS MATT, a pace factor from the start, came back on in the final furlong to prevail by a narrow margin in a stiff drive. SIBERIAN HERO, permitted to settle into stride early, rallied to have the lead a furlong out but could not quite outfinish the winner. HIGH REGARDS, outrun early, came into the stretch four wide and lacked the needed response in the drive. BRONZE TUDOR, far back early, finished strongly to just miss the show. LEMMON JUICE, far back early, found his best stride too late. SILVER SURFER, outrun early, lacked the necessary response in the last quarter. AMATAR was four wide into the stretch. MAUI MELODY, a pace factor for six furlongs, ga way. TIO NINO, far back early, was never close and entered the stretch four wide. DENNIS D., wide down backstretch, was five wide into the stretch. MONDANITE, prominent early, faltered badly and was not persev· with late when far back.

Brohamer's run ended here. During the streak, lasting thirteen racing days, he won with 65 percent of 40 prime bets; 26 red-hot winners!

Ahead $3000 when the surge began, Brohamer raked in another $6000 boosting his bank to $9000 for the hereafter.

MIDWAY

By comparison with the rabbits alongside in the box, my game continued unspectacular, perhaps, but steady as the hands of time.

During the thirty racing days, January 15 to February 21, my bottom line showed profits of $3958. Among 18 winning days, 12 losing, the longest losing run amounted to 3 days, and the best winning run 3 days.

Dollar amounts proved similarly steady. Largest one-day haul was $796, largest one-day loss $275. Bets routinely ranging from $50 to $200 create that soporific effect.

Any possibility of crushing the races disappears, excepting a phenomenal triple or Pick 6, but more overlays and exotics can be risked, the pedestrian strategy for challenging a season of four months. Where consistency flourishes in win betting, profits inexorably outstrip losses, and increasingly so as the meeting progresses. That is, winning days will be worth hundreds, losing days will cost a couple hundred or less. Of the twelve losing days, five cost me less than $100. Only drawing day-long blanks can pinch. Of the eighteen winning days, alternately, seven were worth more than $400. The ratio of dollars won to dollars lost per day is a robust 3–1.

Though idiosyncratic to me, this betting strategy is recreational, transportable, and worth a brief discussion. In the past five years my handicapping for profit has been restricted to the winter seasons at Santa Anita, approximately ninety racing days. Many recreational handicappers have similar habits. If I find three prime bets daily, on average, that's 270 prime shots during the season.

My handicapping edge, best estimate, is .26, the ROI on the invested dollar. If the prime bets become moderately large, say $250, the investment at Santa Anita will be $67,500. Profit estimates are equal to the total investment multiplied by the single-race edge, or $67,500×.26. My profit should be $17,550.

I apply a different strategy, based upon experience. Bet size to win can be lowered, in between $50 and $100 normally, and overlays and exotics pursued more aggressively. Experience teaches the strategy finds enough overlays—not prime bets—to yield $1000 a week in profits, or $15,000 season long. That remains the goal, somewhat less, unimportantly less, than a prime-bet strategy at $250 to win would yield.

The pedestrian strategy allows the possibility, however unlikely, of the big score. Triples can be challenged often, the Pick 6 occasionally, exactas daily, without outrageous capital requirements. In effect, I can play to a single bank, of $5,000 or less.

Where consistency characterizes the win betting, a critical

assumption, and seasonal play abides, this kind of unit-betting strategy works well enough. Profits accumulate, losses are minimized. Chances for assorted scores are retained. Handicappers get profits and action simultaneously. Many relish the combination.

Of handicapping, naturally I collected on a number of the same horses my colleagues did during the exciting and productive period.

On January 22, to cite the most intriguing, my hero would be a grass horse nobody else supported. It was a classified allowance mile on turf, the conditions bringing together the kind of highly competitive field that in my peculiar way I like. I present the guts of the race. Try to find the main contenders.

8th Santa Anita

*Any Song

SHOEMAKER W — 118 — Dk. b. or br. m. 5, by Bold Lad—Flute, by Luthier

Own.—Chilngwrth-Slivan-Tuerk etal — Br.—Collinstown Stud Farm (Ire) — 1987 6 1 1 1 $105,844

Tr.—Sullivan John — 1986 9 4 0 2 $30,573

Lifetime 18 5 1 3 $136,417 — Turf 18 5 1 3 $136,417

24Dec87-8Hol 1 1/16 (T):483 1:121 1:431fm 2 116 2hd 2hd 2½ 2nk ShmrW2 (F)Dahila H 78-22 Top Corsage, AnySong,Aberuschka 6

24Dec87—Grade III; Run in divisions

6Dec87-8Hol 1⅛ (T):493 1:134 1:51 yl 8½ 123 21½ 21½ 32½ 33¼ ShmrW5 (F)Matrh Iv 70-29 Asteroid Field,Nashmeel,AnySong 10

6Dec87—Grade I

27Nov87-8Hol 1 1/16 (T):461 1:10 1:404fm 5¾ 114 86½ 42½ 2½ 12½ ShmrW8 (F)[R]Alz Fr H 90-14 AnySong,DownAgin,MyVirginiReel 11

27Nov87—Run in divisions

11Nov87-8SA 1 (T):474 1:12 1:382fm 12 114 76 75 43½ 41¼ ShmrW6 (F)Midwick H 82-14 Aberuschka, Smooch, WordHarvest 7

11Nov87—Run in divisions

12Oct87-7SA 1⅛ (T):47 1:121 1:512fm 5½ 116 65½ 32½ 73¾ 44½ ShoemkrW2 (F)Aw36000 65-30 Smooch,FrauleinLieber,MrgezLes 10

2Sep87-7Dmr 1 (T):48 1:121 1:374fm 11 116 86¾ 85½ 86½ 53½ ShoemkrW4 (F)Aw28000 78-18 Tropical Holiday, Safeera, Laz'sJoy 8

12Oct86♦6PhoenixPk(Ire) 1 1:421gd 5½ 130 (T) 32½ Craine S (F)TaylorMade Lake Champlain, Ladina, AnySong 12

20Sep86♦5Leopardst'n(Ire) 1⅛ 1:54 fm *2 127 (T) 11½ Craine S HennessyH Any Song, DromondHill,IrishFolly 13

13Sep86♦5Curragh(Ire) 1 1:42 gd 7 127 (T) 15 CrineS Irsh Cmbrdgshr H AnySong,CorrptCommtt,AlldForc 26

Jan 11 SA (T) 5f fm 1:022 h (d) Jan 4 SA (T) 4f fm :512 h (d) ●Dec 21 Hol (T) 4f fm :49 h (d) Nov 25 Hol (T) 3f fm :362 h (d)

Davie's Lamb

TORO F — 120 — B. f. 4, by Unpredictable—Davie Lady, by Bold and Brave

Own.—Deals On Stable — Br.—Meadowbrook Farms Inc (Fla) — 1988 1 0 0 0 $4,500

Tr.—Canani Julio C — 1987 15 4 1 4 $142,250

Lifetime 22 5 1 7 $157,905 — Turf 9 3 1 2 $127,950

6Jan88-3SA 1⅛ (T):482 1:131 1:50 gd 4½ 117 43 42½ 31½ 44¾ VlenzulPA5 (F)Aw60000 72-23 MyVirginiReel,MissAlto,HcllyDonn 9

31Oct87-9BM 1 1/16 (T):471 1:131 1:48 yl *3 121 37 31½ 31 41¼ Toro F7 (F)B M Oaks 77-22 Soft Copy, Fraulein Lieber,Abrojo 10

11Oct87-8BM 1 (T):472 1:121 1:374fm 3 116 74½ 54 1hd 11¼ DizAL10 (F)San Jose H 87-16 Dvie'sLmb,WildMnor,RtherHomly 12

11Oct87—Bumped start

30Aug87-8Dmr 1⅛ (T):47 1:121 1:502fm 3 117 85¾ 52¾ 94¾ 63 TorF12 (F)Dmr Oaks 78-21 LizzyHre,ChpelOfDrems,DcwnAgin 13

30Aug87—Grade II; 5 wide into drive

14Aug87-5Dmr 1 1/16 (T):472 1:12 1:424fm *3-2 115 22½ 2½ 11 13½ Toro F2 (F)[R]Sn Clmnt 86-18 Davie's Lamb, Develop, WildManor 7

14Aug87—Run in divisions

3Aug87-5Dmr 1 1/16 (T):47 1:113 1:431fm 2½ 117 43½ 42 31½ 11¾ Toro F4 (F)Aw23000 84-14 Davie'sLamb,Develop,GoldenGalxy 10

10Jun87-8Hol 1 1/16 :464 1:114 1:44 ft 6½ 115 63¼ 75½ 78 714¼ Toro F3 (F)[R]Itsn T Ar 75-16 HelloSweetThing,KeyBid,LdyyNskr 7

17May87-8Hol 1 1/16 (T):462 1:103 1:411fm 5½ 115 72¾ 73¾ 53 32½ ToroF5 (F)Hnyman H 85-09 PenBlLdy,SomeSenstion,Dvi'sLmb 10

17May87—Grade III

25Apr87-8Hol 1 (T):47 1:111 1:352fm 17 115 55 42 21½ 32½ Sibille R6 (F)Senorita 87-14 PenBalLady,Sweettuc,Davie'sLamb 6

8Apr87-8SA 1⅛ (T):453 1:112 1:481fm 35 113 39 32 2hd 2¾ OrtegaLE5 (F)[R]Prvdnc 85-14 SomeSenstion,Dvi'sLmb,PinkSlipr 7

8Apr87—Veered out start

Jan 20 SA 4f ft :492 h Jan 14 SA 4f ft :472 h Jan 2 SA 6f gd 1:141 h Dec 27 SA 4f ft :473 h

My Virginia Reel *

SOLIS A — 121 — B. m. 6, by Roanoke Island—Tizonada, by Tinajero

Own.—Dodderidge R R — Br.—Dodderidge R R (Va) — 1988 2 1 0 1 $48,000

Tr.—Barrera Lazaro S — 1987 16 4 2 2 $104,530

Lifetime 30 8 6 6 $226,180 — Turf 6 4 0 1 $98,800

18Jan88-8SA 1⅛ :464 1:104 1:491m 3 115 2½ 2½ 1hd 31¾ SolisA5 (F)Sn Grgno H 81-17 MissAlto,TopCorsge,MyVirginiReel 6

18Jan88—Grade II

6Jan88-3SA 1⅛ (T):482 1:131 1:50 gd 8½ 118 32 31½ 1hd 12½ Solis A3 (F)Aw60000 77-23 MyVirginiReel,MissAlto,HcllyDonn 9

16Dec87-8Hol 1 1/16 :471 1:12 1:444sy 2½ 1105 41¼ 31½ 11½ 11¾ BandersAL3 (F)Aw45000 79-21 My Virginia Reel,SarosBrig,Griddle 5

5Dec87-8Hol 1 1/16 :47 1:12 1:453m 8 1105 63¾ 43½ 44½ 32¾ BandersAL5 (F)Aw40000 72-17 HollywoodGlittr,SrosBrg,MyVrgnRl 8

27Nov87-8Hol 1 1/16 (T):461 1:10 1:404fm 18f 110 11½ 11½ 1½ 32½ BdrsAL10 (F)[R]Alz Fr H 87-14 AnySong,DownAgin,MyVirginiReel 11

27Nov87—Run in divisions

8Nov87-4Aqu 1 1/16 (T):491 1:13 1:441fm 5½ 1075 11½ 13 14 13¼ Ortega P Jr7 (F) 75000 84-16 MyVirginiRl,FirstShot,LuckyTouch 9

2Nov87-2Aqu 1 1/16 (T):484 1:133 1:453fm 12 1085 11½ 14 18 18 Ortega P Jr10 (F) 45000 77-24 MyVirginiReel,SwetJllyBinn,Alitin 10

23Oct87-1Aqu 1 :47 1:111 1:36 ft 11 1125 2½ 1hd 21½ 26¾ Ortega P Jr5 (F) 35000 79-18 RoylDiscovry,MyVirginiRl,SpcFlowr 7

27Sep87-5Bel 7f :224 :46 1:234ft 14 115 31½ 55 813 818½ Santos J A1 (F) 47500 64-19 Superb Time, Flantasia, Wan'aFella 8

18May87-1Bel 7f :224 :452 1:232ft 6 117 32 43½ 56 55½ Cruguet J3 (F) 50000 79-15 LdyBeRgl,MrryWidowWltz GrtLdy 10

Jan 15 SA 4f ft :484 h Jan 3 SA 4f ft :482 h Dec 26 SA 4f ft :473 h Nov 22 Hol 4f ft :473 h

Turn And Dance

VALENZUELA P A — 114 — B. m. 5, by Dance Bid—Turn the Blade, by Best Turn

Own.—Seldin M — Br.—Seldin M (Ky) — 1987 12 2 1 2 $84,235

Tr.—Drysdale Neil — 1986 9 1 0 3 $73,797

Lifetime 30 4 4 8 $201,514 — Turf 5 1 1 0 $37,730

25Nov87-8CD 1 1/16 :481 1:14 1:474gd 12 113 44½ 64 79½ 713½ SmthME6 (F)Sun Snow 55-33 BrightTiming,BuckeyeGal,BriefFme 8

12Nov87-8CD 1 (T):474 1:141 1:404fm 11 116 89 87½ 78 67¾ EspinozJC2 (F)Aw27850 77-15 Acquire, Bright Timing,BaldWitch 10

29Oct87-7Kee 1 1/16 :461 1:102 1:424ft 3½e 121 612 714 716 722 McKnight J5 Aw23000 70-14 Cope, Fantasy Lover, Don't'sPride 7

18Jly87-10Aks 1⅛ :471 1:113 1:502ft 6 113 78 75½ 58¼ 59 LivelyJ2 (F)Queen's H 76-25 SoclBsnss,FmlyStyl,HppyHollwMss 8

18Jly87—Grade III

5Jly87-10Aks 1 1/16 :461 1:102 1:442ft 7¾ 114 812 713 58½ 34 MzRQ1 (F)Bud Brd Cup 77-24 ExplosiveGirl,FmilyStyl,TurnndDnc 9

14Jun87-9CD 1⅛ :472 1:121 1:503ft 12 114 89½ 89 79½ 712¼ LivlyJ4 (F)Flr D Lis H 77-16 Infinidad,Mrinn'sGirl,QueenAlexndr 8

24May87-10Cby 1 (T):443 1:09 1:34 fm 36 113 1019 86¾ 46 2nk WrhlVL1 (F)Ldy Cby H 106 — Ntur'sWy,TurnndDnc,PrfctMtchII 10

26Apr87-10Cby 170 :481 1:122 1:413ft 2¾ 121 95½ 68 48½ 310¼ LivelyJ7 (F)Cty O Minn 83-12 HppyHollowMss,WknTnk,TrnndDnc 9

16Apr87-8OP 1 1/16 :46 1:11 1:43 ft *8-5 114 617 46 1½ 11 Lively J6 (F)Aw21000 86-18 TurnndDnce,SurburbnSu,StormOut 7

3Apr87-9OP 1 1/16 :461 1:111 1:421ft 46 110 813 89 68 58¼ LvlJ5 (F)Bud Brd Cp H 82-17 NorthSider,QueenAlexndr,Ann'sBid 8

Jan 20 Hol 6f ft :364 h ●Jan 15 Hol 6f ft 1:123 h Jan 9 Hol 6f ft 1:142 h Nov 23 CD 3f ft :37 h

Mausie * B. m. 6, by Mariache—Magnala, by Mount Athos
STEVENS G L 121 Br.—Haras El Turf (Arg) Tr.—Jones Gary
Own.—De Burgh & Lima Lifetime 20 7 1 5 $105,165
1987 10 4 1 3 $88,537
1986 9 3 0 2 $16,628
Turf 18 6 1 5 $80,415

24Dec87-5Hol 1⅛Ⓣ:4731:1211:432fm 19 116 21 2hd 22½ 62¾ VlnzlPA5 ⒻDahlia H 74-22 Invited Guest, Secuencia, Smooch 9
24Dec87—Grade III; Run in divisions; Bumped early drive
11Dec87-8Hol 1 1/16Ⓣ:4811:1211:43 fm 4 119 11 11 2hd 31½ VlnzulPA 10 ⒻAw55000 77-21 Smooch, Miss Alto, Mausie 10
11Nov87-5SA 1 Ⓣ:4641:1111:371fm 8 114 2hd 1½ 1hd 1hd StnsGL 8 ⒻMidwick H 89-14 Mausie, Down Again, Benzina 10
11Nov87—Run in divisions
31Oct87-7SA 6½f:213 :443 1:17 sy 3½ 114 1hd 1½ 2hd 1¾ StevensGL 2ⒻAw45000 85-25 Musie,Comprbility,OnYourOwnTim 6
7Oct87-8SA a6½f Ⓣ:22 :4441:144fm 22 116 21 21 2hd 62¾ StnsGL 8 ⒻAtm Dys H 82-16 Aberuschka, Luisant, Down Again 11
29Apr87♦10SanIsidro(Arg) a7f 1:24 fm 9-5 121 Ⓣ 32 VldvsoJ ⒻPr Lmbrdo H Sweet Clover, Funny Blue, Mausie 10
30Mar87♦9SanIsidro(Arg) a1 1:343gd 9¾ 121 Ⓣ 22½ Zarate J ⒻCl Orbit Kieenia, Mausie, Fliper 7
25Feb87♦10SanIsidro(Arg) a6f 1:142sf 9-5 118 Ⓣ 1hd Zarate J ⒻPr Pipiolo H Mausie, Danseuse, Grenache 6
4Feb87♦9SanIsidro(Arg) a6f 1:092fm 24 121 Ⓣ 31 ZarateJ ⒻCl Make Trcks Mori, La Fugada, Mausie 11
7Jan87♦1SanIsidro(Arg) a5f :564fm 9-5 119 Ⓣ 1¾ Zarate J ⒻPr Zillertal(Alw) Mausie, Far Famed,LaGuainitaPora 4
●Jan 16 SA 6f ft 1:113 h ●Jan 11 SA 5f ft :593 h Jan 6 SA 4f ft :48 h Jan 1 SA 3f gd :36 h

Perfect Match II B. m. 6, by Kris—Vwonica, by Val de Loir
MCCARRON C J 116 Br.—Clore A (Fra) Tr.—Gosden John H M
Own.—Clore A Lifetime 21 5 2 5 $136,909
1987 7 1 0 3 $78,275
1986 5 4 0 0 $57,758
Turf 21 5 2 5 $136,909

10Oct87-8BM a1⅛Ⓣ 1:482fm 10 115 64 42 33½ 58 ChpTM3 ⒻHlsbrgh H 85-11 ShortSleeves,AdorableMicol,Safeer 7
10Oct87—Grade III
13Sep87-8Dmr 1⅛Ⓣ:4911:1321:501fm 14 117 11 11 2hd 62 PcLJr1 ⒻRamona H 80-17 Short Sleeves,Festivity,Auspiciante 9
13Sep87—Grade I
24Aug87-7Dmr 1 1/16Ⓣ:4731:12 1:433fm 8-5 119 32½ 32½ 22½ 3½ Pincay LJr5 ⒻAw40000 81-20 Micenas,JungleDwn,PerfectMtchII 5
6Jun87-8GG 1 Ⓣ:4831:1221:37 fm 3¾ 116 2½ 2hd 1hd 43¾ Toro F5 ⒻMis Amr H 78-20 Solva, Adorable Micol, River Char 7
24May87-10Cby 1 Ⓣ:4431:09 1:34 fm*8-5 115 24 2hd 2hd 31¾ MezaRQ2 ⒻLdy Cby H 105 — Ntur'sWy,TurnndDnc,PrfctMtchII 10
3May87-8Hol 1 1/16Ⓣ:47 1:1041:41 fm 10 116 1hd 31½ 31½ 32¾ DihssE3 ⒻWlshre H 86-11 Galunpe,TopSocilite,PerfectMtchII 6
3May87—Grade II
24Apr87-8Hol 1 Ⓣ:47 1:1131:36 fm*4-5 115 11 1½ 11½ 11½ McCrrnCJ1 ⒻⓈCnvnc 87-13 PerfectMtchII,FshionBook,Fellinin 8
25Oct86-5SA 1⅛Ⓣ:4711:1141:484fm *2 116 51¾ 31 21½ 1nk DihoussyE1 ⒻAw35000 83-17 PerfectMtchII,Rekindling,StllCloud 9
25Oct86—Stumbled badly start; crowded 3/8 turn
7Sep86-8Dmr 1⅛Ⓣ:4711:11 1:482fm 12 116 54½ 63 58 77 Toro F2 ⒻRmna H 85-08 Auspiciante, Justicara, Sauna 9
7Sep86—Grade I
7Aug86-8Dmr 1 1/16Ⓣ:4721:1211:432fm*7-5 122 42 41½ 5¾ 1nk McCrrnCJ3 ⒻAw27000 89-11 PerfectMatchII,Miranda,P'umTasty 9
Jan 16 Hol 7f ft 1:262 h Jan 10 Hol 7f ft 1:263 h Dec 29 Hol 6f ft 1:134 h Dec 24 Hol 5f ft :594 h

Serve N' Volley B. f. 4, by Music Boy—Acknowledgement, by Fleet Nasrullah
GRYDER A T 108[5] Br.—Wellery-Poley Mrs J H (Eng) Tr.—Vienna Darrell
Own.—Bollinger & Milhous Lifetime 14 3 3 2 $60,875
1988 1 0 0 1 $6,000
1987 12 3 3 1 $54,875
Turf 14 3 3 2 $60,875

7Jan88-8SA a6½f Ⓣ:221 :4531:162fm 7 1095 53½ 53 42 31½ Gryder AT9 ⒻAw40000 76-23 Annoconnor,DownAgin,SrvN'Volly 12
7Jan88—Steadied start
17Oct87♦5Newmarket(Eng) 5f 1:024gd 12 119 Ⓣ 56½ Barnard P Bentinck Perion, GovernorGeneral,Cragside 11
26Sep87♦5Ascot(Eng) 6f 1:143gd 100 121 Ⓣ 33½ BarnrdP Diadem(Gr3) Dowsing,GovGenerl,ServeN'Volley 17
18Sep87♦4Ayr(Scot) 6f 1:151gd 22 124 Ⓣ 2nk BarnrdP Ayr Gld Cp H NotSoSilly,ServeN'Volley,Norgbie 29
9Jly87♦5Newmarket(Eng) 7f 1:244gd 10 112 Ⓣ 8 BarnardP ⒻBahrain H Leyali, Nuryana, Clear Her Stage 13
8Jly87♦4Brighton(Eng) 6f 1:101fm *3 127 Ⓣ 1½ BarnardP Prsto Prk H ServeN'Volley,Exert,BchwoodCottg 7
27Jun87♦5N'wcastle(Eng) 6f 1:134gd 11 105 Ⓣ 11 BrrdP Nrthmblnd Spnt H ServeN'Volley,PickOfThePck,Nefut 9
29May87♦1Hamilton(Scot) 6f 1:114fm 5½ 123 Ⓣ 11½ WllsT Ptarmigan (Mdn) ServeN'Volley,ApplRings,RisAFlyr 10
14Apr87♦2Newmarket(Eng) 7f 1:292gd 14 123 Ⓣ 79½ Hills R ⒻG Barlng (Mdn) Morconett,GustPrformr,InThHbit 17
Jan 14 SA 3f ft :364 h Jan 1 SA 6f gd 1:161 h Dec 26 SA 6f ft 1:172 h Dec 21 SA 6f ft 1:164 h

After surveying the conditions of eligibility, class handicappers would have recognized a relatively restricted event that bars multiple route winners of first money exceeding $17,000 (a minor share at Santa Anita) for five months. Multiple stakes winners will be barred, but winners of a single stakes will be eligible. Multiple classified winners will be barred, but winners of one, two, or three nonwinners races will be eligible. Claiming-race winners have been exempted.

What do class handicappers now know?

First, in any relatively restricted classified race, the likeliest winner is an especially sharp horse (form), particularly well-suited to the distance, footing, and probable pace. Class counts, but not decisively. In any final showdown, class bows to form.

If Grade 1 or Grade 2 horses have been entered, they should *not* be well-intended. Why?

Stakes winners are prepared to win additional stakes. Graded stakes winners absolutely so. Classified events are meaningless to their prestige, incidental to their money won. All-out efforts for minor pots make no sense, and might blunt the conditioning edge needed to win in the stakes. The Graded-stakes stars may win regardless (they certainly possess the ability), but they have not been primed to explode today.

What specific types should handicappers prefer here?

An obvious preference would be a winner of a single stakes since the specified date (August 15), provided the animal remains sharp and will be well-suited to the distance (mile), footing (grass), and probable pace. The more impressive the horse's record just prior to the specified data, the better.

A second preference, less obvious, would be a multiple high-priced claiming-race winner that also has won a similar classified event and has finished close enough in Graded or Listed stakes. An in-the-money finish in an open stakes having a purse of $100,000 or more also qualifies well.

With those guidelines in mind, let's revisit the past performances and consider the records.

Frau Altiva. Away since July 5, this Grade 2 winner does not reveal the sharp form handicappers prefer in this spot, and is not well-intended either. No bet.

Hairless Heiress. Much prefers to sprint, so is not particularly well-suited to today's distance, as handicappers prefer. No bet.

Any Song. Restricted stakes winner on November 27, and currently sharp. A mile may be too short, and therefore uncomfortable, notably since the mare favors a slow pace that lets her reach contention early, or an extra-quick pace to run them down late. Contender.

Davie's Lamb. Open stakes winner at Bay Meadows on October 11, and won the restricted San Clemente stakes at Del Mar on August 14, the day before the specified date. Barely eligible. Sharp form. Likes the mile. Well suited to the probable pace.

My Virginia Reel. Grade 2 runner-up four days ago, on dirt. Won pair of allowance races prior to that, one classified, one closed. Barely eligible. Won both claiming events it entered on turf, and 4 for 6 lifetime on grass. Can attend rapid pace. Draws off if allowed a slow pace on the lead. Contender.

Mausie. Stakes winner at the distance, November 11, and before that won a closed allowance race. Good race in Grade 3 event on December 24, and extra-sharp, best-of-morning workouts since. Very sharp form. Contender.

Perfect Mach II. Short form, no bet.

Serve N' Volley. Sprinter shows a one-sprint stretchout following a layoff, a negative pattern. Probably needs more conditioning, and a softer field too. No bet.

Here are the contenders and post-time odds on each:

Any Song	6–5
Davie's Lamb	9–1
My Virginia Reel	7–1
Mausie	4–1

Carrying basic concerns about today's distance and probable pace, Any Song at 6–5 can be dismissed now. I trust handicappers understand that.

Although Davie's Lamb should improve its five-length loss to My Virginia Reel sixteen days ago, the interplay of its current class-form places it a cut below the other two contenders here. In peak form, Davie's Lamb can no doubt win, but she looks overextended today.

A crucial consideration is whether My Virginia Reel or Mausie will unleash the more powerful stretch punch after tracking Serve N' Volley for six furlongs. Late pace, from the second call to the wire, is decisive routinely in turf routes.

On January 6 My Virginia Reel finished the final three furlongs of a nine-furlong grass route in 36 2/5, winning clear. On December 24, at Hollywood, Mausie finished the final 5/16ths of 1 1/16M on grass in 31 4/5, losing three lengths off a slow pace. Review of other races reinforced the first impression: the stronger finisher is My Virginia Reel.

Lee Rousso liked Mausie from just behind the pace, a tactical advantage.

Brohamer was disinterested in the race.

I liked My Virginia Reel, lots, in part because her form looked extra sharp in a pattern of continuous improvement. Four days ago, in the mud, the six-year-old mare had contested a rapid pace all the way, before tiring inside the sixteenth pole, an impressive Grade 2 performance. Laz Barrera swung My Virginia Reel to the turf course because she relished the footing, the race was there (in the book), and the animal remained razor-sharp.

Without exception, handicappers I consulted on the contest discounted My Virginia Reel precisely because the mare had competed in a rugged race just four days ago. They judged the quick return too much, too soon. Yet handicappers understand the fast turnaround as a positive sign among sharp horses, and statistics reveal the five-day return is even more positive than the seven-day return. Trainer Barrera, less active, and less successful, since his second triple-bypass operation, is without weakness with good horses nonetheless, and handicappers had to assume he knew My Virginia Reel could withstand the four-day reversal.

At 7–1, besides, I found the maneuver irresistible. It's with fond recollection I present the result chart, and I dearly wish, as did Rousso, the exacta had been offered here.

EIGHTH RACE
Santa Anita
JANUARY 22, 1988

1 MILE.(Turf). (1.35) CLASSIFIED ALLOWANCE. Purse $60,000. Fillies and mares. 4-year-olds and upward which are non-winners of $17,000 twice other than closed or claiming at one mile or over since August 15. Weights, 4-year-olds, 120 lbs.; older, 121 lbs. Non-winners of $18,000 twice since June 15 allowed 3 lbs.; of $19,250 at one mile or over since October 1, 5 lbs.; of such a race since July 27 or $22,000 any distance since April 20, 7 lbs. (Claiming races not considered.)

Value of race $60,000; value to winner $33,000; second $12,000; third $9,000; fourth $4,500; fifth $1,500. Mutuel pool $572,243.

Last Raced	Horse	Eqt.	A.	Wt	PP	St	¼	½	¾	Str	Fin	Jockey	Odds $1
18Jan88 8SA3	My Virginia Reel		6	121	6	1	3hd	31	31½	32	1¾	Solis A	7.10
24Dec87 5Hol6	Mausie	b	6	121	7	4	21½	2½	22½	1½	21¼	Stevens G L	4.10
6Jan88 3SA4	Davie's Lamb		4	120	5	6	64	5hd	5hd	4½	3¾	Toro F	9.30
6Dec87 8Hol6	Micenas		6	116	3	8	81	8½	82	51½	42	Velasquez J	16.60
7Jan88 8SA3	Serve N' Volley		4	108	9	3	1½	11	1hd	21½	52¾	Gryder A T5	11.10
24Dec87 8Hol2	Any Song		5	118	4	9	9	9	9	81½	6hd	Shoemaker W	1.30
5Jly87 8Hol5	Frau Altiva		6	114	1	7	72	73½	71	71	73	Olivares F	25.30
27Dec87 7SA1	Hairless Heiress		5	121	2	2	41½	4½	41	61	82½	Vasquez J	13.10
10Oct87 8BM5	Perfect Match II		6	116	8	5	5hd	62	6½	9	9	McCarron C J	9.00

OFF AT 4:19. Start good. Won driving. Time, :23⅖, :47⅖, 1:11⅗, 1:24⅖, 1:37⅗ Course firm.

$2 Mutuel Prices:

6–MY VIRGINIA REEL	16.20	6.80	4.60
7–MAUSIE		5.20	4.00
5–DAVIE'S LAMB			5.20

B. m, by Roanoke Island—Tizonada, by Tinajero. Trainer Barrera Lazaro S. Bred by Dodderidge R R (Va).

MY VIRGINIA REEL lurked within close range of the early lead, responded when called upon in the stretch, took the lead in deep stretch and proved best. MAUSIE forced the early pace, vied for the lead inside SERVE N' VOLLEY around the far turn and in the upper stretch, drew clear briefly between calls in midstretch but could not outfinish the winner. DAVIE'S LAMB, unhurried while being outrun early, was steadied and shuffled back a bit when in tight quarters along the inner rail approaching the end of the backstretch, then rallied for the show. MICENAS, devoid of early speed, improved her position after six furlongs but could not gain the necessary ground in the drive. SERVE N' VOLLEY, a pace factor for a little more than seven furlongs, weakened. ANY SONG, taken in hand to trail early, failed to threaten and had no apparent mishap. FRAU ALTIVA was four wide into the stretch. HAIRLESS HEIRESS, close up early, gave way. PERFECT MATCH II, within easy striking distance early, lacked a sufficient response when called upon

At the meeting's midpoint, the handicapping trio find themselves in splendid spirits, flying high above the madding crowd. Profit margins have been full. Our conversations bear a lighthearted tone, and humor abounds. Brohamer uses understatement, Rousso irony. A unique handicapping experience has begun to bloom like the colors of rainbows.

The midway accounting explains it all:

Brohamer	$ 9,000
Quinn	$ 8,500
Rousso	$16,000

WHISTLES AND BELLS

Expectations stirred the air as Santa Anita's second half commenced. A truly outstanding horse race was blowing in the wind, and everybody from the principals to the most casual occasional racegoers knew it.

The Fifty-first running of the million-dollar Santa Anita Handicap (Grade 1) would match successive Kentucky Derby heroes Ferdinand and Alysheba at the classic 1¼M, and that pair against the other two leading handicap horses on the grounds, Judge Angelucci and Super Diamond.

The square-off would present a fascinating handicapping puzzle besides.

Ferdinand had barely whipped the then three-year-old Alysheba in the Breeders' Cup Classic three months before, emerging as Horse of the Year on a split ballot. But on February 7, in Santa Anita's Strub Stakes (Grade 1), limited to new four-year-olds, also at ten furlongs, Alysheba had dispensed a magnificent performance, earning stratospheric figures, and had triumphed with obvious reserves of speed and power.

I had no doubt the Santa Anita Handicap would bear witness to the passing of the crown.

Yet Judge Angelucci and Super Diamond had looked sensational recently while winning, and Ferdinand had prepped for the Big 'Cap in the Grade 1 San Antonio Stakes, won by stablemate Judge Angelucci, finishing a perfectly calibrated second, while neither all-out nor even doing its best.

About ten days prior to the title match, Brohamer remarked idly that Judge Angelucci might steal the race. Rousso nodded in agreement. I kept my peace for the moment, but soon asserted that Judge Angelucci had little hope of winning, citing in explanation my oft-repeated disclaimer that in definitive Grade 1 events, "class laughs at pace."

As the Big 'Cap drew nearer, debates grew louder among supporters of Ferdinand and Alysheba. A legitimate minority persisted in the opinion the Judge could be a rabbit that never would be caught. I held firm in opposition, insisting simply the Judge would be outclassed.

The past performances for this unique confrontation can be found below.

Here for handicappers' review are the latest speed and pace figures, race shapes, and class ratings for the quartet of handicap stars. The class ratings, to the far right, reflect a measure of speed and competitiveness in combination, and can vary from 10 to 100. The Grade 1 class par is 48.

Jan. 31	Super Diamond	118	113	113	AA	90
Feb. 7	Alysheba	123	122	118	FF	100
Feb. 14	Judge Angelucci	120	115	114	AA	54
Feb. 14	Ferdinand	110	108	110	AA	50

Ferdinand's figures represent his warm-up race. The champion could be expected to improve dramatically, which he did.

8th Santa Anita

1¼ MILES
SANTA ANITA
START FINISH

1 ¼ MILES. (1.57⅖) 51st Running of THE SANTA ANITA HANDICAP (Grade I). Purse $1,000,000 guaranteed. 4-year-olds and upward. By subscription of $2,000 each (regular nomination) due on or before Tuesday, December 1, 1987, fee to accompany the nomination. A sustaining payment of $2,500 each is due on or before Thursday, January 14, 1988. Supplementary nominations may be made by Friday, February 26, 1988 by payment of $25,000. All horses shall pay $5,000 to pass the entry box and $10,000 additional to start, with $550,000 guaranteed to the winner, $200,000 to second, $150,000 to third, $75,000 to fourth and $25,000 to fifth. Weights, Sunday, February 28. Starters to be named through the entry box by the closing time of entries. Trophies will be presented to the winning owner, breeder, trainer and jockey. Early bird nominations closed Friday, August 14, 1987 with 60 nominations at $500 each. Regular nominations closed Tuesday, December 1, 1987 with 24 at $2,000 each. 24 remained eligible at $2,500 each by Thursday, January 14, 1988.

Super Diamond — **B. g. 8, by Pass the Glass—One Chicken Inn, by Gaelic Dancer**
PINCAY L JR 124 — **Br.—Sahm R (Cal)** — **1988 2 1 1 0 $112,300**
Own.—Sahm R & Ramona — **Tr.—Gregson Edwin** — **1987 3 2 1 0 $129,550**
Lifetime 33 15 5 4 $1,152,133 — **Turf 7 1 1 2 $36,850**

31Jan88-8SA 1 1/16 :46 1:10^3 1:43 ft *4-5 125 4^4 3^2 1^{hd} 1^{nk} PincyLJr^2 Sn Psql H 86-21 SuprDimond,JudgAnglucc,H'sASros 5
31Jan88—Grade II
9Jan88-8SA 7f :22^1 :44^1 1:22 ft *6-5 125 7^{11} 7^{13} 7^9 2no Black CA^2 Sn Crls H 90-17 Epidurus,SuperDimond,LordRuckus 7
9Jan88—Grade II; Wide into, through stretch
12Oct87-8SA 1 1/16 :45^4 1:09^2 1:40^{4}ft *1-3 125 4^{2½} 3^2 2^1 1^{¾} PncyLJr^1 Ynkee Vlr H 97-15 SuprDimond,StopThFightrg,Infndd 5
29Aug87-8Dmr 1⅛ :45^3 1:09^1 1:47^{2}ft *2-3 124 1^1 1^{hd} 2^{hd} 2^2 Pincay LJr^3 Cabrillo H 91-12 Ferdinnd,SuperDimond,Nostlgi'sStr 3
8Aug87-8Dmr 1 1/16 :45^4 1:10 1:40^{4}ft 8-5 123 2^2 2^1 2^1 1^{½} PncyLJr^3 San Diego H 96-10 SprDmond,Nostlg'sStr,GodCmmnd 7
8Aug87—Grade III
27Nov86-8Hol 1 :46 1:10^1 1:35 ft *1-3 126 4^{¾} 1^{½} 1^{½} 1^{¾} PncLJr^5 [S]On Trust H 88-18 SuperDiamond,Nostalgia'sStr,Bozin 5
27Nov86—Wide
26Oct86-8SA 1 1/16 :46^3 1:10^2 1:41^{1}ft *1 122 2^{1½} 2^{½} 1^{hd} 1^{2¼} PncyLJr^4 Goodwd H 95-16 SuperDimond,Epidurus,PrincDonB 8
26Oct86—Grade III
20Jly86-9Hol 1¼ :45^4 1:34^3 2:00^{2}ft 3 118 3^{4½} 3^2 1^{hd} 1^{1¼} PncLJr^2 Hol Gd Cp H 90-10 SuperDimond,Alphbtim,Precisionist 6
20Jly86—Grade I
22Jun86-8Hol 1⅛ :46^3 1:10^2 1:47^{3}ft *8-5 117 4^1 4^{1½} 1^{½} 1^{1¾} PincayLJr^1 Bel Air H 99-08 SuperDiamond,Alphbtim,‡Skywlker 8
22Jun86—Grade III
1Jun86-8Hol 1 :44^1 1:08^2 1:33^{3}ft 17 117 4^{5½} 4^{3½} 2^{1½} 2^{½} Pincay LJr^4 Calfrn 94-14 Precisionist,SuperDimond,Skywlkr 7
1Jun86—Grade I

Mar 2 SA 5f m :59^3 b ●Feb 25 SA 1 ft 1:38^1 b ●Feb 19 SA 7f ft 1:27^1 b ●Feb 13 SA 6f ft 1:12^4 b

Alysheba B. c. 4, by Alydar—Bel Sheba, by Lt Stevens

MCCARRON C J 126 Br.—Madden P (Ky) 1988 1 1 0 0 $275,000

Tr.—Van Berg Jack C 1987 10 3 3 1 $2,511,156

Own.—Scharbauer Dorothy&Pamela Lifetime 18 5 7 2 $3,145,642

7Feb88-8SA 1¼ :45^{3} 1:35^{1} 2:00^{2}ft *4-5 126 58½ 1hd 1hd 13 McCrrCJ3 C H Strb 87-16 Alysheba, Candi's Gold, OrTheLine 6

7Feb88—Grade I

21Nov87-7Hol 1¼ :46^{2} 1:35^{2} 2:01^{2}ft 3½ 122 98¼ 54 41 2no McCrrCJ9 Br Cp Clsc 85-12 Ferdinnd,Alysheb,JudgeArgelucci 12

21Nov87—Grade I

27Sep87-10LaD 1¼ :47 1:36^{2} 2:03^{1}ft *1-2 126 76½ 32½ 21 1½ McCrrCJ2 Super Dby 85-19 Alysheba, Candi's Gold, Parochial 8

27Sep87—Grade I; Brushed rival

22Aug87-8Sar 1¼ :46^{1} 1:36^{2} 2:02 sy *2½ 126 712 78½ 69 620½ McCrrnCJ6 Travers 70-16 JavaGold,Cryptoclearnce,PolishNvy 9

22Aug87—Grade I

1Aug87-9Mth 1⅛ :46^{3} 1:09^{3} 1:47 ft 3-2 126 32½ 21 32½ 2nk McCrrCJ4 Haskell H 99-07 Bet Twice, Alysheba, Lost Code 5

1Aug87—Grade I; In close turn

6Jun87-8Bel 1½ :49^{2} 2:03 2:28^{1}ft *4-5 126 47 47 39 414½ McCrrCJ3 Belmont 65-15 Bet Twice, Cryptoclearance, Gulch 9

6Jun87—Grade I; Rough trip

16May87-9Pim 1$\frac{3}{16}$:47^{1} 1:11^{3} 1:55^{4}ft *2 126 56½ 43 2hd 1½ McCrrCJ6 Preakness 88-18 Alysheba,BetTwice,Cryptoclearnce 9

16May87—Grade I

2May87-8CD 1¼ :46^{2} 1:36^{4} 2:03^{2}ft 8½ 126 1312 31½ 21 1¾ McCrrCJ3 Ky Dby 80-09 Alysheba, Bet Twice, Avies Copy 17

2May87—Grade I; Stumbled 3/16

23Apr87-7Kee 1⅛ :46^{4} 1:10^{2} 1:48^{2}ft *4-5 121 32 42½ 2hd 1hd † McCrrCJ4 Blue Grass 95-13 ‡Alysheba, War, Leo Castelli 5

23Apr87—Grade I; †Disqualified and placed third

22Mar87-8SA 1$\frac{1}{16}$:46^{2} 1:10^{4} 1:43 gd 3½ 120 76½ 63½ 4¾ 2¾ Day P3 Sn Flpe H 85-23 ChartTheStrs,Alysheb,TemperteSil 8

22Mar87—Grade I; Lugged in stretch

Mar 3 SA 5f ft 1:00^{3} b Feb 24 Hol 1 ft 1:39^{3} h ●Feb 19 Hol 7f ft 1:25^{4} b Feb 4 SA 5f ft 1:00 h

Judge Angelucci Ch. h. 5, by Honest Pleasure—Victorian Queen, by Victoria Park

DELAHOUSSAYE E 123 Br.—Gentry T (Ky) 1988 2 1 1 0 $186,700

Tr.—Whittingham Charles 1987 11 7 1 1 $1,110,450

Own.—Gentry O B Lifetime 18 9 3 1 $1,306,515

14Feb88-8SA 1¼ :45^{4} 1:10^{2} 1:48^{3}ft 2 122 22 1hd 12½ 13½ DlhssyE3 Sn Antn H 86-20 JudgeAnglucci,Frdinnd,CrimsonSlw 6

14Feb88—Grade I

31Jan88-8SA 1$\frac{1}{16}$:46 1:10^{3} 1:43 ft 8-5 122 2hd 1½ 2hd 2nk DlhossyE5 Sn Psql H 86-21 SuprDimond,JudgAnglucc,H'sASros 5

31Jan88—Grade II

21Nov87-7Hol 1¼ :46^{2} 1:35^{2} 2:01^{2}ft 17 126 1hd 1hd 1hd 31½ DlhossyE3 Br Cp Clsc 84-12 Ferdinnd,Alysheb,JudgeAngelucci 12

21Nov87—Grade I

24Oct87-8BM 1⅛ :46^{1} 1:10 1:48^{1}ft *2-5 122 1hd 1hd 11½ 11 Baze G4 Bd Brs Cp 90-20 JudgeAnglucci,H'sASros,ShowDncr 4

12Sep87-8Dmr 1 :45 1:09^{1} 1:34^{4}ft *4-5 123 1½ 1hd 3½ 65½ Baze G5 Bd Br Cp H 89-14 GodCmmnd,StpThFghtng,Cnd'sGld 6

12Sep87—Bumped, steadied late

23Aug87-10Lga 1 :45^{3} 1:09^{3} 1:34^{1}ft *1-3 121 11 12 12½ 14 Baze G4 Lga Ml H 98-18 JudgAnglucci,LdingHour,SlylyGiftd 8

23Aug87—Grade II

18Jly87-9Hol 1$\frac{1}{16}$:46^{3} 1:10^{2} 1:40^{3}ft *4-5 118 11 11 12½ 13 Baze G2 Bel Air H 106-07 JdgAnglcc,BoldrThnBold,HopflWrd 5

18Jly87—Grade II

28Jun87-8Hol 1¼ :46 1:34^{3} 2:00^{3}ft *2-5e118 11 11 1½ 21½ ♦ Baze G10 Hol Gd Cp H 88-12 Ferdinand, Judge Angelucci,Tasso 11

28Jun87—Grade I; ♦Dead heat

7Jun87-8Hol 1⅛ :46^{4} 1:10^{4} 1:48^{1}ft 18 118 11 1½ 11½ 11 Baze G7 Clfrn 96-17 JudgeAngelucci,IronEyes,SnowChif 8

7Jun87—Grade I

25May87-8Hol 1 :45 1:09^{3} 1:34^{4}ft 2½ 117 1hd 2hd 2½ 44 ShmrW5 M Le Roy H 85-15 Zabaleta, Nostalgia's Star, Sabona 7

25May87—Grade II

Mar 2 SA 5f gd :59^{1} h Feb 26 SA 1 ft 1:39^{2} h Feb 21 SA 4f ft :49^{3} h ●Feb 11 SA 5f ft :59^{4} h

Ferdinand Ch. h. 5, by Nijinsky II—Banja Luka, by Double Jay

SHOEMAKER W 127 Br.—Keck H B (Ky) 1988 1 0 1 0 $50,000

Tr.—Whittingham Charles 1987 10 4 2 1 $2,185,150

Own.—Keck Mrs H B Lifetime 24 8 7 5 $3,395,478 Turf 2 0 0 1 $37,500

14Feb88-8SA 1¼ :45^{4} 1:10^{2} 1:48^{3}ft *2-3 128 612 56½ 35½ 23½ ShmkrW1 Sn Antn H 82-20 JudgeAnglucci,Frdinnd,CrimsonSlw 6

14Feb88—Grade I

21Nov87-7Hol 1¼ :46^{2} 1:35^{2} 2:01^{2}ft *1 126 64¾ 31½ 3½ 1no ShmkrW6 Br Cp Clsc 85-12 Ferdinnd,Alysheb,JudgeAngelucci 12

21Nov87—Grade I

7Nov87-8SA 1⅛ :48^{3} 1:13^{1} 1:50^{4}m 8-5 127 53½ 52 21 11 ShmkrW4 Gdwd H 75-26 Ferdinand, Candi's Gold,Skywalker 5

7Nov87—Grade III; Wide into stretch

29Aug87-8Dmr 1⅛ :45^{3} 1:09^{1} 1:47^{2}ft 3-2 126 21 2hd 1hd 12 ShomkrW2 Cabrillo H 93-12 Ferdinnd,SuperDimond,Nostlgi'sStr 3

28Jun87-8Hol 1¼ :46 1:34^{3} 2:00^{3}ft *2-5e124 42 21 2½ 11½ ShmrW5 Hol Gd Cp H 89-12 Ferdinand, Judge Angelucci,Tasso 11

28Jun87—Grade I

7Jun87-8Hol 1⅛ :46^{4} 1:10^{4} 1:48^{1}ft *8-5 126 65 53½ 54 43¾ ShoemkrW1 Clfrn 92-17 JudgeAngelucci,IronEyes,SnowChif 8

7Jun87—Grade I

10May87-8Hol 1⅛ Ⓣ:49 1:12^{2} 1:47 fm 9-5 123 2½ 2hd 21½ 32½ ShmkrW5 Jhn Hnry H 91-09 AlMamoon,SkipOutFront,Ferdinand 5

10May87—Grade I

29Mar87-8SA 1½ Ⓣ:49^{3} 2:03^{1} 2:27^{1}fm *3-2 126 1½ 2hd 3nk 42½ ShmkrW2 Sn Ls Ry 77-19 Zoffany, Louis Le Grand,LongMick 5

29Mar87—Grade I; Broke stride 1/8, 1st time around

8Mar87-8SA 1¼ :45^{4} 1:35 2:00^{3}ft *6-5e125 55¾ 1hd 11 2no ShomkrW9 S A H 86-15 BroadBrush,Ferdinnd,HopefulWord 9

8Mar87—Grade I

8Feb87-8SA 1¼ :46^{4} 1:34^{3} 2:00 ft *2 126 31 2½ 21½ 2no DlhossyE4 C H Strb 89-14 Snow Chief, Ferdinand,BroadBrush 8

8Feb87—Grade I; Bumped hard late

●Mar 2 SA 5f m :58^{3} h Feb 26 SA 1 ft 1:39^{2} h Feb 21 SA 4f ft :50^{2} h Feb 12 SA 4f ft :47^{1} h

Temperate Sil $6-0$

VELASQUEZ J   **117**

Own.—Frankfurt Stb &Whittingham

Ro. c. 4, by Temperence Hill—Rukann, by Ruken							
Br.—Frankfurt Stable (Ky)					1988	2 1 0 0	$30,250
Tr.—Whittingham Charles					1987	10 2 2 1	$533,900
Lifetime	17 6 2 1 $1,113,775				Turf	3 1 1 0	$52,000

7Feb88-8SA	1¼:45³ 1:35¹ 2:00²ft	3½ 123	1½ 4² 5¹¹ 625½	ShmkrW¹	C H Strb	61-16	Alysheba, Candi's Gold, OnTheLine 6
7Feb88—Grade I							
21Jan88-8SA	1⅛①:473 1:12 1:503fm*4-5 120		1¹ 1¹½ 13½ 12¾	ShoemkerW⁹	Aw55000	74-26	TemperateSil,Ivor'sImge,Steinlen 12
26Dec87-8SA	7f :221 :442 1:21 ft	3½ 126	94¾ 6⁴ 3⁶ 27½	ShomkrW²	Malibu	87-16	OnTheLine,TemperteSil,Cndi'sGold 9
26Dec87—Grade II							
21Nov87-4Hol	1 ①:453 1:09 1:324fm 5½e 123		2¹ 2¹½ 86½ 8⁷	ShmrW¹³	Br Cp Mile	96 —	Miesque, Show Dancer, SonicLady 14
21Nov87—Grade I							
18Oct87-8SA	1⅛①:454 1:102 1:474fm	3½ 122	1³ 1½ 1¹ 2hd	DlhossyE³	Volante H	88-15	TheMedic,TmprtSil,HotAndSmoggy 9
18Oct87—Grade III							
27Sep87-10LaD	1¼:47 1:362 2:031ft	2½ 126	54½ 4³ 42½ 45½	ShmkrW⁶	Super Dby	80-19	Alysheba, Candi's Gold, Parochial 8
27Sep87—Grade I							

The pace figures indicated Alysheba would be capable of overtaking Judge Angelucci before the horses traveled four furlongs, and could bury that frontrunner at six furlongs. In any case, Alysheba could outfinish the Judge easily. It should be no contest.

It was no contest. Moving furiously in tandem, the two champions surged past Judge Angelucci and Super Diamond so effortlessly as the four entered the far turn, the pair of pacesetters literally appeared to be going nowhere.

Jockeys Laffit Pincay (Super Diamond) and Eddie Delahoussaye (Judge Angelucci) each were moved to comment on the explosion that left them lying for dead.

"I couldn't believe they went by so fast like that," said Delahoussaye. "They just left us standing there."

Many handicappers could hardly believe it, either, and many of them, I submit, will not learn the lesson they observed. When blue-chip champions contest definitive Grade 1 stakes at classic distances, the other horses, regardless of pace, or (should I stoop to mention it?) weight, have virtually no chance.

Whenever showdowns like the 1988 Santa Anita Handicap come to pass, a Judge Angelucci will always be in the lineup. Handicappers will ponder long and hard whether that good horse can steal the race. It cannot. In the supreme tests of flesh and will, class rules. There can be no finer example than Alysheba and Ferdinand roaring by the other two handicap stars at Santa Anita as if the two were not even present, and before the real fighting had even begun. Handicappers should not forget that.

Alysheba outslugged a courageous Ferdinand throughout the entire stretch that day, winning by a secure half length. Final time was brilliant, a 1:59 ⅘ clocking, among the handful of Big 'Caps completed in less than two minutes. Par was 111, and Alysheba's figures were 110–115–116 The new champion

Nobody on our team bet, as the horses were underlays, even Judge Angelucci, at 5–1. He finished a dismal, well-beaten last. Not only was it a memorable race, but also an instructive one. The result chart is worth reviewing in full.

EIGHTH RACE

Santa Anita

MARCH 6, 1988

1 ¼ MILES. (1.57⅘) 51st Running of THE SANTA ANITA HANDICAP (Grade I). Purse $1,000,000 guaranteed. 4-year-olds and upward. By subscription of $2,000 each (regular nomination) due on or before Tuesday, December 1, 1987, fee to accompany the nomination. A sustaining payment of $2,500 each is due on or before Thursday, January 14, 1988. Supplementary nominations may be made by Friday, February 26, 1988 by payment of $25,000. All horses shall pay $5,000 to pass the entry box and $10,000 additional to start, with $550,000 guaranteed to the winner, $200,000 to second, $150,000 to third, $75,000 to fourth and $25,000 to fifth. Weights, Sunday, February 28. Starters to be named through the entry box by the closing time of entries. Trophies will be presented to the winning owner, breeder, trainer and jockey. Early bird nominations closed Friday, August 14, 1987 with 60 nominations at $500 each. Regular nominations closed Tuesday, December 1, 1987 with 24 at $2,000 each. 24 remained eligible at $2,500 each by Thursday, January 14, 1988. Total purse $1,000,000. Value of race $975,000; value to winner $550,000; second $200,000; third $150,000; fourth $75,000. $25,000 reverts to Association. Mutuel pool $1,160,501. Exacta pool $851,670.

Last Raced	Horse	Eqt.A.Wt	PP	¼	½	¾	1	Str	Fin	Jockey	Odds $1
7Feb88 8SA1	Alysheba	b 4 126	2	3½	32½	3½	1½	1¹	1½	McCarron C J	1.00
14Feb88 8SA2	Ferdinand	5 127	4	4	4	4	2¹½	2½	22½	Shoemaker W	1.70
31Jan88 8SA1	Super Diamond	8 124	1	2¹	1hd	1hd	3hd	3²	32½	Pincay L Jr	4.70
14Feb88 8SA1	Judge Angelucci	5 123	3	1¹	23	24	4	4	4	Delahoussaye E	5.30

OFF AT 5:11. Start good. Won driving. Time, :23⅕, :46⅗, 1:10, 1:34⅗, 1:59⅘ Track fast.

$2 Mutuel Prices:

2–ALYSHEBA	4.00	2.60 —
4–FERDINAND		2.80 —
1–SUPER DIAMOND		—

(No Show Wagering)
$5 EXACTA 2–4 PAID $18.00

B. c, by Alydar—Bel Sheba, by Lt Stevens. Trainer Van Berg Jack C. Bred by Madden P (Ky).

ALYSHEBA, away in alert fashion and close up early after brushing with SUPER DIAMOND in the initial strides, dropped back early in the run down the backstretch while being unhurried, moved with a rush without being hard ridden to take the lead nearing the three-eighths pole while three wide, continued in front through the final three furlongs, responded when roused with the whip once right-handed soon after passing the furlong marker and once left handed at the sixteenth marker, held on tenaciously in the last sixteenth, to respond while being hard ridden and proved best. FERDINAND trailed while being patiently handled early after breaking in good order, moved with a rush at the same time as ALYSHEBA to get near the lead approaching the three-eighths pole while four wide, forced the issue on the far turn while outside ALYSHEBA, kept after that rival through the drive but could never get past that rival while being shown the whip right handed at intervals in the final furlong. SUPER DIAMOND forced the early pace after brushing with ALYSHEBA in the opening strides, dueled for the lead on the clubhouse turn and all the way down the backstretch while inside JUDGE ANGELUCCI, continued close up along the inside on the far turn and in the upper stretch, then weakened a bit in the final furlong. JUDGE ANGELUCCI established the early pace after breaking alertly, dueled for the lead on the clubhouse turn and all the way down the backstretch while outside SUPER DIAMOND, continued close up on the far turn, came into the stretch four wide and weakened in the drive. TEMPERATE SIL (5) WAS WITHDRAWN. ALL WAGERS ON HIM IN THE REGULAR AND EXACTA POOLS WERE ORDERED REFUNDED AND ALL OF HIS PICK SIX, PICK NINE AND DAILY TRIPLE SELECTIONS WERE SWITCHED TO THE FAVORITE, ALYSHEBA (2).

Owners— 1, Scharbauer Dorothy & Pamela; 2, Keck Mrs H B; 3, Sahm R & Ramona; 4, Gentry O B.
Trainers— 1, Van Berg Jack C; 2, Whittingham Charles; 3, Gregson Edwin; 4, Whittingham Charles.
Scratched—Temperate Sil (7Feb88 8SA6).

Where winter racing occurs, Florida, California, New York, and Oaklawn Park, handicappers who keep a log of figures earned by three-year-olds in stakes can convert the numbers to dollars.

Table 1 presents the ten stakes-winning three-year-olds in routes at Santa Anita (1988) through April 9, date of the Santa Anita Derby (Grade 1), with speed and pace figures, race shapes, and class ratings. Developing horses, three-year-olds vary widely in real abilities. One stakes winner does not equal another. The figures of stakes will be telescopes to the near future. The tabulations below guided three handicappers to small pots of gold in the Kentucky Derby, not to mention the Santa Anita Derby itself.

Even more. When the season began, Brohamer and Rousso agreed Mi Preferido would be the colt to beat in Santa Anita's derby. Brohamer recited its impressive figures in the Grade 2 Hollywood Juvenile, a key race on the two-year-old calendar. Runners-up and other graduates from the field had won repeatedly in their next races.

As events proceeded, the three of us benefitted as Mi Preferido won the Grade 1 San Felipe Handicap at 4–1, when he should have been 6–5. Examine its record just prior to the Grade 1 stakes.

Mi Preferido

Dk. b. or br. c. 3, by Island Whirl—Exacting Lady, by Disciplinarian

MCCARRON C J   **119**   Br.—Saiden A (Fla)   1988   2 1 0 0 $49,025
Own.—Barrera & Saiden   Tr.—Barrera Lazaro S   1987   2 2 0 0 $86,350
Lifetime   4 3 0 0 $135,375

27Feb88-8SA   1 :45¹ 1:10² 1:38 ft   *4-5 118   22½ 2¹ 3² 5¹½   Solis A⁴   Sn Rafl   77-17 WhtADplmt,FlyngVctr,SccssExprss 9
   27Feb88—Grade II; Broke out, bumped; bumped again late
27Jan88-8SA   7f :22   :44¹ 1:22³ft   3-2 120   2hd 1hd 1½ 14½   Solis A³   Sn Vcnt   87-19 MPrfrdo,NoCmmtmnt,SccssExprss 5
   27Jan88—Grade III; Broke through gate
25Jly87-8Hol   6f :21³   :44³ 1:10 ft   4½ 117   3¹ 3² 2¹½ 1³   Solis A⁵   Hol Juv Chp   93-16 MiPreferido,MixedPlsur,PurduKing 8
   25Jly87—Grade II
20Jun87-4Hol   5½f :22   :45³ 1:04²ft   3-2 117   2hd 1hd 1¹ 1⁵   Solis A⁵   Mdn   92-11 Mi Preferido, Iz A Saros, Scientific 6
●Mar 17 SA 6f ft :58¹ h   Mar 11 SA 5f ft :59² h   Feb 25 SA 4f ft :47¹ h   ●Feb 19 SA 5f ft :59² h

Brohamer had bet Mi Preferido on its comeback January 27 at 3–2, second choice that day to Breeders' Cup Juvenile hero Success Express. After breaking through the starting gate, Mi Preferido won handily.

What happened February 27, when Mi Preferido disappointed at 4–5?

Date	Horse	4F	6F	Final	Shape	Class
	Table 1: 3YO Stakes Winner, Routes, Santa Anita 1988 Figures, Shapes, Class Ratings					
1/13	Please Remit	120	112	107	AA	40
1/20	Winning Colors	120	111	105	FA	42
	Lively One	104	100	109	SF	56
2/10	Goodbye Halo (G1)	134	112	106	AA	72
2/20	What A Diplomat	140	115	103	AS	36
2/27	Jeanne Jones	118	106	105	AA	42
3/2	Stalwars	88	96	108	SF	42
3/9	Winning Colors (Gr. 1)	118	112	111	FF	100
3/13	Mi Preferido (Gr. 1)	114	104	109	AF	54
3/20	Winning Colors (Gr. 1)	116	107	114	AF	90
4/9						

Notes.
1. Prior to the Santa Anita Derby (April 9), Lively One and Winning Colors rated two lengths apart on speed figures, and the filly had clear pace advantages and significant class advantages.
2. Mi Preferido has a speed figure (109) within shouting distance of the division leader, but its victory March 13 suggests the colt might need a breather on the pace to show its best.
3. The Stalwars speed figure (108) can be discounted, perhaps significantly, due to inordinately slow pace figures. If forced to attend a fast early pace, what would the colt do? No one knows.

Mi Preferido "bounced."

The pace January 27 had been vicious, lasting until the horses passed the sixteenth pole. After attending another rapid pace at the route February 27, Mi Preferido just collapsed. The slow final time misled the crowd. But the colt "bounced back" on March 20, trouncing the odds-on Lively One in one of the ripest prime bets of the season.

EIGHTH RACE
Santa Anita
MARCH 20, 1988

1 1/16 MILES. (1.40⅕) 51st Running of THE SAN FELIPE HANDICAP (Grade I). $150,000 added. 3-year-olds. By subscription of $100 each to accompany the nomination, $1,500 additional to start with $150,000 added, of which $30,000 to second, $22,500 to third, $11,250 to fourth and $3,750 to fifth. Weights Tuesday, March 15. Starters to be named through the entry box by the closing time of entries. A trophy will be presented to the owner of the winner. Closed Wednesday, March 9, 1988 with 18 nominations.

Value of race $163,800; value to winner $96,300; second $30,000; third $22,500; fourth $11,250; fifth $3,750. Mutuel pool $743,765. Exacta Pool $643,905.

Last Raced	Horse	Eqt.	A.	Wt	PP	St	¼	½	¾	Str	Fin	Jockey	Odds $1
27Feb88 $^{8}SA^{5}$	Mi Preferido		3	119	1	1	$1^{1\frac{1}{2}}$	$1^{\frac{1}{2}}$	$1^{\frac{1}{2}}$	$1^{\frac{1}{2}}$	$1^{2\frac{3}{4}}$	McCarron C J	4.30
27Feb88 $^{8}SA^{6}$	Purdue King		3	119	2	2	$3^{1\frac{1}{2}}$	2^{1}	2^{1}	2^{2}	$2^{\frac{1}{2}}$	Toro F	16.00
24Feb88 $^{8}SA^{2}$	Tejano		3	122	5	4	4^{1}	4^{1}	$4^{1\frac{1}{2}}$	3^{1}	$3^{3\frac{1}{2}}$	Delahoussaye E	3.50
10Feb88 $^{8}SA^{1}$	Lively One		3	122	4	5	$6^{2\frac{1}{2}}$	$6^{\frac{1}{2}}$	5^{3}	$4^{\frac{1}{2}}$	4^{hd}	Shoemaker W	.80
27Feb88 $^{8}SA^{1}$	What A Diplomat		3	117	7	3	$2^{\frac{1}{2}}$	$3^{1\frac{1}{2}}$	$3^{\frac{1}{2}}$	5^{6}	$5^{9\frac{1}{2}}$	Stevens G L	11.30
31Oct87 $^{8}SA^{1}$	Saratoga Passage	b	3	119	6	7	8	8	6^{4}	6^{7}	6^{11}	Steiner J J	13.60
24Feb88 $^{7}GP^{1}$	Jet Charlie		3	114	8	8	$7^{\frac{1}{2}}$	7^{hd}	7^{hd}	7^{hd}	7^{4}	Velasquez J	81.90
27Feb88 $^{8}SA^{4}$	Please Remit		3	117	3	6	$5^{\frac{1}{2}}$	$5^{\frac{1}{2}}$	8	8	8	Hawley S	36.30

OFF AT 4:57. Start good. Won driving. Time, :22⅗, :46⅖, 1:10⅘, 1:35⅘, 1:42⅕ Track fast.

$2 Mutuel Prices:				
	1-MI PREFERIDO	10.60	6.80	4.80
	2-PURDUE KING		11.20	5.40
	5-TEJANO			3.80

$5 EXACTA 1-2 PAID $205.00.

Dk. b. or br. c, by Island Whirl—Exacting Lady, by Disciplinarian. Trainer Barrera Lazaro S. Bred by Saiden A (Fla).

MI PREFERIDO, off alertly, established the early pace while under a snug rating hold, responded in the drive to edge clear coming to the sixteenth marker, then extended his advantage in the final sixteenth when continuing to respond while being hard ridden. PURDUE KING, reserved early while close up, pressed the issue while inside MI PREFERIDO from midway down the backstretch to midstretch, could not keep pace with that rival from midstretch to finish but held on for the place. TAJANO, never far back, menaced on the far turn and in the upper stretch but lacked the needed response in the last furlong. LIVELY ONE, permitted to settle into stride early and bumped entering the clubhouse turn, moved up to get within easy striking distance on the far turn while along the inside rail but failed to sustain his rally in the drive. WHAT A DIPLOMAT, close up to the stretch, weakened. JET CHARLIE broke a bit awkwardly and stumbled in the initial strides, then was wide down the backstretch. PLEASE REMIT bumped with MI PREFERIDO entering the clubhouse turn

Meanwhile, Lee Rousso had succumbed to the charms of Winning Colors before the filly even won a stakes. He admired the manner in which she had breezed on the lead, throwing elegant fractions at opponents, as she eliminated her eligibility conditions.

I waited to see more.

When Winning Colors was defeated in her inaugural Grade 1 try against division leader Goodbye Halo, the 4F pace figure was a super 134. The final figure was par, at 106. Winning Colors had lost by a neck in a strong performance, thrashing the third finisher by eight lengths.

I now was impressed, as I understood how talented Goodbye Halo was.

When the two next met, March 13, in the Santa Anita Oaks (Grade 1), Winning Colors devastated Goodbye Halo, trouncing her by eight in a fast-fast race, forcing the outstanding division leader to spit it out.

Brohamer, Quinn, and Rousso jointly announced the filly would win the Santa Anita Derby as she pleased.

Brohamer announced further his intention to visit the Kentucky Derby future books in Las Vegas the following week.

Rousso predicted the Kentucky Derby would be a war between Winning Colors, of the west, and Forty Niner, of the east. Quite a prediction.

Ten days later Brohamer drove to Vegas, and while there bet $60 to win on Winning Colors in the Kentucky Derby. The delay cost him plenty. He got 20–1 at the Gold Coast. If Brohamer had scurried to Caliente, in Mexico, the Monday morning following the Oaks, he would have been tendered 50–1. Not a few believers did, allegedly including a band of grooms and hot walkers from the Lukas barn, toting $2000. They eventually would go back, to pick up $100,000.

Curiously, none of us cared a trifle for Lively One, widely considered the leading colt for the Santa Anita Derby. Spokesmen for the excellent *Handicapper's Report* thought Lively One a virtual cinch. Numerous public selectors agreed.

The numbers appeared clear and convincing on the issue, and not in Lively One's favor. Check the speed and pace figures, and class ratings, for the colt and filly, respectively, below:

	Date	4F	6F	Final	Shape	Class
Lively One	1/14	112	107	104	AA	21
	2/10	104	100	109	SF	56
	3/20	109	100	102	AF	47
Winning Colors	1/20	120	111	105	FA	42
	2/20	134	112	106	AA	72
	3/13	118	112	111	FF	100

Lively One's single impressive figure, a 109, had resulted from a slow pace. Its races in the aggregate had suggested Lively One suffered a pace weakness, and the figures broadcast it loudly. A one-run type, Lively One could not expect to attend the pace or chase the pace of a Winning Colors and hope to prevail. Yet one-run horses, 3YOs in particular, lose more of their punch as distances lengthen. Lively One's dilemma in fast-fast Grade 1 competition should be classical: damned if you do, damned if you don't.

At 5–2, Winning Colors appealed to many handicappers as an overlay in the Santa Anita Derby, and she won like it. Three prime bets to win were cashed in our box, but I goofed by taking several exactas to Mi Preferido, some others to Tejano. I felt Lively One would run out, and wanted to capitalize. In my defense, Mi Preferido chased the filly's brilliant pace of 22 1/5, 45 3/5, 1:09 2/5, 1:34 4/5, and weakened. Lively One got up for second—a dull, tortured placing, beaten 7½ lengths. A softer pace, I insist, and Mi Preferido stays for second.

Winning Colors's derby figure of 114 trailed Alysheba's top figure of 118 by four lengths, a remarkable achievement for a developing three-year-old filly. She was a gem, to be sure.

When the Kentucky Derby had run its course, Brohamer cashed his future-book ticket, pocketing $1200, and Rousso cashed his Winning Colors–Forty Niner exactas, pocketing a grand.

Me?

In Kentucky the week of the Bluegrass Stakes (Grade 1), ten days prior to the Derby, I might have found my fortune betting head to head with locals who despised the California filly's chances. As far as a California handicapper could tell, no one in Kentucky accorded Winning Colors a decent shot. I went to the well person to person for $400, and cashed the checks when they arrived.

On March 18, 4th race, as Brohamer and I sat impassively, Lee Rousso counted out $1000 and put it on the nose of the filly below under the maiden-claiming conditions specified.

4th Santa Anita

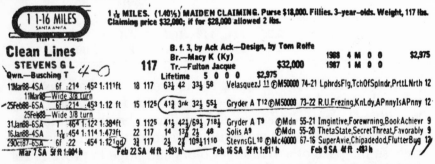

Loser of consecutive maiden-claiming sprints at the $50,000 selling price, Clean Lines was dropping to $32,000 today and stretching out.

On cold dope, Clean Lines shaped up as a classic good news–bad news proposition. At 8–5, a top handicapper invests his largest bet of the season on this ordinary-looking filly competing under the cheapest racing conditions at Santa Anita. How come?

The bad news?

First, on March 11, versus $50,000 maiden claimers, par 99, Clean Lines earned figures of 97 (pace) and 90 (final).

Because the pars at Santa Anita for $32,000 maiden claimers were slower by three lengths for six furlongs and by four lengths at 1 1/16M than pars for $50,000 maiden claimers, I had approached the 1988 season with the notion of capitalizing on these frequent dropdowns. I had come up empty so far, reinforcing my traditional attitude that changes in selling prices under maiden-claiming conditions are unreliable and therefore meaningless.

Second, by Brohamer's early-energy requirements, Clean Lines might be clearly uncomfortable at the route. Her early-energy distribution February 25 was 54.57 fps, and on March 11 was 54.17 fps, when route winners were averaging 52.20 fps. The differences looked enormous, approximately 14 to 15 lengths.

Third, Clean Lines had lost ground, not only in the stretch of every race it had started, but between the prestretch and stretch calls as well. Its losses while sprinting under maiden-claiming conditions looked depressingly similar.

Now, for the good news.

Clean Lines would be moving from the far outside in sprints to the rail in a route. Its early speed would be a potent factor here.

Clean Lines was handled by Jacque Fulton, one of the most impressive new faces at the meeting.

Clean Lines was returning in seven days, with the price drop accompanied by a jockey switch to leading rider Gary Stevens, plus factors associated with form, class, and jockey.

Rousso supplied the bottom line.

"Beginning March first, a two-turn speed bias in routes has helped frontrunners tremendously. That bias has been especially strong the past two days."

In a laugher, Clean Lines controlled the pace from the outset, led by ten at the stretch call, and won by 7½. Rousso netted $1600 so easily it seemed like stealing.

When the filly dominated so powerfully, we discussed the race. Rousso stressed the strength of track biases.

"When a speed bias is strong, it supersedes all else. It supersedes figures. It supersedes pace, including early energy.

It just propels the speed horses to victory. Clean Lines is another undeniable illustration."

Lee Rousso's radio colleague Aaron Hess twice invited Tom Brohamer to be the guest handicapper at a weekend-morning seminar he hosted near the racetrack.

On the two occasions, Brohamer picked ten horses for the customers, and eight of them won. Ah, consistency!

The best, and the boldest, involved Brohamer's meeting-long benefactor Mischievous Matt, a horse Tom understands like nobody else, I suppose.

Earlier handicappers saw how Mischievous Matt went from sprint to route while double-jumped in class successfully, essentially because the horse's early energy fit the route pace of winners so snugly.

Now Mischievous was being double-jumped in class anew, to $32,000 following a claim for $20,000, a difficult rise at Santa Anita, and would be simultaneously switching distance from route to sprint, a difficult change of distance He faced a 6–5 favorite named Cliff's Place, who had finished second at the distance for $32,000 claimers last out, after recording a high pace figure and running a turn time of 22 4/5.

Examine the figures and records below:

Cliff's Place	Feb. 3	104/	111	104	FA	
	Jan. 3	103/	111	102	FA	
Mischievous Matt	Mar. 3	102/	106	106	99	AS
	Feb. 17	102/	112	101	102	AA
	Feb. 11	100/	100	104	AF	

Not unlike numerous effective sprinters, Cliff's Place regularly set a blazing pace and finished at par. Its preferred shape is fast-average.

Mischievous Matt possessed tactical speed in long sprints, and finished strongly. Its preferred sprint is average-fast.

Aaron Hess, age twenty-one, dismissed a Mischievous Matt shortening up on the double rise. He conceded the race to the favorite, which had not competed in thirty-seven days.

Brohamer countered, anticipating the probable pace.

"If Cliff's Place weakens at six-and-a-half furlongs, as is his tendency, Mischievous Matt will be close enough to collar him. At the odds, Mischievous Matt should be a good bet today."

The good odds Brohamer hinted at would be 11–1, an overlay. Alive for a $130 double, Brohamer bolstered his position in the race with a prime bet to win.

Cliff's Place did falter, and Mischievous Matt blew past, to win by 4½ lengths. He paid a premium $24.20.

SECOND RACE
Santa Anita
MARCH 13, 1988

6½ FURLONGS. (1.14) CLAIMING. Purse $25,000. 4-year-olds and upward. Weight, 121 lbs. Non-winners of two races since December 25 allowed 3 lbs.; of a race since then, 5 lbs. Claiming price $32,000; for each $2,000 to $28,000 allowed 1 lb. (Races when entered for $25,000 or less not considered.)

Value of race $25,000; value to winner $13,750; second $5,000; third $3,750; fourth $1,875; fifth $625. Mutuel pool $304,131.

Last Raced	Horse	Eqt.	A.	Wt	PP	St	¼	½	Str	Fin	Jockey	Cl'g Pr	Odds $1
3Mar88 5SA4	Mischievous Matt		5	115	3	3	2 1½	2 1	1½	1 4½	Castanon A L	28000	11.10
17Feb88 5SA6	Time To Smoke	b	5	118	10	2	3 1½	3 3½	3 3½	2¾	Gryder A T	32000	12.00
3Feb88 5SA2	Cliff's Place	b	4	116	2	1	1 2½	1 2½	2 2½	3½	Meza R Q	32000	1.30
17Feb88 5SA4	Fuzzy Bear		5	117	9	5	6hd	6hd	5½	4½	Pincay L Jr	32000	3.30
28Feb88 5SA4	Breu	b	7	116	11	4	4hd	5 2	6 2½	5 2¾	McHargue D G	32000	12.20
14Feb88 5SA5	Tropical Whip	b	5	111	6	11	11	9 1	7½	6 1½	Banderas A L5	32000	4.90
6Dec87 7Hol7	Mon Legionnaire	b	4	116	7	10	9½	7 2	8 1½	7½	Shoemaker W	32000	58.00
20Feb88 9SA9	Nordicus	b	6	116	1	9	8½	8 1½	9 3½	8hd	Sibille R	32000	23.00
5Mar88 2SA4	Sasebo	b	5	116	4	7	5 2	4hd	4hd	9 6	Pedroza M A	32000	22.50
3Mar88 7SA6	Wily	b	4	116	5	6	7½	11	10 1½	10 2½	Ortiz M F Jr	32000	50.00
21Feb87 9SA10	Kilauea		8	116	8	8	10 3½	10 1	11	11	Patton D B	32000	116.90

OFF AT 1:34. Start good. Won ridden out. Time, :21⅗, :44⅘, 1:09⅘, 1:16⅘ Track fast.

$2 Mutuel Prices:			
3–MISCHIEVOUS MATT	24.20	11.40	5.60
11–TIME TO SMOKE		12.00	6.40
2–CLIFF'S PLACE			2.80

Dk. b. or br. h, by Run of Luck—Classic Caper, by Pilot John. Trainer Hess R B Jr. Bred by Waller H E (Wash).

MISCHIEVOUS MATT, nearest to CLIFF'S PLACE while that rival set the early pace, took over in the upper stretch and pulled away in the last furlong while under periodic right handed pressure. TIME TO SMOKE, in a forward position throughout, gained the place. CLIFF'S PLACE made the early pace and weakened in the drive. FUZZY BEAR, outrun early, could not gain the needed ground in the drive. BREU, in contention early after bobbling at the start, lacked the necessary response when called upon. TROPICAL WHIP broke slowly and was never prominent. MON LEGIONNAIRE was wide down the backstretch. NORDICUS was four wide into the stretch.

Andrew Beyer has written that speed figures can be particularly useful to predict which claiming horses can stand the rise. Tom Brohamer adores high-figure claiming horses taking a double-jump in class, notably out of a competent barn, and definitely if the probable pace will be favorable. Handicappers are urged to partake of this claiming pie themselves.

For keepers of figures, windfalls in exactas will come to them from this special angle. In contentious claiming sprints, two horses possess clearly superior speed and pace figures. Both figures must be higher than par. The two horses alone exhibit fast-fast race shapes.

It was February 28, 5th race, a $32,000 claiming sprint, 4up, with the favorite in a full field a dismissive 5–1. To naked eyes, eyeballing unadjusted actual times, the race looked far more contentious than it was. Below are the latest speed and pace figures of the six main contenders. The $32,000 claiming par, 6F, at Santa Anita, was 104. Find the cold exacta:

Social Diamond	104/	102	104	AA
Sasebo	106/	100	101	AA
Cactus Clipper	106/	104	97	AA
Sundance Square	103/	108	108	FF
Growler Sandue	104/	108	100	FF
Ruler of Fleets	103/	109	105	FF

The cold exacta links Sundance Square and Ruler of Fleets. Growler Sandue exits a fast-fast race, comparable class, but fell apart the second half. Following a rapid pace, numerous sprinters do the same.

I relished a win bet here as well. The horse exhibited improving figures in each of its four starts at the meeting, and resided in the hot Craig Lewis stable. Here are the running lines and figures for Sundance Square.

Speed & Pace Figures, Race Shapes

February 20	103/	108	108	FF
February 10	103/	110	105	FF
January 24	103/	111	103	FA
January 3	103/	109	101	FA

Ruler of Fleets showed the improvement pattern also, its last figure its best, but had tailed off consistently above $25,000.

I split a prime bet, half to win, half to exactas, using Sundance Square predominantly on top.

Sundance Square fought off pace-pusher Growler Sandue and won straight, paying a sweet $13. Not far back at the quarter pole, Ruler of Fleets chased the winner evenly through the late stages. The exacta paid $179.50. I took my largest single-race dividend from the pools, $2254.

DOLDRUMS

On February 3, the thirtieth day, Lee Rousso began to co-host, Wednesday through Sunday, a thirty-minute radio show on racing and handicapping. The show went on the air at 8 A.M.

At ten-thirty A.M. every racing day, Rousso appeared at his mid-morning seminar at a restaurant near Santa Anita.

From the seminar Rousso hustled to the racetrack, where he stayed active until closing, five-thirty to six P.M.

At seven-thirty every racing night, Rousso sat glued to the television replays of the afternoon's races.

At eight nightly Rousso confronted the concentrated two-hour task of handicapping the next day's program. After that he prepared a mini-script for the next morning's radio show.

This amounts to a timetable for disaster, and frankly, I told him so more than once.

Rousso's antidote, a palliative, was an afternoon's nap on Thursdays, bum cards he was willing to miss.

The first nap was indulged on Thursday, February 18. That morning, on the radio, Rousso nudged the audience toward Double The Charm in the 5th, a nonwinners-once allowance heat at nine furlongs over grass, for older fillies and mares.

Double The Charm looked like so in the past performances:

Double The Charm Ch. f. 4, by Nodouble—Album, by Never Bend
GRYDER A T 1115 Br.—Mabee Mr-Mrs J C (Cal) 1988 2 1 0 1 $16,800
Own.—Evans & GMBreedingFmsInc Tr.—Lewis Craig A 1987 8 1 1 0 $17,950
Lifetime 10 2 1 1 $34,750 Turf 1 0 0 0

31Jan88-2SA	1 1/16 :471 1:123 1:461ft	9	115	32½	2½	11	15	Stevens G L 12	Ⓕ 25000	70-21	DoubleTheChrm,ElevnSirrs,Bstilli	12
6Jan88-9SA	1 1/16 :462 1:113 1:444ft	8¼	115	2hd	2½	21½	34¼	Stevens G L 1	Ⓕ 25000	73-19	SmmrGlow,BoldArrgnc,DblThChrm	8
27Dec87-1SA	1 1/16 :47 1:122 1:463ft	26	1085	1½	1hd	2hd	2hd	Sherman A B 7	Ⓕ 20000	68-17	GrnEmoton,DblThChrm,LftHrMrk	11
10Dec87-1Hol	6f :221 :45 1:093ft	40	115	85½	1011	1123	1118½	Toro F 11	ⒻⓈ 25000	75-11	LaSierra,Divest,SweetExpecttions	12
10Dec87—Wide 3/8 turn												
28Nov87-7Hol	1 1/16 :47 1:112 1:443ft	6¼	117	66	67	46	55¾	Pincay L Jr 3	Ⓕ 32000	74-18	FirstSilverHwk,Divest,DoubleDent	10
30Oct87-3SA	1 1/16 :473 1:123 1:443gd	22	1125	31½	41½	642	71¾	Gryder A T 5	ⒻAw29000	63-21	VryClssyLdy,BhindThScns,C'sVigor	8
30Oct87—Wide 3/8 turn												
16Oct87-5SA	1⅛ Ⓣ:46 1:1121:491fm	35	117	44	2½	31½	96½	Hawley S 9	ⒻAw30000	74-19	TimeForHart,JustMine,SlyChrmer	10
16Oct87—Broke out, bumped												
4Oct87-8Fpx	1 1/16 :463 1:122 1:443ft	6¾	114	32	95¼	99½	712	PttnDB 1	ⒻⓇAmnda S	75-12	Beseya,Annastance,John'sLdyLuck	9
20Sep87-6Fpx	1 1/16 :464 1:124 1:452ft	6	1085	1hd	12	15	111	Patton D B 8	ⒻMdn	84-16	DoublThChrm,StrOfLov,Ninpythln	10
2Sep87-4Dmr	6f :22 :45 1:102ft	9¼	1125	98	812	613	410½	GrydrAT5	ⒻⓈMc32000	76-17	LdyKell,TimeToSweep,ChicMoren	11
2Sep87—Fractious gate												

Feb 11 SA tr.t 6f ft 1:15 h

The four-year-old displayed the charms Rousso can hardly resist, and most handicappers fail to perceive, in these elementary allowances limited to older horses. Double The Charm exits a big win for a hot trainer versus mid-level claiming-race winners. She boasts a leading turf sire, and will be making only her second start on the grass.

Nodouble, 13 percent lifetime on the turf, in the not-too-distant past had qualified for Quirin's top-ten list among Master Grass Sires, meaning his turf progeny pay generously when they win. Quirin urges handicappers to bet these types on their first and second grass attempts.

While Rousso was sleeping, Double The Charm scampered wire to wire against a nondescript allowance group, and paid $51. A predictable exacta returned $1934.

The bad omen ushered in a period of six weeks where Rousso's streaks consisted of small peaks and deep valleys. He treaded water the last part of February, and donated $3000 during March. The March contribution might have been greater, but a two-turn speed bias that endured throughout the month saved his bacon.

On March 17, St. Patrick's Day, Rousso felt like a lucky Irishman as he knocked down a $1000 profit for the first time in a month, cashing a triple worth $173 multiple times on top of a $200 win bet assisted by the bias.

The next afternoon he followed with the major wager on Clean Lines, who rode the bias to a ridiculously facile victory.

On March 20 he found another thousand aided by the bias. He exploited the route bias a final time March 23, harvesting $1300 from the 1st and 9th races.

Before and after the seven days, victories of any kind managed to escape. Prime horses lost, and exactas, triples, and Pick 6 investments kept adding up. The overtime hours began to extract an enormous energy toll.

By early April, Rousso had resigned himself to the season's first long losing streak. He had begun to slice the bets.

"I try to cheat my losing streaks by betting less," he announced, following a galling loss he deserved to win.

A second adjustment went unannounced, but not unobserved. Beginning April 1, Rousso took two afternoon naps, on Fridays as well as Thursdays. Andy Beyer would not approve. The extra rest, I'm pleased to report, did not cost Rousso an additional $50 winner.

In the meantime, Tom Brohamer himself had crashed into the seven-week wall. The smashup was predictable, its victim prepared for the calamity.

"It's virtually the same for me at Santa Anita each season. Toward late February, about the seven-week mark, I hit a wall. Mental fatigue sets in and I need a break."

Brohamer took a two-week vacation. He went camping and fly-fishing, while keeping variants and a casual eye peeled to the races from afar. While at the track in March, however, Brohamer could accomplish little more than treading water, a fisherman awaiting the big catch that did not bite.

"During downturns," he said, "my goal is to play them even."

For six weeks, roughly March 1 until the second week of April, Brohamer fastened on few prime bets. When prime horses offered inadequate value, smartly, he abstained. He played a pat hand for the most part, advancing a little, sliding back a little more. During the dry spell, Brohamer dropped $1200.

Until the final days of March, my game remained consistent, my spirits bright. Looking back after the season, I was surprised to learn that half my profits in March had resulted from a few highly selective wagers in maiden-claiming races. With so many of these doleful processions crowding the cards of major tracks nowadays, let's pause here to look at two special situations handicappers might exploit.

On March 2, the fifty-first day, I found a play, at last, I had been thirsting for since opening week. I owe the outcome to San Francisco professional Ron Cox, which I shall explain shortly. First, examine the past performances below, and try to pick the winner.

2nd Santa Anita

START
6 FURLONGS
SANTA ANITA
FINISH

6 FURLONGS. (1.07⅗) **MAIDEN CLAIMING. Purse $16,000. 3-year-olds. Weight, 118 lbs.; Claiming price $32,000; if for $28,000 allowed 2 lbs.**

Don Scala
GRYDER A T 118
Own.—Christando & Gatto
Dk. b. or br. c. 3, by Eridanus—Pappa's Chrissy, by Struck Out
Br.—Gatto & Christando (Cal) 1988 1 M 0 0
Tr.—Mayer V James $32,000 1987 0 M 0 0
Lifetime 1 0 0 0
13Feb88-6SA 1 :463 1:13 1:393ft 123 117 1018 1019 1027 1037½ Black C A2 Mdn 33-22 Mister W., Script, Recitation Spin 10
Mar 1 SA 3f m :372 h (d) Feb 25 SA 5f ft 1:023 hg Feb 11 SA 3f ft :351 h Feb 5 SA 5f ft 1:021 h

Angel J.
SOLIS A 118
Own.—Weaver K
B. g. 3, by Boitron—Round the Market, by Rising Market
Br.—Dollase W A (Cal) 1988 2 M 1 0 $3,200
Tr.—Velasquez Danny $32,000 1987 1 M 0 0
Lifetime 3 0 1 0 $3,200
3Feb88-6SA 6f :213 :451 1:111ft 10 118 84½ 85¾ 65½ 1014½ Solis A11 M50000 68-20 BurnAnnie,Hnd'sScrt,FirstToArriv 11
3Feb88—Veered in start
22Jan88-4SA 6f :221 :461 1:121ft 3 118 1hd 2½ 21½ 2hd Solis A6 [S]M32000 77-17 Vancealot, Angel J., Finski 12

Arco's Fancy Guy
FERNANDEZ A L 118
Own.—Hampton J & D
B. c. 3, by Arco—Fancy Tassle, by Space Ruler
Br.—Warren H H DVM (Cal) 1988 2 M 0 0
Tr.—Landers Dale $32,000 1987 0 M 0 0
Lifetime 2 0 0 0
12Feb88-4SA 6f :214 :452 1:12 ft 130 116 77½ 78 911 913½ Fernandez A L4 M35000 64-24 Mikes Lad, Mr.Rusty,GranaAmigo 12
12Feb88—Bumped start
27Jan88-2SA 6f :214 :452 1:114ft 109 118 84½ 1013 1016 920 Fernandez A L7 M32000 59-19 ChrlesTheGret,Dndyroo,JetSkiing 12
Feb 26 SA 4f ft :483 h Feb 9 SA 3f ft :353 h Jan 20 SA 5f ft 1:03 hg Jan 13 SA 3f ft :364 hg

Liberalartsdiploma
PEDROZA M A 118
Own.—Siegel M-Jan-Samantha
Dk. b. or br. c. 3, by In Reality—Sheepskin, by Arts and Letters
Br.—Marriott W D (Ky) 1988 1 M 0 0
Tr.—Mayberry Brian A $32,000 1987 1 M 0 0
Lifetime 2 0 0 0
3Feb88-6SA 6f :213 :451 1:111ft 50 118 3½ 74½ 1071 913½ Pedroza M A9 M50000 69-20 BurnAnnie,Hnd'sScrt,FirstToArriv 11
18Jly87-4Hol 6f :221 :453 1:102ft 21 117 52 711 812 818¾ McHargue D G6 Mdn 72-07 Bold Second, Balote, Running Over 8
Feb 25 SA 4f ft :484 h Feb 16 SA 4f ft :492 h Jan 29 SA 4f ft :493 h Jan 10 SA 4f ft :49 h

P. Tonker
MCCARRON C J 118
Own.—Stockseth W O & Norma
Ch. g. 3, by Beat Inflation—Tutoyer, by Faliraki
Br.—Sterling L J & Judy (Fla) 1988 1 M 0 0
Tr.—Heap Blake $32,000 1987 0 M 0 0
Lifetime 1 0 0 0
18Feb88-6SA 6f :214 :451 1:121ft 38 116 53¾ 65½ 109¼ 98¾ McCarron C J6 M45000 68-30 Field Of View, ‡Pevikson,F.H.King 12
18Feb88—Placed eighth through disqualification; Jostled start
Feb 26 SA 6f ft 1:183 h Feb 18 SA 3f ft :381 h Feb 12 SA 3f ft :353 hg Feb 6 SA 6f ft 1:16 hg

Milk N Quacker's
VALENZUELA P A 118
Own.—Belles H J (Lessee)
Ch. c. 3, by Sumarlid—Milkmaid, by Inverness Drive
Br.—Manzi J (Cal) 1988 2 M 0 0
Tr.—Manzi Joseph $32,000 1987 0 M 0 0
Lifetime 2 0 0 0
10Feb88-4SA 1 1/16 :474 1:133 1:481ft 5½ 117 54 75½ 86½ 99 Hawley S12 [S]M32000 51-23 Cori'sPrinc,CutiousEgl,NothngLft 12
22Jan88-4SA 6f :221 :461 1:121ft 20 118 1111 97½ 76 74½ Hawley S1 [S]M32000 73-17 Vancealot, Angel J., Finski 12
22Jan88—Broke slowly; wide into stretch
Feb 28 SA tr.t 4f ft :493 h Feb 5 SA 7f ft 1:301 h Jan 31 SA 4f ft :501 h Jan 19 SA 4f gd :484 h

Denew
ORTEGA L E 118
Own.—Cooke J K
B. c. 3, by Explodent—Newfoundland, by Prince John
Br.—Elmendorf Farm Inc (Ky) 1988 2 M 0 0 $425
Tr.—McAnally Ronald $32,000 1987 4 M 2 0 $7,275
Lifetime 6 0 2 0 $7,700
20Jan88-6SA 7f :224 :46 1:25 ft 23 116 42 76½ 1012 916½ Velasquez J12 M45000 59-22 SlvrCrcs,Gntlmn'sHonor,IcyAmbr 12
14Jan88-2SA 1 1/16 :47 1:12 1:461ft 5½ 117 79 67½ 57½ 54 Velasquez J6 M32000 66-21 MiSueRe,Zchnie,AMnToRemembr 12
14Jan88—Bumped start, wide
17Dec87-6Hol 6f :222 :463 1:113sy 22 118 86¾ 86¾ 56 25 Velasquez J3 M32000 79-22 MiddleConcho,Denew,PlnImprssiv 12
12Nov87-4SA 6f :221 :451 1:12ft 4½ 118 79¾ 1012 1015 911½ ValenzuelaPA1 M32000 65-21 PubliclyProper,TemperT.,Natntive 12
23Aug87-3Dmr 1 :462 1:114 1:372ft 2½e 116 612 58½ 512 519¾ Delahoussaye E5 Mdn 62-14 ChineseGold,OurNtivWish,Cougrizd 6
5Jly87-4Hol 6f :223 :471 1:124ft 11 117 98¾ 76¾ 63½ 25 Delahoussaye E7 Mdn 74-11 Blade OfTheBall,Denew,MiSueRae 10
5Jly87—Bumped hard start; bore out early drive
Feb 24 Hol 4f ft :48 h Feb 17 Hol 4f ft :48 h Feb 10 SA 6f ft 1:142 h Feb 4 SA 5f ft 1:011 h

Explosive Wing
CASTANON A L 118
Own.—Citro J & F
Ch. c. 3, by Wing Out—Jane's Honey, by Windy Tide
Br.—Citro J & F (Cal) 1988 0 M 0 0
Tr.—Stute Warren $32,000 1987 0 M 0 0
Lifetime 0 0 0 0
Feb 29 SA 3f m :391 h (d) Feb 24 SA 5f ft 1:013 h Feb 19 SA 5f ft 1:041 hg Feb 14 SA 7f ft 1:312 h

Fun Is First

BLACK C A		**118**	B. g. 3, by It's the One—Skate Board, by Green Dancer
Own.—Dick R			Br.—Dick R (Ky)
			Tr.—Speckert Christopher

B. g. 3, by It's the One—Skate Board, by Green Dancer
Br.—Dick R (Ky)　　　　1988　2 M 0 0
Tr.—Speckert Christopher　$32,000　1987　3 M 0 0
Lifetime　5 0 0 0

18Feb88-2SA 6¼f :22² :46¹ 1:19²ft 43 118 11⁹¾109¼ 8⁷ 6¹0¼ Black C A 7 M32000 62-30 Hgley'sLion,Potter'sPride,Hdwind 12
　18Feb88—Jostled early
14Jan88-2SA 1¼ :47 1:12 1:46¹ft 88 117 4⁷ 5⁵ 7¹¹ 8¹² Black C A 3 M32000 58-21 MiSueRe,Zchnie,AMnToRemembr 12
20Nov87-6Hol 1 :45² 1:10¹ 1:35⁴ft 169 117 18¹²10¹⁵11²⁵11³⁶½ Ortega L E 2 Mdn 47-13 Ruhlmann, SpottedRaj,Wo⁻ryation 12
　20Nov87—Lugged out backstretch
1Nov87-6SA 6f :21³ :45 1:11 m 45 119 9¹⁴ 9¹¹ 8¹¹ 8⁹½ Ortega L E 2 Mdn 74-12 GrnMusico,SweetNGo,BelAirDncr 10
　1Nov87—Steadied start
15Oct87-6SA 6f :21³ :45¹ 1:11³ft 45 115 11¹⁶10¹⁵10¹²10¹⁴¾ Ortega L E 5 M45000 65-19 PocktBld,HonstJohnSilvr,Hdwind 11
　Feb 25 SA 3f ft :37² h 　Feb 16 SA 3f ft :36² h 　Feb 11 SA 4f ft :48³ h 　Feb 6 SA 5f ft 1:01¹ h

Self Contained

DELAHOUSSAYE E		**118**	B. g. 3, by Cougar II—Circle Game, by Jacinto
Own.—Duckett-Hinds-Robbins			Br.—Hancock-Bowen-Peters (Ky)
			Tr.—Robbins Jay M

B. g. 3, by Cougar II—Circle Game, by Jacinto
Br.—Hancock-Bowen-Peters (Ky)　　　1988　1 M 0 0　$400
Tr.—Robbins Jay M　　$32,000　1987　4 M 1 0　$4,400
Lifetime　5 0 1 0　$4,800

27Jan88-7SA 6f :21⁴ :44³ 1:11²ft 8½ 118 8⁹¾ 7¹² 6⁹ 5⁹½ Solis A 6 M32000 71-19 Triquitrque,DonMrio,Somkindguy 12
　27Jan88—Fanned wide into stretch
27Dec87-6SA 1¼ :46⁴ 1:12¹ 1:44⁴ft 30 117 31½ 9¹⁵ 9²⁴ — Toro F 7 Mdn — — GladMusic,Freeskate,RecittionSpin 9
　27Dec87—Eased; off slowly
9Dec87-6SA 1¼ :46⁴ 1:12² 1:45⁴ft 54 117 85½ 74½ 66½ 79½ Toro F 10 Mdn 65-16 SpottdRj,GldMusic,SouthrnSpruc 11
22Nov87-4Hol 6f :21³ :44³ 1:09⁴ft 20 117 66½ 78½ 8¹0 9¹5½ Toro F 7 Mdn 77-14 Overbrook, Switch Codes, Peace 11
8Nov87-6SA 6f :22¹ :45¹ 1:11²gd 16 117 32 34 25 29½ Toro F 7 Mdn 71-25 SweetNGo,SelfContined,LivelyOne 10
　Feb 22 SA 5f ft 1:01⁴ h 　Feb 15 SA 5f ft 1:00⁴ h 　Feb 9 SA 4f ft :48¹ h 　Jan 22 SA 5f ft 1:01¹ h

My hope was Liberalartsdiploma, who a month earlier at 50–1 had flashed first-quarter speed at $50,000 maiden claimers. Today the 3YO was entered for $32,000 by a clever trainer. The colt had "blinkers on."

Consider the six-furlong par-time differences between $50,000 and $32,000 maiden claimers at Santa Anita.

Mdn-Clm	$50	45	1:10 4/5	101
Mdn-Clm	$32	45 1/5	1:11 2/5	98

After setting a faster pace, $50,000 maiden claimers typically ran three lengths faster at six furlongs than the $32,000 brand. I had ached to take advantage of these differences on the drop, but had spotted few opportunities and had had no success.

Liberalartsdiploma's early speed from the outside versus $50,000 maiden claimers February 3 alerted me to the possibility the colt could grab the lead at the cheaper slower level. With blinkers on today, I was persuaded the dropdown would secure the lead, and merely had to hold.

The chart documents how easily it happened. At the odds, Liberalartsdiploma was worth the wait.

SECOND RACE **6 FURLONGS. ($1.07\frac{4}{5}$) MAIDEN CLAIMING. Purse $16,000. 3-year-olds. Weight, 118 lbs.; Claiming price $32,000; if for $28,000 allowed 2 lbs.**

Santa Anita

MARCH 2, 1988

Value of race $16,000; value to winner $8,800; second $3,200; third $2,400; fourth $1,200; fifth $400. Mutuel pool $374,086.

Last Raced	Horse	Eqt.	A.	Wt	PP	St	¼	½	Str	Fin	Jockey	Cl'g Pr	Odds $1
3Feb88 $^{6}SA^{9}$	Liberalartsdiploma	b	3	118	4	2	$1^{1\frac{1}{2}}$	1^{2}	1^{5}	$1^{4\frac{1}{2}}$	Pedroza M A	32000	6.10
27Jan88 $^{4}SA^{5}$	Self Contained		3	118	10	5	$8^{\frac{1}{2}}$	$6^{3\frac{1}{2}}$	$3^{\frac{1}{2}}$	2^{4}	Delahoussaye E	32000	5.20
	Eagle's Dream		3	118	12	4	$5^{1\frac{1}{2}}$	5^{hd}	5^{2}	3^{1}	Black C A	32000	13.60
3Feb88 $^{6}SA^{10}$	Angel J.		3	118	2	10	2^{hd}	$3^{\frac{1}{2}}$	$2^{\frac{1}{2}}$	4^{hd}	Solis A	32000	3.10
20Jan88 $^{6}SA^{9}$	Denew	b	3	118	7	9	$11^{\frac{1}{2}}$	$10^{\frac{1}{2}}$	$8^{1\frac{1}{2}}$	$5^{\frac{1}{2}}$	Ortega L E	32000	9.10
18Feb88 $^{2}SA^{6}$	Fun Is First	b	3	118	9	6	$10^{3\frac{1}{2}}$	7^{hd}	$7^{1\frac{1}{2}}$	6no	Hawley S	32000	52.00
18Feb88 $^{6}SA^{8}$	P. Tonker	b	3	118	5	3	3^{hd}	2^{hd}	4^{2}	$7^{3\frac{1}{2}}$	Patterson A	32000	15.10
18Feb88 $^{2}SA^{5}$	Able Hughes		3	118	11	1	$4^{3\frac{1}{2}}$	4^{3}	6^{hd}	8^{hd}	Stevens G L	32000	3.50
10Feb88 $^{4}SA^{9}$	Milk N Quacker's	b	3	118	6	7	7^{hd}	$8^{\frac{1}{2}}$	$9^{1\frac{1}{2}}$	$9^{1\frac{1}{2}}$	Meza R Q	32000	12.90
12Feb88 $^{4}SA^{9}$	Arco's Fancy Guy	b	3	118	3	8	6^{hd}	11^{3}	10^{6}	10^{9}	Fernandez A L	32000	105.60
13Feb88 $^{6}SA^{10}$	Don Scala	b	3	118	1	12	12	12	12	$11^{2\frac{1}{2}}$	Gryder A T	32000	67.70
	Explosive Wing		3	118	8	11	9^{2}	9^{1}	$11^{1\frac{1}{2}}$	12	Sibille R	32000	12.00

OFF AT 1:34. Start good. Won ridden out. Time, $:21\frac{4}{5}$, $:45\frac{1}{5}$, $:57\frac{4}{5}$, 1:11 Track good.

$2 Mutuel Prices:			
4-LIBERALARTSDIPLOMA	14.20	8.40	6.40
10-SELF CONTAINED		6.40	4.20
12-EAGLE'S DREAM			9.00

Dk. b. or br. c, by In Reality—Sheepskin, by Arts and Letters. Trainer Mayberry Brian A. Bred by Marriott W D (Ky).

LIBERALARTSDIPLOMA outsprinted rivals for the early lead, drew away in the upper stretch and remained well clear in the last furlong. SELF CONTAINED, outrun early, rallied for the place. EAGLE'S DREAM, outrun early and wide down the backstretch, improved his position in the stretch but was no match for the top two in the drive. ANGEL J. prominent early after being a bit slow to begin, gave way. DENEW was five wide into the stretch. FUN IS FIRST and P. TONKER, prominent early, gave way. ABLE HUGHES, prominent early after an alert start, faltered. DON SCALA broke slowly. EXPLOSIVE WING, wide down the backstretch after breaking a bit awkwardly, was four wide into the far turn.

Owners— 1, Siegel M-Jan-Samantha; 2, Duckett-Hinds-Robbins; 3, Golden Eagle Farm; 4, Weaver K; 5, Cooke J K; 6, Dick R; 7, Stockseth W O & Norma; 8, Brazos Thoroughbred Unit; 9, Belles H J (Lessee); 10, Hampton J & D; 11, Christando & Gatto; 12, Citro J & F.

Trainers— 1, Mayberry Brian A; 2, Robbins Jay M; 3, Jory Ian; 4, Velasquez Danny; 5, McAnally Ronald; 6, Speckert Christopher; 7, Heap Blake; 8, Stidham Michael; 9, Manzi Joseph; 10, Landers Dale; 11, Mayer V James; 12, Stute Warren.

Scratched—Somekindaguy (12Feb88 $^{4}SA^{5}$); Spectacular Fire (4Feb88 $^{4}SA^{10}$); Table Paw (12Feb88 $^{4}SA^{7}$); Rakhiim (10Feb88 $^{4}SA^{7}$); Teleran (13Jan88 $^{4}SA^{8}$); Buckobob.

$2 Daily Double 6–4 Paid $71.60. Daily Double Pool $341,296.

Ron Cox for years has advocated what he has called the "gap" handicapping of maiden-claming affairs. Where par times differ by more than two lengths in the maiden-claiming division, handicappers watch for the relevant drops. If the faster horses can claim the front prior to the stretch call, slower maidens for sale cannot catch them.

I have an aversion to maiden-claiming races, and confess to have not chased this type of bet before. I intend to again, however, in the near future.

Another kind of opportunity, and I've converted many, handicappers cannot afford to ignore in these pitiful contests. Now the handicapping is conventional, isolating the drop-downs from straight maiden competition as contenders.

Examine four such contenders below, the records, figures, race shapes, and post-time odds.

4th Santa Anita *P 99/45.3 111'/Cᴸᴸᴸᴸᴸ*

6 FURLONGS. (1.07⅘) MAIDEN CLAIMING. Purse $19,000. Fillies. 3-year-olds. Weight, 117 lbs. Claiming price $50,000; if for $45,000 allowed 2 lbs.

Jody's Choice

jod/ick 30 FA

PINCAY L JR 3-N	B. f. 3, by Gunflint—Jetting Jody, by Tri Jet	
Own.—Hooper F W	**117** Br.—Hooper F W (Fla)	1988 2 M 0 1 $2,850
	Tr.—Russell John W $50,000	1987 0 M 0 0
	Lifetime 2 0 0 1 $2,850	

13Feb88-4SA 6f :213 :444 1:11 ft 11 117 21 44 47 713 Sibille R2 ⑥Mdn 70-22 Y'Amor, Scrod, Good Going Gracie 12
21Jan88-6SA 6f :213 :441 1:093ft 51 117 53½ 55½ 37 39½ Sibille R4 ⑥M50000 80-19 WrningZone,L.Mexicn,Jody'sChoic 11
21Jan88—Broke slowly
Mar 9 Hol 4f ft :52 h Feb 21 SA 5f ft 1:00 h Jan 29 SA 4f ft :511 h Jan 14 Hol 6f ft 1:143 h

Pretty Lake North

Lov/91 87

CORDERO A JR	Ch. f. 3, by Upper Case—Lake North, by Northern Answer	
Own.—Clearman-Dunn-Pollock	**117** Br.—Morrenie C & Lois (Fla)	1988 3 M 0 0 $3,175
	Tr.—Mulhall Richard W $50,000	1987 1 M 1 0 $5,000
	Lifetime 4 0 1 0 $8,175	

14Feb88-3SA 1¹⁄₁₆:462 1:114 1:444ft 16 117 712 616 513 513 Stevens G L4 ⑥Mdn 64-20 SettleSngue,SecretThrt,Lori'sLight 7
6Feb88-3SA 6½f:221 :453 1:17 ft 7 117 63½ 54½ 56½ 511½ DelahoussyeE3 ⑥Mdn 74-18 GoldSeal,Forewrning,SummerAmbo 7
9Jan88-4SA 6½f:22 :452 1:181ft 3½ 117 106½ 77½ 76½ 42 DelahoussyeE5 ⑥Mdn 77-17 Jovr,SugrplumGl,YouBetterBeliev 12
9Jan88—Wide into stretch
27Dec87-4SA 6f :211 :442 1:104ft 41 117 56½ 511 45½ 24½ Stevens G L1 ⑥Mdn 79-17 PtternStep,PrettyLkNorth,ScrtThrt 9
Mar 4 SA 3f ft :342 h Feb 24 SA 5f ft 1:013 h Jan 27 SA 5f ft 1:013 h Jan 22 SA 5f ft 1:01 h

Touch Of Splendor

SHERMAN A B 3-O	B. f. 3, by Al Nasr—Touch of Fame, by Prove Out	
Own.—Ritter H & Juanita	**1125** Br.—Floyd & Spendthrift Farm (Ky)	1988 3 M 0 0 $625
	Tr.—Tinsley J E Jr $50,000	1987 0 M 0 0
	Lifetime 3 0 0 0 $625	

27Feb88-6SA 6f :214 :45 1:101ft 53 117 75½ 98½ 913 916½ Velasquez J2 ⑥Mdn 71-17 CherryD'or,Ahwhnee,FortuneBrbr 12
13Feb88-4SA 6f :213 :444 1:11 ft 17 1125 63½ 55½ 64½ 611½ Gryder A12 ⑥Mdn 71-22 Y'Amor, Scrod, Good Going Gracie 12
30Jan88-4SA 6f :213 :453 1:114ft 27 117 3½ 1hd 21 57½ Valenzuela PA8 ⑥Mdn 71-20 Noble Brandy, Lost Lode, IcyToes 11
30Jan88—Wide 3/8 turn
Mar 5 SA 4f ft :472 hg Feb 22 SA 5f ft 1:02 h Feb 6 SA 4f ft :473 h Jan 25 SA 6f ft 1:152 hg

Lyphard's Flag

DELAHOUSSAYE E	B. f. 3, by Lyphard's Wish—Lady's Flag, by Fifth Marine	
Own.—Hartstone & ParrishHillFarm	**117** Br.—Parrish Hill Farm (Ky)	1988 3 M 0 0
	Tr.—Hartstone George D $50,000	1987 1 M 0 0
	Lifetime 4 0 0 0	

14Feb88-3SA 1¹⁄₁₆:462 1:114 1:444ft 47 117 38½ 515 620 627 Meza R Q1 ⑥Mdn 58-20 SettleSngue,SecretThrt,Lori'sLight 7
30Jan88-4SA 6f :214 :453 1:114ft 47 117 96½ 78½ 75 68 Meza R Q2 ⑥Mdn 71-20 Noble Brandy, Lost Lode, Icy Toes 11
30Jan88—Rough start
9Jan88-4SA 6½f:22 :452 1:181ft 53 117 74½ 52½ 87 87½ Hawley S4 ⑥Mdn 72-17 Jovr,SugrplumGl,YouBetterBeliev 12
9Jan88—Broke slowly; bumped at 3 1/2
20Dec87-6Hol 6f :222 :46 1:113ft 40 118 3½ 74½ 712 78½ Cordero A Jr 7 ⑥Mdn 75-00 SumthngRr,WlkInThPrk,SgrplmGl 11
Mar 6 SA 5f ft :59 h Feb 9 SA 4f ft :49 h Jan 27 SA 3f ft :364 h Jan 21 SA 5f ft 1:00 h

---

Par for maiden-claiming $50,000, fillies, at 6F, is 99.

Jody's Choice	102/	104	90	FA	9–2
Pretty Lake North	102/	91	89	SA	3–1
Touch Of Splendor	102/	102	91	FA	15–1
Lyphard's Flag	102/	95	91	AA	24–1

Which dropdown do handicappers prefer?

Pretty Lake North can be tossed. She has the lowest figures and lowest odds, but no speed, a deadly combination.

The other three are difficult to separate. Jody's Choice has lost a maiden-claiming race, but the swiftest of the season, an authentically impressive performance by the winner. Of the dropdowns, as well, Jody's Choice enjoys an early-speed advantage she will use from the rail position, although Touch Of Splendor is adding blinkers and may challenge.

What to do?

Take the odds.

It's that simple, really. Let's establish a rule. In maiden-claiming events, when separating dropdowns that figure, always court the odds. It pays, and will pay handsomely long-term.

I split a nonprime amount on Lyphard's Flag and Touch Of Splendor, the majority on the higher-odds horse. Lee Rousso supported Touch Of Splendor because the filly was adding blinkers and Lasix simultaneously, a double-edged angle he favored throughout the meeting, but ignored the other long shot. I hoped Lyphard's Flag would pick up a collapsing pace under the unexcelled one-run specialist Eddie Delahoussaye.

So I am delighted to present the result chart.

FOURTH RACE **6 FURLONGS. (1.07⅗) MAIDEN CLAIMING. Purse $19,000. Fillies. 3-year-olds. Weight, 117 lbs. Claiming price $50,000; if for $45,000 allowed 2 lbs.**

Santa Anita

MARCH 11, 1988

Value of race $19,000; value to winner $10,450; second $3,800; third $2,850; fourth $1,425; fifth $475. Mutuel pool $445,545.

Last Raced	Horse	Eqt.	A.	Wt	PP	St	¼	½	Str	Fin	Jockey	Cl'g Pr	Odds $1
14Feb88 ^{3}SA^{6}	Lyphard's Flag		3	117	9	12	12	$10^{3\frac{1}{2}}$	6^{1}	1^{3}	Delahoussaye E	50000	24.50
27Feb88 ^{6}SA^{9}	Touch Of Splendor	b	3	112	8	3	1^{hd}	1^{1}	1^{2}	$2^{1\frac{3}{4}}$	Sherman A B^{5}	50000	15.50
14Feb88 ^{3}SA^{5}	Pretty Lake North		3	117	7	2	7^{3}	$6^{\frac{1}{2}}$	4^{1}	$3^{1\frac{1}{4}}$	Cordero A Jr	50000	3.20
4Mar88 ^{4}SA^{3}	Aunt Charlotte		3	112	3	9	8^{4}	7^{1}	7^{hd}	4^{2}	Banderas A L^{5}	50000	14.70
25Feb88 ^{6}SA^{5}	Clean Lines	b	3	117	11	6	$6^{1\frac{1}{2}}$	4^{1}	3^{hd}	$5^{\frac{3}{4}}$	Velasquez J	50000	17.80
13Feb88 ^{4}SA^{7}	Jody's Choice		3	117	1	4	$3^{1\frac{1}{2}}$	$2^{\frac{1}{2}}$	$2^{1\frac{1}{2}}$	6^{nk}	Pincay L Jr	50000	4.70
10Feb88 ^{6}SA^{3}	Love You Darling	b	3	115	10	7	5^{hd}	5^{hd}	$5^{\frac{1}{2}}$	$7^{1\frac{1}{4}}$	Toro F	45000	11.60
27Feb88 ^{6}SA^{8}	Audene's Bid		3	117	12	1	2^{1}	$3^{\frac{1}{2}}$	8^{2}	$8^{\frac{3}{4}}$	Stevens G L	50000	2.40
	Whatchagonnado		3	117	2	10	$10^{1\frac{1}{2}}$	9^{1}	9^{5}	9^{4}	McCarron C J	50000	11.00
2Jly87 ^{4}Hol^{2}	Lickatsplit		3	117	4	8	9^{1}	12	11^{1}	$10^{3\frac{1}{2}}$	Hawley S	50000	29.80
25Feb88 ^{6}SA^{10}	Namasu	b	3	112	6	11	$11^{\frac{1}{2}}$	11^{2}	12	11^{hd}	Valenzuela F H^{5}	50000	199.10
	Exeters	b	3	115	5	5	$4^{\frac{1}{2}}$	$8^{2\frac{1}{2}}$	$10^{\frac{1}{2}}$	12	Meza R Q	45000	14.70

OFF AT 2:42. Start good. Won driving. Time, :21⅘, :45⅖, :58⅕, 1:11⅕ Track fast.

$2 Mutuel Prices:			
9-LYPHARD'S FLAG	51.00	19.40	10.80
8-TOUCH OF SPLENDOR		19.40	10.80
7-PRETTY LAKE NORTH			4.20

B. f, by Lyphard's Wish—Lady's Flag, by Fifth Marine. Trainer Hartstone George D. Bred by Parrish Hill Farm (Ky).

LYPHARD'S FLAG, devoid of early speed, angled out to the middle of the track soon after straightening away in the stretch, closed with a rush to take the lead in the final sixteenth and won going away. TOUCH OF SPLENDOR vied for the early lead, had a clear advantage a furlong out, could not resist the winner's charge to relinquish command in the last sixteenth but held on for the place. PRETTY LAKE NORTH, outrun early after an alert start, came into the stretch five wide and lacked the needed response in the drive. AUNT CHARLOTTE, outrun early, was

Handicappers should notice the maiden dropdowns finished one-two-three.

At the outcome, a chagrined Rousso remarked wistfully, "Wouldn't this have made us a nice exacta?"

The week of March 23 I lost for five consecutive racing days. I could not sing the blues, having experienced only my second losing week of the season. March profits would total $3,069

and with twenty racing days remaining, I felt within grasp of
my goal.

As March closed, our discussion of handicapping had turned
maudlin. We especially moaned how the triple had eluded our
best efforts. Rousso was comfortably in front of the exotic wager, without "killing" it, but Brohamer and I barely had stayed
abreast of it. Expectations here had run high. For good handicappers, a three-race series is manageable, as six is not, and the
triple's payout so frequently amounts to a gigantic overlay.

I moaned that I had not rebounded from my blunder costing
$1600, while scrambling the triple opening day. Brohamer could
not recount a single windfall. Rousso said he expected to make
a few killings at least, but had not. We pondered our mistakes
and omissions.

We reminisced, too, about the big ones that got away. Unan-
imously, we regretted a beauty none of us will forget.

It was January 20, 6th race, the first leg of a triple we might
have clobbered. The 6th was a maiden-claiming sprint at seven
furlongs. The three of us found ourselves swooning over a horse
that was not only a maiden dropdown, but had arrived at the
long sprint with the kind of four-furlong pace figure in its latest
route that we had already come to expect might upset at a price.

The pace figures of the route, in fact, are instructive. The
maiden-claiming $50,000 par at 7F was 99. The horse we rallied
to was Vigors Commander, and its December 27 route figures
against straight maidens looked like this: 101/ 121 97 101 AA.

Vigors Commander had outrun the four-furlong par at the
route against better by five lengths. Its two-furlong time had been
a sprintlike 22 4/5.

We expected the colt would assume the lead against the
maiden claimers and maintain its advantage all the way.

At 7–1, Vigors Commander broke smoothly and indeed
grabbed the lead immediately. Challenged mildly midway around
the turn, Vigors Commander just as quickly fell to pieces.

As Brohamer explained, our pace analysis had been faulty.
Five lengths fast for four furlongs, the horse had been two lengths
slow (97) after six furlongs.

If instead of 97, its six-furlong figure had been 105, two
lengths fast, Vigors Commander probably would have stayed.
The colt suffered a severe pace weakness at the second call. In
our enthusiasm about the four-furlong figure, we had conveniently ignored that. Brohamer felt particularly guilty, noting
the Sartin procedures, which he had abandoned for the day,

were designed specifically to identify any second-quarter pace weaknesses.

Coincidentally, this would be the afternoon our good thing Valiant Cougar blasted the field at 5–1 in the 7th and Winning Colors cakewalked in the 8th.

The disappointing loss in the 6th cost the three of us prime bets to win plus multiple triples each. Vigors Commander also denied Brohamer the Pick 6, the unkindest cut of all.

HOMESTRETCH

In the final weeks of a lengthy meeting, regular handicappers who have collected speed and pace figures, class ratings, trip and bias notes, and the rest, operate at a tremendous advantage. Barns maneuver horses, claiming horses especially, into striking positions, and well-informed handicappers can spring well-set traps of their own.

A common tactic with older claiming horses is to drop them drastically in selling price. The objective is the purse, but both the claim and the bet will be accepted as bonuses. If the drop-downs have earned the top figures and have not since declined, they win.

On April 7, day seventy-seven, the five-year-old below was lowered to $10,000 claiming, after breaking slowly for $16,000 seven days before. Its figures at the $12,500 level on February 25 can be found beneath the past performances. Was this gelding a stickout or not at $10,000, where par, as all now know, is 100?

Follow The Dancer — B. g. 5, by Barachois—Head Spy, by Chieftain

PEDROZA M A — 118 — Br.—North Ridge Farm (Ky) — 1988 4 1 0 1 $11,050

Own.—Steimle A B — Tr.—Azcarate Dan — $10,000 — 1987 15 2 3 3 $38,250

Lifetime 25 4 5 5 $72,350

31Mar88-5SA	6f	$:21^4$	$:44^3$	$1:09^4$ft	$6\frac34$	115	3^2	4^4	$5^{7\frac12}$	$5^{7\frac34}$	Pedroza M A^1	15000	81-20	ClssicQuicki,RockEnSm,FirlyOmn	12
31Mar88—Broke slowly															
25Feb88-3SA	6f	$:21^4$	:45	$1:10^2$ft	$4\frac34$	114	1^1	1^1	1^4	$1^{5\frac12}$	Pedroza M A^5	10500	86-22	FllwThDncr,WstL'Ost,Ex6rnt'sImg	10
15Feb88-1SA	$6\frac12$f	$:21^2$	$:44^1$	1:17 ft	$4\frac14$	116	4^3	2^3	$2^{3\frac12}$	$3^{4\frac12}$	Pedroza M A^4	10000	80-22	BlzngZl,BoldAndGrn,FollwThDncr	12
3Jan88-1SA	6f	:22	$:45^3$	$1:11^1$ft	9	116	$10^{5\frac34}$	$10^{7\frac14}$	$8^{4\frac14}$	5^6	Pedroza M A^7	16000	76-17	FbulousPretndr,Mlchip,BlzingZulu	12
3Jan88—Broke slowly, bumped															
29Nov87-2Hol	6f	$:21^4$	:45	$1:10^2$ft	*9-5	116	11^{12}	12^{16}	12^{15}	$12^{19\frac14}$	ValenzuelaPA^9	c12500	71-12	Move Free, Savio,ElectricMoment	12
29Nov87—Lugged out, wide															
11Oct87-9SA	6f	$:21^4$	$:44^1$	$1:08^4$ft	$3\frac12$	117	$5^{1\frac14}$	$4^{3\frac12}$	3^6	3^6	Pincay L Jr^6	c25000	88-14	SuprbMomnt,QpStr,FollowThDncr	12
11Oct87—Steadied 1/2															
20Sep87-10Fpx	$6\frac12$f	$:21^1$	$:45^3$	$1:17^2$ft	3	120	$4^{1\frac12}$	3^2	8^{11}	$8^{14\frac14}$	Pedroza MA^1	Aw25000	75-16	JustNeverMind,Krestig,Ack'sRply	10
22Aug87-3Dmr	6f	:22	:45	$1:09^1$ft	4	117	$4^{2\frac12}$	3^2	3^2	$2^{2\frac34}$	Pincay L Jr^6	32000	89-15	MchFnGold,FollwThDncr,LdThWgn	8
16Aug87-2Dmr	$6\frac12$f	$:22^1$	$:45^1$	$1:15^3$ft	$*2\frac14$	116	1^2	1^2	1^1	$1^{\frac12}$	Stevens G L^{10}	c20000	94-11	FollwThDncr,MschvsMtt,Brl'sAnt	11
5Aug87-3Dmr	6f	$:21^3$	$:44^4$	$1:10^2$ft	*2	116	4^2	$4^{1\frac12}$	2^2	$3^{2\frac12}$	Stevens G L^7	32000	83-20	DshonrblGst,MchFnGld,FllwThDncr	7
5Aug87—Wide 3/8 turn															

Mar 27 SA 3f ft $:36^2$ h

February 25: 101/ 105 107 FF.

Follow The Dancer won by three while well clear throughout the late stages, and paid $7.60.

Numerous claiming horses look the same, do the same, and pay the same in the final days. I call them low-priced overlays, which they are. The trick is to accept the edge at face value. Many handicappers alter tactics themselves as the curtains close, shopping for exotic values rather than settling for low-priced overlays that figure to win. That can be costly.

As Brohamer heated up again, cashing low-priced overlays galore during the last fifteen days, and I felt determined to rebound from two consecutive losing weeks, Lee Rousso came face to face with his final glorious day of the season. It was Sunday, April 10, and Rousso would have a chance to sweep the pools for more than $10,000, in the style that has marked his career.

The day before, April 9, Santa Anita Derby day, the track afforded properly armed handicappers a day-long special on late-season low-priced overlays. Two or more of our trio caught Athlone ($7.40) in the 1st, Romantic Prince ($6.40) in the 2nd, the daily double at $22.60, Blue Jean Baby ($9) in the 3rd, a Rousso prime bet, Winning Colors ($7.20) in the 5th, Davie's Lamb ($5) in the 8th, and Spacecapiat ($6) in the 9th. I cashed the six winners, but contributed a sizable rebate pursuing exactas and triples, as did my partners.

The next afternoon, Rousso began in the 3rd with $100 to win on Stop The Fighting ($7.40) on a solo lead at nine furlongs in a paceless turf route.

At another nine furlongs on grass, the 5th was for $80,000 claiming horses, 4up. We unanimously fancied a Golden Gate shipper that was 4–1 on the program and looked like this in the past performances:

Minutes Away had become a mild legend on the turf in northern California, winning nine of ten, while second once. Ron Cox's *Northern California Track Record* had informed me Minutes Away in his last had won "geared down."

With the Santa Anita turf variants Slow 5–Slow 10, or slower, most days, Brohamer had stopped making figures on the lawn, but he wanted a share of Minutes Away too.

Despite the shipment and rise in class, southern California handicappers rated Minutes Away 2–1 to win. Rousso and I spread ourselves across exactas. Brohamer bet to win and covered a few exactas. Brohamer cashed the win bet, plus the exacta at $141. I cashed the exacta twice. Rousso cashed the exacta six times.

Regular jockey Chris Hummel, riding the Santa Anita turf course infrequently or not at all, mishandled Minutes Away and permitted the six-year-old to drift out badly coming out of the far turn, but the hard-knocking gelding righted itself and prevailed by a long neck.

Rousso wagered $120 to win on his figure horse in the 6th. It won, paid $10.80.

One of four contenders he used in the 7th on a triple ticket won, another 4–1 horse, paying $10.60.

Rousso was now alive with a $15 triple to a three-horse Charles Whittingham entry in the 8th at even money. The projected payout was $183.

None of the Whittingham horses hit the board.

"My record with odds-on Whittingham horses when I need them must be pathetic," complained Rousso. "I may be batting zero with them."

The nightcap on April 10 would be the most important race of the season for Rousso. It was a $40,000 claiming race, 4up, at 1 1/16M, and brought together four competitive horses that had peppered the fields at this class-distance throughout the season. This time Rousso held a strong opinion, and he exercised it.

Here are the speed and pace figures, race shapes, and today's odds on the four contenders:

L.A. Fire	104/	102	100	104	AA	3–1
Varennes	104/	100	110	103	AA	7–2
Siberian Hero	104/	114	107	106	AA	8–5
Ono Gummo	106/	112	100	105	FA	5–2

Rousso likes improving horses in contentious fields. In his opinion, two horses here were improving, two had passed their peaks already. The high-figure horse, speed and pace, Siberian Hero, was Rousso's choice on the improve. Making a strong middle move into a hot pace last out, Varennes was the second improving horse.

Rousso bought a $150 exacta box coupling Siberian Hero and Varennes, a $300 investment.

To intensify the drama, Rousso had stayed alive to Siberian Hero, a single, in the day's Pick 6, five times! The six-horse parlay, if Siberian Hero won, would register at odds of 1–1, 2–1, 4–1, 4–1, 4–1, and 8–5. Rousso estimated the payout on his five tickets between $8000 and $10,000.

In a fast-fast race contested severely at each call, Varennes took the lead down the backstretch and Siberian Hero challenged him into the lane. It was these two, Rousso's two, period. Siberian Hero stuck a neck in front midway home. Varennes fought gamely. The two began a bumping match inside the sixteenth pole. Quickly it was over. The photo sign was lit.

Watching in the turf club, I called the favorite. I hurried to view the immediate replay of the stretch drive. Indeed, the television showed Siberian Hero had held—I thought. Here is the result chart.

NINTH RACE
Santa Anita
APRIL 10, 1988

$1\frac{1}{16}$ MILES. (1.40⅕) CLAIMING. Purse $32,000. 4-year-olds and upward. Weight, 121 lbs. Non-winners of two races at one mile or over since February 1 allowed 3 lbs.; of such a race since then, 5 lbs. Claiming price $40,000; if for $35,000 allowed 2 lbs. (Claiming and starter races for $32,000 or less not considered.)

Value of race $32,000; value to winner $17,600; second $6,400; third $4,800; fourth $2,400; fifth $800. Mutuel pool $460,493. Exacta pool $728,719.

Last Raced	Horse	Eqt.	A.	Wt	PP	St	¼	½	¾	Str	Fin	Jockey	Cl'g Pr	Odds $1
20Mar88 $^{9}SA^{2}$	Varennes	b	5	116	2	4	$2^{\frac{1}{2}}$	$1^{1\frac{1}{2}}$	$1^{\frac{1}{2}}$	2^{2}	1no	Delahoussaye E	40000	3.60
3Apr88 $^{9}SA^{1}$	Siberian Hero	b	6	116	3	2	4^{hd}	$4^{\frac{1}{2}}$	4^{hd}	1^{hd}	2^{5}	Stevens G L	40000	1.70
27Mar88 $^{9}SA^{3}$	Ono Gummo		6	118	6	3	3^{1}	$3^{\frac{1}{2}}$	$3^{\frac{1}{2}}$	3^{1}	3^{1}	McCarron C J	40000	2.60
20Mar88 $^{9}SA^{3}$	Tokyo Boy		4	116	5	5	5^{6}	5^{6}	5^{7}	$4^{\frac{1}{2}}$	4^{4}	Sibille R	40000	15.30
20Mar88 $^{9}SA^{1}$	L. A. Fire		5	118	1	1	1^{1}	2^{hd}	2^{1}	5^{8}	5^{10}	Hawley S	40000	3.20
27Mar88 $^{9}SA^{8}$	Ultimate Pleasure	b	6	116	4	6	6	6	6	6	6	Pedroza M A	40000	25.90

OFF AT 5:31. Start good. Won driving. Time, :23⅕, :46⅗, 1:11⅕, 1:36⅘, 1:43⅕ Track fast.

$2 Mutuel Prices:			
2-VARENNES	9.20	4.00	3.00
3-SIBERIAN HERO		3.00	2.40
6-ONO GUMMO			2.60

$5 EXACTA 2–3 PAID $73.00.

B. h, by L'Enjoleur—Tyrant's Escape, by Tyrant. Trainer Gregson Edwin. Bred by Loch Lea Farm Inc (Ky).

VARENNES moved up along the inner rail to get the lead going into the backstretch, set the pace down the backstretch and on the far turn, battled for command through the stretch while inside SIBERIAN HERO, bumped with that rival approaching the furlong marker, bumped at intervals with that rival in the final sixteenth and prevailed by a slim margin. SIBERIAN HERO, never far back and boxed in on the far turn, found room to engage for the lead outside VARENNES at the head of the stretch, battled for command with that rival through the stretch, bumped with that rival approaching the furlong marker, bumped at intervals with that rival in the final sixteenth and lost by a slim margin. A claim of foul against VARENNES by the rider of SIBERIAN HERO, for alleged interference in the stretch drive, was not allowed by the stewards when they ruled that both horses were responsible for the contact in the stretch. ONO GUMMO, close up to midstretch, weakened. TOKYO BOY, in contention early, came into the stretch four wide, continued in contention to midstretch and weakened. L. A. FIRE set or forced the pace to the stretch and gave way.

A remarkably composed well-dressed young man joined me beneath the turf-club TV monitor, saying he thought for sure Siberian Hero had won it, even after watching the finish on television. He showed me a Pick 6 ticket he stood to exchange if Siberian Hero had prevailed.

I almost told him about a guy I knew who had the Pick 6 live to Siberian Hero—five times—but decided it was hardly a moment for oneupsmanship.

Suddenly the Inquiry sign lit up, flashing! The stewards wanted to inspect the bumping near the finish. A belated chance for the killing.

After a tortuous wait, the stewards determined both horses had been at fault. A cruel game, racing; sometimes.

I accompanied Tom Brohamer to Las Vegas for handicapping seminars the next-to-last week. I would be addressing several hundred Sartin clients on picking contenders and pace lines in claiming races.

Brohamer junkets to Vegas several times a year. He likes the racing books. In preparation, Tom for weeks had compiled variants and figures for New York racing. He challenged Santa Anita, Aqueduct, and Golden Gate daily, and humbled all three, not losing at any track, any day. I sputtered, and lost, throughout the week.

Saturday, April 16, our next-to-last day in town, I bought a $90 triple linking three favorites at Santa Anita. Brohamer covered two other horses in the 7th on his triple, including Double The Charm, the 50–1 Nodouble horse that had upset on the grass while Rousso lay dreaming. Double The Charm was 9–1 now, facing nonwinners three times other than maiden or claiming, new company, much better.

With the favorite boxed in for at least 1/16th mile in the stretch, Double The Charm drew clear and survived the favorite's late rush by a disappearing head. Brohamer collected a $447.90 triple three times. I added up my fourth, and worst, losing week to $1200.

Getaway week passed by unremarkably, until Sunday, day ninety, the next-to-last day of the meeting. I had agreed to appear with Brohamer at Aaron Hess's morning seminar, an activity I shy from, due to a vaguely discomforting notion I've internalized about touting the public, which I find distasteful.

In fact, the seminars are harmless, an entertainment, and potentially informative sessions for participants, whether the designated experts pick six winners or none, extremes the experts manage to reach from week to week.

Our host, a fine handicapper, opened the session by naming the speedy Bold Vegas in the 1st as his best bet of the day.

Brohamer followed by telling the customers that if Bold Vegas were the easiest winner of the afternoon, he (Brohamer) could expect to have a lousy day. Brohamer thought the likeliest winner appeared in the 1st, too, but it was Lady Helcha, not Bold Vegas. So there you are. Examine the records, figures, shapes, and post-time odds.

Bold Vegas	103/	101	99	AS	11–1
Lady Helcha	100/	96	100	SA	3–1

How many handicappers noticed Lady Helcha qualifies as a candidate for the "bounce-bounce back" pattern described here previously? Take another glance if you did not notice.

Away four months, Lady Helcha wins on the comeback, then

loses on the rise at 9–5. The third race following the layoff, today, Lady Helcha can be expected to "bounce back," and at juicier odds. Brohamer noted Lady Helcha should be expected to improve her comeback figure, which she did by five lengths.

In a cakewalk April 24, Lady Helcha displayed keen speed and galloped by six. She paid $8.40. Brohamer, and his colleagues in the box, caught a $46 double as well, when Rock Em Sam went wire to wire in the second half.

In the 7th, a $32,000 claiming race, 4up, at six furlongs, our host strongly preferred Bizeboy and Savio, in that order, and recommended a cold exacta box. My personal best was entered here, a seven-year-old named Alitak. The horse was returning to the more suitable sprint after a solid six furlongs in a route for $25,000, in which it had been haltered by the fine young trainer John Sadler. Consider the speed and pace figures of the three.

Alitak	102/	103	104	AF	9–1
Bizeboy	104/	109	104	FA	7–5
Savio	104/	108	101	FA	8–1

Pace analysis here was textbook basic. With blazing pace figures but ordinary final figures, if Bizeboy and Savio weakened one another, Alitak could drive by both in the stretch.

It happened exactly as predicted, Alitak winning late on the inside, paying $20.60. Savio held second, and a generous exacta returned $343.50.

Brohamer supported Alitak, and keyed the exacta to the front pair as well. He cleared $2000 for the afternoon.

When Alitak won, I not only pocketed a grand, but had a last chance for a score on the triple. I was alive on a $30 ticket to the favorite in the feature, the Grade 1 San Juan Capistrano Invitational, at 1 3/4M, and beginning down the unique hillside turf course at Santa Anita, arguably the prettiest grass stakes on the national calendar.

My hope, Putting, could not get the marathon distance and finished next to last. I netted $1225 for the afternoon.

Closing day Tom Brohamer drove to Palm Springs and I boarded an early flight to Lexington, Kentucky.

Lee Rousso sat alone in the box and chased the Pick 9, which this day provided an automatic payout of a $503,612 pool to the customers selecting the most winners. Rousso played tough, losing only the 2nd, 3rd, and 7th, the last by a head on a 13–1 shot.

One lucky customer had eight winners and took home $464,037. Another 123 tickets identified seven winners, earning $808.40 apiece. Rousso held one of 1621 tickets naming six winners. Each got $61.20.

Chasing the same exotics that had served him so well in the first half, Rousso abandoned another $1000 of profits in April, unable to catch the big ones.

The final accounting came back squarely in the black for each of us.

Brohamer	$11,500
Quinn	$13,500
Rousso	$12,000

In essence, the three professional handicappers had won the same amounts across ninety-one hectic days, while agreeing they had never experienced better times doing it.

TAGLINES

Recreational handicappers crave to comprehend the machinations of the professional. They especially long to know how much money the competent professional wins.

Now handicappers know.

The preceding discussion represents the racetrack realities extremely well. It tells it rather like it is.

The trio of pros on these pages play a fast, informed, highly refined game. They are rarely unprepared, rarely fooled. They do not often lose for the season. Yet they do not often win significantly greater amounts than they did at Santa Anita 1988. After ninety-one days the three had won ballpark amounts, an average profit of $12,333.33. Nonreproducible windfalls apart, if the three repeated the experience for each of the next five Santa Anita seasons, and bet the same, the amounts won would not vary dramatically up or down.

If anyone cares to dispute that assertion, let them first consider the following.

The professional finds two or three prime horses a day. He

invests conventional amounts, approximately $200 to win on the prime choices. The investment for ninety-one racing days amounts to $54,600.

Assuming the professional has developed into an outstanding handicapper, he gets 35 percent winners at average odds of 2.5–1. The proficient professional's edge is 22.5 percent.

Money won will be equal to the total amount wagered ($54,600) multiplied by the edge (.225). This amounts to a season's profit of—would you believe it—$12,285.

That is the stark reality, and our threesome won precisely what they should have expected to win.

If the trio continued to invest in the horses for a year, each would net between $25,000 and $42,000, depending upon the bet size and money management methods.

Of all racetrack realities, this might be the cruelest body blow to the dreamers. The ceiling on seasonal profits attributable to conventional levels of handicapping proficiency is not sky-high. The ceiling instead curves low.

The ways to generate heavier profits are to increase the normal bet size (significantly), or to crush the exotics, not a particularly predictable or replicable exploit.

Suppose a newborn professional set a goal of winning $50,000 a year at the races. If he prefers to bet $200 to win or thereabouts, how much must he invest, and how long must he persist, at the desired levels of proficiency? That is, 35 percent winners at average odds of 2.5–1.

The investment must be $50,000/.225, or $222,222.22. At $200 a prime, the pro must endure 1111 bets to net the $50,000. At two or three win bets a day, 250 racing days a year, the investment traverses two years, not one. The income will be $25,000 to $40,000 a year, which is where we started. To earn $50,000 a year, bet size must be hyped to $350 to $400, with no slack in proficiency. Many handicappers cannot stand the raise, and therefore would not play as well.

Moreover, a handicapping win proficiency of 35 percent at average odds of 2.5–1, while attainable, will be challenging, even for experienced, highly skilled, well-informed handicappers. More realistic win percentages range from 33 percent to 30 percent, and the profit margin is most sensitive to the win percentage. A rise of three percentage points, from 30 to 33 percent, for example, causes profits to triple. A similar decline holds out similar consequences.

It's true, too, that winning at the races culminates in periodic runs, such as Brohamer and Rousso completed in January–February. Professionals succeed at other times as well, rather consistently, only at moderate profits. Professionals lose infrequently, and not too much capital, so that when winning runs occur, profits multiply.

Nothing about the patterns of winning and losing reflected by the Santa Anita experiences of Brohamer-Quinn-Rousso should be thought uncommon or atypical. They instead have been representative of real life.

Tom Brohamer continued to play, and the first week of Hollywood Park he cleared an additional $3000. Tom relishes the changeover to new tracks on local circuits, arguing that regulars who draw accurate beads on the local tracks have a sharp edge the first several days.

In the ensuing weeks,Brohamer redeposited a moderate proportion of his early winnings, and by the final third of the Hollywood meeting his motivation had slackened anew. Tom went camping again with his wife for three weeks.

Brohamer attended Del Mar sporadically, and played lightly. Will Brohamer win $25,000 to $30,000 for the whole of 1988? Very probably not.

Shortly following Santa Anita, Lee Rousso flew to Cabo San Lucas, in Mexico, where he relaxed with his wife Elayne for twenty-one days. On his return, Rousso played at Hollywood Park irregularly, not enjoying it much.

On June 1 Rousso did something brainy. He moved to a condominium rental in the plush resort La Costa, north of San Diego, and while waiting for the Del Mar season himself, he played the remainder of the Hollywood season at the Del Mar inter-track site.

Lee struggled during the opening weeks of Del Mar, rebounded some, but not entirely. Will Rousso win $25,000 to $30,000 for the whole of 1988? Maybe, if he scores, but probably not.

Following the Santa Anita season, adhering to my custom, I stopped cold turkey. I began to write this manuscript.

The last year I traveled the southern California circuit full circle, 1979, and kept accurate records, I won precisely $26,600. So, what's new?

It brings to mind the unkind allusion of money management

expert Dick Mitchell on the financial rewards of successful professional handicapping as "not exactly Rolls-Royce wages."

Handicapping the thoroughbreds is a fabulous pastime, a stimulating challenging avocation, but a difficult and frustrating profession; amen.